The Teaching American History Project

"As this volume attests, the TAH program has reinvigorated a teaching force and breathed new life into history teaching. The papers gathered here burst with enthusiasm, renewed energy, and creative ideas for reforming practice. The variety of programs—from interventions at the elementary level (where history had all but choked in the miasma of 'expanding horizons') to collaborations with state and local historical societies, engaging archivists, museum directors, and professional educators—is simply dazzling. One can feel the energy."

Sam Wineburg, Stanford University, From the Foreword

"… the first scholarly look at the mammoth Teaching American History program. This book is the prism that will set the agenda for future discussions of what is the largest-ever federal investment in history education."

Larry Cebula, Eastern Washington University

The premise of the Teaching American History (TAH) project—a discretionary grant program funded under the U.S. Department of Education's Elementary and Secondary Education Act—is that in order to teach history better, teachers need to know more history. Unique among professional development programs in emphasizing specific content to be taught rather than a particular pedagogical approach, TAH grants assist schools in implementing scientifically based research methods for improving the quality of instruction, professional development, and teacher education in American history.

This collection of essays and research reports from TAH participants provides models for historians, teachers, teacher educators, and others interested in the teaching and learning of American history, and presents examples of lessons learned from a cross-section of TAH projects.

Rachel G. Ragland is Assistant Professor of Education at Lake Forest College. She currently serves as the Director of Clinical Partnerships for the Education Department and is a national co-editor for the H-NET Humanities and Social Sciences Online Discussion Network on Teaching American History. She was Assistant Academic Director for the Model Collaboration: Rethinking American History TAH grant from 2001-2004 and a TAH grant reviewer in 2007.

Kelly A. Woestman is Professor of History and History Education Director at Pittsburg (KS) State University. She has written or co-written twelve Teaching American History grants, and has served as Project Director for five grants in Kansas and as external evaluator for TAH grants in Missouri, New Mexico, Colorado, and Maryland. A founding editor of the H-TAH list community, she was elected President of H-Net Humanities and Social Sciences Online (www.h-net.org) for 2009.

The Teaching American History Project

Lessons for History Educators and Historians

Edited by

Rachel G. Ragland
Lake Forest College

Kelly A. Woestman
Pittsburg (KS) State University

Routledge
Taylor & Francis Group

NEW YORK AND LONDON

First published 2009
by Routledge
270 Madison Ave, New York, NY 10016

Simultaneously published in the UK
by Routledge
2 Park Square, Milton Park, Abingdon, Oxon OX14 4RN

Routledge is an imprint of the Taylor & Francis Group, an informa business

© 2009 Taylor & Francis

Typeset in Minion and Gill Sans by EvS Communication Networx, Inc.
Printed and bound in the United States of America on acid-free paper by Edwards Brothers, Inc.

All rights reserved. No part of this book may be reprinted or reproduced or utilized in any form or by any electronic, mechanical, or other means, now known or hereafter invented, including photocopying and recording, or in any information storage or retrieval system, without permission in writing from the publishers.

Trademark Notice: Product or corporate names may be trademarks or registered trademarks, and are used only for identification and explanation without intent to infringe.

Library of Congress Cataloging in Publication Data
The Teaching American History Project: lessons for history educators and historians / [edited by] Rachel G. Ragland, Kelly A. Woestman.
p. cm.
Includes bibliographical references and index.
1. United States—History—Study and teaching. I. Ragland, Rachel G. II. Woestman, Kelly A.
E175.8.T413 2009
973.071—dc22
2008047462

ISBN10: 0-415-98881-0 (hbk)
ISBN10: 0-415-98882-9 (pbk)
ISBN10: 0-203-87820-5 (ebk)

ISBN13: 978-0-415-98881-0 (hbk)
ISBN13: 978-0-415-98882-7 (pbk)
ISBN13: 978-0-203-87820-0 (ebk)

Foreword

The *Teaching American History* Program
A Venerable Past and a Challenging Future

Sam Wineburg
Stanford University

It would have been easy to overlook the amendment to the 2000 Education appropriation budget. Buried in the bureaucratese of Title X ("Repeals, Redesignation, and Amendments to Other Statutes") was a proposal by Senator Robert C. Byrd (D-West Virginia) to provide $50 million "to develop, implement and strengthen programs to teach American history (not social studies) as a separate subject within school curricula."[1] Byrd expanded on the program's rationale by warning of a "hybrid called 'social studies' [that] has taken hold in our schools." The purpose of the "Teaching Traditional American History" program (the "Traditional" eventually dropped, hence TAH) would be to restore history to its rightful place in the curriculum, thus insuring that "our Nation's core ideals—life, liberty, justice—will survive."[2]

Byrd's introduction of the proposal on June 30, 2000 seemed to catch many by surprise. Congress approved the legislation three months later and the first request for proposals appeared in the Federal Registrar on May 23, 2001. Applicants nationwide rushed to put their ideas on paper and submit their proposals by the July 23 deadline. With the end of the fiscal year looming, Department of Education officials set selection criteria, processed the proposals, assigned them to raters, and completed the selection process by September 21, 2001. The TAH grant program had officially begun.

Few in the profession saw the TAH windfall coming, especially those familiar with the annals of federal incursions into history (and social studies). Some still remembered the thrashing that academics got during the hearings on Jerome Bruner's fifth-grade curriculum, *Man: A Course of Study* (MACOS). Representative John Conlan (R-Arizona) warned members of the House of Representatives of school materials, disseminated with federal funds, that promoted "adultery, cannibalism, killing female babies and old people, trial marriage and wife-swapping," in short "not the kind of material Congress or any Federal agency should be promoting."[3] More recent efforts to influence school curricula by members of the academy haven't fared much better: Lest we forget, there was the hemorrhaging of the "National Standards for United States History" before they died a violent death on the floors of Congress in a 99–1 censure (the lone dissenter angry that the rebuke was insufficiently harsh).

Naysayers who predicted a similar fate for TAH have been proven wrong, very

wrong. Eight years after its appearance, TAH has not merely survived but flour-
ished, more than doubling its yearly allocation (from $50 million in 2000 to $120
million in the successive budgets of 2004, 2005, and 2006), gaining influential
backers (from Lamar Alexander and Ted Kennedy in the Senate to the nation's
unofficial history laureate, David McCullough), and boldly redrawing the landscape of teacher professional development in history. Federal dollars have coaxed
reluctant historians out of their ivy-covered lairs to work side by side with middle
school and high school teachers, often receiving pedagogic aid from teacher educators and other specialists.

If historians' newfound interest in elementary and secondary education seems
to have a surreal quality, it should. Among the disciplines, history's track record
of school involvement is hardly sterling. A variety of reasons contribute to this.
As Peter Novick explained in *That Noble Dream*, historians' efforts to gain professional stature meant distancing themselves from practice—especially from fields
dominated by women and ministering to children.[4] Other reasons have to do with
history's status as one element (and not always the most dominant) in the con-
glomeration that is social studies. And, as Robert Orrill and Linn Shapiro argued
in a recent essay, the professional associations also own a share of the blame—the
nadir coming in 1969 when the American Historical Association shut its Service
Center for Teachers of History, a unit that under Paul Ward had authored some
of the finest materials for teachers ever produced.[5] Add to this an allergic reaction to things pedagogical infecting some quarters of the profession (more than
fifty years after its publication, Arthur Bestor's *Educational Wastelands* still commands adherents) and the new collaborative flowering among teachers, historians, and educationists (chapter 10, Abt-Perkins) is all the more impressive.[6] As
Peter Knupfer notes (chapter 2), "money has a way of thawing even the chilliest of
professional relations."

And we're talkin' money. The TAH largess ($838,172,000 at the time of this
writing) has been a boon—especially to professional historians, providing steady
summer work to many, along with funding PhD students in history programs
at Michigan State University, the University of Maryland-Baltimore County,
Ohio State University, Arizona State University, and the University of Houston
(chapter 2). Buoyed by TAH dollars, new MA programs in "History Education"
have sprung up (at Arizona State), and moribund MA programs, now enrolling
TAH teacher participants, have coursed with new blood (see Woestman, chapter
1). Throughout the land, school teachers have been treated to historian "dream
teams." In my involvement with a Wisconsin TAH project, I've sat with teachers from communities like Washburn (population 2,280) and Bayfield (population 578) as they have welcomed the likes of Gary Nash, Eric Foner, and Mary
Beth Norton to their rural hamlets. A veritable Chautauqua, with the profession's
leading lights barnstorming the nation. Who would've thunk it?

The needs could not be greater. As data gathered by the National Center for
Education Statistics showed in 1997, more than 80 percent of those teaching
social studies at the middle or high school level possessed neither an undergraduate major nor minor in history.[7] With the exception of some isolated projects, few
professional development opportunities exist for teachers seeking to ratchet up

their content knowledge.[8] For the thousands of TAH participants throughout the nation this is obviously no longer true.

As this volume attests, the TAH program has reinvigorated a teaching force and breathed new life into history teaching. The papers gathered here burst with enthusiasm, renewed energy, and creative ideas for reforming practice. The variety of programs—from interventions at the elementary level (where history had all but choked in the miasma of "expanding horizons") to collaborations with state and local historical societies, engaging archivists, museum directors, and professional educators—is simply dazzling. One can feel the energy.

We owe a great debt to this volume's able editors, Rachel Ragland and Kelly Woestman, for throwing into sharp relief the variety, scope, and progress made by history education during the last decade. (While we're at it, we should all sit down and write Senator Byrd a thank you card.) At the same time, the collection before us provides an invitation to step back from the buzz of activity and ponder what we might call the $838,000,000 question. What has TAH wrought?

Let's begin with a thought experiment. If our goal were to overhaul history education on a national scale, would our efforts take the form of our present program? In other words, would we sink a billion dollars into reforming history education by retooling veteran teachers with knowledge many would claim they should have acquired in college? Or would our tack be different, charting a course in the policy arena by working with state legislatures to enact subject matter requirements for new teachers? Would we work to change requirements for education majors, putting teeth into their much maligned methods courses, and socializing teaching cadets to the centrality of content knowledge from the moment they enter the profession?

TAH has given teachers voice (see Gerwin, chapter 7) and in the process reenergized historians by reminding them of their public mission. To be sure, marrying enthused teachers with engaged historians is an important outcome. Important, yes, but in many ways, beside the point: As taxpayers, we fund programs for teachers not to make them (or historians) happy—though, as a byproduct, happiness is pretty good thing. Rather, we invest in teachers so they can help students learn. And it is imperative to document such learning in demonstrable, not just anecdotal, ways.

With few exceptions, the connection that links our hefty investment in teacher professional development and verifiable gains in student learning remains elusive.[9] Forging this connection must be the TAH program's next frontier. We must redouble our efforts to invent new measures that document how programs for teachers lead to measurable changes in student learning. Lest this be taken as a plea for more testing (particularly of the multiple choice variety), my record is clear.[10] What we need, instead, are a host of new measures for gauging students' understanding of history as an interpretive discipline, with analysis and critical thought at the center, as students grapple with questions about the formation of American government, the resilience of the Constitution, and the debates over American Exceptionalism, among other topics. We need reliable and cost-effective ways to measure children's ability to craft written arguments from historical evidence. No longer can we restrict to a small elite the reasoning skills embedded in the "Document-Based Question" (DBQ) of the Advanced Placement exam: such skills must be extended to all. For those who have watched the evaporation of serious reading and writing from social studies classes, we must cultivate a crop of programs that show a skeptical public how history promotes a textured and perspicacious literacy.

In short, let's ask ourselves how we can do better, particularly in showing the link between teacher knowledge and student achievement. In a program designed to improve how teachers teach our past, this goal must be the beacon that guides our future.

Note: This essay reflects this author's personal opinion and does not represent an official endorsement of the views by any government agency.

Notes

1. Cary D. Wintz, "*Teaching American History*: Observations from the Fringes," chapter 15, this volume.
2. Ibid.
3. Conlan cited in Harry E. Wolcott, "The Middlemen of MACOS," *Anthropology and Education Quarterly* 5 (2007): 195–206. For an account by a major participant in MACOS, see Peter Dow, *Schoolhouse Politics: Lessons from the Sputnik Era* (Cambridge, MA: Harvard University Press, 1991).
4. Peter Novick, *That Noble Dream: The "Objectivity Question" and the American Historical Profession* (New York: Cambridge University Press, 1988).
5. Robert Orrill and Linn Shapiro, "From Bold Beginnings to an Uncertain Future: The Discipline of History and History Education," *American Historical Review* 110, no. 3 (2005): 727–751.
6. Arthur E. Bestor, *Educational Wastelands: The Retreat from Learning in Our Public Schools* (Urbana: University of Illinois Press, 1953). An indication of this book's resilience is that a second edition, with retrospectives by Clarence J. Karier and Foster McMurray, appeared in 1985.
7. Diane Ravitch, "The Educational Background of History Teachers," in *Knowing, Teaching, and Learning History: National and International Perspectives*, eds. Peter N. Stearns, Peter Seixas, and Sam Wineburg, 143–155 (New York: New York University Press, 2000).
8. Notable exceptions include California's History-Social Science project, UCLA's National Center for History in the Schools, and the workshops offered by the Gilder Lehrman Institute.
9. By verifiable, I mean peer-reviewed. As Wintz notes in chapter 15, internal evaluations (as well as many external evaluations contracted by project directors) tend to be of dubious quality. Even if technically sound, they rely too often on self-reports, either by teachers or by students. To my knowledge, there is but a single report from a TAH project that has survived the rigors of review by a journal with the expertise to evaluate research design and inferential statistics: Susan De La Paz, "Effects of Historical Reasoning Instruction and Writing Strategy Mastery in Culturally and Academically Diverse Middle School Classrooms," *Journal of Educational Psychology* 97, no. 2 (2005): 137–156.
10. Sam Wineburg, "Crazy for History," *Journal of American History* 90, no. 4 (2004): 1401–1414.

Preface

Rachel G. Ragland
Lake Forest College

Kelly A. Woestman
Pittsburg (KS) State University

Purpose and Audience for the Volume

This collection of essays and research reports from participants in the U.S. Department of Education's more than $800 million investment in the *Teaching American History* (TAH) grant program illustrates the diversity of these programs as they have been implemented in local education agencies throughout the nation. The reports provide models for historians, teachers, teacher educators, and others interested in the teaching and learning of American history. The collection presents examples of lessons learned from a cross-section of TAH projects arranged in various categories including new ideas in the content of American history, American history pedagogical innovations, featuring historical cognition, professional development models for American history teachers and teacher educators, and school/university collaboration models. Each chapter presents a narrative of innovation, documenting collaboration between classroom, community, and the academy that gives immediate and obvious relevance to the teaching and learning process of American history. By sharing these narratives, we hope to expand the impact of emerging practices from individual TAH projects to reach a larger audience across the nation.

The TAH program is a discretionary grant program funded under Title II-C, Subpart 4 of the Elementary and Secondary Education Act. The program supports competitive grants to local educational agencies. The purpose of these grants is not only to promote the teaching of American history in elementary and secondary schools but also to improve the quality of history instruction by supporting professional development for teachers of American history. The underlying thesis of the TAH program is that in order to teach history better, teachers need to know more history. This aspect of the *Teaching American History* grant program makes it unique among most professional development programs that often emphasize a particular pedagogical approach over specific content to be taught.

To achieve these goals, the grants are designed to assist schools in implementing scientifically based research methods for improving the quality of instruction, professional development, and teacher education in American history. The local educational agencies carry out their activities in partnership with an institution of higher education, or a nonprofit history or humanities organization, and/or a library or museum. According to the U.S. Department of Education, "the goal of the program is to demonstrate how school districts and institutions with expertise in American history can collaborate over a three-year period to ensure that teachers develop the knowledge and skills necessary to teach traditional American history in an exciting and engaging way. Through these projects, districts will demonstrate comprehensive professional development approaches for providing high-quality American history instruction."[1] It is the first program to make history professional development needs of the school district primary.[2] This is in contrast to similar programs, such as those administered by the National Endowment for the Humanities, that place scholars at the center of the grant program with the assumption that the impact will be an automatic result of teacher participation in seminarlike experiences with these scholars.

This volume will provide insight into issues being raised in the current national dialogue on the impact of the *Teaching American History* grant program on diverse stakeholders involved in the teaching of American history across the nation and underscored by the annual TAH Symposium cosponsored by H-Net Humanities and Social Sciences Online and the Organization of American Historians. Some of these issues include: the role of historians as content experts and as actual providers of content; the facilitation of communication between historians and teachers; how TAH has changed the way historians teach at their colleges; the creation of enduring partnerships between history departments and local schools; the nature of productive relationships between history departments and colleges of education; how historians are assessing the work products of the projects; the impact of ongoing follow-up on the work of teachers in their classrooms; how teachers are being prepared to do the work of historians, such as thinking historically and using primary sources; the sustainability of the results of these projects after the period of the grant; and generalizable knowledge that is being discovered to inform a national perspective.

This volume contributes to the discipline by significantly extending the dialogue, and adding to the important national conversation now underway, concerning the impact of the Teaching American History grant program, through which the federal government has funded over 900 grant projects at a cost of over $800 million since 2001. Due to the structure of the projects and partnerships, educators, historians, and teachers of history at all levels have been engaged in a collaborative enterprise on a scale not previously experienced.

The chapters contained in this volume address the interests of historians and history researchers, teachers of American history, public historians, archivists, history educators and researchers, teacher educators and researchers, and professional development practitioners and researchers. We hope that readers will use the materials to inform their own participation in professional development activities involving collaborations between teachers and professors, schools, colleges, academic societies, and other resource providers. The lessons learned from the projects profiled in this book can also be applied to disciplines other than American history as models of professional development practices and collaborations in all academic areas. The larger public that is interested in how American history is being taught in the public schools will also find this volume insightful. Preservice history and social studies methods instructors across the nation should find this volume useful for both undergraduate and graduate teaching methods classes.

This volume is the first to take a comprehensive look at the impact of the Teaching American History program. This collection is also distinctive in its attempt to address a variety of audiences that represent the variety of constituencies involved in the collaborative process of the grants. Contributors to this volume have written essays describing emerging practices that have developed from their personal experience with *Teaching American History* grant projects all across the country. Each chapter documents lessons learned from these projects and how readers in the various constituencies can benefit from applying these lessons in future work in various aspects of the history education field as well as how their involvement has changed their outlook and sometimes even their approach to their chosen profession of history.

Organization of the Volume

The chapters in this volume are organized into four parts. Each part presents emerging practices that are addressed primarily to a particular segment of readers. More detailed information on the focus and key ideas in each part can be found in the introduction to each part. Part I focuses on emerging practices most relevant to historians. In this section, Kelly Woestman discusses the emerging field of cognitive history and explores how this research has been applied to *Teaching American History* grant programs through case studies of five Kansas projects. Working with teachers to further develop their historical habits of mind is the first step toward their being better able to teach their students to develop these same historical habits of mind. Peter Knupfer's chapter emphasizes that historians—academic historians, professionals in public history or the public sector—can have a bigger, more powerful, and more enduring impact on history education in the public schools than they had previously thought. He examines the ways that history departments and historians have adapted their university teaching, their research, and their grant development and collaborative skills to the new audience of school teachers. Next, Gus Seligman describes a project designed to improve American history teaching by reshaping the course itself as well as training teachers to teach the new material. The course offered covers the military history of the United States and lures disinterested students into the classroom to introduce them to the ambiguities, subtleties, and nuances that make history the great study that it is. Finally, Laura Westhoff discusses that we need to not only use primary sources to help teachers and students "do history," we need to teach them how to use primary sources to actually improve historical thinking. She advocates going beyond using primary sources as mere illustrations and turning them into more effective tools for actively engaging students in the study of history so that they learn more actual content along the way.

Part II is primarily directed toward emerging practices that can be used by classroom teachers. In this section, Don Owen and Kathy Barbour explore the results of a project designed to provide teachers with direct access to historical artifacts and primary sources so that they can better view national issues in history through the lens of local events. This gives teachers, and their students, the unique opportunity to become practitioners of history. Archivist Tim Rives shares successful practices for introducing teachers to archival research and archivists to classroom teachers. A portion of the essay is devoted to an archives research primer for novice teacher researchers. David Gerwin's chapter focuses on the importance of honoring the classroom teacher's voice in the planning and delivery of a successful professional development experience. His narrative demonstrates many parallels in the processes that historians and teachers use in their respective work with history. Finally, Elise Fillpot shares a model for preparing entire elementary teaching staffs to incorporate constructivist history explorations in their K-5 classrooms. The model inventories essential lessons teachers learned as a consequence of their grant participation that will inform and inspire other K-5 history professional development project designers and participants.

The emerging practices of Part III focus on lessons addressed primarily to history educators involved in professional development for teachers. Rachel Ragland shares evidence-based conclusions based on a study designed to see if there are similarities in terms of what was successful across five TAH projects, both in achieving the goals set by the project and in terms of the types of professional development activities and collaborations preferred by the participants. A model for professional development for history teachers is presented that focuses on the "4Ps" of partnerships, preparedness and planning, pedagogical content knowledge, and practical applications. Dawn Abt-Perkins suggests a model that leads to a productive partnership that binds history faculty and teacher educators in the common goal of supporting middle and high school teachers of history. The model for collaboration creates a common ground by using strategies such as metateaching, study groups, and focused curriculum innovation projects around the practices of historians. The chapter by Ann Marie Ryan and Frank Valadez offers a case study of a *Teaching American History* grant project in Chicago that also offers insights on the implementation of programs attempting to enhance the content-knowledge of middle and high school history teachers. Evidence collected from all partners in the project informs the emerging practices recommended for a successful project. Lynn McRainey and Heidi Moisan of the Chicago History Museum describe how museum educators can serve as a pedagogical bridge for teachers, helping to link the graduate level reading and work they were accomplishing with concrete examples of classroom applications of that content. An explanation of how working on TAH projects gave them the opportunity to be part of a community of learners and develop new products and approaches for working with teachers is included. Finally, Julie Kearney, Emily Lai, and Donald Yarbrough of the University of Iowa present a comprehensive look at how to evaluate TAH projects. The chapter describes evaluation approaches that provide information for improving project quality and documenting the value and worth of the program as implemented. Using logic models, program directors and evaluators collaborate to focus evaluations on the most important questions and create feasible evaluation designs that result in the most useful information.

Part IV puts the emerging practices from many grant projects into a larger perspective. Robert Rook's chapter explores the clash of agendas often present in TAH programs that highlight assessment issues by expressing a desire to "improve student achievement." These programs frequently find themselves caught between great opportunities to develop skill and content bases on the one hand and the specter of state assessment requirements on the other hand. Finally, Cary Wintz brings his expertise as both a history faculty member and grant reviewer to look at TAH projects from a unique perspective. He provides an intimate but outsider's assessment of the program, including a summary discussion of the program's strengths and weaknesses, successes and failures.

Acknowledgments

The editors would like to acknowledge the many invaluable contributions of our editor at Routledge Press, Naomi Silverman. The other talented staff at Routledge, including the reviewers of our initial proposal who provided excellent suggestions for revision, also contributed to the quality of our final product. We also deeply appreciate the support of professional colleagues in the TAH community, especially those who join us each day as part of the H-TAH community and have joined us each year since 2006 to participate in the interactive examination of the larger impact of these grants at the annual TAH Symposium.

We would also like to individually thank those who have inspired our work, including Michael Ebner, who brought a first round TAH grant to Lake Forest College and helped launch the involvement that eventually led to this volume, as well as other supportive colleagues at Lake Forest College including Education Department chair, Shelley Sherman. We would also like to thank our colleagues in both the Pittsburg (KS) State University Department of History and the College of Education, along with each of the university administrators whose signatures were graciously offered for their support of my active involvement in these grants. Mike Bodensteiner at the Southeast Kansas Education Service Center-Greenbush first believed in my ability to write grants and patiently educated me about the realities of actual grant implementation. My fellow grant directors at Greenbush, Jim Rodman and Julie Sneed, have provided infinite expertise in effective program implementation and genuine wisdom when it comes to effectively working with teachers and adequately meeting both their needs and their expectations.

Thanks to the teachers throughout Waukegan and Lake County, Illinois and eastern Kansas and beyond, without whom these experiences would not have been nearly as beneficial, and from whom we learned so much that we share each semester with the students who will one day be their colleagues, and who every day teach the students we will see in our classrooms in a few years.

Finally, thanks to our personal support systems including Bob and Jason Ragland, Sara and Marc Berzenski, Miriam Giguere, and Jim, Pat, and Sam Woestman, whose enduring love and support make everything we endeavor to do possible in the first place.

Notes

1. http://www.ed.gov/programs/teachinghistory/index.html (accessed January 20, 2009).
2. Alex Stein, "The Teaching American History Program: An Introduction and Overview," *The History Teacher* 36, no. 2 (February 2003): 178–185.

Part I

Emerging Practices
for Historians

Introduction

Part I addresses emerging practices from the *Teaching American History* projects which historians may find of primary interest. Historians who have had broad ranges of experiences from conceptualizing TAH grants to writing them to actually implementing them share their experiences here. Whether historians have already been actively involved in these grants, are just beginning their involvement, or wish to learn more about what being a historian in a TAH grant may or can entail, they will find something of interest in this chapter.

Overarching themes

In examining the chapters in this section, four overarching themes emerge from the work of these diverse projects that are relevant to historians. These are: (1) the pivotal role that academic historians can and do play in TAH grants; (2) the importance of TAH grants to all members of a department of history; (3) the important role of primary sources in teaching American history; (4) the importance of contextualizing primary sources both within historical context and the context of an individual teacher's classroom so that they can be effectively implemented in any history classroom. Most importantly, the authors of this group of essays discuss the role of primary source repositories in teaching history, the use of a specific field of history such as military history as a lens through which to understand and teach the larger view of American history, and what history departments are missing if they aren't taking an active role in TAH grants or do not make the most of the opportunity to address other long-standing cultural issues inside the walls of the academy.

Emerging practices chapter by chapter

In chapter 1, Kelly Woestman describes the emerging practices of teachers as historians through the work that she has done to implement five *Teaching American History* grants. Woestman is a Professor of History and oversees the department's undergraduate teacher preparation program as its Director of History Education and discusses how being closely involved with TAH grants has broadened her collaborative interaction with teachers throughout the university's community service area and beyond. Woestman used the research base that surrounds historical cognition, with an emphasis on the work of Sam Wineburg at Stanford University, to work with teachers to first enhance the American history knowledge base of teachers so that they would know more history to teach and, most importantly, use the state standards to support the important work they were doing instead of feeling constrained by the very specific state standards set forth by the Kansas State Department of Education. Woestman then describes the evolving nature of grant partnerships to support the work of teachers as they collaborate to incorporate their new knowledge not only of American history but also of content-specific teaching strategies to implement in their classrooms to improve student learning.

Woestman's experience with TAH grants dates back to the initial year of the U.S. Department of Education's program grant competition and implementation in 2001 and she describes the evolving nature and diverse approaches of the five grants that her project team has been awarded and has implemented through the 2008 TAH awards. She includes a discussion of her projects' emphases on assisting teachers in more fully utilizing the vast number of free primary sources repositories available online as one way of enabling sustainability of program goals to endure beyond the end of grant funding. Finally, she urges her colleagues at colleges and universities to better understand that we are all colleagues who can learn from one another no matter what the label on the outside of the building in which we teach.

In chapter 2, Peter Knupfer shares his insight regarding the evolving nature of college and university history departments in connection with their colleagues teaching history in K-12 settings. An Associate Professor of History at Michigan State University and the Executive Director of H-Net (Humanities and Social Sciences Online), he asserts that even though most academic historians have had no formal preparation or education in the work being done at the precollegiate level, these historians have the opportunity to have a bigger, more powerful, and more enduring impact on history education in the public schools than they had previously thought possible. Knupfer points out that active involvement in TAH grants can give academic historians the opportunity to tear down traditional barriers to not only improve their own teaching to more effectively reach students in their college and university classrooms but also can lead to more engaging involvement with the various public communities served by land-grant colleges and universities with a strong community service mission.

Knupfer also calls for an end to the "cold war between Colleges of Education and Departments of History" so that everyone can benefit. He includes in his essay a discussion of the American Historical Association's Benchmarks for Professional Development as well as the 2006 report, "The Next Generation of History Teachers," and their role in the evolution of history, education, and history education.

Chapter 3 takes a look at how Gus Seligman of the University of North Texas used his love of military history as a lens through which to explore the larger scope of American history and form the foundation of his TAH grant in which he worked with the local Denton Independent School District. Working with fellow military historians and local history education professionals in the school district, including mentor teachers, he developed a TAH program that utilized military history as the "hook" to more actively engage at-risk students in learning American history. Knowing that teenage students, especially males, are more interested in fights and battles and the sometimes gruesome details associated with military history, Seligmann decided to use this existing interest to help teachers more fully understand how to use military history as a gateway into also teaching political and social history in their classrooms.

In the final chapter in this section of the book, Associate Professor of History and History Education at the University of Missouri-St. Louis Laura Westhoff examines the use of primary sources in not only teaching preservice and in-service teachers but, more importantly, in assisting teachers in translating that new knowledge into their classrooms. She points out that it is not uncommon for academic historians to incorporate primary sources in their lectures and presentations to teachers but that teachers often struggle to edit these same primary sources for use in their classrooms. The issue of lack of time is one factor but Westhoff digs deeper to explore how the Missouri projects in which she has been actively engaged offer teachers the opportunity to "do history" by becoming familiar with local museum collections and archives. She includes examples of teachers' work and discusses how this work has not only given teachers a broader understand of their local history and how it fits in the larger context of American history but also how it has changed the way that curators and archivists view their relationships with schools. Finally, she discusses the point that we have to discover how to better use primary sources effectively if we want to be ultimately successful in helping students, teachers, and historians at any level "do history."

Chapter 1

Teachers as Historians

A Historian's Experiences with TAH Projects

Kelly A. Woestman
Pittsburg (KS) State University

As a former secondary history teacher and a professor who teaches preservice teachers in a history department, the U.S. Department of Education's *Teaching American History* (TAH) grant program has provided unprecedented opportunities not only to work with a diverse group of teachers throughout the eastern half of Kansas but also to improve the work I do to prepare future teachers. Throughout the nation, TAH grants should and do take unique forms depending on the institutions, the people, and the settings involved. Having participated in TAH grants since the U.S. Department of Education announced its first request for proposals (RFPs) in 2001, our journey through the current implementation of TAH grants seven years later will illustrate the diverse goals as well as the unique implementations of these American history-centric grant programs in primarily rural districts in the nation's heartland. By the middle of the implementation of our first TAH grant, I had become aware of the work surrounding history teaching and learning and worked to implement that expanding knowledge base into the rest of our TAH grants and grant proposals. This chapter will describe our approaches and methodology for incorporating the study of historical cognition into our work with teachers as they enhanced their knowledge not only of American history but also of content-specific teaching strategies to increase student learning in their classrooms.

The first step in understanding how to support the work of teachers in increasing their own knowledge of American history so that they can enhance their teaching of history in their classrooms and, most importantly, impact the knowledge and thinking abilities of their students is to explore some of the literature surrounding historical cognition. A key and sometimes controversial leader in this field of study is Stanford professor Sam Wineburg. A former middle school and high school history teacher himself, Wineburg earned a PhD from Stanford University in psychological studies in education and is currently a professor of education at Stanford University. He also serves as a professor of history at the institution as a courtesy appointment and is director of "The Stanford Education Working Group."[1] In exploring the research surrounding historical cognition, I first came across Wineburg's *Historical Thinking and Other Unnatural Acts: Charting the Future of Teaching the Past*[2] and the collection of essays he coedited with Peter M. Stearns and Peter Seixas, *Knowing, Teaching, and Learning*

History: National and International Perspectives.[3] Published in 2001 and 2000, respectively, these works presented a coherent collection of work that explains the relevant research base. From that point, I began exploring the numerous articles published in history, education, and psychology journals to supplement the knowledge base we made available to teachers through our TAH grants.

The study of primary sources was not a new concept to teachers but effectively implementing them into their classrooms to enhance student learning was a new concept. As Wineburg and others point out in their published research,[4] the natural tendency of most teachers is to rely primarily on the textbook to guide them in teaching historical knowledge. The biggest downside to this approach is that it makes it difficult to effectively teach historical thinking skills, or historical cognition, because of the usually overwhelming number of facts and dates that have to be memorized in order to succeed not only on school tests but on state-mandated tests to meet the increasing accountability demands of the federal government's No Child Left Behind (NCLB) initiative. In Kansas, this depth versus breadth conundrum is especially contentious given the extremely detailed nature of the Kansas State Department of Education's standards.[5] The good news is that Kansas standards are strong in the individual disciplines usually grouped under the less clear umbrella of social studies. The bad news is that it is an almost impossible task for even veteran teachers to cover every standard for which they are held accountable not only each year, but before the test is given in either March or April of the designated years, the most recent of which were 2005 and 2008; the tentative upcoming date is 2010.

Adding to the complexity of this problem is that many history teachers, even those at the secondary level, often have only had a modest number of undergraduate history courses. As we examined the content backgrounds of middle school and elementary teachers teaching in the districts our grants would ultimately serve, we found that their undergraduate preparation to meet state licensure requirements may have only included one course in history and that course did not necessarily have to be American history. As some of our participating teachers have verbalized and were later quoted in our grants' annual evaluation reports, they did not know how much they did not know until they began participating in a TAH grant. Prior to that point, they had no choice but to rely on the textbook as their "Bible" for teaching to meet the state standards.[6] This impending pressure to teach all of the standards—and securing a textbook for their district or their school that appeared to be the closest to meeting these standards—provided teachers with a resource to do their jobs. However, they often did not realize that reliance on a textbook was severely limiting not only in terms of their knowledge and their students' knowledge of American history but also their options for effectively teaching American history. One elementary teacher even commented that she did not realize how much her fourth grade textbook left out until she became more aware of the numerous monographs, articles, and primary sources she could have easy access to in order to enhance her already highly rated teaching. One of the most important successes of our TAH grants is helping elementary teachers understand that, according to one of our participating teachers, "I can teach history all day." One of our challenges in writing funded TAH grants is to explain that at the elementary and middle school levels, it is almost impossible to ask teachers to teach American history as a separate discipline as stated in the grant program's founding legislation and official RFPs each year. As a result, we work collaboratively with teachers to learn more effective ways to incorporate American history throughout their daily curricula.

To be fair, the demands placed on any teacher of history go well beyond the content or even the analysis skills necessary to understand any individual content discipline such as history. Unlike college professors, they have supervision duties including but not limited to lunches, bathrooms, and buses but, especially at the secondary level, they also have coaching duties that can often leave little of their day for planning their history classes. The problem is even more acute for middle school teachers who may teach more broad-ranging social studies courses that range from geography to civics to current events. The challenge is most clearly evident in the daily teaching lives of elementary teachers who usually have to teach every subject within the curriculum. Furthermore, the state often specifies the exact number of minutes in their day that have to be spent on reading and math and, most commonly, history is left until the end of the day or the end of the week if they have a chance to get to it at all.

What we did know going into our TAH grants was that we had some talented and more than competent teachers in our area who were already experts in how to teach students and, sometimes even more importantly, manage their classrooms.[7] What even these teachers lacked, however, was not only the access, but more critically, the time to learn more about how to incorporate scientifically based research strategies into their classrooms and to locate and adapt the primary sources that they knew were critical to developing students' skill sets in history. The expanding research base in historical cognition was just what we were looking for to help bridge the gap between theory and practice and offer teachers an alternative to the primarily generic professional development opportunities to which they had ready access throughout our region and, eventually, online.[8] By generic, I mean the approach that teaching skills are similar across disciplines and are not specific to the content being taught. The work of Wineburg and others underscores the importance of content-based teaching strategies that ultimately result in student learning of content and content-related skills such as historical analysis. We worked hard to incorporate practical applications of historical cognition strategies throughout each of our grants.

One vital key to the success of all five of our TAH grants is the effective utilization of a teacher leadership team for each grant. For our first grant, area superintendents identified five veteran teachers who met with the grant's administrative staff at least twice each year in addition to participating in the actual grant activities. From these meetings, we gained formal insight into how to keep improving our program offerings and make them relevant to teachers so that they would ultimately impact student learning. Sometimes even more important was the informal feedback they would give us, either during or just after the conclusion of an event, regarding how teachers responded to particular activities or speakers as well as insight on how to handle the people management aspects of having a group of individuals working together in a much different environment from their daily work environment in which they are in charge.

One of the most important aspects of management I have learned as the Program Director for our grants is how I can bring a horse to water, but I can't make it drink. Some of my earliest frustrations with TAH grant workshops and institutes were personified by the teachers who were expecting a ready-made lesson plan to take home with them and wanted no more than that. Furthermore, if it didn't fit the exact content of their grade level, a few teachers did not think there was any reason for them to learn the content. To more efficiently achieve the goal of convincing teachers that it would be useful for them to learn the American history content beyond the scope of their teaching day, we utilized the study of historical cognition to help transcend the limitations of only covering smaller topics with their limited facts and dates to utilizing our teacher leadership team members to help them "transfer" what they were learning to the content in their classrooms.[9]

So, through our TAH grants, we concentrated on the practical implementation of the historical cognition research of Wineburg and others doing complementary work.[10] I want to focus on some of the key points that Wineburg makes in his research and writing to underscore our approach to working with teachers in our TAH grants. In his 1991 article, "On the Reading of Historical Texts: Notes on the Breach between School and Academy," Wineburg explores what it means to read a historical text and draws on his research with both historians and high school students. He discusses what is referred to by some as the think aloud protocol in which the student verbalizes what he or she is thinking at each step of the process of reading a document. Wineburg asserts that comparing the approaches of high school students and historians to reading the same documents is much more complex than comparing an "expert" to a "novice" and that it takes something much different than students simply learning "more" history to develop a broader historical background. He takes a metacognitive stance "in which knowledge is constructed by students questioning themselves about a fixed and friendly text." He emphasizes teachers working with students to bring their own existing insight to reading a document and building on that particular skill set instead of asserting that by becoming an expert on "all things history," a student will be better able to identify both the "text and subtext" of a particular document.[11] More recently, Wineburg published an article in *The Journal of American History* asserting that the challenges we face today in adequately assessing student knowledge of American history are not new and that objective testing will always fail to accurately measure this knowledge. "Light rail excursions through mounds of factual information may be entertaining, but such dizzying tours leave few traces in memory. The mind demands pattern and form, and both are built up slowly and require repeated passes, with each pass going deeper and probing further."[12]

We adapted some of the same approaches described above to working with TAH grant teachers and eventually did so successfully after numerous trials and efforts on our part. Unlike other disciplines, history does not have "one answer" to most of its questions and, in fact, often has competing answers or interpretations. One of the interpersonal skills we had to develop was how to get teachers to the point where they knew it was okay, and actually felt comfortable questioning a particular document or historical text or history textbook.[13] In their world, they had been told that their textbooks were the "holders of the knowledge" they were required to teach their students. Through our TAH grants, we worked interactively with teachers not only to teach teachers but to learn from them how best to help them understand how to go beyond the text and get to the "good stuff" of history. One of the foundations for this historical analysis work was the utilization of the study of primary sources to enhance not only their knowledge of American history but then to provide them with access to historians who were expert in the field they were studying, master teachers who had successfully taught the topic, and, most importantly, access and effective approaches to utilizing the vast and diverse primary sources available free online.

To accomplish the goal of surrounding teachers with primary sources so that they could choose what would work best with their particular set of students, we purposely chose not to spend money on commercial databases that provided gateways to these sites but instead spent the money on the teachers themselves. We paid for their time, provided the technology, and, in some cases, their travel to regional archives throughout the country, so that they could spend time exploring these online and physical sites. Most importantly, we provided them with the opportunities for both the formal and informal collaboration that is often lacking in the traditional school day in which each teacher is firmly ensconced in her or his classroom with the students most of the day with little interaction beyond a few in-service days with colleagues. We went into our TAH grants knowing that we had teachers with a great deal of knowledge about effective teaching strategies but with little time or opportunity to share that expertise, especially in a non-threatening environment in which the state standards were important but were not the be-all and end-all of what was actually going on.

In the early years of our grants, Google and other search engines were not nearly as effective as they are now and most Web sites for primary source repositories were not necessarily user friendly. Effectively navigating some archival and library Web sites sometimes seemed to require a graduate degree in Boolean searching, and we worked side-by-side with teachers to help discover more efficient ways for them to find what they needed and find it much more quickly. Even at the beginning, however, teachers enjoyed having a span of an hour or more to just "surf" the Web. They often discovered the most interesting sources when they were not looking for them and they didn't have to deal with the frustration of having only ten minutes to find something for a classroom lesson and not being able to find it.

Our first grant, Project Mine, which initially emphasized technology integration much more than history, focused on the local history of southeast Kansas and our region's coal mining heritage. As we looked for primary sources related to our cultural heritage, we were able to bring in primary source documents from our university's Special Collections department (http://library.pittstate.edu/spcoll/) and, ultimately, take teachers there to do their own in-person research. It was important that many teachers had family connections or had grown up in the area or at least close by. The discoveries of personal angles on history helped teachers experience for themselves what the research was telling us about getting students actively engaged in history. Just as they bring their own context to any historical document, students are intrigued when they can connect themselves or a family member to a historical occurrence or issue. Those types of sources were abundant in our Special Collections department since many of our students trace their immigrant ancestors to the coal mining that dominated the region's landscape beginning over a century ago. Primarily as a result of this first grant, four area teachers taught local history courses separate from their other courses while most of the others started incorporating at least a local history unit into their curriculum. We had achieved a small yet important step in helping teachers not only deepen their appreciation of American history but, more importantly, in reaching out to their students in ways that would more actively engage them in their study not only of local history but of how that local history fit into the larger scope of American history. Ultimately, we hoped that this increased knowledge would also translate into higher test scores on the state assessments.

We also began exploring what was then the online database system at the National Archives and Records Administration (http://www.archives.gov). Since that time, the easier-to-use Archival Research Catalog (ARC) system has replaced the National Archives Information Locator (NAIL) database system for making archival records and records descriptions available online. One of our first challenges in dealing with access to the National Archives was helping teachers ensure that once they found something, they could find it again. While identifier numbers were intended for this purpose, they often just simply didn't make sense to teachers. So, just as we expected teachers to go to their students' existing knowledge bases to learn more, we had to do the same thing as we planned for online access opportunities within our grant activities. This was especially important if we wanted any sustained impact beyond the life of the grant since few individuals will voluntarily engage in such an often frustrating process. One of the questions that we did not expect helped us to better understand meeting teachers at their point of need. When we worked with them to search for mining photographs, we talked about a project conducted by the federal government in coal mining communities in Kentucky. After we painstakingly guided teachers through learning how to use ARC and they were able to access digital copies of photographs on their screens, more than one commented that they did not know why it would help them to see pictures of coal mining in Kentucky. They wanted to see pictures of coal mining in Kansas. In response, we tried to explain to them that these pictures existed only because of a federal government project to document the living conditions in the coal mining communities at the time and that the coal mining region in the eastern United States was much larger than the one in our state and that the federal government could not document all of the coal mining communities.

So, even though we had shown them a few local pictures available at Special Collections, some teachers saw no use for ARC if they could not find exactly what they were seeking. Later, we discovered pictures of lead and zinc mining available from the Library of Congress Web site which many of the teachers found much more useful in their teaching and much more accessible given their subject/topic organization in contrast to the record groups schema of the National Archives (see chapter 6 for more on archival research with teachers).

While it is clear that teachers did use the primary sources they could either print out or save on a flash drive, the data we gathered from grant evaluations indicated that most of the Project Mine teachers did not continue to search the ARC database at the conclusion of the grant. This may also have been due to the fact that the majority of this group of teachers were elementary teachers and considered it a much lower priority to continue to access these types of primary sources than did teachers at the middle and secondary levels who had more content to cover in their state standards and much more formally scheduled time to teach American history.

As mentioned previously, another important primary source repository readily available to teachers is the Library of Congress Web site (http://www.loc.gov), including the American Memory site (http://memory.loc.gov). Organized by subject and topic area, teachers more readily gravitated toward using this particular Web site. Initially teachers discovered more easily accessible local sources here, and they also found that the way sources were more often presented as part of larger groups fit within their existing expectations for finding appropriate sources, especially visual sources, for their classrooms. It was interesting trying to answer teachers' questions about why particular sources are in the National Archives and why others are held by the Library of Congress. We explained that the National Archives can only collect documents created by the federal government and specific government projects and interests determined what types of records were created in the first place. Because they represented many of the records of the executive branch, the presidential libraries were initially the most user friendly sites within the National Archives system. In general, however, the court records that represented the work of the judicial branch were much more difficult to use not only because of the difficulty of navigating legal terminology but also because of the sheer complexity of the evolution of a court case and the usually voluminous paperwork documenting court cases. As with all of NARA's holdings, archivists were invaluable in evaluating record groups to determine if their contents would be of interest to teachers.

In contrast, the Library of Congress exists as a comprehensive "reference desk" for members of Congress and is not limited to records created by Congress. Because the interests of Congress and our nation's federal representatives are both broad and deep, the collections initially appear to be more comprehensive than those maintained by NARA, at least in the eyes of teachers. As we progressed through subsequent TAH grants, we were able to help teachers more fully understand how to effectively navigate both sites and ask themselves questions about what they might find in each repository. Both the collections of the National Archives and those of the Library of Congress are so voluminous, there is usually relevant information to be found for their teaching of American history. The challenge is to find it easily. The Smithsonian Institution (www.si.edu), most notably the National Museum of American History (americanhistory.

si.edu), also contained a wealth of primary sources and exhibits that comple-mented those available from the National Archives and the Library of Congress.

Also during our first TAH grant, we had the opportunity to meet a represen-tative of the Gilder Lehrman Institute of American History (GLI) (http://www.gilderlehrman.org) at the National Council for the Social Studies (NCSS; http://www.ncss.org) annual meeting. We were simply amazed by their list of summer seminars for teachers and asked how we could make those opportunities avail-able for teachers (http://www.gilderlehrman.org/teachers/seminars.html).

Through our third TAH grant, we sent the first teacher from Kansas to one of these engaging seminars focused on primary sources that involved working with leading historians and master teachers. This type of access also heightened the interest of our teachers in doing more work with primary sources because they saw teachers from all over the country exploring the same types of learn-ing opportunities to enhance their classroom teaching and, ultimately, student learning. We continued to partner with GLI on all subsequent grants not only to provide unprecedented access to senior scholars but to provide these unique collaboration opportunities with other teachers that built on our local approach to that same goal.

What is important to note about the GLI Seminar is its methodology for using primary sources. The historians and educators who work for and with the insti-tute have designed an effective, simple, and flexible approach to incorporating primary sources into the classroom. Instead of creating a complex lesson plan with numerous sources, they provide teachers with collaborative opportunities to design a one-to-two page primary source document activity. Teachers can if they wish design more complex activities that are also flexible because they can usually be divided into parts that are usable within an individual class period. The three major components of these activities are the historical background that provides the necessary historical context, an excerpt from the document that ensures that student attention is not lost because a document is too long for them to effectively comprehend within the scope of the particular activity, and questions that emphasize higher level thinking skills related to history. In other words, the GLI approach makes what otherwise might be overwhelming man-ageable and, most importantly, they have a wide variety of these primary source activities along with a large repository of primary sources that are especially rich in representing the pre-twentieth century history of the United States.

To further complement this primary source work, GLI has created several pri-mary source collections titled, "People, Places, Politics: History in a Box." These boxes contain rich resources not only of primary source documents, but also the work of expert historians that provides historical context, and multimedia resources including music and recorded speeches, and posters and display qual-ity pictures and illustrations that are easy for any teacher to use in his or her classroom. Not only has the institute developed these comprehensive units for topics such as the Founding Era, Alexander Hamilton, and Abraham Lincoln, it recently developed one specifically for elementary teachers and one the history of the American West. These resources can be part of TAH partnership agreements with GLI or are available for purchase from their Web site.

It is important to note that there has been some controversy surrounding the political leanings of the GLI founders, but closer inspection shows that their choice of historians to work with teachers represents all sides of the spectrum of political ideas in the nation.[14] Furthermore, like the government agencies mentioned above, they were providing free resources to teachers before the TAH grants and will continue to make these resources available to teachers after the grants are no longer funded. This is the greatest contrast to the commercial, for-profit vendors and their products sometimes used by TAH grants, since we knew that after grant money was no longer available to pay the annual fees associated with access to them, most of our school districts would not be able to continue making them available to teachers. We decided along with our teacher leadership team that there were so many free resources that it was a more responsible use of federal grant funds to provide teachers with the knowledge of how to fish rather than give them just a few fish for a short period of time.

Another free site, created by historian Steve Mintz, Digital History (http://www.digitalhistory.uh.edu/), which also provides not only primary source documents but numerous approaches to providing critical historical context information to teachers. Designed in an easily accessible fashion with numerous cross-references to related materials, our TAH grant teachers have also found this site useful in enhancing their knowledge of American history as well as the knowledge base of their students. This is yet another example where we observed and talked with teachers about what primary source repositories worked best for them. While initially some wanted to move away from the National Archives site given its inherent complexity, as we developed specific examples of the great resources there, we were able to convince them that it was well worth their time and effort to acquire new online searching skills, especially to obtain free resources that were history content-specific for their classrooms. This also translated into being easily accessible to their students and, when conducting follow-up classroom observations, I observed at least three instances of teachers working with students either in their classrooms or taking them to the school's computer lab to find resources to present in class, often as part of larger PowerPoint presentations, activities which they used to enhance students' inquiry and technology skills along with their knowledge of American history.

A central part of another of our TAH grants was that all participating teachers would work together to complete a master's degree in history, Project eHIKES (enhancing History Instruction for Kansas Educators and Students) provided us with a unique opportunity to work with a captive audience to more closely study how to incorporate the historical cognition research base into an organized course of graduate study offered to both novice and veteran teachers. In Project Mine, teachers primarily took the option of professional development credit instead of the graduate credit offerings first in education and then in history as the program became more history-centric over its three-year life. Another innovative opportunity provided by Project eHIKES TAH for funding was to offer a delivered master's degree in history through two-week summer institutes and academic year online course offerings. The timing was crucial given that our state governing board had issued a new requirement that the university not only had to have students in our graduate classes, we had to have at least five graduates a year. Given the lack of need for a master's in history in the job market in southeast Kansas, teachers were our critical opportunity to sustain our graduate program in the Department of History. In the past, most teachers had pursued graduate work in education and Project eHIKES allowed us the opportunity to demonstrate to them that we could provide an academically rigorous program in history that also, and more importantly to them, met their immediate needs in the classroom and their more long-term needs for career advancement, as well as meeting the more rigid demands of NCLB.

Initially basing the grant proposal on a successful grant from 2002, we modified the course offerings to fit our master's program instead of the MAT offered by their Institution of Higher Education (IHE) partner, Emporia State University. Although we have a uniquely collegial relationship between the College of Education and the College of Arts and Sciences in which the Department of History is housed at Pittsburg State University, we do compete with them for potential graduate students, and this was an opportunity to provide area history teachers with a more content-specific graduate degree option as well as the chance to work more directly with historians not only from PSU but also with scholars representing the Organization of American Historians (OAH) (http://www.oah. org) whom we brought to the host district, Parsons USD No. 503 (http://www. vikingnet.net).

In customizing the components of the Project eHIKES grants to the needs and interests of the teachers in the Parsons USD No. 503, we met with the superintendent and then the assistant superintendent several times. Then, we held an informational meeting with teachers after school and discussed what the program would entail as well as established meeting times that would work for the teachers' busy schedules. Given the size of the district and the common connection between the district's history teachers and its athletic coaches, we scheduled around fall and spring sports practices and aimed for the short break between seasons. During the summer we made sure that we did not interfere with football camp and teachers' other obligations such as summer church camps. Most of our teachers are heavily involved in their communities because even if they are not a native of their particular town, they know more people in the community each year as more and more of the town's children pass through their classroom doors.

In contrast to Project Mine, we started with more records that we pulled from archival sources to illustrate what was possible. This was part of our learning curve in effectively teaching American history to teachers and how to access relevant primary sources. Here is one teacher's response to the primary source methodology we used:

> I started Project eHIKES thinking I knew quite a bit about American History. My dad was a history teacher and I had read plenty of textbooks covering history as well as taking classes in college. I thought I was a good teacher, not necessarily of American History but a good teacher in my content area [social studies]. But Project eHIKES made me realize I was good at teaching facts in a textbook and areas covered

on assessments but not really very good at actually teaching history and the many ways it can be interpreted. Project eHIKES has really made me discover quite a few things about teaching history.

But by far the best part of the summer sessions was discovering how important primary sources can be in teaching history. Reading and analyzing primary sources to an actual event really made the event so much more exciting and real. I had a section on primary and secondary sources in my textbook but never realized the potential in using primary sources until Project eHIKES. Using photographs, video, and audio help the students make real connections in the subjects they are studying.... So definitely the enthusiasm that eHIKES rekindled in me was the first way my classroom was impacted.[15]

Project eHIKES teachers primarily taught middle and high school social studies and represented the host district but also 12 other districts in southeast Kansas. Elementary teachers had dominated the Project Mine grant and we were not as comfortable with the significant numbers whose primary interest was taking home new lesson plans and who were somewhat resistant to learning new historical content, especially if it did not tie directly to their curriculum. Most importantly, this did not differ from existing professional development programs that were widely available from Greenbush, the Southeast Kansas Education Service Center. In contrast to the teachers served by Project Mine, Parsons USD No. 503, however, had several elementary teachers that were interested in Project eHIKES, including earning the master's degree. We had several discussions so that they understood the academic expectations of the program.

We also discussed this critical issue within our department because these same elementary teachers did not have the adequate undergraduate preparation (normally 24 hours) in history content classes to be eligible for admission to the master's in history. We offered them conditional admission and then would review their status in the program once they completed the two-week summer course and the fall online historical research and historiography class. This historiography class is the only specific course required in the department's master's program. It introduces the advanced study of history and emphasizes historical analysis and understanding the history of history—historiography. It is also taught by the department's graduate adviser who oversees the History Department's master's program.

Following the introductory graduate research course, Project eHIKES teachers took a spring online course centered on historical cognition. Books assigned in this course included Wineburg's *Historical Thinking and Other Unnatural Acts*, Stearns, Seixas, and Wineburg's edited volume, *Knowing, Teaching, and Learning History*; Rosenzweig and Thelen's *Presence of the Past*;[16] Joyce Kasson's *Buffalo Bill's Wild West: Celebrity, Memory, and Popular History*;[17] John Lewis Gaddis's *Surprise, Security and the American Experience*;[18] Diane Ravitch's *The Language Police*,[19] Davidson and Lytle's *After the Fact: The Art of Historical Detection*,[20] and Emily Rosenberg's *A Date Which Will Live: Pearl Harbor in American Memory*.[21] After exploring the foundation information about historical cognition in the Wineburg texts, we asked teachers to apply this new knowledge to specific topics that they teach. Recently published works related to September 11, Pearl Harbor, and Buffalo Bill offered an opportunity to further explore the practical application of historical cognition. We provided reading guides for the individual monographs along with an online folder in the course management system that provided teachers with quickly accessible links to information related to each text, including book reviews, interviews with the authors, and guides to related primary sources (these included detailed guidelines for accessing specific primary sources in the ARC system). Since we first started exploring how to assist teachers in making more efficient use of its online database system, the National Archives has published several useful topic guides (http://archives.gov/research/arc/topics/).

Below are two examples of the reading guides we developed to more efficiently utilize the teachers' time as they read the required historical cognition material:

> Reading Guide for Wineburg's *Historical Thinking and Other Unnatural Acts*: This book is the foundation text for this online course on historical cognition. The author is one of the preeminent experts on the topic of historical cognition.
>
> Note that there are two reviews and other works by Wineburg as well as others who based their work on his in the same folder as this reading guide.
>
> Make sure to look at the bibliography at the end of each chapter to get a better feel of how Wineburg formulates his ideas and assertions as well as further reading possibilities for ideas and strategies that interest you.
>
> Some important concepts and ideas you want to be able to define, utilize, and apply, after reading this monograph:
>
>> historical cognition
>> cognitive approaches
>> ways of knowing (and progression from ways of reading)
>> contextualized thinking
>> disciplinary perspectives
>> moral ambiguity
>> collective memory

The following is the guide we used for Diane Ravitch's work that closely examines the textbook development process. We discovered through informal conversations with teachers, that many were simply unaware of the numerous and diverse "versions" of almost every historical event. By having them read this book, we found that they developed a keener sense of the business end of the textbook development process and, more importantly, the politics behind the scenes that often dominate the history portrayed in the final published book. Many assumed that if a historian's name was on the outside of the book that he or she had written it rather than the multiauthor process of adapting higher level content to appropriate grade-reading levels. Furthermore, the book explores some of the sometimes vastly differing viewpoints surrounding what historians think is important about history and what social studies educators think is crucial to learn about the discipline of American history. In other words, our goal was to illuminate the fact that textbooks brought to the table their own "historiography" and that as teachers of history they should feel much more confident in questioning anything in the text. Previously, many teachers had felt comfortable only in identifying the occasional errant fact or caption. As a result, teachers became more critical consumers not only of the sources of history but developed a keener sense of the place of textbooks in supplementing but not controlling what they chose as the best teaching options for ensuring student learning in history.

> Reading Guide for Ravitch, *The Language Police: How Pressure Groups Restrict What Students Learn*
>
> You may already know that Diane Ravitch is one of the people that interprets the findings of what is known as "The Nation's Report Card" on History. This is part of the NAEP testing. (You may Google all of these terms if you want to find out more).
>
> You may also go to the Web site http://www.langugagepolice.com for more information.
>
> As you are reading this monograph, think about how the processes described by Ravitch have affected the history or history-related textbooks that you use in your classrooms.
>
> Also make note of some of the paragraphs in one or more of your textbooks that you think might possibly be the result of some of the processes that Ravitch describes.
>
> Now, the big question—do you think Ravitch has valid concerns? Why or why not? Or is she just a critic to be a critic?
>
> If you wish to discuss this topic more this summer, we can also continue the discussion then.

We discovered that teachers now found Wineburg's and Ravitch's works more accessible along with the other monographs and articles assigned to further illustrate how people think about history. Additionally, learning more about historical cognition and how to apply that knowledge to the incorporation of primary sources into their teaching, gives teachers more effective tools to engage not only with each other but with students in their classrooms. In future offerings of this graduate course, we will include Wineburg's most recent article[22] about students' perceptions of heroes of American history as yet another tool to more closely examine student learning and understanding of American history.

In her 2005 Reflection Paper, Pittsburg, KS Community Middle School teacher Teri Blancho stated,

> This semester's class, Historical Cognition, has helped me understand how history can and should be taught. I have taken several classes on learning styles, teaching strategies, and classroom management. However, this class has specifically dealt with teaching history and how to help students learn. This has been very helpful in my class. It has made me stop and think about my day to day lesson plans and how to engage the students. They don't want lectures and facts, they want to explore and make their own discoveries. With eighth graders, this can be a challenge but they are excited when they discover something interesting and it is rewarding to both them and me to have them share this new information.

Another veteran teacher, Mark Boyd, who teaches at Iola, KS Middle School asserted in his 2005 Reflection Paper that:

Project eHIKES has been something of a second wind. It's given me the energy to take a fresh look at what I do and the resources to make some valuable adjustments.

Because of Dr. Woestman's emphasis on primary sources and her training of us in how to find them, I think they will become a more integral part of my teaching. I have a better understanding of how the concept of primary sources is developed in the state standards and how to profit from their use. As a teacher of what is still essentially a survey history course, I'll continue to rely heavily on secondary materials but I'm more certain than ever that the textbook is a kind of last resort.

Beginning with the Project eHIKES grant, we designed each of our TAH grants to keep the initial cohort of teachers together for three years. We believed that if we wanted to go beyond more traditional "one-shot" professional development offerings and effect systematic change in not only enhancing teachers' understandings of American history but also in ensuring classroom impact on student learning of American history, we would have to work with a cohort for more than two weeks each summer. We also knew that this cohort cohesion was invaluable to ensure long-term sustainability of a grant's impact in classrooms throughout eastern Kansas.

With our third TAH grant, Project Primary Sources, we returned to offering a program to a consortium of school districts as we had done with Project Mine. Again, the close connections that Greenbush has with area school districts made this possible. We used what we had learned from Project Mine and Project eHIKES to offer numerous options to teachers who were interested in learning more American history along with content-specific teaching strategies. Each two-week summer institute would be required, and we could keep the initial cohort together for three years.

We incorporated an initial required archival research experience into Project Primary Sources with the requirement that any teacher who wanted to go to other regional NARA facilities had to participate in the initial Kansas City educator workshop. This was a simple financial decision based on using grant funding responsibly. We decided we should utilize local facilities that were cheaper given less travel and housing cost before supporting more distant work that would require more expensive travel and housing support. Graduate coursework was not required. However, it was expanded to reach those who already had a master's degree in fields such as curriculum and instruction and educational administration.

Teaching American History with Primary Sources (TAHPS) was our fourth grant effort but was different from the previous TAH grants we had implemented because of its focus on teachers in northeastern Kansas. Greenbush had existing relationships with Valley Heights, the lead school district in this TAH project. As we had done before, we designed the program based on teacher feedback from our previous three grants and then revised the program according to the interests of teachers actually participating in the grant as the three years progressed. As I write this chapter, we have completed Year 2 of this grant and are offering this new group of teachers experiences similar to what we made available to teachers in southeast Kansas in regard to content and travel to archival facilities. The TAHPS teaching fellows have been able to research the resources of the National Archives in Kansas City and Chicago and will visit those in Boston in Year 3 of the grant. We added the Eisenhower Library to their list of archival research experiences because of its close proximity to the host school district. Our other grant partners remained virtually the same with this grant as with the most recent grant, Project Primary Sources.

During summer 2008, the U.S. Department of Education informed the Andover Unified School District No. 385 (http://www.usd385.org/) that they had been awarded their first TAH grant. Just outside of Wichita, Andover is a town with a growing population and a superintendent and high school principal who were former history teachers and who were quite happy to hear the news after two previous applications were unsuccessful. Throughout this grant-writing period, I corresponded by e-mail and on the phone with one of the high school history teachers who had been identified as the lead teacher by the school administration. I explained to him what had and had not worked with previous grants. And, during this three-year time span, Andover fell into the lower dollar grant parameters because the district serves fewer than 20,000 students. To accommodate the reality that we could only ask for up to $500,000 instead of up to $1 million, we primarily cut out travel funding in order to ensure that we could continue to have the high quality level of historians we had brought in with earlier programs. In many ways, this is going to be similar to our second grant, Project eHIKES, which like our third and fourth TAH grants did not emphasize travel. Another way to empower teachers participating in TAH grants as fellow professionals and to ensure wider dissemination of the results of grant activities is to financially support their membership in the history profession's historical organizations. We included teachers in our presentation focusing on primary sources in the classroom that was part of the 2003 Innovations in Collaboration Conference.[23] Starting with our second grant, we included the Organization of American Historians (OAH) as a partner not only to offer memberships to teachers but also to take advantage of the OAH Distinguished Lectureship Program. This component of the organization's offerings gave us another avenue of access to well-known historians whom we might not otherwise have been able to include in our grants. The *OAH Magazine of History* was another attractive feature of this partnership with the accessibility it provides to the latest historical scholarship in a teacher friendly approach.

We have supported teachers who wanted to attend the annual OAH meeting each year that we have had funds available. It provides them not only with a chance to interact with historians and other history teachers but also allows them to visit places that they might not otherwise have the opportunity to see. And, being history teachers, they tend to gravitate toward the historic sites a particular location may have. Teachers from our TAH grants have had the opportunity to attend conferences in San José, Washington, DC, Minneapolis, and New York City. Both formal and informal interactions during these professional conferences provide opportunities not only for professional growth and learning but also the development of personal relationships with others who share the same interests and some of the same challenges.

Another useful opportunity for teachers is the annual TAH Symposium cosponsored by H-Net Humanities and Social Sciences Online (http://www.h-net.org) and OAH, which I have helped organize. We have supported teachers' participation in this component of the OAH meeting each year but were the most successful the last two years. In 2008, one of our teachers was a panelist for the symposium, and he shared his insights about being involved in four TAH grants and how it had directly impacted his classroom.[24]

The existing Kansas TAH grant on which we modeled Project eHIKES included a partnership with the National Council for History Education (NCHE). Mike Bruner, a teacher in Chanute, KS, utilized TAH funding in partnership with other area TAH grants to develop a state chapter of NCHE—KsCHE. We purchased memberships in NCHE during Project eHIKES and then paid for our teachers in the three later grants to join KsCHE after it came into existence. These memberships also included membership in the national organization. I worked with four teachers in Project eHIKES to assist them in applying to be on the program for the NCHE annual meeting in Austin in 2006 and they were successful. I also worked with three Project Primary Sources teachers to apply to be on the program but that effort was less successful although it did help the teachers involved learn more about the process of presenting at professional meetings and they later presented at state-level conferences.

We also found attending and participating in conferences empowering for teachers because they also became aware of what resources they had available to them that other schools do not necessary have. They also slowly began to realize that, especially if they had been teaching more than ten years, they had skills and expertise they could share with other teachers to build a true collaborative learning environment. This is in contrast to the traditional "sit and get" professional development that was the primary delivery mode of "expert instruction" in years past. With good reason, teachers are often skeptical of the experts brought in to teach them that do not face the day-to-day realities of a middle school or high school history classroom that are governed by the state standards that must be covered each and every day.

One of the areas in which we had to work was to find a balance in creating teacher learning experiences that went beyond traditional lesson planning sessions while also reassuring teachers that we were not wasting their valuable time. While in theory most of us realize that a great deal of learning takes place informally, schedules imposed upon the teachers' class days often confined their comfort zones to expecting that same sort of regimentation in any professional development offerings. This contrasted with our expectations that we allow for teacher collaboration time that might take fifteen minutes or might take several hours to accomplish its goals. Furthermore, as we attempted to get teachers to be more forthcoming about what they expected and what they needed from professional development beyond "I want it to be standards-based," we found that it was a difficult question for them to answer because no one had really asked them before.

This underscores one of the main tenets of all of our TAH grants—treating teachers as fellow professionals and not as subjects that we are forcing to undergo some type of "treatment" primarily so that we could compare a control group and an experimental group. As noted in the AHA Benchmarks for Professional Development in Teaching History as a Discipline (http://www.historians.org/teaching/policy/Benchmarks.htm), "[c]ollaboration should involve K–12 teachers from the beginning as part of an Advisory Committee to consider the interests for their schools and how they perceive development of their history program." There is a strong correlation to teacher recruitment and retention given that a successful TAH program has to provide teachers with professional development opportunities that are attractive not only in terms of content but also in modes of delivery. By offering a wide variety of modes of delivery with online interaction being the common thread that weaves the rest together, we have worked together with teachers to both teach them and learn from them as we implement each successive TAH grant.

One of the ways in which we tried to effectively convey to teachers what they would be offered to them and what demonstration of enhanced knowledge of American history would be expected from them was to include detailed information in a "Dear Applicant" letter, as seen below.

Dear TAHPS Fellowship Applicant:

We are excited about offering this unique opportunity to deliver professional development opportunities centered around the study of American History from Pittsburg State University and the Greenbush Wolf River Center to area history and social studies teachers in Kansas who teach middle school and high school. TAHPS (Teaching American History with Primary Sources) is a grant funded by the U.S. Department of Education's Teaching American History Program. School districts throughout northeastern Kansas compose the core grant group and will have first priority for participation in all grant activities. You are receiving this letter because yours is one of the participating school districts.

Participants in TAHPS will fulfill the teacher quality requirements of No Child Left Behind in Kansas by earning Greenbush Professional Development Credits and/or PSU Graduate Credit in a content field—history. Besides increasing your content knowledge, you will also learn more research-based teaching strategies to help you incorporate this enhanced knowledge in your classroom and earn the designation of "Highly Qualified" in Kansas. Assessment of what your students demonstrate they have learned is an integral part of the program and is hopefully a positive point for both you and your district and/or building administrator.

Because of grant funding, we will be able to bring in nationally-ranked historians to work with you side-by-side as you both learn more history and learn how to apply this enhanced content knowledge in history to your classrooms. These historians will work with PSU faculty to offer you the workshops and coursework through summer institutes in 2007, 2008, and 2009 and online courses offered through the 2007–2008 and 2008–2009 academic years. Stipends for demonstration of enhanced content knowledge in American history and effective classroom implementation will be available. More information will be discussed during the required initial meeting on November 2, 2006, at the Greenbush Wolf River Center. Substitute pay will be provided or teachers accepted into TAHPS for any grant activities on school days.

You will find additional information about this program on the following pages. Please contact us if you have any questions about participating in TAHPS. We look forward to hearing from you.

Then we all signed the letter and along the bottom listed the Grant ID 3 along with each of the grant partners: Greenbush Wolf River Center, Pittsburg State University, the Gilder Lehrman Institute of American History, the Organization of American Historians, H-Net, and the National Archives (Kansas City, Chicago, Boston, DC & MD, Eisenhower Library).

Besides identifying their educational background, teaching experience, and current teaching assignment, we asked them to prepare a typed, double-spaced essay of two to four pages that explained their interest in this *Teaching American History* grant program and references the following: teaching experience, interest in American history (if they didn't currently teach U.S. history, we asked them how they would address applying the material and strategies learned in their classrooms), classroom impact, intent to share knowledge with other teachers, and why they were interested in participating in this particular grant.

Utilizing increasingly user friendly online technology options to reach teachers was also a key not only in the success of our TAH grants but in effectively reaching out to teachers beyond the physical boundaries of time and place. In our mostly rural area, there has been a forthright effort to prepare our students for the increasing demands of the world and the workforce they will enter as adults and the physical distance between many of our schools and within most of our school districts has necessitated utilizing technology as the most cost and time efficient way to support enhanced learning opportunities for teachers and students. Online course management systems such as Blackboard (http://www.blackboard.com) originally allowed us to post information and resources for teachers and provided a venue for us to share their work products, including everything from historical background information to primary sources to fully developed lesson plans. This provided an easy to access environment while also attempting to deal with sometimes less than clear copyright issues. During the last two years, however, we have moved more distinctly into the freely available online tools from Google and found that teachers appreciate the "instant sharing." In fact, one of the positive side effects of using Google Docs is that teachers have learned to use free online tools such as Picassa to share images without having to worry about cyberspace transfer rates associated with e-mailing pictures.

Since our second grant, we had taken advantage of the free blogging tool then available through Blogger.com and now available through Google as part of iGoogle.com. Because the teachers in Project eHIKES were all working on the master's in history, we had better ways of ensuring cooperation as we pushed them to explore new frontiers not only in historical learning and understanding but also in utilizing online tools to expedite that entire process. This same group of teachers was the first to participate in online courses from Pittsburg State University during the fall and spring semester. These courses included not only the previously mentioned historical research and historiography and historical cognitions but graduate courses focused on American history in the twentieth century and specifically on primary sources of an individual teacher's choosing.

How did we make all of these approaches unique from previous professional development offerings for teachers in our area work and how did a professor at a small regional state university come to be so intimately involved in TAH grants?

The Southeast Kansas Education Service Center-Greenbush (http://www.green-bush.org) in rural southeast Kansas serves sixty primarily rural school districts in southeast Kansas with almost every possible service schools and students might need from the classrooms to the physical plants to the personnel. In the more than thirty years of its existence, Greenbush had focused on serving teachers at the elementary level and primarily focused on science and math when it offered content-specific professional development opportunities for teachers. Because it depends primarily on grant funding to sustain its programming, Greenbush was able to take advantage of the initial announcement of TAH grants despite the short time frame allowed for grant submission.

One of my graduate students had recently begun work at Greenbush and she had already recommended me to design some history-focused professional development programs and online advanced placement offerings. As a result, the organization's grant writers asked me history-specific questions that I later discovered became part of its first successful TAH grant application. Project Mine, funded in 2001 and offering summer institutes for teachers and camps for students, focused on the area's mining history and explored the local connections utilizing the history of coal, lead, and zinc mining in the school curriculum. The teachers worked together for a week each summer to design a camp for students to be held the following week in order to ensure immediate implementation of the lesson plans developed by teachers. Most importantly, technology was initially emphasized much more than American history content because of the interests of the project director as well as institutional expectations. During the first year, the grant provided teachers with a PocketPC with which to do their work and many of the teachers signed up primarily to receive "the computer." In contrast to Project Mine and, as the grants evolved, however, teachers were expected to demonstrate an increase in their own knowledge of American history as well as that of their students.

Over the course of the three-year life of Project Mine, I served as the historical consultant. The responsibilities that went with this position also grew throughout this period as I learned more about the stated goals of the TAH program as well as the expectations of the TAH program staff at the U.S. Department of Education. As I gradually became aware of how much money "nonhistory" presenters were being paid to speak with teachers, I suggested that, for the same amount of money, we could bring in nationally known historians and history education specialists to work with teachers to provide a unique experience that enhanced the work of local professional development specialists who already worked with Greenbush. In the process, I learned a great deal about contracting with individuals and the various approaches to effectively securing their services as well as ensuring that what they brought to Project Mine met the goals of the program and also met teacher expectations.

This opportunity presented itself at a time when my university was under the microscope of our state governing board, the Board of Regents, which, in order to deal with budget shortfalls, was eliminating programs that did not graduate at least five students a year. While we had a number of students earning graduate credit, even some of our best undergraduate programs did not always have either professional or personal incentives to actually complete a master's degree. As the Department of History discussed how to meet this challenge from the Board of Regents, we agreed to utilize our partnership role in a TAH grant to deliver a master's degree to the school district that was thirty-five miles from our campus. Although that seems like a short distance, the reality of teachers who worked until after 6 p.m. and even later on game nights, in addition to the planning and grading work they took home with them each night did not allow for them to easily drive to campus. Furthermore, we saw an opportunity to expand our increasing use of online technology to meet the needs and interests of our students as well as allow teachers to spend time reading and studying history that would have normally been spent driving.

Through Project eHIKES, we were able to give teachers laptop computers to ensure that they had the fullest possible access to the technology required to take online classes. They would also be expected to bring the laptops with them to their two-week summer institutes and their one-day fall and spring institutes that were all part of the delivered master's coursework. This hybrid approach allowed us to test the waters in a variety of ways to maintain rigorous academic standards while also being flexible in how teachers participated in graduate coursework.

I began teaching at Pittsburg State in 1993 after being a junior high and high school social studies and history teacher for four years and teaching and running two teacher education programs for the Department of History at the University of West Florida. Pittsburg State hired me to teach twentieth century U.S. history and to lead the department's teacher education program, including teaching the required education methods course and supervising teachers. While I had attempted in the past to work with teachers to offer graduate credit that was specific to the content they taught in contrast to the more common general or interdisciplinary course offerings most often offered by our College of Education, most teachers simply did not have time to contemplate what would best serve their needs until a few of them became a captive audience as part of our Project Mine grant. Through our two-week summer institutes and the numerous opportunities for less formal interaction, the teachers became more comfortable voicing their opinions about what they needed from professional development and what types of program offerings would attract them to participate. Since 2001, I have certainly learned more about American history from the well-respected historians we've been able to work with because of TAH grant funding but, more importantly, from the teachers who teach the students who show up in my university classroom. Since almost 80 percent of our majors are planning to become teachers, this also enhances my ability to effectively teach the undergraduate teaching methods class that is required as part of our teacher education program.

Tracy Hutton, a teacher who has participated in three of our TAH grants, including twice as part of our Teacher Leadership Team, has shared her insight as part of the materials published on the National History Education Clearinghouse. Her essay underscores the challenges teachers face as they move away from primary reliance on textbooks and begin exploring how to incorporate primary sources from a variety of sources to enhance student learning in their classrooms:

All the success I enjoyed using primary sources did not come without some difficulties. Because this method of teaching goes against the traditional lecture approach to teaching history, it took some time for my students, their parents, and the school administration to really understand that this was the "meat and potatoes" of the content and not the "dessert." By using primary sources, my class became student-centered. Rarely did I lecture. Instead, my students were engaged in inquiry and research. They were seeking to answer their own questions. Because they did not have lecture notes, many of my military dads—who were avid history buffs—questioned my approach. However, I did not back down and soon my school administrators realized that my students were performing better on state tests than their peers.

It is important to keep expectations high in this type of classroom setting. The teacher must have a strong classroom management system in place and provide clear instructions. It is essential that the teacher roam the room and converse with all groups to gauge the level of understanding and involvement of students. This is where differentiation can really happen and problems can be solved.[25]

Teachers will continue to face these and other challenges and what teachers need from historians is going to change over time. This change is most dependent on how often the state standards are rewritten and how often state assessments are given and at what grade level. As historians, if we want to ensure the most accurate and the most engaging history is taught to our students before they arrive on our doorsteps, we need to work collaboratively and move well beyond the "sage on the stage" model of content delivery. In exchange, we can learn a great deal from precollegiate teachers and will, as a result, connect more to the students who show up each year in our college and university classrooms. Following the guidelines set forth in the collaborative report, *The Next Generation of History Teachers: A Challenge to Departments of History at American Colleges and Universities*,[26] is one way to do this. Another approach to consider is to be sure to allow collaboration time during the TAH sessions among teachers with the historian(s) still in the room listening and available to field questions related to the history, the historiography, and the primary sources discussed. In her grant Reflection paper, Pittsburg High School teacher Marjorie Giffin shared their beliefs about the importance of teacher collaboration:

> Even though, as I stated, most of the topics were earlier than what I directly teach in the classroom, I am always able to take away bits and pieces from nearly every lesson that I attended. One of the great things about listening to other teachers, attending seminars, listening to renowned scholars, etc., is that no matter what the topic or what era is at the center of the lesson, there is always something good that can be taken from it. Aside from the general knowledge acquired, there are ideas, strategies, anecdotes, and connections to what I do teach that are always welcomed.

As we move forward to implement current and future *Teaching American History* grants, we continue to incorporate both formal and informal feedback to ensure that we are meeting both the statutory guidelines for this federal grant program that is critical to ensuring change in how we teach history at all levels and meet the inherent needs of teachers already overwhelmed by what is expected of them each day. We treat teachers as fellow professionals and continue to work with them side-by-side to meet the real-world demands that dominate their teaching days. State standards and state assessments are political battles in many states and historians need to be sure to engage in these more local debates where they can make a difference. Those of us working at state-funded institutions of higher learning especially owe it to the teachers in our service area to reach out to them even after funding ends to ensure that elementary, middle, and secondary teachers have access to the latest knowledge of American history being published in the larger historical community. And, most importantly, we need to keep learning from the teachers who eventually send their students to our classrooms and whom we train to go back to the local precollegiate classrooms. As the research base surrounding historical cognition expands, we can only achieve the most benefit for all of our students by simply working together.

Notes

1. Wineburg's most recent grant award was $7 million from the U.S. Department of Education to support the National History Education Clearinghouse (NHEC; www.historical-thinkingmatters.org). The clearinghouse is a joint project of the Center for History and New Media (CHNM) at George Mason University, Stanford University, the American Historical Association, and the National History Center; the work is also supported by funding from the William and Flora Hewlett Foundation, and the Carnegie Corporation of New York. The purpose of NHEC is to provide a central repository of the most current research related to how we understand and study history along with providing tangible examples and case studies for teachers of how to apply this research into their classrooms in order to more actively engage students in the complex task of historical thinking. This project addresses a critical need clearly identified by many TAH grantees to preserve the important work being done throughout the country within the scope of TAH grants and to ensure long-term sustainability of what we are learning about history teaching and learning so that project outcomes are not lost once grant funding ends. Not only is the clearing house making available online a diverse set of narratives and active learning resources, it is working to identify the best work produced by TAH grantees to include in its vast database so that these critical assets are much more widely available. Making these vital resources easily available to teachers using the latest technological tools is also a key component of the NHEC and builds on the existing strengths of George Mason University's Center for History and New Media (www.chumn.gmu.edu). With an infinite number of resources already available on the Internet, what teachers most need is an effective means of accessing those resources in an easy-to-use and efficient way to alleviate hours of Web surfing. The clearinghouse is beginning to address some of those same critical needs for all teachers of history.
2. Sam Wineburg, *Historical Thinking and Other Unnatural Acts: Charting the Future of Teaching the Past* (Critical Perspectives on the Past). (Philadelphia: Temple University Press, 2001).
3. Peter Stearns, Peter Seixas, and Sam Wineburg, eds., *Knowing, Teaching, and Learning History: National and International Perspectives* (New York: New York University Press, 2000).
4. Robert Bain, "'They Thought the World Was Flat?' Applying the Principles of How People Learn in Teaching High School History," in *How Students Learn History in the Classroom*, ed. National Research Council (Washington, DC: National Academies Press, 2005), 179–213; Joan E. Talbert, Milbrey Wallin McLaughlin, and Brian Rowan, "Understanding Context Effects on Secondary School Teaching," *Teachers College Record* 95, no. 1 (1993): 45–68, http://www.tcrecord.org/Content.asp?ContentId=110 (accessed May 14, 2008); and Thomas Andrews and Flannery Burke, "What Does It Mean to Think Historically?" *AHA Perspec-*

tives 45, no. 1(2007), http://www.historians.org/perspectives/issues/2007/0701/0701tea2.cfm (accessed March 15, 2008).

5. Kansas State Department of Education, "History and Government; Economics and Geography," Kansas State Department of Education, http://www.ksde.org/Default.aspx?tabid=1715 (accessed August 1, 2008).

6. For more on teachers and textbooks, see David Kobrin, Sarah Faulkner, Stephanie Lai, and Laura Nally, "Benchmarks for High School History: Why Even Good Textbooks and Good Standardized Tests Aren't Enough," *AHA Perspectives* 41, no. 1 (2003), http://www.historians.org/perspectives/issues/2003/0301/0301tec1.cfm (accessed July 27, 2008).

7. An article related to this topic, "Integrating Teacher Feedback and Teaching American History Grants" previously appeared in the Teaching Column of the 2007 *AHA Perspectives,* http://www.historians.org/perspectives/issues/2007/0702/0702tea1.cfm. In the same issue, Bruce VanSledright published, "Why Should Historians Care about History Teaching?" that might also be of interest to readers.

8. For additional research on this topic, see three articles in the special section on the Teaching American History Program in the February 2007 issue of *The History Teacher*: Wilson J. Warren, "Closing the Distance Between Authentic History Pedagogy and Everyday Classroom Practice," *The History Teacher* 36, no. 2 (2007), http://www.historycooperative.org/journals/ht/40.2/warren.html (accessed May 3, 2008); Timothy D. Hall and Renay Scott, "Closing the Gap Between Professors and Teachers: 'Uncoverage' as a Model of Professional Development for History Teachers," *The History Teacher* 36, no. 2 (2007), http://www.historycooperative.org/journals/ht/40.2/hall.html (accessed May 3, 2008); and Stephen Mucher, "Building a Culture of Evidence Through Professional Development," *The History Teacher* 36, no. 2 (2007), http://www.historycooperative.org/journals/ht/40.2/mucher.html (accessed May 3, 2008).

9. For more on TAH grants and their potential for impacting ongoing teacher education, see Jack Bareilles, "Using Teaching American History Grants to Build Ongoing Teacher Education," *OAH Newsletter* 32, no. 3 (2004), http://www.oah.org/pubs/nl/2004aug/bareilles.html (accessed June 1, 2008).

10. Bruce A. VanSledright, "And Santayana Lives On: Students' Views on the Purposes of Studying American History," *Journal of Curriculum Studies* 29, no. 5 (1997): 529–557. Academic Search Premier, EBSCOhost (accessed May 26, 2008).

11. Samuel S. Wineburg, "On the Reading of Historical Texts: Notes on the Breach between School and Academy," *American Educational Research Journal* 28, no. 3 (1991), Database online. Available from CSA, Education: A SAGE Full-Text Collection (accessed March 3, 2008). Earlier articles by Wineburg on similar topics include Suzanne Wilson and Samuel S. Wineburg, "Peering at History through Different Lenses: The Role of Disciplinary Perspectives in Teaching History," *Teachers College Record* 89, no. 4 (1988), http://www.tcrecord.org/Content.asp?ContentId=540 (accessed May 14, 2008); and Samuel S. Wineburg, "Historical Problem Solving: A Study of the Cognitive Processes Used in the Evaluation of Documentary and Pictorial Evidence," *Journal of Educational Psychology* 83, no. 1 (1991): 73–87.

12. Sam Wineburg. "Crazy for History," *Journal of American History* 90, no. 4 (March 2004): 1401–1414. Academic Search Premier, EBSCOhost (accessed May 26, 2008).

13. For more information about this, consult Robert Bain, "Rounding Up Unusual Suspects: Facing the Authority Hidden in the History Classroom," *Teachers College Record* 108, no. 10 (2006): 2080–2114, http://www.tcrecord.org/Content.asp?ContentId=12723 (accessed May 14, 2008).

14. For more information about this topic, go to Bonnie Goodman's article, "Richard Gilder and Lewis Lehrman: Interviewed on C-Span," published on the History News Network online site, http://hnn.us/articles/12738.html#.

15. Rob Barcus is a teacher at Parsons USD No. 503 High School and wrote this comment in his grant Reflection Paper.

16. Roy Rosenzweig and David Thelen, *Presence of the Past: Popular Uses of History in American Life* (New York: Columbia University Press, 1998).

17. Joy S. Kasson. *Buffalo Bill's Wild West: Celebrity, Memory, and Popular History* (New York: Hill and Wang, 2000).

18. John Lewis Gaddis, *Surprise, Security, and the American Experience* (Cambridge, MA: Harvard University Press, 2004).

19. Diane Ravitch, *The Language Police: How Pressure Groups Restrict What Students Learn* (New York: Knopf, 2003).

20. James West Davidson and Mark Hamilton Lytle, *After the Fact: The Art of Historical Detection* (New York: McGraw-Hill, 2004).

21. Emily S. Rosenberg. *A Date Which Will Live: Pearl Harbor in American Memory* (Durham, NC: Duke University Press, 2003).

22. Sam Wineburg and Chauncey Monte-Sano, "'Famous Americans': The Changing Pantheon of American Heroes," *The Journal of American History* 94, no. 4 (2008), http://www.history-cooperative.org/journals/jah/94.4/wineburg.html (accessed April 15, 2008).

23. For more on the Innovations in Collaboration conference, see William Weber, "'Innovations in Collaboration': A Report," *AHA Perspectives* 41, no. 7 (2003), http://www.historians.org/perspectives/issues/2003/0310/0310aha1.cfm (accessed August 1, 2008).

24. For more information on the TAH Symposium, see Kelly Woestman, "How TAH Grants Educate Professors: A Report from the Third Annual TAH Symposium," *OAH Newsletter* 36, no. 3 (2008), http://www.oah.org/pubs/nl/2008aug/woestman.html (accessed August 15, 2008); and Peter Knupfer and Kelly A. Woestman, "Second Annual TAH Symposium Builds on Success of 2006 Gathering, *OAH Newsletter* 34, no. 4 (2006), http://www.oah.org/pubs/nl/2006nov/tahsymposium.html (accessed June 16, 2008).

25. Tracy Hutton, "The Power of Primary Sources: How Teaching American History Grants Changed My Classroom [Kansas]," National History Education Clearinghouse http://teachinghistory.org/tah-grants/lessons-learned/14951 (accessed July 27, 2008).

26. Edward L. Ayers, et al., "The Next Generation of Teachers: A Challenge to Departments of History at American Colleges and Universities" (n.p.: University of Virginia, 2007), http://historians.org/pubs/Free/historyteaching/index.htm (accessed February 15, 2008).

Chapter 2

A New Focus for the History Professoriate

Professional Development for History Teachers as Professional Development for Historians

Peter B. Knupfer
Michigan State University

Writing in the summer of 2006, historian Kelly Ann Long recounted the "transformative" experience of serving as a consultant, instructor, and curriculum designer for Project TEACH, a professional development program serving 200 K-12 history and social studies teachers from five nearby school districts. "As my work with the project took my intellectual interests in new directions over time, my focus shifted from a desire to communicate with a small group of historians whose interests corresponded to my own, toward a will to communicate more broadly about my discipline and to share a broad base of content knowledge with a wider public audience," she recalled. Long's work for the program changed "from that of information deliverer to resource provider ... [that] included not only carefully selected materials, but also pedagogical approaches focused on higher-order concepts ... and content skills." By the end of the program's three-year cycle, she and her fellow historians in the project "recognized that our interaction with precollegiate educators had strengthened our own teaching and provided an important audience," and as a consequence, "illustrating the reciprocal learning that can result through such grants, my approach to teaching my own courses has been transformed." Long redesigned her traditional lecture courses back at Colorado State to employ the techniques, philosophy, and objectives learned from her experience with the public school teachers. Such "powerful reciprocal processes entail potential risk for untenured faculty," she warned, and echoing the words of James Horton, past president of the Organization of American Historians, she urged that "history departments must support individual historians in ways that will sustain outreach and networking between educators."[2]

How many of the literally hundreds of academic historians participating in professional development programs seized the opportunity afforded by intensive exposure to public school teaching practices to reflect on what happens in their own classrooms back at the university? How many departments responded to the unprecedented infusion of resources for history education and professional development to begin institutionalizing and professionalizing their new connections both to in-service and preservice teachers? No one knows. Long's experience documented the unintended collateral effects of participating in a professional development program for history and social studies school teachers:

professional development for them became professional development for historians, an intriguing outcome with tremendous potential consequences for the historical profession.

Not coincidentally, an institutional response to her experience occurred that very summer, when a host of luminaries in the burgeoning cottage industry of history education met at the University of Virginia under the auspices of the Carnegie Corporation of New York's Teachers for a New Era project, the Thomas Jefferson Foundation, the University of Virginia College and Graduate School of Arts and Sciences, and the Virginia Center for Digital History to discuss and eventually issue a manifesto ambitiously titled "The Next Generation of History Teachers: A Challenge to Departments of History at American Colleges and Universities."[3] The document, endorsed by several leading historical associations (as well as such major players in the U.S. Department of Education's *Teaching American History* program as the Gilder Lehrman Institute of American History and the National Council for History Education), lamented the "neglect" of teacher education by departments of history, especially at major research universities where, presumably, depth of specialization, rich information resources, a long tradition of outreach or extension service, and the presence of well-funded professional schools of education should provide a fertile ground for innovative and extensive involvement by the historical profession in teacher education. The paper urged departments to reengage in teacher education, offer incentives (or at least remove barriers) to junior scholars and instructors who participate in outreach and professional development efforts, and to collaborate with professional schools of education in rethinking history classroom instruction for preservice teachers.

By the time of its publication in 2007, the white paper offered little that was new, however. Jeremiads about the historical profession's indifference to teacher education stretch back to the beginnings of the profession itself, often followed by episodic and fitful attempts at correction at the policy, institutional, and classroom levels.[4] And for the two years prior to its issuance, the Organization of American Historians and H-Net: Humanities & Social Sciences Online, had been pursuing a partnership to undertake a national conversation about the impact of the U.S. Department of Education's *Teaching American History* program on historians in public, heritage, and academic institutions.[5] But the paper's appearance did signal a major change in the offing for the budding discipline of history education: it was signed by prominent researchers in this field from colleges of education (such as Keith Barton, Susan Levstik, Bruce VanSledright, Bill McDiarmid, and Peter Seixas) as well as noted historians (such as Edward Ayers, Carol Lasser, Peter Stearns, Deborah Gray White, and David Oshinsky). The document announced, rather than presaged, a growing mutuality of interest and collaboration between professional historians on the one hand and researchers in educational psychology, learning theory, and teaching methods on the other. The catalyst for this collaboration between camps that normally keep each other at arm's length undoubtedly has been the unprecedented public investment in history and history education over the past decade; money has a way of thawing even the chilliest of professional relations, after all.

The Carnegie Corporation's Teachers for a New Era program invested $110 million in eleven institutions of higher education to reform the teacher education curriculum, with significant attention to be paid to the arts and sciences; one of the program's fundamental working assumptions has been that "faculty in the disciplines of the arts and sciences must be fully engaged in the education of prospective teachers, especially in the areas of subject matter understanding and general and liberal education."[6] The funding and leadership for this program passes through the professional schools of education on the assumption that partnerships between experts in pedagogy and experts in the content disciplines are more likely to produce reform than are curricular changes in the education schools alone. The results of this massive effort—especially in the social sciences and humanities, traditionally a backwater for curricular reform at universities when compared to math, science, and literacy—have yet to be seen, but its working philosophy underscores the collaborations necessary to effective teacher education in history.[7]

And an estimated $500 million per year over the past decade has gone into federal programs for professional development for history teachers, history digitization projects, museum and library services targeted to historical research and collections development, and training programs for social scientists that include graduate programs in history. Although much of this funding has been allocated separately and with little to no coordination across the departments, centers, agencies, and school districts that disbursed or received it, the number of professional historians and teacher educators in the United States is small enough for the profession to take notice, take stock, and ponder the kind of collaboration and institutional attention that the white paper advocates. Many of these projects, although not directed to history education and teacher training specifically, have had curricular and teaching spin-offs in their dissemination phases that have attracted attention to the basic problem of history education in the schools.

The Role of the TAH Program

Perhaps the most visible of these federal programs has been the U.S. Department of Education's *Teaching American History* program launched the same year as Teachers for a New Era, which has dispensed $838,172,000 million alone in the past eight years through 906 grants for local professional development programs in school districts across the nation. The program's keystone—partnerships between content providers (especially departments of history, but also public history sites and museums, publishers, and centers for historical study such as the Gilder Lehrman Institute) and school districts or regional education agencies—has bridged the historic divide between town and gown in history education. Whereas a small percentage of history departments have in the past been institutionally and officially engaged in the training of teachers on or off campus through certification programs, TAH potentially opened the door for academic historians to move into the public schools in large numbers to influence the teaching of American history in ways never previously imagined.[8]

Indeed, few people foresaw the potential ripple effects into the college history classroom that this program presaged. Launched with little fanfare, hidden among the mountain of U.S. Department of Education grant and professional development opportunities, overshadowed by the ongoing dust storm of national concern about math, science, and literacy education, funded with a tiny staff at a paltry $50 million for its first cycle, and targeted at understaffed local school districts rather than at universities with the capacity to manage large grant projects, the *Teaching American History* program at first received scant attention from professional historians outside the DC Beltway. The staff of the program called upon the usual suspects—the Organization of American Historians, the American Historical Association, and the National Council for the Social Studies—to create a set of benchmarks for professional development in "teaching history as a discipline." Published in 2003 and updated a year later,[9] these widely cited and influential "Benchmarks for Professional Development in Teaching of History" strongly encouraged the use of multiple learning styles, collaborative planning, active learning, an emphasis on "historical thinking," extensive follow-through for continuing education during the program cycle as opposed to injections of expertise at intensive summer institutes, and effective pre- and post assessments to determine the effectiveness of teacher learning.[10] Given the nature of the task, it's understandable that the focus of the benchmarks was on in-service professional development for teachers, but it's still remarkable that none of the benchmarks relates to where the problem of history education begins, in the history departments and college classrooms where historians educate future teachers largely with the same techniques they would use in professional development programs. Two years later an update to the benchmarks inched closer to the real problem and urged that "university faculty who possess a firm knowledge of the needs of K-12 teachers and students in a local area are best equipped to help provide content expertise as well as other guidance to their K-12 colleagues." How many academic historians in the United States fit those qualifications? And is it possible that the *Teaching American History* program could offer a clear opportunity for historians to learn "the needs of K-12 teachers and students" in order to improve history instruction both in-service and preservice?[11]

The Historian's Role in TAH

The instructional styles of history faculty who participated in the early years of the TAH program reflected the idea that historians are scholars first and educators second. Although nationwide data on instructional methods are scarce, both anecdotal evidence and a brief study by one TAH project strongly suggest that those who participated in the project's formative years largely exported their college classroom teaching styles and content to the summer institutes that came to dominate the typical TAH program cycle. A brief survey conducted by TAH personnel at Arizona State University in 2005 indicated that the engagement by academic historians was limited largely to lectures, tours, and short seminars—extensions, basically, of their college classrooms. "We discovered that participation [by professional historians] is at a moderate level," the latter study concluded, "driven predominately by school districts rather than history departments, and characterized by 'workshops' and 'summer institutes' that fit traditional professorial styles":

> Only about a fifth demonstrated vigorous participation by historians in shaping and managing project activities. Among these, almost none mentioned graduate student involvement and few indicated much use of internet resources or distance learning technology. With important exceptions, historians' roles were passive, and largely oriented toward giving traditional lectures; or as one director noted, we "stand and deliver." Evaluations confirm this judgment. Directors were generally satisfied with the role of historians, but there were repeated complaints that professors were not able to adapt content to grade level, integrate state standards, or contemplate teachers' classroom needs. As one director put it, "They do not know about teaching kids."[12]

Of course history professors "do not know about teaching kids" because they teach adults, not children, and the TAH program focuses on adult education as the first step in improving children's education. The findings of this survey do, however, document the weakness of the partnership between academic historians and their counterparts in teacher preparation schools where teachers do learn to "adapt content to grade level, integrate state standards, or contemplate teachers' classroom needs." The missing ingredient in these early years was a collaborative instructional model whereby everyone at the table—historians, school teachers, curriculum developers, and administrators—came first and foremost as *educators* each with something in particular to contribute. Instead, historians came as scholars first and educators a distant second, and they tended to employ instructional methods used in their survey or historical methods classes that rarely, if ever, had been field-tested in professional development situations.

This continues to occur even though everyone admits that the typical public school teacher's work setting is very different from the typical professor's. The former invariably involves teamwork: close collaboration with colleagues to create and align curriculum to external standards, team-teaching, direct and frequent engagement with parents and community, and a command-style administrative and legislative environment with significant influence over content. The typical professor is a solo practitioner working in a classroom with little or no supervision or collaboration beyond "tips 'n quips" shared with colleagues at the water cooler. Indeed, the history professoriate specifically bases its teaching styles on the post-World War II research model ingrained through graduate training, which involves the rigorous, individualized application of a few straightforward methodological principles rather than elaborate scientific practices or discipline-wide technical skills. To research is to teach.

Higher education in the arts and sciences largely is geared to such a result, which mitigates against collaboration between specialists in pedagogy and history. Diana Rigden notes in a recent review of this issue that

> faculty in the arts and sciences are educated and trained to explore their disciplines in isolation and, in some cases, to protect the discipline from the dirty fingers of application. Faculty rewards of promotion, tenure, and salary increases are almost

exclusively linked to pure scholarship rather than the kinds of service and pedagogy-oriented work that collaboration requires. On the other hand, K-12 education, and by extension teacher education, are caught up with the processes of moving children from the ignorance of pre-kindergarten into the experiences and knowledge of 12th grade and citizenship. While teachers' subject matter knowledge is a key piece of this process, it is only one piece and for many education faculty not a very interesting piece. The administrative processes dear to the hearts of education faculty bore others who would, rightly speaking, rather engage their minds on comparative sonnet sequences or experiments to stop light. In the hierarchy of higher education, the best minds are assumed not to be those who bother with teacher preparation.[13]

Historian's Approaches to Professional Development

In its early years, the instructional method used in TAH professional development frequently tried to fit a highly intuitive and personal *research* strategy—historical method—into essentially two *teaching* venues, sometimes blended with each other: (1) The in-service as boot camp model that organizes raw recruits into platoons of teachers and field experts, and aims to have them think like historians in a week or two. (2) The Dalai Lama approach, where teachers sit at the foot of a master in a summer institute and come out with some curriculum and their spirit invigorated. Neither of these approaches—even when supplemented by extensive travel, discussion, reading, or seminar activities—intrinsically builds in either the kind of follow-up in the teacher's classroom that is essential to effective professional development or the habits of professional practice whereby thinking historically transcends a particular building or range of working hours. Most districts did not involve administrators or curriculum personnel capable of disseminating new ideas or reforms in history teaching, so that successful results often were fragmentary and isolated to a single building or classroom.[14] And we all know that the modern middle-class disease—multitasking—makes it well-nigh impossible for teachers, especially in the elementary grades, to engage in yearlong professional development and continuing education in one subject, let alone all of the subjects they have to teach.[15] That condition alone forces much professional development and on-site history instruction into highly compressed time frames that are rarely conducive to the central requirement of any disciplinary intellectual endeavor: reflection. In the flood of presentations at national conferences by appreciative and inspired teachers and project directors over the next few years one could hear of the remarkable synergy between teachers and participating historians, yet the silence of historians about how all of this work affected their practice, or even if it should affect their practice, has been deafening.

The consequences of an instructional method largely drawn from defining the "doing" of history as research, writing, and publishing from primary sources, as opposed to how one learns, collaborates, and shares history with different audiences (itself a variant on the definition of "public history"),[16] were evident in the early years of TAH, when historians stopped by in person or by satellite to tell teachers how to do history. In effect, historians either replicated the teaching strategies they used in the standard college historical methods course (usually offered as an introduction to history, sometimes as a seminar sometimes as a lecture course, but normally entailing a sequence of historiography, primary source research, and the creation of a research paper), or adapted a lecture from a course in their field by folding in recommendations and resources for school teachers. The successful graduate of this in-service would "think historically," the central objective of hundreds of TAH programs, consistent with the National Assessment of Educational Progress U.S. History Framework[17] as well as the benchmarks proposals.

Seizing an Opportunity: Applying K-12 Pedagogy to the College History Classroom

But now consider how historians might benefit from exposure to new teaching methods through their work with TAH projects. For instance, the Oakland Public Schools' "History Grows in Oakland" TAH program in 2006 offered a rich array of presentations by historians, followed a year later by intensive collaborative lesson plan development by teams of teachers. The curriculum development strategy, "Lesson Study," was based on a growing literature in support of team-based lesson plan development in mathematics.[18] Like many recent developments in the scholarship of learning history, "Lesson Study" is intuitively simple and makes sense to teachers at all levels: a group of teachers working the same curriculum set learning objectives collaboratively, design the unit and its lesson plans, and then take turns teaching the unit while the other group members observe. The group then gathers to critique, adapt, and fine tune the plan. The Oakland project rarely involved the project historians in that process—they provided traditional instruction in content the year before the lesson planning occurred. What would be the benefits of, say, applying this simple model to the development of a survey course at a major university, with an audience of perhaps 500 students per year (including a significant number of teacher education majors)? The instructors would be modeling teaching practices that future teachers are likely to use and they would improve their own practice through collaboration with their colleagues.[19] Nothing in the literature about Lesson Study suggests that this method of curriculum development is suited only for children or teenagers and therefore irrelevant to college instruction. Just as school teachers work with their colleagues to adapt advanced content and method to the needs of their young audience, so can postsecondary instructors make the same adjustments in their classrooms for the needs of an adult, preprofessional audience. Indeed, Lesson Study's chief advocate in the United States, who led its implementation in Oakland, noted in an earlier paper about how this method could be spread from Japan to American schools, that "subject matter specialists ... also often participate in lesson study in Japan."[20] Why not here? The same observations could be made about the widespread use of the ubiquitous *Understanding by Design*, Lesson Study's intellectual cousin (in that both use "backwards design" principles), which both intuitively and practically resonate with history instruction at the college level.[21]

Changing College History Teaching

It is not my intention to propose that the *Teaching American History* program or other professional development programs for school teachers be recast to show academic historians how to teach. It is my intention to argue that the opportunity for historians to learn new methods, principles, and practices will not be there for long, that we do well to seize that opportunity, and that improving history education back at the university is a vital link in the chain of education that leads to improved student history achievement in the schools. The *Teaching American History* program remains enormously popular with participants, especially teachers, who almost uniformly praise the approachability and collegiality of participating historians.[22] Thus, it can be a remarkably cost-effective way for historians to get professional development that could only improve their instruction. In order for that to happen, several things must be in place: history departments must treat history education as both a discipline and a collaborative enterprise, and therefore do more than dispatch field experts to lecture teachers; academic historians must be more open to the idea that reaching multiple audiences requires skills they acquire by neither nature nor scholarship per se; and that effective partnerships with professional schools of education, as opposed to each poaching on the other's territory or ignoring the problem altogether, can especially bring progress in postsecondary history education for future teachers.

Some of these elements are already sliding into place and offer a launching point for real improvements in the college history classroom. The institutional response—both through the Virginia white paper and the various initiatives taken by departments—suggests that history departments may be awakening to the opportunities not only for stronger engagement with the public schools, but also for improvements in postsecondary teaching.

The TAH program has in particular given history departments a major opportunity to expand their involvement in teacher education beyond in-service instruction. History departments that previously performed only cursory instruction of teachers outside the survey course now find themselves with major outreach projects that needed to be staffed. This means hiring new faculty, both regular and temporary, encouraging the growth of a new breed of historian—the project director equipped by training and experience to assess content, coordinate programs, manage budgets, hire and handle staff, and work effectively with school districts, other content partners, and the university. Whereas in the past such a position might have been regarded as a cast-off job for adjuncts with better things to do (like complete the degree), they now take on an even stronger professional importance at the intersection of so many vital interests in history education. Graduate training in history needs to take these kinds of professional opportunities into account. How many major universities prepare their graduate history students for the job described in this advertisement for the project director of a TAH grant:

> The Project Director must hold an advanced degree in American History or related field and will be responsible for the overall daily operation of History is Central. Pre-

ferred qualifications include teaching experience, administrative competence and experience, technology proficiency including web site maintenance, grant writing experience, collaborative project experience, and a record of interest and involvement in K-12 education. The ability to relate history content to students of diverse backgrounds and learning abilities and styles is also preferred. The search committee will look for candidates with a rich understanding of American history, a passion for teaching, demonstrated organizational ability, and outstanding leadership, writing, and communication skills.[23]

The addition of history education specialists and project directors to history department staff exposes regular faculty to the ideas, practices, and needs of K-12 educators and encourages them to see this field as an important subdiscipline of the scholarship of teaching and learning.

In addition, some history departments, such as Arizona State, Ohio State, Michigan State, the University of Maryland-Baltimore County, and the University of Houston, funded graduate students, history education faculty, and regular faculty service portfolios with TAH money. In some cases, the leveraging of TAH funds along with other grant opportunities and legislative mandates permitted the creation of new university centers for teaching history, where advanced degrees for teachers (such as a master's in teaching), state certification and professional development accreditation, and historical methods instruction, in addition to conventional research on history learning, could be promoted.[24] The creation of soft-funded centers is a significant development because it combines the flexibility of grant-supported project work with the stable academic structures of line history departments that have major curricular and service responsibilities, especially at land-grant universities where outreach and extension are integral to the institution's mission.

Another advance in history education stimulated by this surge of federal dollars has been the creation of more durable partnerships between universities and public schools in addition to the training programs of professional schools of education. Unfortunately the TAH program itself does not collect data about content partners for the various grants it dispenses, and the one national evaluation of the program so far, of the first two cohorts of TAH grantees in 2001 and 2002, has little to say about the nature and extent of these partnerships. But the surveys conducted by the evaluation team turned up a consensus by project directors that these partnerships were the key to success; 88 percent of the project directors responding to the survey mentioned the need for effective partnerships with nearby historical institutions and academic departments in order to improve the teaching of history.[25]

A New Type of Academic Partnership

But partnerships *within* the university can be just as vital as partnerships between departments and schools, and on that point the evidence of progress is less encouraging. Some departments have responded to new opportunities in history education by creating their own history education programs parallel to, but not coordinated with, social studies or history education up the street at the campus's College of Education. Such an approach typically entails unilaterally creating history courses on the teaching of history in the schools in order to "rescue" history from the methodologists and make sure it's "done right," and to launch professional development through outreach, in-class, summer, and on-campus institutes, seminars, tours, and Web sites packed with lesson plans, lists of links, video, and bibliography. For example, the History Department at Arizona State University has adopted both of these strategies. Supported by the College, three TAH grants, and foundation funding, it has conducted almost six years of outreach instruction in local schools and offers its own history teaching methods class for teacher candidates at the university. It hired faculty dedicated to history education, assigned existing faculty to work in the program, and formed alliances with local public history organizations through the department's flagship public history program. Declaring its purpose to be "serving history teachers and their students," the department crafted a Web site[26] that is well-maintained, up to date, and filled with useful material for in-service teachers.

Integrating History and Pedagogy

But do such efforts entail rethinking the college history classroom? How many of them forge new alliances with local educational methods and field instructors whose courses very often enroll the same students as the home department? A common complaint among teacher candidates is that there is no connection between the history they learn from historians and the methods they learn from their field instructors. Instead of segregating teacher preparation issues to a new track of courses, have history departments found ways to incorporate assessments, teaching strategies, and learning activities in the regular curriculum, so that preservice teachers are exposed to pedagogical issues and new learning theory at the same time they are immersed in conventional historical reading, writing, and analysis?

Even though historians care a lot about teaching and discuss it frequently, they are loathe to open their classrooms to the kinds of observation, critique, and new ideas grounded in research-based scholarship of learning that could resolve that problem. "This reluctance to be accountable for what happens in the classroom is the largest obstacle to the progress of a scholarship of teaching and learning in history," one recent review of the field has observed. "The greatest challenge ahead will be to convince skeptical [college] history teachers that they have an intellectual opportunity as well as a moral responsibility to bring the scholar's playfulness and piety into their classrooms."[27] The authors of this review properly defend the flexibility and spontaneity of college instruction and eschew any intention of subjecting it to the more rigid and stultifying consequences of formal peer review. Yet the typical form of evaluation for college history instructors—the student survey accompanied on rare occasions by a class visit by a committee or department chair—comes nowhere near the kind of reflective, searching critique of instructional method to which public school teachers are accustomed.

Their experience with team teaching, collaborative curriculum construction, and repeated rethinking and experimentation in their practice can be of enormous value to college history instructors.

The traditional reluctance to consider the possibility that classroom practices and teaching methods in the historical profession play a major role in creating the very problem that teacher professional development tries to solve, is more than evident in the remarkable indifference of history departments to the opportunities inherent in the *Teaching American History* program. Despite the tremendous potential for professional development in the pedagogy of history in higher education, department after department that participates in the program simply sends historians to local schools to replay the stand-and-deliver methods of the typical college classroom—lectures, punctuated by ubiquitous, mind-numbing PowerPoint presentations with occasional question-and-answer formats. In some cases, teachers endure discussions and minilectures about what it takes to write a history monograph or why a teacher who wants to escape from "teaching to the test" should just read good books and find a way for that knowledge to "filter into the classroom." Little of this takes the form of conversation among fellow educators who share a common intellectual challenge of teaching history. Both groups are, in fact, educators, and by approaching professional development activities as opportunities for both to learn as well as teach, the ultimate audience they want to reach—their students—could well benefit[28] (see chapter 9 of this volume for an alternate approach).

Although one might argue that academic historians and public school history teachers can both "think historically," the fact remains that their very different audiences dictate different forms of "teaching historically," and of assessing the extent of learning history. This important distinction is often lost in courses that stress historical method while leaving it to the future public school teacher to figure out how researching and writing a twenty-page paper based on primary sources will prepare them to show squirming eighth-graders how to "think historically."[29]

Changing Paradigms in College History Classrooms

Indeed, the last barrier to rethinking the college teacher preparation curriculum in history remains the professor's classroom, which remains largely screened from the prying eyes of colleagues and departments. Some historians have begun to see this, as Kelly Long did, and to make incremental changes in their approach to teaching. Prize-winning historian Carol Berkin has told multiple audiences of her experience in over two dozen teacher institutes that "I have rethought why I teach and how. I have reevaluated my relationship with nonacademics; and I have redefined what being a member of my profession means to me."[30] Now she enters her classroom with a different outlook, asking herself: "Who are your students? Not who do I wish they were? But, who *are* they? And how can I best reach them?" Will this epiphany for an influential historian and popular teacher stretch beyond significant changes to the way she lectured, and to further incorporate different forms of instruction, assessment, and learning activities that might relate the "doing" of history to the "doing" of the students' intended professions, however vaguely those might be defined for students in an introductory course?

Professor Karen Halttunen of the University of Southern California has made that leap. Responding to the "dramatic" influence of collaboration with school teachers, she

> began to move away from what learner-centered education proponents call the "sage-on-the-stage" model of teaching towards the "guide-on-the-side." I have learned the value of pedagogical variety, and particularly the cultivation of different teaching modalities for different types of learners. I have a new appreciation for the value of kinesthetic learning: rearranging chairs for in-class discussions, taking trips to museums and historic sites, attending movies and plays with my students. In my classrooms, I have come to privilege academic history less, and public history more; and I now try to identify potential K-12 teachers among my students, to encourage their interest, and help prepare them for their own classrooms. I have learned the value of collaborative research towards a single larger project, such as a public-history installation or a website.[31]

Suggestions for Widespread Change: Placing Teaching in the Forefront

What can history departments do to encourage the kind of reinvigoration of the classroom that Halttunen and Long have been experiencing? First, they need to seize whatever opportunities present themselves for faculty to work with teachers in the role of educators who happen to have published, and not as scholars who happen to teach a few times a week. By placing education and teaching in the forefront of outreach, curriculum development, and other history teaching activities, the department reinforces both its pedagogical role and the importance of students (and teacher candidates in particular) in the undergraduate curriculum, as well as in the local schools.

Departments also can revisit the service courses that teacher candidates frequent (mainly because they are required to take them). The introductory surveys and the methods or historiography classes that commonly make up the core of the history major or minor offer a common curriculum and a shared emphasis on methods that make them the perfect beginning for the department's efforts to cater to the needs of future teachers. The writing requirement that these courses usually must meet should be examined in light of the kinds of learning activities and assessments that teachers must design. For example, the alternative to the term paper need not be simplistic PowerPoint presentations, but could instead involve storyboarding of biography or a primary documents assignment supported by an extensive narrative that justifies the selection of materials and explains the historiographical and educational basis for the design and content of the assignment. Such an activity can be just as challenging to a young history teacher as a major research paper would be.

Departments also can begin to harvest the wealth of learning and information that their staff acquires from involvement in professional development and outreach by creating a department library and archive of successful grant applications, recent literature on the scholarship of history learning and teaching, and a digital repository of video, lesson plans, and curriculum that their staff works on with teachers. Faculty members who incorporate some of these ideas into their college courses should be encouraged to share them and to work with others to adapt them to their courses.

Finally, it is time to end the cold war over history and social studies education between colleges of education and departments of history. Both have a deep, vested interest in fostering generations of successful history teachers and both bring unique strengths to the effort. History departments that launch their own methods courses should collaborate with their colleagues in education so as to introduce and reinforce content and method that meet disciplinary standards. Social studies and history methods and field instructors in departments of teacher education or curriculum and instruction should work with graduate students and faculty in history to use sample content drawn from history courses that their common students are likely to have taken by the time they approach graduation. Capstone courses such as senior seminars for majors, intern teaching in the schools, and senior methods courses or masters' for teachers programs should benefit from collaboration between historians and instructors in the college of education to demonstrate that the division of labor between the content disciplines and the professional methods disciplines can produce more light than heat.

The unprecedented investment and interest in history education has yet to be examined systematically, and no study of its backward linkages to the college curriculum or the history classroom has been conducted. If there is any symbiotic relationship between professional development for school teachers and pedagogy in the typical college history classroom, it has yet to surface beyond anecdotal evidence of the kind sketched here. In sum, the great strides of recent decades in history education—especially in research on learning theory, experience with professional development programs in partnership with schools, and the creation of history education centers at major universities—have yet to breach the last redoubt of the academic fortress, the college history classroom, where all future teachers learn the history that eventually they will be teaching.

Notes

1. I wish to thank the editors, Sam Wineburg, Bethany Hicks, Ted Mitchell, the inspiring teachers and staff of the Battle Creek Teaching American History Project, Robert Floden and the Teachers for a New Era Project at Michigan State University, and the Department of History at Michigan State University, for research and resources in support of this essay.
2. Kelly Ann Long, "Reflections on TAH and the Historian's Role: Reciprocal Exchanges and Transformative Contributions to History Education," *The History Teacher* 39, no. 4(August 2006): 498, 500, 501, 505. Retrieved January 20, 2009, from http://www.historycooperative. org/journals/ht/39.4/long.html. For a similar self-discovery, see Karen Halttunen, "From K-12 Outreach to K-16 Collaboration," *National History Education Clearinghouse* (2008), http://teachinghistory.org/tah-grants/lessons-learned/19347 (accessed January 20, 2009).

3. Edward L. Ayers et al., "The Next Generation of Teachers: A Challenge to Departments of History at American Colleges and Universities" (n.p.: University of Virginia, 2007), http://historians.org/pubs/Free/historyteaching/index.htm (accessed January 20, 2009). On Teachers for a New Era, see http://www.teachersforanewera.org/ (accessed January 20, 2009). The document opened auspiciously with the challenge that "every department...devote at least one departmental meeting in 2007 to discussing this message."

4. For some recent reviews of this topic, see Ian Tyrrell, *Historians in Public: The Practice of American History, 1890–1970* (Chicago: University of Chicago Press, 2005); Robert Orrill and Linn Shapiro, "Forum Essay: From Bold Beginnings to an Uncertain Future: The Discipline of History and History Education," *American Historical Review* 110, no.3 (June 2005), http://www.historycooperative.org/journals/ahr/110.3/orrill.html (accessed January 20, 2009).; Allan E. Yarema, "A Decade of Debate: Improving Content and Interest in History Education," *The History Teacher* 35, no. (May 2002):389–99 and a brief discussion in David Wrobel, "A Lesson from the Past and Some Hope for the Future: The History Academy and the Schools, 1880–2007," *The History Teacher* 41, no. 2 (February 2008): 151–62.

5. The programs for the annual OAH/H-Net Symposia on TAH, which have continued up to the present, may be found by following the links from the 2006, 2007, and 2008 annual meetings of the OAH, at http://www.oah.org/meetings/, and at http://www.h-net.org/~tah/ (accessed January 20, 2009).

6. "About Teachers for a New Era," http://www.teachersforanewera.org/index.cfm?fuse action=home.about TNE.

7. Dr. Diana W. Rigden, *A Feasibility Study of the Arts and Sciences / Teacher Education Collaborative (ASTEC)* (New York: Carnegie Corporation of New York, 2005), 2, n4, PDF in author's possession.

8. The program's home page is http://www.ed.gov/programs/teachinghistory/index.html; the figures on awards are compiled from: http://www.ed.gov/programs/teachinghistory/awards.html and http://www.ed.gov/programs/teachinghistory/funding.html (accessed January 20, 2009).

9. Noralee Frankel and Peter Stearns, "Benchmarks for Professional Development in Teaching of History as a Discipline," *Perspectives Online* 41, no. 5 (May 2003), http://www.historians.org/Perspectives/issues/2003/0305/index.cfm (accessed January 20, 2009). Noralee Frankel and Peter Stearns, "The Development of Benchmarks for Professional Development in the Teaching of History as a Discipline," *Perspectives Online* 42 (April 2004), http://www.historians.org/perspectives/issues/2004/0404/0404tea1.cfm (accessed January 20, 2009).

10. The benchmarks have influenced some history education programs, such as the one at Illinois State University; see that program's handbook, linked from http://www.history.ilstu.edu/historyed/students/ (accessed January 20, 2009).

11. Bruce VanSledright, "Why Should Historians Care About History Teaching?" *AHA Perspectives* 45 (February 2007), http://www.historians.org/perspectives/issues/2007/0702/0702tea2.cfm (accessed January 20, 2009).

12. Will McArthur et al., "Improving the Contribution of Historians to TAH Projects," *OAH Newsletter* 33 (May 2005), http://www.oah.org/pubs/nl/2005may/mcarthur.html (accessed January 20, 2009).

13. Rigden, *Feasibility Study*, 10.

14. According to the SRI national evaluation of the first two cohorts of TAH grants, "The follow-up activities, however, did not directly focus on the teachers' work in their classrooms. TAH participants reported that follow-up activities were more likely to take the form of information delivery than visits to classrooms. In fact, only 31 percent of participants reported more than one visit to their classroom from a TAH project representative." The most frequent follow-up method was e-mail. From these findings it is hardly a leap of faith to surmise that the vast majority of professional historians involved in TAH programs were neither invited on, nor sought, nor ended up conducting, visits to teacher classrooms to see the results of their handiwork. Daniel C. Humphrey et al., *Evaluation of the Teaching American History Program* (Washing-

ton: U.S. Department of Education Office of Planning, Evaluation and Policy Development, 2005), 35–36, http://www.ed.gov/rschstat/eval/teaching/us-history/teaching-exec-sum.html (accessed January 20, 2009).

15. For an interesting discussion by TAH project directors about the report's criticisms of project follow-up and other issues, see the month-long conversation in February 2006 on H-TAH@H-Net.msu.edu: http://h-net.msu.edu/cgi-bin/logbrowse.pl?trx=lx&list=h-tah&user=&pw=&month=0602.

16. The issue of finding a "usable past" for "applied history" is an old one in the profession. The latest extended discussion of it and its relevance to public education—is in Tyrrell, *Historians in Public*, 111–52.

17. The Document is available via ERIC: U.S. Department of Education National Assessment Governing Board, *U.S. History Framework for the 1994 and 2001 National Assessment of Educational Progress*, NAEP U.S. History Consensus Project (Washington: Author, 2001), ERIC# ED444928.

18. See references below, and additional material collected by the Lesson Study Research Group at Teachers College, Columbia University, http://www.tc.edu/centers/lessonstudy/articles_papers.html (accessed January 20, 2009).

19. See the elaborate video and research documentation on "Lesson Study" in American history, at http://www.teachingamericanhistory.us/lesson_study/index.html (accessed January 20, 2009). The project's final year evaluation report offers no new or innovative role for scholars beyond recommending that the program continue to "use scholars to deliver content lectures at professional development meetings," http://californiaschools.net/americanhistory/evalReports.html (accessed January 20, 2009), *Oakland Unified School District Teaching American History Project Third Year Evaluation Report, July 1, 2006–June 30, 2007* (Redding, CA: Center for Evaluation and Research, LLC, 2007), 19, http://californiaschools.net/americanhistory/evalReports.html (accessed January 20, 2009).

20. Catherine Lewis, "Does Lesson Study Have a Future in the United States?" *Nagoya Journal of Education and Human Development* 1 (January 2002): 16, linked from http://www.lesson-research.net/resources1.html (accessed January 20, 2009). See also Catherine Lewis, "Lesson Study in North America: Progress and Challenges," in *Lesson Study: International Perspective on Policy and Practice*, vol. 1, ed. M. Matoba, K. A. Crawford, and M. R. Sarkar Arani (Beijing: Educational Science Publishing House, 2006), 12, linked from http://www.lessonresearch.net/resources1.html (accessed January 20, 2009).

21. Grant Wiggins and Jay McTighe, *Understanding by Design* (Alexandria, VA: Association for Supervision and Curriculum Development, 2005).

22. Humphrey et al., *Evaluation of the Teaching American History Program*, 17, 51.

23. See, for instance, http://www.h-net.org/jobs/display_job.php?jobID=30381 (accessed January 20, 2009). For similar positions, see Ohio State University—Marion, http://www.h-net.org/jobs/display_job.php?jobID=26489 (accessed January 20, 2009); University of Pittsburgh "professional developer in history" for outreach in the schools, http://www.h-net.org/jobs/display_job.php?jobID=25914; University of Virginia "Director of Outreach and K-12 Education," http://www.h-net.org/jobs/display_job.php?jobID=4956 (accessed January 20, 2009).

24. For instance, the Center for History Teaching and Learning (Michigan State, http://history.msu.edu/center.php); the History Teaching Institute (Ohio State, http://hti.osu.edu); Center for History Education (University of Maryland Baltimore County, http://www.umbc.edu/che/); Center for the Teaching of American History (SUNY Binghamton, http://www.binghamton.edu/ctah/); in addition to older centers such as UCLA's National Center for History in the Schools, http://www.sscnet.ucla.edu/nchs/. The blend of research and outreach in these centers should be distinguished from the exclusive teacher-preparation and training role already taken by many departments, either through alliances with professional schools of education or by themselves, such as Illinois State University's highly visible History-Social Sciences Education Program, http://www.history.ilstu.edu/historyed (all URLs accessed January 20, 2009).

25. Humphrey, et al., *Evaluation of the Teaching American History Program*, 10, 26, 36–37, 49–50.
26. http://history.clas.asu.edu/teaching (accessed January 20, 2009).
27. Lendol Calder, William W. Cutler III, and T. Mills Kelly, "History Lessons: Historians and the Scholarship of Teaching and Learning," in *Disciplinary Styles in the Scholarship of Teaching and Learning: Exploring Common Ground*, ed. Mary Taylor Huber and Sherwyn P. Morreale (Menlo Park, CA: American Association for Higher Education; Carnegie Foundation for the Advancement of Teaching, 2002), 54.
28. See, for example, the instructive video of colloquia involving history professors and teachers at Illinois State University's Professional Development School Network for Learning and Teaching American History, where even the discussions among teachers and historians involve little or no exchange of information between the two *as educators*. http://www.history.ilstu.edu/tahg/video_gallery/roundtable_5.mov (accessed January 20, 2009). The larger professional development program of which this discussion was a part featured rich discussions of historical materials by historians and teachers, http://www.history.ilstu.edu/tahg/video_gallery/index.html (accessed January 20, 2009).
29. For a defense of the traditional research paper as "an endangered species" in the high school, see Will Fitzhugh, "The Making of a Relic," *Teacher Magazine* 13, no. 6 (March 2002): 37–39, ERIC EJ775888. For a striking example of a history methods course that intentionally instructs prospective teachers that even the most innovative teaching of historical method still should eventuate in a standard research paper that bears little relationship to what those teachers will be doing five years later, see G. Williamson McDiarmid and Peter Vinten-Johannsen, *The Teaching and Learning of History—from the Inside Out*, NCRTL Special Report (East Lansing, MI: National Center for Research on Teacher Learning, 1993), http://ncrtl.msu.edu/special.htm. The authors defend the construction of historical narratives as the essence of historical thinking in a later work, Peter Vinten-Johansen and G. Williamson McDiarmid, *Stalking the Schoolwork Module: Teaching Prospective Teachers to Write Historical Narratives*, NCRTL Special Reports (East Lansing, MI: National Center for Research on Teaching and Learning, 1997), http://ncrtl.msu.edu/special.htm.
30. Carol Berkin, "Doing History: How the Worlds of the Scholar and the Popular Historian Come Together," *Common-Place* 6, no. 4 (July 2006), http://www.common-place.org/vol-06/no-04/author/ (accessed January 20, 2009).
31. Halttunen, "From K-12 Outreach to K-16 Collaboration."

Bibliography

Ayers, Edward L., Keith Barton, Titus Brown, et al. "The Next Generation of Teachers: A Challenge to Departments of History at American Colleges and Universities." N.p.: University of Virginia, 2007. http://historians.org/pubs/Free/historyteaching/index.htm (accessed January 20, 2009).

Berkin, Carol. "Doing History: How the Worlds of the Scholar and the Popular Historian Come Together." *Common-Place* 6, no. 4 (July 2006), http://www.common-place.org/vol-06/no-04/author / (accessed January 20, 2009).

Calder, Lendol, William W. Cutler III, and T. Mills Kelly. "History Lessons: Historians and the Scholarship of Teaching and Learning." In *Disciplinary Styles in the Scholarship of Teaching and Learning: Exploring Common Ground*, edited by Mary Taylor Huber and Sherwyn P. Morreale, 45–68. Menlo Park, CA: American Association for Higher Education; Carnegie Foundation for the Advancement of Teaching, 2002.

Fitzhugh, Will. "The Making of a Relic." *Teacher Magazine* 13, no. 6 (March 2002): 37–39. ERIC EJ775888.

Frankel, Noralee, and Peter Stearns. "Benchmarks for Professional Development in Teaching of History as a Discipline." *Perspectives Online* 41, no. 5 (May 2003), http://www.historians.org/Perspectives/issues/2003/0305/index.cfm (accessed January 20, 2009).

———. "The Development of Benchmarks for Professional Development in the Teaching of History as a Discipline." *Perspectives Online* 42 (April 2004), http://www.historians.org/perspectives/issues/2004/0404/0404tea1.cfm (accessed January 20, 2009).

Halttunen, Karen. "From K-12 Outreach to K-16 Collaboration." *National History Education Clearinghouse* (2008), http://teachinghistory.org/tah-grants/lessons-learned/19347 (accessed January 20, 2009).

Humphrey, Daniel C., Christopher Chang-Ross, Mary Beth Donnelly, Lauren Hersh, Heidi Skolnick, and SRI International. *Evaluation of the Teaching American History Program.* Washington, DC: U.S. Department of Education Office of Planning, Evaluation and Policy Development, 2005. http://www.ed.gov/rschstat/eval/teaching/us-history/teaching-exec-sum.html (accessed January 20, 2009).

Lewis, Catherine. "Does Lesson Study Have a Future in the United States?" *Nagoya Journal of Education and Human Development* 1 (January 2002): 1–23. Linked from http://www.lessonresearch.net/res.html (accessed January 20, 2009).

———. "Lesson Study in North America: Progress and Challenges." In *Lesson Study: International Perspective on Policy and Practice*, vol. 1, edited by M. Matoba, K. A. Crawford, and M. R. Sarkar Arani. Beijing: Educational Science Publishing House, 2006. Linked from http://www.lessonresearch.net/res.html (accessed January 20, 2009).

Long, Kelly Ann. "Reflections on TAH and the Historian's Role: Reciprocal Exchanges and Transformative Contributions to History Education." *The History Teacher* 39, no. 4 (August 2006): 493–507, http://www.historycooperative.org/journals/ht/39.4/long.html (accessed January 20, 2009).

McArthur, Will, Brian Gratton, Robert M. Barnes, Laura Blandford, and Ian Johnson. "Improving the Contribution of Historians to TAH Projects." *OAH Newsletter* 33 (May 2005), http://www.oah.org/pubs/nl/2005may/mcarthur.html (accessed January 20, 2009).

McDiarmid, G. Williamson, and Peter Vinten-Johannsen. *The Teaching and Learning of History—From the Inside Out.* NCRTL Special Report. East Lansing: National Center for Research on Teacher Learning, 1993, http://ncrtl.msu.edu/special.htm (accessed January 20, 2009).

National Assessment Governing Board, U.S. Department of Education. *U.S. History Framework for the 1994 and 2001 National Assessment of Educational Progress.* NAEP U.S. History Consensus Project. Washington, DC: Author, 2001. http://www.nagb.org/pubs/hframework2001.pdf (accessed January 20, 2009).

Oakland Unified School District Teaching American History Project Third Year Evaluation Report, July 1, 2006–June 30, 2007. Redding, CA: Center for Evaluation and Research, LLC, 2007. http://californiaschools.net/americanhistory/evalReports.html (accessed January 20, 2009).

Orrill, Robert, and Linn Shapiro. "Forum Essay: From Bold Beginnings to an Uncertain Future: The Discipline of History and History Education." *American Historical Review* 110, no. 3 (June 2005). http://www.historycooperative.org/journals/ahr/110.3/orrill.html (accessed January 20, 2009).

Rigden, Diana W. *A Feasibility Study of the Arts and Sciences/Teacher Education Collaborative (ASTEC).* New York: Carnegie Corporation of New York, 2005. PDF in author's possession.

Tyrrell, Ian. *Historians in Public: The Practice of American History, 1890–1970.* Chicago: University of Chicago Press, 2005.

U.S. Department of Education National Asssessment Governing Board. *U.S. History Framework for the 1994 and 2001 National Assessment of Educational Progress.* NAEP U.S. History Consensus Project (Washington: Author, 2001). ERIC# ED444928.

VanSledright, Bruce. "Why Should Historians Care About History Teaching?" *AHA Perspectives* 45 (February 2007), http://www.historians.org/perspectives/issues/2007/0702/0702tea2.cfm (accessed January 20, 2009).

Vinten-Johansen, Peter, and G. Williamson McDiarmid. *Stalking the Schoolwork Module: Teaching Prospective Teachers to Write Historical Narratives.* NCRTL Special Reports. East Lansing, MI: National Center for Research on Teaching and Learning, 1997, http://ncrtl.msu.edu/special.htm (accessed January 20, 2009).

Wiggins, Grant, and Jay McTighe. *Understanding by Design.* Alexandria, VA: Association for Supervision and Curriculum Development, 2005.

Wrobel, David. "A Lesson from the Past and Some Hope for the Future: The History Academy and the Schools, 1880–2007." *The History Teacher* 41, no. 2 (February 2008): 151–62.

Yarema, Allan E. "A Decade of Debate: Improving Content and Interest in History Education." *The History Teacher* 35, no. 3 (May 2002): 389–99.

Chapter 3

Engaging At-Risk Students
Teaching American Military History

G. L. Seligmann
University of North Texas

Some time ago a cartoon was published that has over time morphed into a metaphor. The cartoon shows two men talking in what is obviously a bathroom while behind them is a bathtub from which four horse feet are projecting. The one man is saying to the other "What dead horse in the bathtub?" The question has of course become a metaphor for ignoring the obvious by attempting to focus on something else. Hold the metaphor, I will return to it in a moment.

Why Rethink the United States History Course?

Why indeed? The U.S. Department of Education through its over 900 *Teaching American History* grants has done an excellent job of supporting the improvement of the teaching skills and knowledge base of K-12 teachers of U.S. history throughout the country. However, almost all of these grants were for programs aimed at improving individual teaching skills. The program discussed in this chapter looked at the problem from a different angle and therefore proposed a different solution. What we proposed to do was to modify the traditional U.S. history course by adding a strong but integrated military history component and we hoped thereby to engage students who previously had looked on U.S. history with attitudes ranging from boredom to outright hostility. In this regard this program was significantly different from the clear majority of TAH programs. Only a very few other programs looked at the course being taught. While teachers may have been taught and taught well how to explicate the Federalist Papers, few were asking why or looking at the fact that their students were not always interested in the Federalist Papers, no matter how well taught nor how important the subject might be. This chapter describes a program that, by proposing to create a course with a large military history component, had as its basic goal the reshaping of the basic course itself.

The content of our course that is focused around U.S. military history examines the underlying diplomatic, political, and economic causes leading to our wars as well as how these wars shaped our nation's constitutional, political, economic, and social development, both during and after the actual struggles. Under the auspices of a *Teaching American History* grant, members of the University of North Texas History Department created a series of summer institutes for secondary school teachers that provided the necessary factual and interpretative materials to integrate major elements of United States military history into their respective curricula, while simultaneously beginning to develop a model course for high school students.

The argument and the facts that students, even those who are university bound, are graduating from high school with a stunning lack of historical knowledge has been made and documented so often that it is almost axiomatic. I refer those who doubt this to the National Assessment of Educational Progress (http://nces.ed.gov/naep3/) as a sample of these criticisms. Unfortunately, as the source noted above indicates, this argument is not only axiomatic, it is accurate. On a note of personal disclosure, I have been teaching the U.S. history survey course at the university level almost every semester since 1967. To put it bluntly, I have found my students are simply not prepared to do what I have defined as college level work in the basic U.S. survey course. Many of them lack any sort of factual knowledge; many claim, and then prove it by their actions, to have never written an essay exam answer; and many of them don't care enough to be concerned.

And just as critique of the students seems beyond challenge, so, too, is the argument that some of these problems can be overcome by improving the teaching of our nation's past. Teaching strategies that accent the close examination of primary documents, professional development programs which familiarize teachers with the locations and ambience of places that have played a major role in our national development, or simply programs which increase the factual knowledge of dedicated teachers forced into areas where they lack training and competence, are all possible solutions for the problems mentioned above. These and similar endeavors are both useful and successful, and they have been supported by the U.S. Department of Education's Teaching American History initiatives, the National Endowment for the Humanities Landmarks of American History program, the various Gilder Lehrman Institute of American History programs, and others of the same sort.

These valuable programs alone, however, will not solve all of the pedagogical problems that face K-12 teachers. The "dead horse in the bathtub" usually not addressed in discussions involving the teaching of history, be it state history, U.S. history, or world history, is that many students, for a variety of reasons, simply do not like history even when well taught by well qualified teachers. These reasons are varied and in many cases valid. Many in this age group demand certitude, and history well taught offers nuances. Or as Reinhold Neibuhr, recently quoted in Newsweek, more elegantly phrased it, "while the drama of history is shot through with moral meaning, the meaning is never exact. Sin and punishment, virtue and reward are never precisely proportioned." Some students demand simple short-term solutions and history offers complex long-term problems.[1] Students may wish to see one group or cause as totally wrong and their opponents as totally right. A good history course might see some virtue along with some accompanying vices in both groups. Thus for a variety of reasons, many students at the K-12 level are simply not motivated to study history traditional or otherwise. Simply put, many high school students see history as either boring or irrelevant. And of course these problems are sometimes multiplied when we enter the world of those students who are "at risk" because of social, economic, or other educational reasons. For example, I often have given what many students rate as a very insightful lecture on the meaning of the Declaration of Independence to a mostly bored classroom and followed it later that same hour with a rather trite lecture discussion of the Battle of Saratoga to the same but now interested class. One could lay this off to the fact that they slept during the Declaration lecture and were now awake for the Saratoga part, but I have seen the same thing reversed with a nondescript discussion of the Battle of Gettysburg followed by a subtle and meaningful discussion of the role of the Gettysburg Address in foreshadowing the reshaping of the American experience. This background of observation supported by the popularity of the History Channel with its emphasis on military history has led me to the inescapable conclusion that students, particularly male students, simply like military history.

Looking at the Course Differently

If one starts with the premise that students are interested in military history, and my anecdotal information suggests that they are, then one must ask why. At first glance it avoids many of the problems discussed above. It offers clear-cut solutions to what are often complex problems. It is often easy to identify virtue or the lack thereof. In short it is a possible hook to attract not only the good but bored or disenchanted students but the disaffected or at-risk students as well.

U.S. military history, as will be demonstrated later, can also serve as a vehicle for articulating and stressing essentially every aspect of American history. As the following pages will demonstrate, United States military history can serve as a basis for a course of study that will examine the underlying diplomatic, political, and economic causes leading to our wars as well as how these wars shaped our nation's constitutional, political, economic, and social development, both during and after the actual struggles. Such a course, were it to attract the interest of students who were previously disaffected, might go a long way toward providing our students with a grasp of the fundamentals of U.S. history and thus help to close the ignorance gap that currently exists. Let me note here that the University of North Texas, in common with most other universities, centers the teaching of pedagogy in the College of Education and that of history content knowledge in the History Department. Consequently the needed overlap between parts what should be interlocking parts is close to nonexistent.

Under the auspices of a *Teaching American History* grant, members of the University of North Texas History Department in the summer of 2004 began planning to create a series of summer institutes or workshops designed to deliver to interested middle and high school teachers the necessary factual and interpretative materials to integrate major elements of U.S. military history into the respective curricula. In addition, the program would simultaneously begin to develop a model course for high school students.

We at UNT believe that this program has the potential of achieving national significance. Because of our ongoing plans to develop detailed and user friendly lesson plans and make them readily available on accessible Web sites, we hope that teachers around the nation can turn to the study of U.S. military history as a vehicle to reach students who are not interested in history as it is currently taught. We believe the uniqueness of this proposal and its appeal to at-risk students; the enrichment that the special speakers bring to the program; the expertise of both the high school teacher mentors, and the academic strengths of the University of North Texas historians, coupled with the sophistication of the proposed Web sites, have an immense potential for engaging this population of students into the richness of American history.

Why the University of North Texas?

The major content provider for this new course, the Department of History, University of North Texas, is very well qualified to provide the historical component of the program. About a decade ago the Department of History made a formal decision to have as one of its two areas of focus the study of military history. This decision has been a major factor in guiding hiring and curriculum decisions in the intervening years. As a result of these hiring decisions, the department can now boast one of the finest military history faculties in the United States. The six military historians in the department regularly offer upper division and graduate classes in all aspects of U.S. and European military history. Of these six military historians, all four U.S. military historians were at one time or another directly involved in this program. As a natural outcome of this sort of topical concentration, the UNT Library holdings in the area of American military history are extensive. Moreover, the UNT Oral History Collection is internationally known for its focus on World War II interviews as well as a strong program in all aspects of U.S. military history.

In addition to this strength in the content area, the University of North Texas brought other strengths to the table. Until university budgetary restrictions forced the ending of the program, the department regularly offered summer institutes covering Texas history, Chicano studies, and U.S. history since World War II for teachers of grades K-12. These accelerated classes were designed to deliver content as well as to suggest new ways to present the material in the K-12 classroom. In addition the department has, since 1978, in cooperation with the American Historical Association, hosted an annual Teaching Conference aimed at teachers of grades eight through twelve. These annual conferences feature sessions devoted primarily to content but also focus on ways in which this content can be transmitted to students. The average attendance at these conferences is around 300 teachers a year. In addition to the content providing function of these conferences, they have also provided a venue for committed teachers to both share teaching strategies and to develop friendships with other devoted teachers. As a result of these activities the University of North Texas has earned an enviable reputation as having a major history department interested in both teaching and research at all levels.

The New Course Described

Our TAH program proposed to introduce at-risk secondary students to the systematic study of U.S. history in general by making use of the popularity of U.S. military history to draw them in. This was to be done by first introducing teachers to this new content knowledge. Anecdotal evidence suggests that this format might be more popular with that age group than the standard approaches to U.S. history. As will be demonstrated below, the content to be presented in these new courses would fit the majority of the criteria mandated by most state standards. The program was designed primarily to appeal to an audience of students who do not normally perform well in traditional U.S. history courses and who seldom take additional U.S. history courses. The popularity of military history was to be the "hook" to entice these disaffected students. It was our hope that once enticed by the "hook" of military history, and then shown the ways that military history connected to other aspects of history, these students might become more interested and engaged.

Structure of the TAH Program

The first of the our grant's three components were a series of four institutes, each two weeks in length, offered for each of the three summers of the grant period. Each of these institutes was projected to enroll twenty teachers for a total of eighty participants, with each individual being able to take up to three of the four institutes during one summer. These participants would be chosen on a first come first served basis with slots being set aside the first year for teachers in the Denton Independent School District, the grantee LEA. The participants could be awarded Continuing Education Credits from the University of North Texas if they wished these credits. Arrangements could also be made with the Toulouse Graduate School of the University of North Texas for participants who qualified for admission to the graduate program to earn history graduate credit for participation in these institutes. All participants would get a $500 stipend per institute completed.

Each of these institutes met five days a week for six hours per day for two weeks. Initially, each Wednesday was set aside for a Plenary Session featuring an off-campus distinguished military historian's lecture. These all day sessions were divided into a formal presentation to be followed by an extensive question/answer and discussion period. The last Friday of each session would be dedicated totally to methods of transferring the factual and interpretative material covered during the previous sessions into a format suitable for an eighth through twelfth grade classroom environment. Four master secondary classroom teachers, each with a special expertise or interest in U.S. military history, selected by the Denton Independent School District, would be present for these Friday sessions.

Historical Content of the Course

These institutes, which ran concurrently, were chronologically organized. The first institute focused first on the American Revolution and the origins of American nationalism and the problems both militarily and politically of creating an army and a nation before an American nationalism existed. As illustrations of this process, the aftermath of the American Revolution and the movement from the Articles of Confederation to the U.S. Constitution and the role of the Revolution in underpinning this move toward centralization were carefully examined. The discussions next addressed the Quasi-Naval War with the French and the earliest manifestations of the tensions that exist between patriotic unity and patriotic dissent. This was examined using the run-up to the Quasi-War as reflected in the debate over Jay's Treaty and the debates swirling around the adoption and implementation of the Alien and Sedition Acts and the role of the debates over Jay's Treaty and the Alien and Sedition Acts in the development of American political parties.

The institute would conclude with a discussion of the diplomacy leading up to the War of 1812, the role of the War of 1812 in forcing James Madison to change his mind as to the necessity and the constitutionality of both a semiprotective tariff and the Second Bank of the United States, and the diplomatic aftereffects of the war culminating in the issuance of the Monroe Doctrine. The unit also covered the importance of the Battle of New Orleans in the creation of an American national identity and the battle's role in the election of Andrew Jackson. Attention was also paid to the opposition to a primarily military figure in politics as reflected by Henry Clay's long-term opposition to Andrew Jackson as a "man on horseback." To be sure much of this was not "military history" as it is usually defined, but it can be easily demonstrated that the impact of wars often last past the end of the war.

This idea of the long-lasting impact of war was to be reinforced in all of the subsequent institutes. In no case would the material be confined to the actual battles. In all cases the longer effects of the causes of the wars and the impact of the wars would be emphasized. It cannot be overemphasized that in this grant military history was indeed the "hook" to catch the students. But, in actual implementation what was actually happening was that we were teaching what has come to be known as the "New Military History." We were placing military history in its broadest political, diplomatic, social and cultural context. We were proposing and implementing a course which discussed what causes wars, how wars are fought, and what the impact of these wars was upon American society in the broadest sense of the word. In other words, we were teaching how to teach a U.S. survey course with an emphasis on military history but not at the expense of the other aspects of our rich past.

The second Institute would cover American history from the Mexican-American War through the Indian Wars of the late nineteenth century. The major political, diplomatic, and constitutional points to be addressed prior to the Civil War were Manifest Destiny and the United States' sense of mission, the role of territorial expansion and the question of the expansion of slavery into these new territories and how the Mexican-American War impacted and made these issues more volatile. The specific issues to be discussed were the conflicting constitutional theories of slavery expansion that culminated in the Compromise of 1850, the birth of the Republican Party, the Dred Scott decision, the Lincoln-Douglas

Debates, and the Election of 1860. While a large number of political, constitutional, and economic issues would be discussed in the sessions devoted to the Civil War, the principal theme of this section would be the unleashed power of the forces of a liberal democracy versus the forces of tyranny as exemplified by what Abraham Lincoln and others called "The Slavocracy," a theme drawn from the works of the eminent military historian Victor Davis Hanson.[1] Central to this approach was a discussion of the tensions involved in the transformation of a War for Union versus a War for Emancipation to a War for Union and Emancipation.

Subsumed under the theme of "Democracy Unleashed" would be a discussion of the growth of industrialism, railroads, banking changes, the introduction of greenbacks, and the other economic changes forced by the magnitude of this war. The constitutional changes would focus on the Thirteenth, Fourteenth, and Fifteenth Amendments and the role they played in the transformation of the United States from "Mr. Madison's Republic to Mr. Lincoln's Nation," and how that change is hinted at in the Gettysburg Address and driven by the exigencies of the war. This section would culminate with a discussion of the political aspects of the abolition of the Three-Fifths Clause of the Constitution, its importance to Reconstruction and to the creation of the Solid South, issues which would continue to shape U.S. electoral politics for the next century. This institute would conclude with a discussion of the Indian Wars and their impact on U.S. Indian policy into the twentieth century.

The third institute would begin with the Spanish-American War and its emphasis on reuniting the nation, and cover the diplomacy of our brief fling with overseas imperialism and the diplomatic rapprochement between the United States and Great Britain. Moving into the diplomacy and several incidents leading to World War I, the lectures would stress the growing realization in the United States that we were an integral part of the North Atlantic community and therefore not immune to the tensions within that area. Economic, social, and political changes prompted by the war such as the harnessing of our industrial might typified by the War Industries Board were accented. In addition the tension between democratic unity and democratic dissent, the migration of African Americans in search of jobs and better living conditions, and the impact of that movement on our electoral politics were also covered. The diplomacy of the interwar period as it pertains to the outbreak of World War II was also discussed. Central to the discussion of World War II is the theme of the power of the forces of democracy when pitted against the forces of tyranny.

On the military side, the successes of Eisenhower, Bradley, and Patton (the U.S. Army did not lose a major battle after the Battle of Kasserine Pass in 1943) were discussed as would be the eventual triumph of the traditions of freedom versus Bushido in the Pacific War. On the domestic scene attention was paid to a variety of themes such as the decline of hyphenated Americanism, the broadening of the base of the Civil Rights movement as Black veterans returned home to a segregated America (the idea of victory against the enemy abroad and victory against prejudice at home, the Double V movement), the intellectual impact of the Holocaust on American thinking about race, and the postwar impact of the war as exemplified by the G.I. Bill of Rights and its broadening of home owner-ship and educational benefits. Diplomatically the various wartime conferences and their impact on the postwar world and the creation of the United Nations held center stage.

The last of the four institutes concentrated on the Cold War and its aftermath. It began with the impact of rapid demobilization on our military, foreign, and domestic policy and how the beginnings of the Cold War began reshaping our views of diplomatic, political, and economic policy. From that beginning the institute covered the Korean War and the debate over limited versus total war. Next on the agenda were the Vietnam War and the limits of limited war. Under-lying all of these discussions was the role of diplomacy and the changing nature of our electoral politics particularly as influenced by the dissent over the Vietnam War and its aftermath. Central to this segment of the course would be the ongo-ing Cold War and its eventual end. This institute culminated with a discussion of the military actions in Granada and Panama and the first Gulf War and the ramifications of American hegemony in a troubled world.

Pedagogical Applications of Historical Content Knowledge

The second major component of this program, and the one that would occupy the faculty during the first full semester of the grant, was the creation of very detailed lesson plans designed to facilitate the transfer of the knowledge and insights gained in these classes to the high school level. Both the military history faculty at the University of North Texas and the four experienced high school teachers included in this project were closely involved in the creation of these lesson plans. Thus the lesson plans were informed by both a scholarly knowledge of the material and a practical knowledge of how to best integrate this knowledge into the actual high school classroom.

Course Dissemination: Web Site Development

The project Web site is designed to be accessible to everyone connected to this grant proposal as well as their students and the general public. When the relevant fair use, copyright, and intellectual property issues are resolved it will be interac-tive and will include such diverse materials as extensive bibliographies, war songs and music, art and cartoons—for example, such cartoons of Bill Mauldin from World War II and battlefield sketches of Tom Lea as might be legally available—digitalized editions of the spoken word as they are made available, and such other materials as might be available. In this last category the Department of Army's recruiting aid war game comes to mind. This public site will be widely advertised by such means as the various H-NET Humanities and Social Sciences (http://www.h-net.org) discussion lists devoted to teaching and those lists devoted to the fields of military history such as H-TAH, H-WAR, and H-CIVWAR. Access to this site will not be limited in any way. Unfortunately at the time of this writing I cannot project when this Web site will become available to the general public.

We believed that the uniqueness of this project and its appeal to at-risk students, and the academic strengths of the University of North Texas historians coupled with the sophistication of the proposed Web site had an immense potential for engaging this vulnerable population of students into the richness of American history. This belief was supported by the Teaching American History division of the U.S. Department of Education and those who reviewed the proposals, and the grant was funded in June 2004.

What Actually Occurred and How It Was Received

We are told in a quote attributed to Field Marshal Helmut von Moltke that "No plan survives contact with the enemy."—which is a statement so obviously true as to be axiomatic.[2] So too it was with this TAH grant. Not that anyone was the enemy, only that things got caught up in "the fog of war," a phrase given currency by Carl von Clausewitz, and began to change before we really got going with the actual classes. Another military analogy might be to borrow from an author on the Napoleonic Wars who wrote to the effect that every soldier in Napoleon's armies had three uniforms: The one they actually wore, the one they were supposed to wear, and the one that historians have said they wore. All of the above is what was supposed to happen. What follows is what actually happened.

The Denton Independent School District (DISD) and the University of North Texas (UNT) were informed by the Department of Education that the DISD with UNT as a content provider had been awarded a three-year *Teaching American History* grant to both teach and prepare a course in American military history beginning in June 2004. UNT was to provide the content assistance and to begin as soon as possible to structure the summer institutes and the materials to give to the enrolling teacher/participants. In this case "as soon as possible," because of preexisting summer teaching and other plans, meant that the formal grant activities would begin with the fall semester. But even this was far too optimistic. For a variety of reasons which were never adequately explained to the UNT Project Director[3] the legal staffs of the DISD and UNT had a great deal of difficulty agreeing on the form and nature of the subcontract although the budget narrative and supporting materials for the grant had been very specific in describing who did what and how much was involved. The end result of this long period of negotiation was that UNT was unable to offer the several faculty involved the course releases that the grant had budgeted to allow them time to develop both the new courses and the lesson plans and other materials called for in the grant.[4] This impasse was not resolved until early May 2005, slightly over a month before the summer institutes were scheduled to begin. This created a major scramble to get ready for the summer made worse by the fact that it was final exam season with the resulting time demands. This delay had also made it impossible for the UNT Director to schedule classrooms in a timely manner because he had no official reason or budgetary account for reserving this valuable classroom space.[5]

This delay also caused major problems in the recruitment of the teacher/participants. UNT has a mailing list of some 2,500 individuals who have attended the UNT/AHA Fall Teaching Conference but the development, printing, and mailing costs for that large a mailing list had to wait until the subcontract issues were resolved. By the time the legal fine points had been ironed out many of the prospective teacher/participants had already finalized their summer plans. To be sure the DISD representative was active in recruitment during this period, and it is due to her efforts that we were able to enroll as many participants as we finally did, although these numbers were far lower than the planning figures.

The one bright note during this period was that despite the legal hang-ups both Directors were able to attend the TAH Director's conference in Pittsburgh and the UNT Director was also able to attend the National Council for History Education (NCHE) meeting that followed the Director's meeting. At the NCHE meeting the UNT Director met with Professor Fred Anderson of the University of Colorado and made tentative arrangements for Professor Anderson to serve as a Guest Lecturer for that summer's sessions.[6] Although almost nothing had actually been done on the TAH grant, attendance at this meeting was to prove invaluable during the subsequent years.

Finally in May the legal issues involving the subcontract with UNT were worked out and serious and formal planning could begin.[7] In short order preliminary lesson plans were produced, potential participants were contacted and enrolled, guest speakers were nailed down, and a myriad of other details attended to on at least an ad hoc basis.

Adapting a Successful High School Course for a Larger Audience

Under the terms of the grant the UNT Director was to have sole control of content which included the guest lecturers. In conjunction with the other UNT faculty and the DISD Director he decided on bringing in a former high school teacher from the Gadsden Independent School District in Southern New Mexico to discuss his success with a similar course which he had pioneered there and which had served as the model for this project. This speaker, Lieutenant Colonel Allan Holmes (USA Ret.) had, upon retirement, earned a master's in history from New Mexico State University along with the necessary teaching credentials and had returned to the troubled high school from which he had graduated.[8] Gadsden High, at the time he returned, was facing a dropout rate of over 50 percent and was generally considered a troubled educational environment. After teaching there several years, Col. Holmes, with the support of the school principal, had surveyed the school's students and found to his surprise that the major academic stumbling blocks were the state mandated U.S. history courses not, as they had assumed, the math requirements. The school had not been able to engage the heavily Hispanic population's interest in studying and learning, or even taking, the state mandated history courses. Col. Holmes, based partially on his own background in the U.S. Army and having noticed the students' interest when he had discussed U.S. military history, thought that a course focusing on the wars of the United States and the impact of these wars might be a hook to capture the attention of the disaffected students. With the agreement of the principal he was assigned a small class of likely dropouts as an experimental class. It proved to be a success. These students soon warmed to the topic and successfully completed the course with a renewed interest in the educational process. With that initial success Holmes was scheduled for several sections the next semester and the course began to flourish. Originally intended for a primary male audience, female students soon began expressing an interest in the course and with their enrollment and strong success rates the course was off to a very successful future. As Holmes noted in his talk to the teacher/participants, by the time of his second retirement his entire teaching load had become the U.S. military history course and a noticeable drop in the dropout rate of the school had occurred. To be sure this improved dropout rate cannot be traced only to his teaching of U.S. military history and, indeed, other programs beyond the scope of this chapter were instituted at his school, but it appears from anecdotal evidence that this new approach to our past had some impact on retention. Given his intellectual mastery of the subject and his experience in teaching the proposed class, Holmes seemed a natural outside speaker with which to begin the program.

And indeed he was. His first day's lecture ran the gamut from course content, to initial student reaction, to male reaction to being bested by female students, to the politics of trying to get the State Board of Education to approve the course for general use throughout the state.[9] In the final evaluation he was easily rated as the best of the three outside speakers. The second of the outside speakers, two weeks later, was Major (now Lt. Col.) John Grenier USAF. At the time Grenier, who holds a PhD in U.S. history from the University of Colorado, was a member of the History Department of the Air Force Academy. Grenier, the author of *The First Way of War: American War Making on the Frontier: 1607–1814* (Cambridge University Press, 2005), and subsequently (*The Far Reaches of Empire: War in Nova Scotia, 1710–1760* (University of Oklahoma Press, 2008), lectured on the reasons and impact of the seventeenth and eighteenth century colonial wars and their impact on the development of the American colonies and the new nation. His lecture too was very well received. The third guest lecturer, Professor Brian Linn of the Texas A&M History Department, spoke to the third two-week session on his particular area of interest—the United States handling of the Filipino insurrection following the capture of the Philippine Islands in the Spanish-American war and the relevance of that experience to the present-day conflict in Iraq. His excellent lecture and the subsequent discussion it evoked was rated as the third best of the three guest lecturers. This rating was perhaps due to the controversial nature of some of his conclusions regarding the relationship between U.S. policy in Iraq and policies in the Spanish-American war—the latter having been for the most part successful. Setting this aside, however, the participants uniformly saw the lecture and following discussion as an excellent example of how one can make the past extremely relevant to the future. It should also be noted here that the guest lecturers were equally impressed with the grant program and its goals and were quite clear that they would be pleased to be invited the next year.

Measuring Success

As good as the guest lecturers were and as well received as they were, it must be stressed that they were transient. The heart of the program was the day-to-day lectures and the interaction between the UNT faculty, the master teachers, and the participants. Here too the first year was a success beyond the hopes of the organizers. One hundred percent of the participants answered "Yes" to the question "Would you recommend these summer institutes to friends and colleagues for next summer?"[10] To the question "If you did not attend one of the sessions this year, will you attend next summer?" an equally stunning 100 percent answered in the affirmative. In examining the comments the participants made on their evaluation sheets one is struck by the varieties of value the participants saw in the program. In short despite the disappointment over the relatively small number of participants, twenty-two in all, and the directors had been warned at the Pittsburgh Director's Conference to expect low first year numbers, the first year could only be judged as an unqualified success.

The Program Moves Forward: Lessons Learned

With an entire year to plan and prepare one would assume that the second year would be a smoother operation than was the first. And indeed it was. With adequate time and internal financing in place lesson plans were revised, external materials added to, and the new faculty addition, Richard McCaslin (PhD, University of Texas) was integrated into the project. In addition to the additions and changes in the materials to be distributed to the participants, fundamental decisions were reached involving the outside speakers. Although the cadre agreed that all of the previous speakers had done an excellent job, a consensus existed that different topics and therefore different speakers should be brought to the program. The exception to this was Col. Holmes. All of the planners agreed that he should be brought back for an encore presentation. The other two speakers to be engaged were Dr. Dennis Showalter, the dean of American World War I historians, and Dr. Susannah Bruce an up and coming Civil War historian. In the final evaluations these choices were again rated outstanding by the participants. Professor Showalter was rated the highest, receiving such comments such as: "The sheer knowledge of history. He is passionate about history," "Great knowledge of twentieth century conflict," to cite but a few. Holmes and Bruce also received excellent evaluations, with Holmes's comments in the line of "actual classroom experience," and Bruce's tending toward "personable, energetic, connected to teaching."

In addition to giving the faculty additional time to prepare materials there was also additional time to recruit participants. This resulted in almost doubling the number of teachers who enrolled in the second set of institutes. The subcontracts being in place also meant that mundane but vital issues, which had inconvenienced everyone the first summer, such as parking and changing rooms on a regular basis could be resolved.

There was, however, one area in which minimal progress occurred. That was in the construction, stocking, and maintaining of the Web site. The grant proposal had called for the construction and maintenance of a state of the art interactive Web site to be constructed under the auspices of H-NET and housed in their computers on the Michigan State campus. This was not to be, although it was not apparent at this early date. It is still not clear to the UNT Project Director what went wrong over the next two years. Whether the problem lay in inexperienced programmers in Michigan or bad advice and muddled expectations emanating from the UNT Project Director, this project never came to completion with Michigan State although it was eventually launched through the auspices of skilled programmers at the University of North Texas.

Once again if the participants' evaluations are to be taken at face value the program was a great success. Again an astounding 100 percent of the participants answered "yes" to the question, "Would you recommend these summer institutes to friends and colleagues for next summer?" Of the 29 percent who indicated they would not be returning, a number did indicate that they had taken all of the institutes, but we could not determine exactly how many of those not returning could return. Despite this glitch the evaluation as a whole was overwhelmingly positive and left all concerned quite pleased with the results and ready for the last year. The lesson here is to be very careful in the construction of evaluation instruments (see chapter 12 for details on successful program evaluation).

Professor Gene Smith, the author of several studies of the U.S. military in the early national period, was chosen to participate in the final summer of the grant. Professor Keith Mitchener, a specialist in naval warfare in World War II, was also selected. Both of these turned out to be extremely good decisions.

With the issue of the teaching faculty settled the team turned to the issue of guest lecturers. They elected to follow the guidelines agreed on earlier of trying to cover all the major aspects of the proposed course. Due to the unavailability of Col. Holmes, we turned to Dr. James Reckner, the Director of the Texas Tech University Vietnam Center, as our first outside speaker. Because we had not, as yet, had an outside speaker specializing in World War II we invited Dr. Gregory Urwin, Temple University, who readily accepted. For our third lecturer we returned to Professor Susannah Bruce, Sam Houston State University. Professor Bruce had received very glowing comments in the second year evaluations both for the factual content of her lecture and for the suggestions for teaching which she had offered in her lecture the previous year. Again all three of the outside speakers received very high evaluations from the teacher/participants.

In terms of the actual conduct of the summer programs very little can be added to what occurred the previous two years. The enrollment essentially doubled and from all accounts the programs were an unqualified success. Again 100 percent of the teacher/participants indicated that were the program to be offered the next year they would recommend it to their friends and colleagues. Essentially everyone who had not taken all four institutes indicated that they would have liked to enroll in those segments that they had missed. Many commented that they were unhappy that this was the third and final year of the program. In short, hallmarks of a very successful program were displayed.[11]

During this summer session the UNT Director devoted his full attention to resolving the issue of the nonexistent Web site. He decided to use UNT expertise and facilities to construct the site. He engaged the services of two Web site specialists from the UNT College of Business Administration and turned them loose on the project. Although they did not finish the project as quickly as the Director had wished, they soon turned out a most creditable Web site.

Lessons Learned and the Future

The primary lesson learned was simple. You cannot begin the planning too soon. The ten-month delay in the first year of the project was the single largest problem that occurred during the three-year period of the grant. The second lesson learned and one that is related to the first is choose your partners well. It is not that DISD was in and of itself a problem. The problem is that it was never on the front burner of the personnel at DISD assigned to work with the program. For them it was simply an additional project they had to shepherd to completion. To the UNT personnel it was their primary summer task. When they were called upon to work on the project during the school semesters they did so willingly because they had been compensated by a reduced teaching load. For the UNT History Department it was a feather in their cap in that this department goes out of its way to perform not only the teaching and research that is expected of a PhD producing department but to be of service to the larger community as well. By demonstrably reaching out to the precollege teaching community the department was performing what it considers to be a major service. In addition the funds which came to the department via the released teaching time and the indirect cost of internal allocations enabled the department to provide funding for several graduate students who needed the additional funds to continue their education. Again none of this is intended to be seen as criticism of DISD, it is simply that the reward structure was greater on the UNT side of the ledger. Given the fact that the impetus for this grant came from the UNT faculty it is not surprising that its strongest support came from the UNT campus.

And where do we go from here? The History Department and the Director are committed to revising and improving the project and resubmitting it to the Department of Education in the next funding cycle. The probability is quite high that the new LEA will be one of Texas Education Agency's (TEA) regional offices thus enabling us to cast a far larger net for teacher/participants and thus broadening the impact of this new approach to the teaching of U.S. history. Engaging the TEA in this project in this manner might also make it easier to add the course in U.S. military history to the state's inventory of acceptable courses and thus perhaps fulfill the goal of creating a course designed to appeal to the less motivated and the more at-risk students in the system. If that is to happen it will be, in my opinion, time, money, and effort well spent.[12]

Notes

1. Hanson, Victor Davis: *The Soul of Battle: From Ancient Times to the Present Day: How Three Great Liberators Vanquished Tyranny* (New York: Random House, 1999).
2. The actual quotation from von Moltke's *On Strategy* is "No plan of operation extends with certainty beyond the first encounter with the enemy's main strength." Daniel J. Hughes ed. *Moltke On the Art of War: Selected Writings* (Novato, CA: Presidio Press, 1993), 45.
3. This observation is based on some 40 years of teaching college freshmen and sophomores. It is not based on empirical research. If any such educational research exists this historian is unaware of it.
4. These lesson plans are still under review by the military history faculty of the University of North Texas and are still subject to tweaking as a result of the interaction between the mili-

tary history faculty, the master teachers, the participants, and the UNT Legal office for fair use issues. All tweaking aside, when these lesson plans are finished and vetted for possible copyright violations they will be placed on an easily accessible web site.

5. The Director for UNT, G. L. Seligmann, had both conceptualized and written the grant. He is also the author of this chapter.

6. The UNT History Department awards the PhD degree in history and consequently is a research oriented department. The most common device for encouraging activities such as working on a TAH grant is to use grant funds to "buy out" a class thus reducing the individual faculty members' teaching responsibilities and creating the time for the grant activity. These funds were budgeted in the grant but could not be released until the subcontract terms were agreed upon. Thus the History Department, which teaches some 6,000 students per semester, could not hire additional faculty to handle the involved professor's courses.

7. UNT did not actually charge the grant for classroom space, this was subsumed under indirect costs, but an account number had to exist before rooms could be reserved.

8. Although Professor Anderson was unable to work this TAH grant into his schedule he did recommend the eventual speaker. This will be discussed later in this essay.

9. To be sure some planning had been ongoing since the notice of acceptance had arrived the previous June. With the formal agreement signed, such things as room assignments, meetings with the master teachers, could now begin on a greatly expedited, if not more precisely frantic, schedule.

10. In the interest of disclosure I should note that Colonel Holmes is my brother-in-law and I had been following this experiment from its earliest days. I should also note that the conception and implementation of the program had been his and his alone. Simply put, I projected his idea to a larger canvas.

11. In this he met with mixed success. The State Board would not accept U.S. military history as a stand-alone course but it would allow U.S. history (with an emphasis on U.S. military history) to count as an acceptable alternative to the traditional requirement.

12. First year evaluations. Copies of these evaluations along with the evaluations of the second and third years are in the possession of the author and are available upon request.

Chapter 4

Lost in Translation

The Use of Primary Sources in Teaching History

Laura M. Westhoff
University of Missouri-St. Louis

> Primary sources drive many lessons.
> I am much more comfortable bringing [documents] in and using them.
> I see primary sources as the foundation to my lessons.
> I try to incorporate a primary source in every lesson.

Feedback such as the above from a recent cohort of *Teaching American History* grant participants should have inspired my colleagues and me to celebrate our success. After all, one of our explicit goals over the two years we worked with this group of teachers was to introduce them to the historical discipline through the use of primary sources and to encourage them to use documents in their own classrooms. So reports from teachers that they are using primary sources to shape their teaching are indeed gratifying. But eight years of working with TAH grants has taught me that much is lost in the translation from grant activities to lesson design. When I read such comments, I want to know more: What function do primary sources serve in their lessons? To what extent do their lessons develop historical thinking skills? How well do the skills we focus on in grant programs translate into classroom activities that actually transform students' understanding of continuity and change, context, complexity, cause and effect, and contingency? In this chapter, I examine the unit and lesson designs of participants in our grants to consider such questions.

With training as a historian rather than an educational researcher, with professional responsibilities as a teacher educator, and with great respect for the daunting job of all K-12 teachers, I approach this task with caution. Over the past two decades, researchers in history education have contributed fascinating and very useful studies on history teaching and learning.[1] My discussion below of teachers' use of primary sources is informed by my reading of this literature, but the issues I raise are not particularly new to anyone familiar with those studies. Nor is my purpose here to be critical of any individual teacher or lesson, nor to suggest a quick fix to problems in history education. Rather I offer my observations to consider how we as historians can use the opportunities afforded by TAH grants to address some of the more typical problems teachers encounter in designing lessons that use primary sources to promote historical thinking.

Like our grant, many TAH grants around the country have explicitly made historical thinking and the use of primary sources a central feature of their programs.[2] This is for good reason. Primary sources are the raw materials of the historical discipline. Learning how to read them as historians do—with attention to details about the source and its context—will not only teach us about the discipline, but might make us better readers and more critical, thoughtful citizens.[3] But primary documents receive far too little attention in K-12 classrooms. While science, literature, writing, and math teachers have long had their students learn the discipline through hands-on practice with experiments, reading and writing, and problem solving, history teaching has long appeared as a game of Trivial Pursuit, with the winners of "A" grades able to remember the most names, dates, and events culled from textbooks and lectures. Too few teachers and students of history use primary sources as historians do—as an open-ended inquiry with sensitivity to bias and context, to build stories about the past, local and national narratives, sometimes with controversial interpretations. The reasons for this state of history education are myriad, ranging from epistemological conceptions of the discipline and competing purposes of history, to arguments of students' limited skills, and teacher's own lack of preparation in the historical discipline.[4]

As the culture wars and struggle over the national standards in American history revealed in the 1990s, Americans are divided in their views of history education, with some arguing that history is primarily composed of factual information—names and dates, with little room for interpretation—and others recognizing that history is primarily an interpretative discipline and that factoids are only the tip of the iceberg of historical knowledge.[5] The debate then is whether history is constructed or whether historical reality is absolute and discovered. Furthermore, conflict reigns over whether the purpose of the discipline is to promote patriotic feelings rooted in pride in the American experience or whether its contribution to education is a set of critical thinking skills and habits of mind. Even those who believe that history is constructed frequently argue that elementary and high school students lack the level of thinking skills to engage in authentic interpretation on their own. And some reports point out that across the United States, history teachers are not prepared to teach the discipline.[6] Most states do not require a history major in order for a teacher to become certified to teach the subject, meaning that teachers themselves may not have the content background and disciplinary knowledge to conduct sophisticated lessons about historical knowledge and thinking.[7] This last argument is one that many TAH grants, including ours, seek to rectify.

But as a growing body of literature on the use of primary sources and historical thinking suggests, even when a teacher understands the discipline and uses primary sources, his or her lessons do not necessarily translate into effective teaching of historical thinking skills.[8] Studies of the differences in the way that historians and teachers read primary sources remind us of a significant gap between their practices.[9] Furthermore, a deep understanding of history and the use of primary sources "only begins the teacher's task. Unlike the researchers who reveal these hidden elements of historical thought, teachers must design activities that engage students in using such thinking in the classroom."[10] To do so, teachers need to understand *students'* historical thinking, as well as the nuances of the discipline. As I reviewed the lessons developed by teachers in our grant, I was reminded of this literature and increasingly aware of the fact that we need to reconsider our strategies for helping teachers use primary sources in their classrooms. In the discussion that follows, I elaborate on these issues.

Grant Design, Goals, and Programs

Since the first round of TAH grants in 2001 I have been closely involved with several grants with my colleagues at the International Education Consortium of Cooperating School Districts (IEC) and participated as a guest presenter in several others. With over twenty years' experience of providing history-specific professional development, IEC is part of a regional network of organizations that seek to improve education in schools.[11] While the specifics of each grant have varied, the overarching goals, programs, and products have remained similar: to deepen teachers' content knowledge of liberty and democracy in American history and their understanding of the historical discipline. To that end, we have invited cohorts of participants to attend a series of colloquia, institutes, and workshops over eighteen month cycles. Most participants have been high school history teachers; all participation is voluntary.

Several sessions included primary source activities and introduced teachers to strategies for incorporating them into their lessons. Guest historians have discussed their craft, particularly their work with documents such as seventeenth century court records, nineteenth century county records, and oral histories. As historians introduced numerous types of primary sources, master teachers modeled strategies for using them. These included Socratic seminar, historical inquiries with multiple primary sources gathered from diverse individuals, groups, and organizations, oral histories, artifacts, and photos and paintings.

These primary source activities highlighted several historical thinking concepts. In each activity, presenters emphasized the importance of placing the document in its historical setting, using what cognitive scientist Sam Wineburg calls a "sourcing heuristic" in which the reader first identifies information about the text and its production—author, intent, date, audience—before reading it.[12] Many speakers used tools, such as the National Archives and Records Administration primary source worksheet or other similar frameworks, to identify the source and place it in context.[13] Understanding the importance of context in decoding primary sources further occupied a significant portion of the hands on activities. We paired presentations on historical content with relevant primary sources and teaching activities in order to emphasize the importance of placing documents in historical context. Both the content presentations and primary source activities emphasized continuity and change, context, cause and effect, contingency, and complexity in history.[14]

Grant activities culminated in a final project: a unit plan organized around open-ended questions and featuring primary sources.[15] By designing units, teachers had the opportunity to translate their new understanding of primary sources and historical thinking into their classrooms. It also gave grant staff a means to evaluate the impact of grant programs on teachers' understanding of the role of primary sources in the historical discipline and ways to use them in their teaching. Teachers were free to pick unit topics that fit into their existing curriculum; units ranged from Japanese internment during World War II, to African-American and women's suffrage movements, the modern Civil Rights movement, and Andrew Jackson's presidency. While teachers were free to develop any topic and teaching strategy they chose, we expected them to use primary sources in their lessons. All the teachers used some primary source material in at least one of their lessons.

Teachers' Use of Primary Sources: Issues of Selection, Relevance, and Presentism

As I reviewed these units, I was struck by two recurring problems with the way teachers used primary sources. The first was a matter of selection and relevance to teaching objectives. While teachers were generally enthusiastic about using primary sources themselves and bringing them to their classrooms, they struggled with the selection of engaging, relevant, and usable sources that served an identifiable teaching purpose. That is, they included primary sources, but they did not always use them in a way that promoted historical thinking. The second problem evident in the units was present-mindedness, or presentism—using current values and knowledge to judge people and actions in the past. It is a struggle that history teachers and researchers at all levels face. For teachers trying to make history more relevant to apathetic students, it is a tempting trap because it engages students on more familiar terrain—what they already know and believe. Yet sound historical thinking that encourages an understanding of context requires us to avoid this pitfall. I discuss these issues in more detail below and offer some examples of how they appeared in the lessons.

Documents for What? Problems of Selection and Relevance

Simply using primary sources does not make a history lesson "better" than one that does not use primary sources. There are indeed limits to their usefulness and these limits are largely determined by the way teachers actually use them in lessons. While grant personnel expected that teachers would use documents to promote historical thinking skills, many lessons failed to do so. As I reviewed the unit designs for this chapter, I asked "What function do these documents serve?" The answer from several lessons was "to provide information." That is, the documents served essentially the same purpose as a textbook, particularly in offering details about the past.[16] It is a stretch then, to suggest that simply bringing a text document or photograph into the classroom will necessarily help students grasp context, the complexity, or contingency of history. Let me offer a couple of examples from the unit designs.

One lesson asked students to read Marcus Garvey's "Declaration of the Rights of Negro Peoples of the World" and identify the "three most striking/important things about the document." While this lesson has potential for helping students understand a moment in African-American history, the lesson unfortunately was not set up to do so. The teacher stopped with the students' lists. Indeed, nowhere does the teacher ask students to do any sourcing of the document, consider Marcus Garvey and his political and racial beliefs and agenda, or the particular historical context of the Great Migration and Harlem Renaissance in which the document was written; nor were the students asked why certain aspects of the document struck them. This exercise puts the emphasis on the document as a source of information about the past. The words stand alone, unmediated, as though they mirror beliefs and events in the past exactly as they occurred. Furthermore, without additional analysis, this lesson further runs the danger of conflating Garvey's particular views with *all* African-American views, a conflation which overlooks the importance of multiple perspectives and complexity in the past. Such conflations are a common mistake, given the limited time in the curriculum and the gaps in historical knowledge of many teachers. Garvey's perspective is the only one that students read; they do no sourcing of the document to understand who Garvey is and whether, for example, his views might be representative of many or few African Americans. They end the lesson with a list only of what they found interesting about the document. The teacher failed then, to connect the primary source to any broader historical interpretation.

In a different lesson, the teacher asked students to read the Declaration of Sentiments from Seneca Falls and list the grievances it outlines. For homework, students wrote a Declaration of Sentiments from a current viewpoint, for example, students' rights, gay rights, African-American rights, illegal immigrants' rights. Here again, the document serves to supply information about the past, in this case, the agenda of the antebellum women's rights movement. But it does not require students to engage in a historical reading of that document. Students read it for information only, not for analytic purposes for deeper understanding of the movement or the convention.

This lesson also illustrates how the teacher misconstrued constructivism. By placing the emphasis on the students' creation of a modern-day Declaration of Sentiments, the teacher asks students to construct their own understanding of a current issue and to take the perspective of another group in constructing that knowledge. But this is not the same as historical understanding. Constructivism does provide a rationale for teachers to use primary sources in their teaching, with the emphasis on a final product that students create. When done well, with attention to the guidelines of evidence and interpretation of the discipline, the process and products can be exciting. But often this is not the case. If lessons do not teach students historical context or require them to consider it in their products, they proceed without a more nuanced understanding of the documents, leading them to make unwarranted judgments about the past. A lesson might ask students to develop an argument using the evidence from the sources, and some arguments can be quite sophisticated. But given the boundaries of the discipline, not all arguments are equal. Unfortunately, students who do not learn about the standards of evidence and warrantability in history may fail to understand why some answers are better than others. And the teachers who do not understand this are left without a basis on which to adequately evaluate students' historical thinking.

These lessons neglected the sourcing and analytic reading skills specific to history. Such an approach suggests that documents are a mirror reflecting an unmediated past, that history is not an interpretive practice. Using documents in this way fails to help students understand the strengths and weaknesses, the limitations, and the relevance or applicability of a source to a particular question; all sources are essentially equal and the past is accessible through a literal reading. Yet the nuances of a document can be as important as the surface meaning of the words themselves. As Wineburg explains, historians consider the subtext of documents; they look at a document as both a rhetorical artifact (the author's intentions, motivations, and goals) and a human artifact (the author's world beliefs, values, and goals).[17] Considering the social location of the author, her connection to the event which she describes, her audience, her purpose for writing, and other events in the recent past that affected her life, all these facets of context may well affect our judgment of the strengths and weaknesses of a given document as a piece of evidence. It also demands more careful, interactive, and critical reading skills, making primary sources and the discipline of history a particularly suitable subject in which to teach literacy.[18]

Another lesson on Japanese internment during World War II included thirty pages of primary source documents for a two-day lesson. The teacher used some strategies learned in the grant, particularly Socratic seminar, to engage students with the sources, but the sheer volume of documents was overwhelming. While the teacher hoped to present multiple perspectives on the matter by presenting different kinds of documents such as executive orders, newspapers, personal accounts, and oral histories all from different participants, the lesson did not facilitate close reading of sources with attention to the different purposes, audiences, or reliability of each. Students simply read the documents without considering how to interpret these different sources and different perspectives.

Teachers' Disciplinary Knowledge

These examples tell us something about the disciplinary knowledge of teachers and their struggle to effectively teach the discipline. They may understand that primary sources are valuable, but they struggle to use them effectively. These lessons primarily use documents to teach the content of history, not the skills of historical thinking. This may not have been the teachers' intent; indeed, each teacher sought to bring multiple perspectives to their classrooms to help students understand the complexity of history. But the way that they *used* the documents did not facilitate such understanding. Rather it reinforced the idea that primary sources are mirrors onto an unmediated past. This was not necessarily a problem with teachers' understanding of the historical discipline. They had a strong background in history, and their contributions to discussions throughout the eighteen-month cycle suggested they understood the nature of history and the role of primary sources within it. Rather it was a problem of teaching strategy. These lessons fell short of using the documents to help *their students* understand the skills of historical interpretation.

The lesson here is one of teachers' disciplinary knowledge—and what we as grant directors need to assess about our participants. What do they understand about history and historical thinking skills? How well do they understand how to teach those skills? What do they understand about *students'* thinking about history? While many studies point out that teachers do not possess a solid grasp of historical thinking themselves, making it impossible to design lessons that teach it, it is important to consider that even teachers who understand the nature of the discipline may not know how to teach it.[19] Or they may not recognize how their own students think about history and how they, as teachers, might facilitate students' growth in historical cognition.

The seeds of this teaching problem are too numerous to explore here but they are certainly nurtured in college history classes. The traditional lecture format of most undergraduate history classes does not model strategies that prepare future teachers to teach active, hands-on history that promotes historical thinking. Instead, it betrays an assumption that all students learn in the same ways and that they should master a particular narrative. It also reinforces a view of history that is authoritarian and promotes passivity.[20] Students receive historical truth from the "expert," whether teacher or textbook. This kind of teaching often obscures the nuances of historical interpretation, the open-ended nature of historical research and knowledge, and the political uses of the discipline.

For teachers (and administrators) preoccupied with content coverage, lectures are an efficient way to meet that goal. Teaching historical thinking is at odds with the pressure on teachers to keep to a schedule and cover state standards. Standards tend to cover breadth of content rather than depth of thinking skills. Even standards that encompass historical thinking offer little guidance and are deemphasized on high stakes tests. Teachers who must cover a set curriculum find it difficult to devote the time to inquiry lessons that give students the opportunity to hone historical thinking in an effective manner. This is certainly a complaint we hear often from grant participants. That they devote *any* time at all to primary sources is, for many, an accomplishment in itself.

Documents and Presentism

Several units also fell prey to the seduction of presentism. As Wineburg has explained, presentism "is not some bad habit we've fallen into. It is, instead, our psychological condition at rest, a way of thinking that requires little effort and comes quite naturally."[21] We assume that others in the past are like ourselves, or that "the past is [the] present waiting to happen."[22] But this kind of thinking promotes simplistic conceptions of the past by flattening the historical terrain so that differences in time, place, and culture no longer matter. All human experience is taken as similar to ours in the present and judged accordingly. One unit, titled "African Americans Protesting Oppression," helps illustrate this problem.

The unit raised questions about historical and current day oppression, racism, and the struggle for civil rights and considered how social change happens in a democracy. These concerns were reflected in the organizing questions for several lessons that used excerpts from a variety of sources, including a quotation from Mary McCleod Bethune: "If we accept and acquiesce in the face of discrimination, we accept the responsibility ourselves. We should, therefore, protest openly everything that smacks of discrimination or slander."[23] The unit asked students to consider a number of thought-provoking questions.

- Is protest an essential part of democracy?
- Do people have the power to change society?
- Can an oppressor put so much fear into people that no one dares protest?
- What does the modern civil rights movement look like in the twenty-first century?

These questions reflected the teachers' interest in long-standing traditions of courage and protest in American democracy, with the last question connecting the unit to the present.

Let me be clear that these are rich questions that we hope young people grapple with; the questions themselves are not the problem. Bringing the discipline of history to bear on such concerns might encourage students to develop skills of analysis sensitive to context, continuity, and change, and produce careful consideration of the differences between motives, conditions, and strategies in the past, even the recent past, and the present.

Unfortunately, the lessons did not help students deepen such historical thinking; instead the focus remained on an ahistorical concern with oppression and protest that suggested all were universal without regard to issues of time, place, or culture. The unit began with students' and dictionary definitions of these terms and then proceeded to have students explore slave narratives from the nineteenth century, Jim Crow Laws, the antilynching and Black nationalist campaigns of the early twentieth century; oral histories of local civil rights activists, and protest songs of the 1960s and 1970s. Exciting though these sources may be, the lessons neglected to address them historically—to engage students in a deeper analysis of why, for example, protest looked different in the 1950s and 1960s than in the 1850s or 1890s, or how racism and oppression are manifested differently today than they were fifty or a hundred, or two hundred years ago. When lessons ask students to consider such issues, historical thinking dovetails with critical thinking skills such as comparison and contrast.

In discussing this unit with the team of teachers who wrote it, it was clear that their lessons had admirable motives. Teaching in a primarily African-American school, the teachers hoped to make history relevant to their students and to promote their sense of identity and agency.[24] Their hope was that the lessons would encourage students to understand that African Americans had worked hard for civil rights and had been able to bring about change, but that the struggle was not over; it was up to their students to continue it. For these teachers, history's power lay in its potential to inspire political engagement and activism today.[25] Thus they asked students, "For what issues would you protest? What are some things that make people want to fight?" But this runs the risk of conflating students' struggles today with those of people in the past; the lesson doesn't ask students to consider their commonalities and differences with historical actors and the reasons for those differences. When not followed with other tasks that help students understand the past on its own terms, such questions can flatten the historical terrain so that all experience of racial oppression in the United States, all motives for opposing it, are the same. Lost in translation is the historical thinking necessary to understand people and problems in the past as products of a given time and place with motivations, constraints, and possibilities different from ours. This is a kind of intellectual narcissism that promotes not only misunderstanding of the past, but misunderstanding of others in the present, as well.[26]

Next Steps: How to Use Documents to Teach Historical Thinking

Lessons that flatten the historical terrain, employ irrelevant sources or unwieldy sources, or disconnect sources from historical thinking suggest that we still have much work to do in future TAH grants. Many grants, including ours, laud the value of introducing teachers to primary sources, but we cannot stop there. Even when TAH grants intend to develop teachers' historical thinking, and even when they are successful at doing so, my experience suggests that teachers still need considerable support in translating that knowledge into effective lessons. While our grants have clearly been successful in developing teachers' understanding of the discipline of history and the role of primary sources in it, what has been lost in translation from grant activities to classroom lessons is fundamental to history education: an understanding of the way to *use* documents to teach historical thinking. While easily recognizable, this problem has proved difficult to solve, as the vast literature on history teaching and learning suggests and as my reading of grant participants' lessons corroborates. We can do much more to link primary sources to historical thinking skills. Luckily there is a growing body of research literature to support such efforts and TAH grants would be wise to help teachers translate this research into their classroom practice.

Reviewing these units then, has reminded me of some obvious, but still very valuable lessons about translating primary source activities into the classroom and how we might do a better job of it in future grants. As I look forward to working with more grants, I have several agenda items. First is the need to clearly define with our participants what historical thinking is and to use consistent and accessible terminology to describe its characteristics. There are numerous models from which to draw. The National Standards on History Education identify five standards in historical thinking: Chronological Thinking; Historical Comprehension, Historical Analysis and Interpretation; Historical Research Capabilities; Historical Issues Analysis and Decision Making. These standards are useful in that they breakdown the skills into discernible tasks to employ when designing and evaluating lessons.[27] The National Council on History Education uses History's Habits of Mind articulated in the Bradley Commission Report.[28] Those who research history teaching and learning talk about "sourcing heuristics," "corroboration," and "contextualization."[29]

All of these frameworks have their virtues and share a concern for both disciplinary skills and analysis and promoting empathy. These various frameworks offer us a starting point for clearer articulation of grant goals among project staff, teachers, and presenters. But with so many frameworks of historical thinking from which to draw, we have run the danger in our grant of further complicating already difficult cognitive skills. One TAH project, "Thinking Like a Historian," avoided this problem by facilitating conversations between teachers and historians as they together developed their own framework of historical thinking.[30] Their model includes:

- Cause and Effect (What were the causes of past events? What were the effects?)
- Change and Continuity (What has changed? What has remained the same?)
- Turning Points (How did past decisions or actions affect future choices?)
- Through Their Eyes (How did people in the past view their world?)
- Using the Past (How does the past help us make sense of the present?)

The virtue of this approach is that it was developed by participants in the grant who then used it to develop and teach their lessons. Since they created it themselves, teachers probably found it more meaningful and useful for their teaching.

Second, with a clearer articulation of a framework for historical thinking, I hope we will wrestle with how to scaffold these skills in the grant without losing sight of the ways they are interconnected. For example, sourcing heuristics that ask about author information, audience, and purpose help teachers grasp that the narratives of history are constructed and often disputed. Hence many teachers had students read multiple sources to gain multiple viewpoints of past events. But we can further build on this understanding. Grant activities can help teachers develop a deeper understanding that multiple viewpoints found in primary sources are not just mirrors onto different perspectives in the past, but help us understand the past as complex terrain. How do we help students sort through what to do with those multiple perspectives—how do we teach them how historians understand multiple and conflicting viewpoints and make sense of them in their interpretations? How then do we connect the practice of sourcing to better understand context and contingency, cause and effect? Carefully making these skills transparent and building them into grant activities that use primary sources is an important next step in deepening teachers' own grasp of historical thinking.

The Importance of the Historian's Role

If we are to do this, the historian's role in the grant becomes even more important. Historians are typically invited into TAH grants as content experts; they arrive for one morning or visit over a weekend to deliver lectures on their research specialties. This approach privileges the idea that school-based historical knowledge is passive, it is transmitted in a neat package with the historian's struggles over interpretation often left out of the story; her or his *historical thinking,* is bypassed. This is in direct conflict with the view of the discipline and the teaching strategies we want to encourage in our grants. Instead, historians must work with teachers as *they* themselves go to the sources and think through the problems of historical interpretation. Then the historian must go a step further and join teachers in wrestling with practical steps and strategies in teaching those skills. Historians' habits of mind and practices must be more transparent, both to themselves and to grant participants, and ideally I hope that we historians use that disciplinary knowledge to provide teachers with feedback on their own lesson design. Such conversations will help further develop a community of historical practice that includes academic and public historians and teachers[31] (see chapter 10 for further discussion of historians' communication with teachers).

To accomplish these goals, not only do we as project staff need to be more careful in articulating of historical thinking skills, scaffolding activities that develop these skills, and better involving historians in making their craft transparent. We also need to work intensively with teachers on their pedagogy and build communities within school buildings, districts, and regionally that are supportive of this type of history education. As a number of studies in historical thinking have shown, and as the lessons here suggest, exposure to content knowledge does not necessarily translate into good lesson design.[32] We need to pay much more attention to the organization and structure of future grants so that teachers have *time* and *opportunities* to practice using primary sources, to practice historical interpretations, and to practice lesson design. We need to provide time for teachers and grant personnel, including historians, to evaluate together the historical habits of mind built into the lessons teachers design. This requires attention to historical thinking, making the *process* of historical interpretation more transparent, not just exposing teachers to the *products* of historians' research. Clearly we needed more time with our teachers to accomplish these goals. A colloquium and summer institute (a total of eight days) was not enough for teachers in our grant to digest and then translate primary source activities that focused on historical thinking into their units.

Fortunately we learned this lesson and have made some valuable changes. In our most recent grant, we have spent much more time with participants, meeting with them every two months in afternoon seminars and scheduling two weekend colloquia and summer institutes, rather than only one as in past grants. In addition, teachers develop a portfolio, which includes not only lesson plans as in our earlier grants, but also an annotated bibliography, history topic reflection, reflection on teaching with primary sources, and student work samples. The reflection on teaching with primary sources has helped them to make the connections between using primary sources indiscriminately or as information only, and using them to develop specific historical thinking skills. They also connect their lessons to classroom practice by including examples of student work and their own analysis of their students' historical thinking. The portfolio addresses the content concerns of the TAH program by asking teachers to include an essay on a historical topic covered in the grant and an annotated bibliography of the materials they used for their essay and lessons.

Evaluation of Teachers' Lessons

Participation in the grant is voluntary and teachers do not receive any graduate credit. Since our grant was not designed to formally assess teachers, a scoring rubric for the portfolio would not have fit its intention or spirit. However, we did articulate several "talking points" to provide teachers with feedback on historical thinking and their use of primary sources, and to help us evaluate the effectiveness of grant activities in developing those skills. These talking points include:

- Lessons include historical knowledge and themes presented in the grant.
- Lessons include teaching strategies presented in the grant.
- Lessons include primary sources.
- Primary sources support teaching objectives; primary source activities encourage historical thinking.
- Bibliography draws from a variety of sources to shape teaching plans.
- Reflection on History Topic includes historical knowledge and themes presented in the grant.
- Reflection on History Topic includes evidence of in-depth engagement with topic, including some familiarity with historiography.
- Reflection on Teaching Primary Sources shows understanding of historical thinking skills and how to teach it.
- Reflection on Teaching Primary Sources demonstrates analysis of student learning and analysis of students' historical thinking skills.
- Student Work Samples correlate with historical thinking teaching objectives.

One of the unintended but important results of these changes is that teachers invite project staff to their classrooms more frequently than in the past and are thus able to get feedback on the actual lessons they teach, not just their lesson design. A particularly enthusiastic teacher organized her American history course around the central questions, "Who is an American?" and "What does freedom mean?" She used these questions to guide many of her primary source selections, choosing those that could speak to these questions in some way. The lessons I observed in her classroom promoted contextual thinking by asking students to consider how people in different time periods and with different identities answered these questions. My observation allowed us to discuss not only how the sources she selected for her lessons on the Civil War (the Gettysburg Address, the Emancipation Proclamation, and letters to Abraham Lincoln from African Americans) addressed those questions and whose voices were missing in her selections. We were also able to discuss how *students* used those documents and how their comments and interpretations revealed their background knowledge and interpretive skills and what skills they still needed to understand the significance of the Emancipation Proclamation and the deeper meaning of the Gettysburg Address.

While I have focused on lesson design here, ultimately we hope to support teachers in their classroom practices. Our latest grant seeks to do this through a mentoring relationship in which teachers who participated in the first two-year cohort team with members of a new cohort. Over the next year they will share their work from the grant, meet with them during planning time, and visit their classrooms. We hope this structure will underscore teachers' role as professional colleagues and create a community of history practitioners dedicated to historical thinking that outlives the grant. This coming year, mentors will have additional training on historical thinking and will work closely with grant personnel in their own classrooms and in after-school meetings to continue to hone their own skills and explore how to help their colleagues deepen their knowledge of historical thinking and teaching.

A Historian's Look at History Education

As a historian, who also works closely with teacher education and professional development, the opportunity to work with *Teaching American History* grants has deepened my understanding of the challenges facing the history education community. It has encouraged me to revise several of my courses, both in Progressive Era history, women's history, and especially the history and social studies methods courses I teach. I focus much more of my energy on historical skills and inquiry than on content coverage. This has been extremely difficult for me as I loath to cut out any information I find so important and fascinating about Progressive Era reformers, political culture, economic changes, social policies, and—well, you get the idea. (I hope this has led me to share a bit of the teachers' concerns about coverage.) Now I try more deliberately to pair content with a historical thinking skill, and I look for sources that support those goals. This is a practice I try to make transparent in my history classes, and I ask students in history methods courses to do the same when they design lessons.

Over the years, as I have observed, reviewed, and experimented with ways to teach historical thinking, my emphasis has moved from an exclusive focus on simply including primary sources in the classroom to *how* to use primary sources in the classroom. And, as history education researchers have been reminding us, the question of how to use primary sources and encourage historical thinking requires us to explore how our students think about history when they enter our classrooms and how we can transform naïve ideas about history into more sophisticated understanding. That is, we must not only develop teachers' content knowledge, we must support teachers' knowledge of historical *learning* as well.

In sum, working with TAH grants has reminded me that focus on content and even introduction to the discipline is not enough to make a major impact on classroom practices. If historians are to influence history education, we must be more transparent about our practices when we work with teachers. My work with TAH grants draws attention to the importance of the research in history teaching and learning and the necessity of helping teachers themselves recognize, analyze, and evaluate the way they are using sources to develop lessons and teach historical thinking. If we want teachers to effectively translate grant activities into their classrooms, historians and grant staff must give them more time, opportunity, and support in doing so.

Notes

1. The recent literature on historical thinking developed out of the field of cognitive science, particularly the study of pedagogical content knowledge articulated by Lee Shulman. Following Shulman, others, such as Sam Wineburg, Peter Seixas, and Bob Bain, have identified the types of thinking specific to history, and teachers' and students' historical understanding. Linda Levstik and Keith Barton have also explored the role of historical understanding among students and the role of history education more generally. These are only a few of a growing number of researchers in historical thinking and history education. For examples of this literature, Lee Shulman, "Knowledge and Teaching: Foundations of the New Reform," *Harvard Educational Review* 57 (February 1987): 1–22; Wineburg's collected essays in *Historical Thinking and Other Unnatural Acts: Charting the Future of Teaching the Past* (Philadelphia: Temple University Press, 2001); Seixas, "Mapping the Terrain of Historical Significance," *Social Education* 61, no.1 (1997): 22–27; Seixas, "Historical Understanding Among Adolescents in a Multicultural Setting," *Curriculum Inquiry* 23 (1993): 301–327; Peter N. Stearns, Peter Seixas, and Sam Wineburg, eds, *Knowing, Teaching, and Learning History: National and International Perspectives* (New York: New York University Press, 2000); Mario Carretero and James F. Voss, eds., *Cognitive and Instructional Processes in History and the Social Sciences* (Hillsdale, NJ: Lawrence Erlbaum, 1994); Keith C. Barton and Linda S. Levstik, *Teaching History for the Common Good* (Hillsdale, NJ: Lawrence Erlbaum, 2004).
2. This approach privileges the development of historical thinking skills akin to those practiced by historians. In our grant, we have been committed to this goal, not because thinking like an historian is, in and of itself, worthwhile, but because the historian's habits of mind promote useful critical thinking skills which are the foundation of thoughtful citizenship. As Keith Barton and Linda Levstik have recently discussed, there are a number of other purposes, or "stances," of history education: the identification stance, the analytic stance, the moral response stance, and the exhibition stance. For their discussion of the limitations of instruction focused on developing the skills of academic disciplines, see *Teaching History for the Common Good,* 258–61. For an alternative perspective, see Peter Seixas, "Schweigen! Die Kinder" in *Knowing, Teaching, and Learning History,* 19–37. My purpose here is not to deal with this debate or defend the value of our particular approach, but to reflect on how we might better design grant activities to achieve our goal of developing historical thinking among teachers and their students.
3. Sam Wineburg and Daisy Martin, "Reading and Rewriting History," *Educational Leadership* 62, no.1 (September 2004): 42–45.
4. Seixas offers a thoughtful discussion of competing epistemologies within history education in "Schweigen! Die Kinder" in *Knowing, Teaching, and Learning History*; Diane Ravitch addresses teacher preparation in "The Educational Backgrounds of History Teachers," in *Knowing, Teaching, and Learning History,* 143–155. See also Barton and Levstik, *Teaching History for the Common Good,* 191–97; 244–61.
5. Gary Nash, Charlotte Crabtree, Ross Dunn, *History on Trial: Culture Wars and the Teaching of the Past* (New York: Random House, 2000); Lynne V. Cheney, *Telling the Truth: Why Our Culture and Our Country Have Stopped Making Sense and What We Can Do About It* (New York: Touchstone, 1996).
6. Ravitch, "The Educational Background of History Teachers"; Sarah Drake Brown and John J. Patrick, *History Education in the United States: A Survey of Teacher Certification and State-Based Standards and Assessments for Teachers and Students* (Washington, DC: American Historical Association and the Organization of American Historians, 2004); Richard M. Ingersoll, "Out-of-Field Teaching and Educational Equality" (Washington, DC: U.S. Department of Education, Office of Educational Research and Improvement, National Center for Education Statistics, (October 1996); National Center for Education Statistics, *America's Teachers: Profile of a Profession, 1993–94* (Washington, DC: National Center for Education Statistics, 1997).
7. No Child Left Behind legislation has attempted to address this concern by requiring secondary teachers to be "highly qualified" in the subject matter they teach. The measures for deter-

mining highly qualified teachers, however, vary from a major in the content area to passing a state test. Such tests, however, may not evaluate the teacher's ability to use primary sources and think historically.

8. See Barton and Levstik's discussion of this issue in *Teaching History for the Common Good*.

9. Sam Wineburg, a cognitive scientist who has been instrumental in shaping the field of history of teaching and learning, has written extensively on differences between the ways historians, teachers, and students read primary sources. See his collection of essays in *Historical Thinking and Other Unnatural Acts*.

10. Bob Bain, "Into the Breach: Using Research and Theory to Shape History Instruction," in *Knowing, Teaching, and Learning History: National and International Perspectives* (New York: New York University Press, 2000), 331–52; 334.

11. My thanks to Dennis Lubeck, IEC director and project director on numerous TAH grants, and John Robinson, IEC research associate, for their work with history teachers over the years and especially their collaboration with me and the University of Missouri-St. Louis on several TAH grants.

12. Wineburg, *Historical Thinking and Other Unnatural Acts*, 76.

13. See for example, the document, artifact, and photograph worksheets at http://www.archives. gov/education/lessons/index.html, Fred Drake's guidelines at http://lilt.ilstu.edu/fddrake/main%20pages/firstsecondthirdorder.html#first,which are also available in Fred D. Drake and Lynn R. Nelson, *Engagement in Teaching History: Theory and Practice for Middle and Secondary Teachers* (New York: Pearson, 2005).

14. Thomas Andrews and Flannery Burke, "What Does It Mean to Think Historically?" *Perspectives* (January 2007): 45:1.

15. We loosely used the model of essential questions from Grant Wiggins and Jay McTighe, *Understanding by Design* (Alexandria, VA: Association for Supervision and Curriculum Development, 1998). Though many districts in our area use UbD, we have not required that teachers use it for their lesson design. However, its notion of essential questions has proven useful in helping teachers understand the discipline of history as one rooted in inquiry with historical interpretation that begins with questions.

16. As Wineburg has noted, high school students do this as well. See "On the Reading of Historical Texts," 76–79.

17. Wineburg, "On the Reading of Historical Texts," 65–66.

18. Wineburg and Martin argue this point in "Reading and Rewriting History," *Educational Leadership*.

19. Bruce VanSledright, "Closing the Gap between School and Disciplinary History? Historian as High School Teacher," in *Advances in Research on Teaching*, vol. 6, *Teaching and Learning History*, ed. Jere Brophy (Greenwich, CT: JAI Press, 1996); G. Williamson McDiarmid, "Understanding History for Teaching: A Study of the Historical Understanding of Prospective Teachers," in *Cognitive and Instructional Practices in History and the Social Sciences*, eds. Mario Carretero and James F. Voss (Hillsdale, NJ: Lawrence Erlbaum, 1994), 159–86.

20. James Loewen, *Lies My Teacher Told Me: Everything Your American History Textbook Got Wrong* (New York: Touchstone, 1995).

21. Wineburg, *Historical Thinking and Other Unnatural Acts*, 19.

22. Barton and Levstik, *Teaching History for the Common Good*, 134.

23. Excerpted from Mary McLeod Bethune, "Certain Unalienable Rights," *What the Negro Wants*, edited by Rayford W. Logan (Chapel Hill: University of North Carolina Press, 1944). Additional documents used in the unit include *Six Women's Slave Narratives, Strange Fruit*, memoirs from Ida B. Wells, W. E. B. DuBois, and A. Philip Randolph, and oral histories from local civil rights activists.

24. Barton and Levstik, *Teaching History for the Common Good*.

25. Ibid., 91–109.

26. Wineburg, "Historical Thinking and Other Unnatural Acts," in *Historical Thinking and Other Unnatural Acts*.

27. Historical Thinking Standards are available online from the National Center for History in the Schools.

28. Bradley Commission on History in Schools, *Building a History Curriculum: Guidelines for Teaching History in Schools* (Westlake, OH: National Council for History Education, 1995), 9. These Habits of Mind include: (1) Understand the significance of the past to their own lives, both private and public, and to their society. (2) Distinguish between the important and the inconsequential, to develop the "discriminating memory" needed for a discerning judgment in public and personal life. (3) Perceive past events and issues as they were experienced by people at the time, to develop historical empathy as opposed to present-mindedness. (4) Acquire at one and the same time a comprehension of diverse cultures and of shared humanity. (5) Understand how things happen and how things change, how human intentions matter, but also how their consequences are shaped by the means of carrying them out, in a tangle of purpose and process. (6) Comprehend the interplay of change and continuity, and avoid assuming that either is somehow more natural, or more to be expected, than the other. (7) Prepare to live with uncertainties and exasperating, even perilous, unfinished business, realizing that not all problems have solutions. (8) Grasp the complexity of historical causation, respect particularity, and avoid excessively abstract generalizations. (9) Appreciate the often tentative nature of judgments about the past, and thereby avoid the temptation to seize upon particular "lessons" or history as cures for present ills. (11) Recognize the importance of individuals who have made a difference in history, and the significance of personal character for both good and ill. (12) Appreciate the force of the nonrational, the irrational, the accidental, in history and human affairs. (13) Understand the relationship between geography and history as a matrix of time and place, and as context for events. (14) Read widely and critically in order to recognize the difference between fact and conjecture, between evidence and assertion, and thereby develop the ability to frame useful questions.

29. See for example, Wineburg, "On the Reading of Historical Texts: Notes on the Breach Between School and the Academy," in *Historical Thinking and Other Unnatural Acts*; Fred D. Drake and Lynn R. Nelson, *Engagement in Teaching History: Theory and Practice for Middle and Secondary Teachers* (New York: Pearson, 2005); M. Anne Britt, Charles A. Perfetti, Julie A. Van Dyke, and Gareth Gabrys, "The Sorcerer's Apprentice: A Tool for Document-Supported History Instruction," in *Knowing, Teaching, and Learning History*, 437–70.

30. Nikki Mandell and Bobbie Malone, "Thinking Like a Historian: Rethinking History Instruction" (2007). My thanks to Nikki Mandell for sharing this work with me. (Madison: Wisconsin Historical Society Press, 2007).

31. Peter Seixas, "The Community of History as the Basis of Knowledge and Learning: The Case of History," *American Educational Research Journal* 30, no. 2 (Summer 1993): 305–24.

32. For discussion of a number of studies that point to gaps between teacher disciplinary knowledge and lesson design, see Barton and Levstik, 246–52.

Part II

Emerging Practices for Classroom Teachers

Introduction

Part II addresses emerging practices from the *Teaching American History* projects that may be of primary interest to classroom teachers of American history. Both those currently working in *Teaching American History* projects and those who are currently teaching history in K-12 classrooms and want to transfer the lessons learned from these grant project to their classrooms will benefit from the insights detailed here. Those involved with mentoring, preparing, and working in other capacities with classroom teachers will also find useful information here.

Overarching Themes

In examining the chapters included in this section, four overarching themes emerge from the work of these projects relevant to classroom teachers. These are: (1) the importance of teachers becoming practitioners of history, especially engaging directly with primary sources; (2) the importance of using teachers' voices to shape successful project decision making; (3) the important of collaboration with colleagues; and (4) the importance of teachers modeling history skills and sharing their enthusiasm for history with their students. Taking a closer look at each of these themes reveals key factors to consider as a classroom history teacher.

When teachers become practitioners of history there are changes in their understanding of many aspects of history instruction. Their understanding of history as a constructed discipline open to interpretation is improved, as is their understanding of the use of archives and local resources. Teachers also improved in their understanding of how to choose and use documents to support inquiry-based classroom practices.

The importance of teachers using their voices to impact their participation and learning in *Teaching American History* projects involves several key features. The project partners benefited in many cases from the educational expertise and suggestions that teachers shared regarding how historians, archivists, and museum staff could improve their interactions with teachers and students. Teachers contributed ideas for integration of content and constructivist pedagogy, such as improving literacy and social studies skills strategies that used active, "doing history" methods. Finally, projects became more successful when they recognized the realities of teachers' working conditions and took them into consideration in project planning and resource development.

Collaboration among partners is a hallmark of all TAH project designs, and those who recognized the importance of including teachers as equal partners demonstrated success in achieving project goals. Sustaining the collaboration with partners such as historians and archivists throughout the project and even beyond was found to be valuable. It also proved useful to engage in peer mentoring which provided inspiration, motivation, professional development, and positive influences for teachers. Another lesson from collaboration was the commonalities that emerged in the roles of teachers and historians.

Finally, by modeling skills for students to use and sharing their enthusiasm for history, teachers learned to improve their instruction in several ways. Teachers learned the process of history and then had students do the process, which led to increased engagement and learning for students. Teachers applied their new knowledge to instructional design of units and lessons, and they used local resources to encourage student enthusiasm and connection with history.

Emerging Practices Chapter By Chapter

In chapter 5, Don Owen and Kathy Barbour, administrators from Urbana, IL School District No. 116, describe lessons learned from the American History Teachers' Collaborative project. Their project involved teachers as practitioners of history through engagement with primary sources with a particular focus on local history. This work increased the teachers' content knowledge, changed their understanding of history and teaching with primary sources, and taught them how to work effectively with archive and museum resources and staff. They describe the guidelines the teachers learned for choosing documents to gain students' attention, enabling them to compare two sides of an issue, and developing critical reading skills. Using teachers' voices was the most effective method of examining the impact of the project as teachers shared their expertise with museum staff and became teacher scholars.

The AHTC project took advantage of local and regional primary documents by having teachers actively doing history in local archives during summer internships where they learned the importance of local history to connect and engage students. In turn, they applied the knowledge they gained in their classroom units and modeled the process for their students. Teachers also came to value their collaborations with colleagues for inspiration and motivation.

Supervisory Archivist Tim Rives of the Eisenhower Presidential Library and Museum in Abilene, KS shares a primer for teachers on the effective use of archives in chapter 6. He provides suggestions for breaking the barrier of previous research experience in libraries and beginning to "think archives." The key to understanding archives is the focus on the record creator, the organic relationship of items in archives, the uniqueness of their holdings, and the principle of provenance. By following Rives's "iron law" of archives and preparing well in advance, research can be productive for teachers and students.

Rives also stresses the importance of maintaining a working relationship with local archivists. He describes a two-way collaboration that includes what archivists can learn by working with teachers and listening to their voices as well as what teachers can learn from the archivists' unique knowledge of their collections. Finally, the goal of civic literacy can be achieved by supporting teachers and students who use primary sources from local archives.

The importance of using teachers' voices in decision making is the focus of David Gerwin's argument in chapter 7. An Associate Professor of Education at Queens College/CUNY, his Inventing the People project used teachers as grant directors and based their project on the interests expressed by the teacher participants. Another lesson from this project is the value of integrating content and pedagogy by having teachers "doing history" to support inquiry-based classroom practices and modeling those practices for students.

Another message that Gerwin emphasizes is the parallel nature of teachers' and historians' roles. Teachers came to understand that history is provisional and open to continual interpretation and became comfortable using primary sources. They learned how to choose documents to connect with and motivate their students. Finally, the importance of creating a teacher community of collaboration with support for each other and collaborative activities featured prominently in the project.

Chapter 8 shines a spotlight on elementary history teachers through the University of Iowa's Visiting Scholar and Professor Elise Fillpot's work on the Bringing History Home projects. The emphasis on recognizing the reality of the time constraints and curriculum pressures on the teachers proved valuable to the success of the project. Teachers made a commitment to their own professional development and curriculum change, and this was strengthened by having all teachers in the school or district participating. A positive peer influence was shown by teachers mentoring each other and building a close teacher community. As in other projects, practices emerged that had the teachers "doing history" and understanding history as an interpretive, constructivist process. They engaged in a new way to learn history that focused on depth and not breadth.

The K-5 teachers used constructivist pedagogy centered on active learning and matching content with pedagogy. Fillpot shares the dynamic strategies the teachers created including new practices with timelines, maps, literacy practices, primary source analysis, and assessment using historical analysis and source analysis. Students became engaged and excited about history because their teachers were also engaged and excited. In turn, student learning enhanced the teachers' interest.

Chapter 5

Through the Lens of Local History
Enriching Instruction Using Regional Primary Sources

Donald D. Owen and Katherine Barbour
Urbana, IL School District No. 116

> Providing teachers direct access to historical artifacts and primary sources so that they can better view national issues in history through the lens of local events [gives] teachers the unique opportunity to become practitioners of history. (Urbana School District's 2005 Teaching American History grant narrative)

The American History Teachers' Collaborative is a *Teaching American History* grant project that has been directed by Urbana School District No. 116, Urbana, Illinois, since 2003 (http://www.americanhistoryteachers.org). Four *Teaching American History* grants (2003, 2005, 2007, 2008) have provided funding for the American History Teachers' Collaborative (AHTC) to serve K-12 teachers in a consortium of small urban and rural school districts. Urbana School District partners with local archives and museums in central Illinois, as well as archives in Springfield and Chicago, to provide unique hands-on historical research experiences for participating teachers. The AHTC provides content-driven in-service opportunities to teachers of American history in the public schools of central Illinois. This project has three specific goals. The first goal is to improve teachers' American history content knowledge. The second goal is to provide teachers with direct access to historical artifacts and primary sources so that they can better view national issues in history through the lens of local events. The final goal is to disseminate content knowledge and foster communication of best practices in the teaching of American history in order to increase student achievement. This chapter explores the impact on teachers and students of this focus on local and regional primary documents.

To accomplish the goals of the AHTC, Urbana School District partners with five institutions that house local, state, and national historical documents and artifacts. These partners are: Champaign County (IL) Forest Preserve District's Early American Museum; Champaign County (IL) Historical Museum at the Cattle Bank; Champaign County (IL) Historical Archives at the Urbana Free Library; the Illinois State Archives; and the Great Lakes Regional Depository of the National Archives and Records Administration. The "local lens" concept of the project design was first explored during an internship at a county historical archives. In 1997, Donald Owen, while completing his master's degree in history at Illinois State University, spent the summer semester researching local history in the Champaign County Historical Archives at the Urbana Free Library. As a culminating project, Owen created a series of lesson plans that was centered on local primary documents (Owen, 1997). The following school year, Owen incorporated several of the lessons into his eighth grade U.S. history class at Urbana Middle School. He immediately noticed that the local documents sparked more questions, interest, and engagement in his students than had been the case previously. The AHTC began as a project to expand teacher and student engagement with history.

The American History Teachers' Collaborative is made up of teachers from seven East Central Illinois school districts. The largest of these districts serves 9,031 students and the smallest serves 556. Altogether these school districts serve almost 21,000 students in a variety of urban and rural settings. Teachers in these districts have limited staff development resources but are willing to work together to improve the teaching of American history. These teachers learn and work together as they take part in summer institutes, participate in day-long focus workshops each of which revolves around a time period or theme in history; engage in the bigger picture through experiential learning trips; conduct research as an AHTC fellow; analyze books and lectures in evening discussion groups; present their ideas to their colleagues and to a larger audience at national conferences; and share their research and lessons with their peers.

Each summer the AHTC holds a five-day summer institute during which teachers examine a major theme of American history through the lens of local historical events and people. Examples of these themes include immigration, transportation, civil rights and liberties, and constitutional issues. These institutes include research using primary documents and artifacts; collaboration with professional historians, museum experts, and fellow teachers; discussion of scholarly works; and the development of model lesson plans.

In addition to the workshops and institutes, teachers have the opportunity to apply for fellowships supported by the grant project. Each summer, a number of participating teachers complete internships at the partner museums and archives. The fellows' role is to act as educational specialists for the museums and help the museums in their educational outreach activities. The fellows spend their time doing in-depth research into the museum's collections looking for connections between the holdings and the American history curriculum. They have the opportunity to spend many hours getting familiar with the partners' collections and to develop unit plans based on the local primary sources. The fellows also are instrumental in the selection of documents and artifacts for the use in workshops and on the project Web page. Fellows are encouraged to present the local primary source units that they create at local, state, and national conferences. The fellowship program is an integral part of the AHTC because it fosters collaboration and sustained use of the local historical institutions and organizations by area schools and teachers.

One of the goals of the American History Teachers' Collaborative is to provide teachers with direct access to historical artifacts and primary sources so that they can better view national issues in history through the lens of local events. This gives teachers the unique opportunity to become practitioners of history. Instead of acquiring all of their content knowledge from listening and reading, teachers conduct research using primary documents. They have the opportunity to spend many hours with the local museum and archive collections. Teachers evaluate the documents and artifacts based on how well they can be used to enrich and explain major themes or watershed events in American history. Teachers also select documents that will be accessible to their students, readable, engaging, and that can be used to reinforce or challenge students' prior knowledge. After selecting the best documents and artifacts, the teachers collaborate to develop unit plans based on the local primary sources to enhance student engagement and learning. AHTC teachers do this as summer fellows working in local museums and archives or as part of the summer institute.

This engagement with primary sources has a broader impact than just increasing the teachers' content knowledge in American history. This chapter examines how teachers' engagement with primary sources changes their understanding of history, their view toward teaching with primary documents, their classroom instruction, and their views of archive and museum resources. The impact of a professional development project can be measured in a variety of ways. In this analysis, the importance of the teachers' own voices was deemed to be the most effective method of examining the impact that the project had on the teachers and their classrooms. The teachers whose voices were selected represent a small cross-section of the participants. Most of the teachers interviewed for this chapter have been involved in the AHTC since the beginning of the project. Seven of the nine teachers interviewed have been AHTC fellows and, therefore, have worked closely with one or more of the partner museums or archives. Two of the teachers are elementary school teachers, two are high school, and five are middle school teachers. Two of the teachers have been in the classroom for less than two years. They were included to represent the voices of novice teachers who often find issues of content, pedagogy, and professional development uniquely challenging.

Teachers' Learning Processes: Increasing and Applying Historical Content Knowledge

Whether it is a Saturday workshop, a summer institute, or an afternoon of lesson study, teachers participate in American History Teachers' Collaborative activities to improve their content knowledge and to find ways to provide a richer American history learning experience for their students. Often content learning occurs in reference to the major topics and themes of history, but sometimes it is as simple as rediscovering events that teachers, or textbook authors, have overlooked. Don Barbour, an eighth grade teacher and social studies department chair, explains how his view of early 20th century history changed:

> The flu epidemic is, for me, a really important chapter...that doesn't appear in our book. We had a focus workshop on it, and we had a book discussion on it, and then other fellows took on the task of creating a lesson from primary sources about it. It is a really interesting look at history, especially given the fact that there is an avian

flu out there that could mutate into something like this from 80 years ago. So, my own consciousness with a particular historical event was raised through at least one AHTC [event]—that's just one example. (personal interview, December, 12, 2007)

Although much of the teachers' learning happens as they interact with curators and archivists or as they listen to historian presenters, they also rely on their colleagues to improve their content knowledge, as well as to provide inspiration, motivation, and professional discussion. First-year teacher Natalee Steffen teaches eighth grade U.S. history. She describes the collegial environment at grant project activities:

> The enthusiasm from other teachers around you at the AHTC events is so great that you just feed off of each other with ideas. Additionally, you learn from other teachers and the ideas that they're using incorporating primary documents into their lessons. I'm walking in here with a blank slate as a new teacher, and I've been given the opportunity to collaborate with veteran teachers who have done this before, are giving me ideas, and are helping me out. (personal interview, December 12, 2007)

This enthusiasm and collegiality often extends outside regular grant activities. Christine Adrian, an eighth grade social studies and writing teacher with over 15 years of classroom experience, said that AHTC teachers in her school district have become the "cohort of teachers that have basically written the curriculum" (personal interview, December 17, 2007). Our project staff sought to capitalize on this transfer of learning after school hours to the regular school day. When Alexis Jones moved from her elementary classroom to take a full-time position with us as AHTC Activity Coordinator, she began facilitating lesson study with teachers in the two largest, and closest, districts served by the AHTC. She explains the process in this way:

> Lesson study is a traditional Japanese form of long-term professional development. In order to improve their teaching and enrich students' learning experiences, teachers collaboratively research and plan a model lesson, implement the lesson in a classroom, collect observation data, and reflect upon the lesson. (Richardson, 2004)

> This process takes place in a cycle. Teachers research and plan the lesson, one teacher teaches while others observe, everyone reflects on the students' learning, and then changes are made to the lesson. At that point, another teacher can teach the refined lesson or the group can continue the process with other ideas. This next lesson would at the very least involve some component of the previous lesson so that the entire process is one continuous learning experience for the teachers involved.

> During the observation, the emphasis is not on observing the teacher as much as it is on thinking about student learning, reflecting and discussing teaching, and identifying knowledge necessary to improve the teaching practice. These lessons are videotaped for future discussions, and a reflection session is held immediately after the model lesson.

> The first year of AHTC lesson study was definitely a learning experience. Giving teachers time to discuss the issues they're dealing with in their history classes, set goals for their students, and collaboratively plan a lesson to address these issues

was quite valuable. It is rare that teachers are able to co-plan or even take the time to discuss common goals, so this initiative was a huge step in the right direction. The lesson plans that were developed were also quite interesting and very thorough. Since there were three to four teachers working on each lesson, they could split up the work, allowing for a more hands-on approach than one teacher would have had the time to prepare.

In my opinion, the most valuable part of lesson study is the postlesson discussion, but this was also what presented the most challenges. Effective teaching requires reflection, but often we are pulled in so many different directions that we don't take the time to consider what went right or wrong with a lesson we have just taught. Lesson study gives teachers the opportunity to engage in this type of reflection, with the help of other members of the research group who are observing the students during the lesson. (personal communication, January 6, 2008)

One of the elementary lesson study teachers was third and fourth grade teacher Tiffany Clark. Clark explains the importance of professional collaboration and discussions with colleagues:

One of the things that is most important is having the time and the framework in which to create these kinds of lessons. That's just been something I'm so thankful for…being able to create these windows of opportunity and set aside the time to be able to be the kind of teacher I want to be. Working with other people and being able to mix in their ideas, and also to hear [their thoughts], allows us to craft an exceptional learning experience for the children. Of course, this is the point of a lesson study…what your colleagues have to say about your lesson and how you did it. Okay, the kids got this. The kids didn't get this. Let's start with that next time. Let's try this next time. And it was interesting how some of that was just teacher style. I tend to be pretty casual and pretty flexible, perhaps to a fault, and some of the other teachers preferred a much more formal, structured arena, so … my kids were kind of wandering around, and they're doing their thing, and it's pretty loud and noisy, and I'm letting them go at it. But the next teacher … had everybody line up and pass the marker in a certain way, and that was just a style issue more than a curriculum issue. But we had some great conversations about "what is history?" We ended up debating the question. The kids had come up with every answer from Abraham Lincoln to the glaciers, all on the same piece of paper. Well, what is history, and where do we want to take them with it? (personal interview, December 17, 2007)

Besides providing opportunities to collaborate with colleagues, the grant project also provides teachers with the time to engage with primary sources and to develop meaningful lessons focusing on primary sources. Mark Foley, a veteran secondary school teacher, describes his experience:

It has given us the opportunity to dig into local history and actually produce lessons that can be used in the classroom and can bring that history alive in the class, and so that's really important. We talked so much about primary sources and how to use them in the classroom. I think, I don't know if I necessarily do it exactly the way we've talked about, but I think having seen what people suggest and then kind of through my own filter as a teacher saying, "I like that part. Don't really like that part." It's helped me to sort of fine tune how to use this ... in the classroom, and I think it's really helped my teaching a lot. (personal interview, December 14, 2007)

In some cases the teachers were unfamiliar with how to use primary sources in the classroom, but, more often, they just needed a refresher and some inspiration. Christine Adrian's experience is typical:

> I think the use of primary sources in general, quite honestly, when I started this project I was a teacher that used a lot more of the book and just the expert sources. Then, when I started coming to these activities at first I was like, "Oh, this is cool. I want [to] come to them because I want to learn more about history, and I enjoy those kinds of activities." But, then when I started using them in the classroom it really changed my outlook from just being a history teacher to trying to be a teacher of investigation. You realize that there are different viewpoints and perspectives that require research and theories and critical thinking on a level that I just didn't think about before. (personal interview, December 17, 2007)

Those that needed more specific guidelines were helped by the work of Drake and Nelson that was shared with them and will be discussed in a later section of the chapter on "Engaging with Primary Sources."

Teachers Learning from Partner Museums and Archives: Forming Sustainable Partnerships

With any grant project, one of the concerns is sustainability and long-term impact. One goal of having local museums and archives as partners is to take advantage of the wonderful resources in the local community. However, teachers' enthusiasm for and commitment to using local primary sources in the classroom has been beyond expectations. The sustainability and long-term impact of the AHTC is already evident in the relationship between the AHTC teachers and partner museums and archives.

Before AHTC activities, even if teachers had been to the local museums and archives, they were there as visitors instead of as researchers and historians. Their personal views of these institutions and of the teachers changed as the grant project provided opportunities for teachers to dig into local history sources and to collaborate with curators, museum directors, and archivists. Several teachers felt intimidated by the local collections, sometimes unsure how to access local resources. Others had not even considered using these institutions for research, lesson planning, or professional growth. Don Barbour explains how his perspective of local museums and archives has changed:

> I didn't used to know they existed. It would have never have occurred to me to go into an archive to look up anything at all. And I've been really fortunate to spend time at our local archive, the state archive, and the regional depository of the federal archive just to see what kind of resources are in their collections and just knowing that I could walk in there now without so much intimidation, and I could ask some-

body, "Do you have any sources about a particular historical event?" or maybe I'm researching a person or maybe there's a name on a street sign, and I want to find out why that street is named for that person. I feel like I could do that. I'm still trying to figure out how to get the kids into the archive, but for now it's nice knowing that I can walk in there and do some research. (personal interview, December 12, 2007)

Alexis Jones, former fifth grade teacher and AHTC Activity Coordinator, agrees:

> I'm just amazed at what is out there that I didn't know anything about. I am much more aware of the people and resources in our small community that can provide a hands-on, local perspective of events in American History. On a personal level, I know I am much more likely to choose to go to a museum in my free time now. I'm more curious, I feel like I have some background information to connect to what I see and hear, and I'm comfortable asking questions. In a way, I'm motivated both by knowing more and not knowing as much as I want to! (personal communication, December 1, 2007)

Being able to share part of the results of historical investigations with students is one aspect of the motivation for teachers to do research in museums and archives. Mark Foley explains that teachers can, "dig into it and bring it into your classroom without having to commit to a dissertation or thesis." Jones also explains why some teachers have not taken advantage of local historical institutions:

> There is simply not time to explore local museums and archives for primary resources that fit into their curriculum. One of the best benefits of the AHTC is the opportunity for teachers to work with museums and archives and receive resources that they can use the next day. Many teachers in our group have changed over the years from not knowing what a primary source is, to experimenting with document analysis, to developing quality lesson plans where students are thinking historically while engaging with a variety of local and national primary documents. (personal communication, December 1, 2007)

Obviously, it is not just about getting the teachers comfortable with the resources of local museums and archives. One of the goals of the grant project is to have teachers use the resources of the local historical institutions with their students, using museums and archives not as field trip destinations, but as valuable collections of primary sources that can be used to enrich the regular curriculum with local connections. Teachers create lessons with local primary sources as part of the summer institute, but it is the summer fellows who create the richest and most in-depth lessons. Because fellows spend 40 hours over the course of a summer in the AHTC partner museums or archives, they have time to engage with the collections and collaborate with the curators and archivists. Alexis Jones describes her fellowship experience with the Champaign County Forest Preserve District's Early American Museum:

> I was apprehensive at first, given my limited interest in museums and archives, and my scant knowledge of American history. However, when I first met with the director of the Early American Museum, she was quite willing to discuss my interests in the classroom. We soon came to realize that we wanted the same thing—to find ways to make it easier for teachers to use the museum's collection in the classroom. (personal communication, December 1, 2007)

And, while most of the teachers have only brought materials from the partner institutions into their classrooms, a few teachers have found ways to give their students the experience of conducting historical research in a local museum or archives. Tiffany Clark's perceptions of archives changed, and now she is seeing to it that her third and fourth grade students do not feel intimidated or unfamiliar with local history resources, "Archives and museums were 'look and don't touch,' now I'm able to get in and see these things and handle them. Watching the kids put on the white gloves to handle the photographs—that's exciting" (personal interview, December 17, 2007).

Engaging with Primary Sources

Like many *Teaching American History* grant projects, the AHTC puts a heavy emphasis on engaging teachers and students with primary documents. The local museums and archives provide unique opportunities for teachers to access primary documents from the community that emphasize the fact that the watershed events in American history impact everyone. Cognitive research tells us that the more closely emotions and actions are tied together, the greater is the focus, attention, and retention of details (Jensen, 1998). It follows that the more teachers work with the historical documents and artifacts from local sites, the greater their appreciation of the trials, tribulations, and successes of the people who built their community. By looking at national themes and events through the lens of local history, teachers and their students will be more likely to appreciate, and also analyze, synthesize, and evaluate our national historic record. Best practices in the teaching of history stress the fact that teachers need to increase the amount of time students are asked to examine and analyze primary documents (Zemelman, Daniels, & Hyde, 2005). What better way to encourage the use of primary documents than to have the teachers themselves be the ones digging for and studying documents in museums and archives? One of the goals of the American History Teachers' Collaborative is to ask teachers to find the local connections that will make the large themes of American history more meaningful for their students. Combining the teachers' hands-on research with presentations by expert historians from the University of Illinois, the Organization of American Historians, and other institutions not only increases the teachers' knowledge of the content, but encourages them to become teacher-scholars who can bring a greater appreciation of the content and the process of history to their students.

The AHTC teachers spend a great deal of time discussing the process of choosing primary documents for use in their classroom. In workshops and at summer institutes, they are given the following guidelines, which were adapted from Drake and Nelson (2005, p. 145):

- Will the document interest my students?
- Will the document activate students' prior knowledge?
- Does the document lend itself to personal connections?
- Does the document relate to state or national content standards?
- Is the document appropriate cognitively for my students?
- Is the document legible?

Teachers report a variety of reasons for using primary documents in the classroom. Many of their reasons relate to providing a richer historical context for their students as well as teaching their students to think critically and historically. Tiffany Clark, a third and fourth grade teacher, describes her thought process, "It was really neat to be able to go to a museum, find documents and artifacts and let them try to paint pictures in my mind. And also help select the things that would paint pictures in other people's minds bringing out the themes that are going to be important for people to consider" (personal interview, December 17, 2007). Middle school teacher, Christine Adrian, adds, "I like to [use primary documents] with kids because I think that the way history books are often constructed reduces an event down to a stereotype and a generalization that is often disconcerting to me. Things just don't happen in isolation" (personal interview, December 17, 2007). Teachers work with primary documents to help their students make connections, build context, and read their texts more critically.

Eighth grade teacher, Krista Ruud, explains that sometimes she uses primary documents to get students' attention, "I think a lot of times primary sources evoke more emotion than reading the book" (personal interview, December 12, 2007). Another way of introducing students to primary documents and grabbing their emotional and personal attention is the way Tiffany Clark first introduces her elementary students to archival research by researching information about the houses they live in: Researching their homes is,

> something that was very personal to them, because [without the personal connection] history would seem hypothetical; there would be nothing concrete for them. [Focusing on a local and personal subject gives] the children something concrete that they can put their hands on, that was meaningful to them. We go to the archives, of course, and we use the city directories and the Sandborn maps. We go onto the archives database and check to see if there's anything in a vertical file, and we check out the photograph files, and we use any other maps they have to locate the approximate year that each student's home was built. (personal interview, December 17, 2007)

Teachers also use primary documents to compare and contrast information. There are times when this strategy is used overtly to compare two sides of an issue or compare what one source, like the textbook, says compared to a firsthand account or a photograph. But there is also the unconscious comparing and contrasting, as Krista Ruud describes, "[the students] compare and contrast their own lives to [the information in the photograph], but without even realizing that they're doing it" (personal interview, December 12, 2007). Another middle school history teacher, Don Barbour, stresses the importance of critical reading to his students, "We still kind of have to go over what a primary source is every time we use one, and then the struggle is getting them to look at those primary documents critically—that just because it's old doesn't mean it's revealed truth" (personal interview, December 12, 2007). The use of primary documents for getting students to think and read critically as well as building historical context are all important strategies that ensure a primary document doesn't just become another reading assignment.

While there are a plethora of books, kits, and Web sites that have primary documents and lessons for teachers to use, one of the challenges of using local primary documents is selecting ones that will meet the needs of the curriculum, teacher, and students. Teachers talked about the various things that they considered when deciding which documents to use with their students. High school history teacher, Mark Foley, indicated that he tried to find a series of documents that would do things simultaneously, convey a clear chronology, and reflect more than one viewpoint. "I was really looking for documents that would make both sides of that case while telling the story at the same time. I just got really lucky with this case [about student protests and curfew laws during the Vietnam era] because it was covered well in the local paper" (personal interview, December 14, 2007). Don Barbour suggests that primary documents help get beyond a simple narrative, "it's really important that you select something that shows history and lets students really get an experience in a different way from somebody telling them the story" (personal interview, December 12, 2007).

"I like to pick things that will make them think about something in a whole different way; something that they're not going to hear anywhere else. It's not going to be in their textbooks, and this is new information, kind of like, okay, it said something here, and this is a whole new spin on the story" (personal interview, K. Ruud, December 12, 2007). Krista Ruud's comments represent a general consensus among the teachers interviewed that the local primary documents help get students beyond the textbook by offering perspectives that either reinforce or contradict the information in the text.

Middle school teacher, Natalee Steffen, summarizes the steps that she uses when selecting primary documents for her middle school students:

> Initially, I look for primary documents that are meaningful to me and then I try to figure out how students with different learning levels will understand the sources that I have chosen. I ask myself questions such as: How will a student at a particular level look at this picture? How will a student at a particular level read this document? Is the document legible? Will students be able to understand the language in it? What information will students observe in this map? Once I analyze these questions, I select differentiated sources according to students' learning levels of comprehension. (personal interview, December 12, 2007)

The power of local primary sources is the personal connection that students automatically form with the photograph or document. Don Barbour describes his students' reactions:

> Students love it because they see, "Oh, I know that street, but why is that big cable car in the middle of that picture." What does this tell us about how you got around back then. They get excited over seeing something that looks familiar and yet looks different at the same time. I think that's the coolest experience I've ever had. Recognizing a street and yet, not recognizing it at the same time. (personal interview, December 12, 2007)

Christine Adrian stresses the importance that local history be connected to national events, "I try to make [the connection between local and national] as natural as possible, because I don't want them to see local history as segmented from the national or world landscape." And yet, she also talks about using local primary sources to help students gain a sense of identity that is tied to the local community. "I often start by having students look at historical pictures of the community and ask them to how they relate to those places in the current time so that we can start conversations on why sense of place is important" (personal interview, December 17, 2007).

Putting It Into Practice: AHTC Local History Lessons in the Classroom

The lesson plans created by the teachers of the American History Teachers' Collaborative are not the end product of the grant project. They are a way of showcasing the teachers' collaboration with grant partners, but it is collaboration and investigation that are at the heart of this work.

Teachers are thoughtful and enthusiastic about their collaboration and investigation and produce outstanding lesson plans that challenge students to engage in similar collaboration and investigation. The lessons highlighted in this section can all be found on the AHTC Web site, (http://www.americanhistoryteachers. org), with complete details and links to the digitized local primary sources that bring these lessons to life.

A Bank, a Library, and a Hospital: The Legacy of Benjamin F. Harris and Julia F. Burnham, Peggy Christensen, Edison Middle School, Champaign, Illinois Summer 2007

Abstract

Students will study aspects of the lives of Benjamin F. Harris and Julia F. Burnham, two prominent residents of Champaign, Illinois in the late 1800s. They will analyze primary and secondary sources to better understand how information about an individual is gathered and will note how this information contributes to and reflects the history of the period.

Essential Questions/Enduring Understandings:

How does an individual's history reflect the history of a particular period?

How does studying the life of an individual help us better understand moments in history?

How do primary and secondary sources differ?

What are some of the limitations that must be recognized when using primary and secondary sources?

How can the use of multiple sources contribute to a more accurate understanding of a particular situation?

Setting the Purpose

The purpose of this unit is for students to learn the difference between primary and secondary sources and the need to use multiple documents to develop an understanding of history.

Primary sources from the collection of the Champaign County Historical Archives at the Urbana Free Library.

This entire lesson plan, including resources, can be found on the American History Teachers' Collaborative Web site at http://www.americanhistoryteachers.org

Veteran teacher Peggy Christensen engaged sixth grade students in this series of lessons as part of her 9-week biography unit for her reading class. She wanted the students to understand how biographies are written. As she explained, "I realized when I started teaching the honors kids that they had not a clue where all the information came from that was in all these different biographies that they were reading. They just sort of thought, 'Oh, well, they got on the Internet and found it all.' So, my goal was to give them some exposure to primary sources—actually digging and finding out the information themselves."

She wanted the students to have an appreciation for the complexities of and discrepancies in primary sources, so she guided them through the analysis of primary sources about the life of B. F. Harris, a prominent resident of Champaign in the late 1800s who was friends with Abraham Lincoln. Using reproductions of sections of Harris's autobiography, a page from the Harris family Bible, a check, letters, divorce papers, census rolls, a will, and court documents, Christensen's students worked to piece together Harris's life. His personal life was complex, with multiple marriages, and his autobiography contained omissions and half-truths about his family. The students did more than find and fill in the gaps to his family history. They also were able to solve the mystery contained in letters between Harris and a chemist, along with a check sent to Harris's third wife. The chemist confirmed Harris's suspicion that his wife was slowly poisoning him. In response, Harris paid her off and filed for divorce.

To build this series of lessons, Christensen drew on her own experience analyzing primary sources as a fellow at the Champaign County Historical Archives:

I wanted to start with something very basic. Who's in this person's family, and how do you go about finding this information? In the archives I pulled the vertical file, and then one thing led to another, and so I built it up from that. I wanted the students to appreciate the fact that even to find out when somebody was born, a researcher had to do some exploring. Somebody had to investigate to find out all of this information, and I wanted my students to have a feel for how it happened and the problems that the researchers might have.

Because there was not one primary source that told the whole story, students had to use a variety of sources that sometimes included conflicting information. They began to think critically about sources that they use every day, such as Web pages. Christensen "wanted them to learn about the limitations of each [source] and about the need to look lots of different places and not to blindly assume that everything that they found on the Internet was accurate." The students were able to begin to think critically about secondary sources because of their research experiences, as Christensen describes:

> The biggest thing that they did was wondered if what they had read was really the full picture of the person. They questioned, and one of them actually said, "Okay, so do you have a better shot of getting more information if you read a fatter book?" And he wasn't being funny. He was just thinking, "Okay, well, just think about the little thin biographies you read when you were younger. You assume you know all about the person, but think of everything that's been omitted." So, I think the biggest connection they made was the need to question and to look in multiple places.

History Pathways: Abel Harwood, Christine Adrian, Jefferson Middle School, Champaign, Illinois, Summer 2004

Abstract

This lesson includes an overview of a unit about Abel Harwood, a man prominent in Champaign's history and formation. Students are encouraged to question and investigate history using local primary sources. This unit can be a connection between Civil War history, Champaign County history, and the Illinois State Constitution.

Essential Questions

How and why do we examine history?

How do we choose what history is "important"? How does history change depending on perspective? Who shapes the history we digest?

Why is examining primary sources important? How can we use multiple primary sources to discover answers to questions we have about history?

How are everyday people important in local or national history?

How does family shape our lives?

What was life like for everyday people around the time of the Civil War?

What motivates a group to change its laws?

Setting the Purpose

The purpose of this unit is to look at history in a critical way and to learn to pose questions about history. The purpose is also to create interest in local history and inspire meaningful critical questions and research for students. This unit is a nice tie into Civil War history and the Illinois State Constitution.

Primary sources from the collection of the Champaign County Historical Museum at the Cattle Bank and the Champaign County Historical Archives at the Urbana Free Library.

This entire lesson plan, including resources, can be found on the American History Teachers' Collaborative Website at http://www.americanhistoryteachers.org

Christine Adrian describes her students' engagement with the primary sources in this lesson:

> This one was particularly interesting because ... the kids really didn't know who this guy was, but they started looking at the letter and seeing things that it connected with things that they were learning about [the] Civil War at the time, and one of the things they noticed was the date that he was talking. He was talking pre-Civil War about the eminence of war, and this was happening on the evening of July 4th. He was talking about how these people were just celebrating in the street in these garish ways, and we have no right to do that ... the kids were really fascinated about that. We used that to start to connect with some of the mentalities, then we talked about pre-Civil War, and once we got into that we started to try to make mystery-type guesses about where this was going.

As with Christensen's lesson, Adrian used multiple primary sources to engage students in an investigation into a person's life. She pointed out inconsistencies and information that would not have necessarily been emphasized in secondary sources about the time period. She encouraged the students to act as investigative historians, solving mysteries and trying to piece together one person's story and how it fit into the larger picture of local, state, and national history.

Urbana's Curfew Laws and their Challenge in Court, Mark Foley, Urbana Middle School, Urbana, Illinois,

Summer 2006

Abstract

During the Vietnam War era many communities responded to protests by instituting curfew laws. Some of these laws were found to be illegal, for various reasons. In this lesson students will use primary sources to explore the actions of their local government in creating a curfew law and the response of the protest community that resulted in the law being overturned. Finally, students will examine current curfew laws in their community and reflect of the meaning of these laws.

Essential Questions

How does local government affect your life?

How can citizens challenge their government's actions?

Why are your freedoms as a young person limited?

Content

Students will research the legal issues involved in the City of Urbana's attempt to grant the Mayor emergency powers of curfew in response to the culture of protest in the late 1960s and 1970s. Students will prepare and defend a position on the issue of the legality of the curfew, and write a persuasive letter to their Mayor arguing for or against the legality of the curfew. Finally, students will search the Code of Ordinances for the City of Urbana, Illinois to locate their current curfew and state their opinion of its merits.

Process

Students will analyze primary sources from this time period and determine important information to use in a debate about this issue. Students will create a formal letter arguing for or against the legality of the curfew.

Setting the Purpose

Students will be asked about the concept of a curfew. What is a curfew? Who has power to make a curfew in your life? What is your curfew right now? Has it changed over the years? Why has it changed? Does the City of Urbana have a curfew for young people? What is the curfew? Have any of you ever broken the curfew? What happened? Do you know anyone who has been in trouble for breaking a curfew? What happened to them? Is curfew fair? What are some reasons a parent and/or the government might set a curfew? What are some reasons the curfew might be stricter or more lenient?

Primary sources from the collection of the Champaign County Historical Archives at the Urbana Free Library.

This entire lesson plan, including resources, can be found on the American History Teachers' Collaborative Website at http://www.americanhistoryteachers.org

By using local primary sources to illustrate the national issues of the time period and by relating the issues to their current lives, Mark Foley was able to pique his high school students' interest in the topic of governmental powers and individual freedoms. Foley explains:

> The documents I have were about the Vietnam era and the antiwar protests, so I worked that into the national by sort of doing a prior knowledge…activity. I asked [the students] what [events] were happening in '69 and '70 … they managed to pretty much recall most of them—civil rights, Vietnam—as far as national things, this particular lesson works really well for that because it's really a reflection of it. What I was trying to get at … was [that] what was happening in the national context probably was a motivator for the mayor to put in the curfew in '69.

Foley understands the power of primary sources to tell a story and does not believe that the documents or photographs always need to be sensational to draw the students in. He describes why:

> And at the end of the lesson … they actually look at the current Urbana curfew law. They look at the statute. I think one of the things with government is that they don't look at, or hold in their hands, the actual laws. We talk about them a lot. To actually look at what it says and actually look at the way that they are made is really interesting. Curfew works well because that is actually the law that applies to them, which is, I think, helpful.

Bringing History Home: Investigating Local History through Personal Connections, Tiffany Clark, Leal Elementary School, Urbana, Illinois, Summer 2004

Abstract

In this lesson on Urbana history, students use their home as a primary source, as well as analyzing information from newspapers, maps, residence directories, photographs, and documents. We will research the year their home was built and use that as a springboard into state and national research. The children will also do a little family research, including oral histories, to find out what brought their family to the area and how long they have been here. The students create poster board displays for presentation to the school and parents at an open house at the end of the unit. The last activity involves taking pictures of our homes and donating them to the archives as part of being responsible to future historians by documenting and preserving information from today.

Goal

The children should begin to recognize that they are part of a living, ongoing history. They are the latest chapter in our town's book.

Primary sources from the collection of the Champaign County Historical Archives at the Urbana Free Library.

This entire lesson plan, including resources, can be found on the American History Teachers' Collaborative Web site at http://www.americanhistoryteachers.org

Tiffany Clark's fourth grade local history lesson is unique in several respects. In creating this lesson, she took advantage of her elementary school's location in historic Urbana. Many of her students live in houses that were built in the early 1900s, and some of those houses belonged to families who played prominent roles in Urbana's history. Clark describes her vision for the students' discussions, "talking about history, our same location through time, and about evidence that is left through time."

For this lesson, Clark took her students to the Champaign County Historical Archives to do their research. That is not something that many teachers have tried, but it meant that the students had access to more resources than they would have in the classroom. They also had the opportunity to be "real" history researchers—wearing white gloves to search through decades-old photographs, using the microfilm machines to look for newspaper articles, and gathering around oversized books of land use maps.

Clark's lesson was also unique in that she concluded her class's study of the school neighborhood by adding to the vertical files at the archives. Clark explains, "After we researched our homes ... I went out and took black and white photos of all the kids' houses. We are donating [a set of prints] to the archives so that we are part of this continuum." One of her students had asked, "Can we give something to the archives?" She agreed that this was a good idea and was pleased to have her students making that connection. "That's a remarkable thing for kids to realize ... the historical importance of what they do in their everyday lives. By encouraging my students to give back to the local archives, I hope it shows a respect for them and their integrity and who they are and what they are capable of ... I would love for all the children in my class to walk away with [that]."

The Influenza Pandemic of 1918, Warner Ferratier, Central High School, Champaign, Illinois, John Kirkpatrick, Edison Middle School, Champaign, Illinois, and Hyung Ro, Marie Murphy Middle School, Wilmette, Illinois, Summer 2005

Abstract

In this multidisciplinary lesson, students will participate in class discussions and activities, produce an Excel database, analyze primary sources using the National Archives Written Documents Worksheet, complete a prewriting graphic organizer, and complete a writing activity in order to show their understanding of the chronology of the Flu Epidemic of 1918 and the public response to the epidemic.

Goal

Students will use primary sources to explain the chronology of the Flu Epidemic of 1918 and the public's response.

Essential Questions

Why is this epidemic considered to be one of the deadliest plagues in human history?

How did this epidemic change Americans' daily life and attitudes about health care?

Primary sources from the collection of the Champaign County Historical Archives at the Urbana Free Library.

This entire lesson plan, including resources, can be found on the American History Teachers' Collaborative Website at http://www.americanhistoryteachers.org

The most engaging primary sources to use with students are not always the obvious ones. High school teacher Warner Ferratier worked with middle school teachers John Kirkpatrick and Hyung Ro to create a strong series of lessons based on students' analysis of local death certificates from the 1918 flu epidemic. They started developing the lesson in the Champaign County Historical Archives, as Warner Ferratier describes:

> The original concept was…this was an international epidemic. What was it like here in Champaign-Urbana? How could we figure that out? I bet a lot of people died, and there would be a record of those deaths. So, we spent several days … photocopying death certificates, and my two partners and I who were involved … originally thought, "Oh, you know, it'll be 10 or 20," and we ended up doing only one month of the three month epidemic, or pandemic more correctly, because there were just so many [death certificates]. In the process of scanning some of the patterns we noticed were things that kids could analyze—the age of the decedents, where they had lived—and then it occurred to us, "I bet you could map where they lived and possibly see how the flu spread through Champaign-Urbana."

Ferratier, Kirkpatrick, and Ro had their students use the death certificates to plot the local spread of the flu on a map. The students also analyzed the death certificates to access the rate of spread of the disease and who was dying from it. They used the death certificates similarly to the way that they might use census rolls—looking at age, job, and gender for each person listed.

Chinese Immigration and the Chinese Exclusion Act of 1882: Why Do Many Large American Cities Have a Chinatown? Don Barbour, Urbana Middle School, Urbana, Illinois, Summer 2006

Abstract

This unit is set up as a Document Based Question, with a final writing prompt assigned to address the question:

How did Chinatown come to be a part of so many American cities?

Goal

Students will examine primary source documents from the late 1800s to get an idea of the racism against Chinese-Americans at the time and what kind of procedures were in place for Chinese immigrants who came to the U.S.

Essential Questions

How did others perceive Chinese immigrants in the 1870s?

What were the specific provisions of Chinese Exclusion Act of 1882?

How did the Chinese Exclusion Act affect Chinese-Americans in the early 20th century?

Background

After the discovery of gold in 1849, thousands of fortune hunters from all over the world descended on California with the dream of finding easy wealth and returning to their homelands to live a life of ease. The allure of "Gold Mountain" beckoned Chinese adventurers as well, but their fate differed from many of their fellow immigrants to California.

Their cultural and physical differences doomed them to becoming the first victims of a racist United States policy barring foreigners from immigrating to this country, to pursue a better life.

Setting the Purpose

Given that students have already studied the California Gold Rush in some detail, understanding how and why such a large influx of people invaded the San Francisco area in the early 1850s, this unit should commence with a brainstorming session, or ideally, an Internet search of the word, "Chinatown." Many large American cities, including San Francisco, Los Angeles, Seattle, Chicago, Philadelphia, Boston and New York, each has a neighborhood called Chinatown. These neighborhoods are as architecturally distinct from the rest of the city as they are ethnically and culturally distinct.

Primary sources from the collection of the Champaign County Historical Archives at the Urbana Free Library and the Great Lakes Regional Depository of the National Archives and Records Administration.

This entire lesson plan, including resources, can be found on the American History Teachers' Collaborative Web site at www.americanhistoryteachers.org

Don Barbour draws his eighth grade students into his lesson by facilitating a discussion about Chinatowns in large cities. He explains:

I like the essential question of this lesson, "Why do so many large American cities have a Chinatown?" Initially, most students assume the answer has something to do with tourism, the same reason why there is an ethnic village at the state fair. Because Chinatowns physically look different than surrounding neighborhoods in terms of architecture, it seems natural that they were created to promote multiculturalism and diversity. But once students really delve into the primary sources, they realize that Chinatowns are ghettos, isolating and segregating nascent Chinese communities. History has become grittier and meaner, but more real and comprehensible at the same time.

Sometimes students think that conflicts in history always happened somewhere else. War, the effects of racism, and protests are often associated with other parts of the nation. With this lesson, Don Barbour encourages his students to see that racism against Chinese immigrants was part of the local culture and not just something that was part of the belief system on the West Coast. Barbour explains:

The first document we look at is an 1878 article from our own hometown newspaper describing what the author views as the horrible impact Chinese immigrants are having on California and how the scourge must be stopped as soon as possible. The 19th century language is archaic and hard to read, but students are fascinated by the vitriol.

Barbour continues engaging the students with other primary sources from the Great Lakes Repository of the National Archives and Records Administration:

> By looking at a Chicago family who merely wants to visit abroad in 1913 yet must endure a tortuous screening process, students can again relate to the immigrant experience in a more meaningful way since Chicago is just up the highway a couple of hours.

Like many of his AHTC colleagues, Barbour believes that local primary sources are a powerful way to interest students and to think like historians:

> Because I relied on local primary sources rather than a nondescript secondary text, the students were keenly aware that this was their history and had a vested interest in learning about it. They were not passive consumers of history, but engaged in historical thinking.

Conclusion

Researchers, project directors, and individuals in charge of staff development can learn several lessons from *Teaching American History* grant projects and from AHTC in particular. By having teachers work closely with museums and archives, use primary documents to research and plan lessons, they not only become more invested in the lessons and learning, but they are modeling skills that they would like their students to use. Teachers in this project have reported an increased understanding and personal interest to a variety of topics in American history. They have also reported an increase in student engagement and historical understanding. Looking at American history through the lens of local events increases student interest and enhances understanding and historical thinking. While all of the data presented in this chapter is anecdotal, the voices of the teachers lend a great deal to the understanding of how and how well staff development activities are translated into personal and professional growth.

The link between public practitioners of history, scholars, and teachers has shown great success in the American History Teachers' Collaborative. One of the strengths of the project is the opportunity for teachers to see history as scholars, researchers, archivists, and, of course, teachers. The format of the AHTC allows teachers to spend a great deal of time not just reading and talking to historians about the key figures and events in American history, but also researching and discovering primary documents that they, the teachers, can bring back to their students. The experience that the teachers gain looking for primary documents helps them model and explain research skills to their students. The result is that teachers are finding their students more engaged and interested in history.

Another aspect of the AHTC which may increase student engagement in historical content is the lens of local history. Teaching local history is not a new concept, but in many history classrooms, potentially interesting and engaging local history is ignored in favor of the textbook. *Teaching American History* grant programs, like the AHTC, have helped advocate for the use of primary sources and historical research as a method of teaching content to students. The AHTC's focus on local history brings primary documents and historical content even closer to the students. When students are reading a primary document that was created blocks away from where they are sitting, there is a connection that helps teachers further spark students' interest.

While the future of the *Teaching American History* grants depends on the political priorities of the Congress, the lessons that have been learned from this one project can inform research into curriculum, pedagogy, and professional development for teachers beyond American history. Student engagement is a key to student learning and achievement. The model of increasing student engagement by viewing events in American history through a local lens seemed to increase student engagement. This statement is so far based on teacher interviews and case study data. Research in measuring student engagement should be conducted at the student level, both through case study and through the development of validated observation tools that measure student engagement. The *Teaching American History* grant projects also provide a rich and varied collection of data that can be used to critically analyze best teaching practices in history. Researchers should tap into the data that the TAH grants have been gathering since 2001, in order to provide further insight about what works in history classrooms. Finally, because these grant projects have a clear and specific focus on professional development for precollegiate educators, these projects must be reviewed to help inform what types of professional development have the biggest impact on improving classroom instruction (see chapter 10.) The American History Teachers' Collaborative is just one of hundreds of TAH grant programs that have had a profound impact on the teaching of American history. The challenge ahead is to compile an analysis of the results of all of these projects to continue to inform future directions.

References

Drake, F. D., & Nelson, L. R. (2005). *Engagement in teaching history: Theory and practice for middle and secondary teachers.* Upper Saddle River, NJ: Pearson Merrill Prentice-Hall.

Jensen, E. (1998). *Teaching with the brain in mind.* Alexandria, VA: ASCD.

Owen, D. (1997). *Champaign County history in the classroom: Primary source lessons from the Champaign County Historical Archives, the Urbana Free Library.* Urbana, IL: The Champaign County Historical Archives.

Richardson, J. (2004, February/March). Lesson study: Teachers learn how to improve instruction. *Tools for Schools.* 1–7.

Zemelman, S., Daniels, H., & Hyde A. (2005). *Best practice* (3rd ed.). Portsmouth, NH: Heinemann.

Chapter 6

Introducing Teachers to Archives and Archivists (and Vice Versa)

Tim Rives
Eisenhower Presidential Library and Museum, Abilene, KS

A day at the archives can literally turn into a treasure hunt, and when you come up with the actual document, the payoff is as good as gold. (Patrick M., Secondary History Teacher)

Introduction

This chapter recounts the experience of a National Archives and Records Administration (NARA) regional staff and its work with teachers participating in *Teaching American History* (TAH) grant-funded research. The main goal of the chapter is to familiarize teachers with archival thinking, theory, and practice. In other words, to give them the map they need to find the research gold described by the teacher quoted above, along with the tools to mine it. A secondary goal is to give archivists who will work with teachers an idea of the challenges they may face.

Section I begins with a brief history of NARA and the development of its system of regional archives, and its regional archivists' work with teachers prior to the advent of TAH grants. Section I proceeds to describe how the staff became involved in TAH-supported programming, retraces the steps they took to prepare the teachers for their research visit, outlines the programs they offered them, and presents the main lesson they learned and the practices that emerged from recognizing that the most immediate barrier to success in the archives research room was built by years of traditional library research.

Section II is a guide to practices that work in overcoming the barrier. It has three parts. Part A provides a historical explanation of archives organizational principles and how this determined the way archives are arranged and described. Part B is a conceptual primer designed to help teachers new to historical records research learn how to "think" archives. Part C of the section examines the people who work in the archives and suggests how teachers can maintain a fruitful relationship with them after they have returned to the classroom. The main lesson to be drawn from Section II is that the most important thing about a record is the identity of its creator; a closely related second lesson is that archives research takes time. A concluding section presents ideas for practices that will enhance teacher and archivist collaboration in the future.

Section I: Introducing Teachers to Archivists

After more than a century of parlous delay, the United States finally established a national archive on June 19, 1934. Before then federal courts and agencies were responsible for maintaining their own records, and as the National Archives Web site describes it, "Some took great care of the materials, but many did not."[1] It was up to early federal archivists to find the documentary survivors of this Dark Age, and to arrange, describe, preserve, and make them available to researchers. NARA's mission then and now involved more than just saving and servicing records, however. There is a higher calling: The National Archives "serves democracy" by providing access to "the essential documentation of the rights of American citizens and the actions of their government."[2]

NARA expanded access beginning in the late 1960s with the establishment of a system of regional archives. The National Archives and Records Administration–Central Plains Region in Kansas City, Missouri, stands today as one of fourteen regional archives. The Central Plains regional branch holds more than 45,000 cubic feet of records created by federal courts and agencies that operated in Iowa, Kansas, Minnesota, Missouri, Nebraska, North Dakota, and South Dakota. Drawn from more than ninety federal entities, the holdings range from the records of the U.S. District Courts to the Bureau of Prisons, and from the National Park Service to the Bureau of Indian Affairs, to name but a few.

Over the years the Central Plains Region's records have drawn historians, anthropologists, scientists, artists, attorneys, environmentalists, federal employees, journalists, private investigators, police officers, screenwriters, graduate students, and genealogists—everyone, it seems, except secondary teachers. This began to change in 2003 when we were approached by Dr. Kelly Woestman of Pittsburg (KS) State University to participate in the TAH program by providing access to the records in our holdings and by training teachers in how to use them. Our first opportunity came in July 2004 when we transmitted a program to Dr. Woestman's Project Mine group over the Interactive Distance Learning Network (IDL) cameras of Pittsburg State's KC Metro Center. Three NARA staff members presented the initial program. They gave the group of fifty teachers an overview of NARA's history and mission, and exhibited original textual records "live" over the IDL network.

This experience was a more technically sophisticated version of the classroom visits that had historically made up our educational outreach programs. And while it exposed the teachers to more "original" records than they might otherwise have seen, it was not the same as working with genuine archival documents in the National Archives. Current IDL technology provides an adequate image of a record, but it is a high altitude overview, not a ground-level close up. Some details are inevitably lost in the virtual landscape. Nor did the teachers get the tactile pleasures of the record—the feel, the smell, the thrill of handling the raw materials of history. The teachers' encounter with authentic records would wait until the following summer when those participating in a second TAH grant program, Project eHikes ("enhancing History Instruction for Kansas Educators and Students"), arrived at the archives.

The teachers prepared for their visit by completing "NARA Investigation Chart Worksheets" that outlined their research topics and listed the "Record Groups" (more on Record Groups in the next section) where they hoped to find relevant records. The worksheets circulated by e-mail between the teacher, Dr. Woestman, and a NARA staff member. An example of the worksheet appears in appendix A.

The worksheets helped to refine the teachers' research objectives and narrow the range of prospective records. The worksheets also gave them an idea at the beginning of the process of the preparatory work that goes into successful archives research. The worksheets further allowed NARA staff sufficient time to review and pull records before the teachers arrived.

The Central Plains Region research room at that time was not big enough to accommodate large groups of researchers, so the teachers were divided into two groups, and worked in our facility over two days, in two half-day sessions. Prior to starting their research, they heard presentations on how to understand the basic differences between archives and libraries, how to compose and read source citations, and how to use archives records in exhibits to capture the interest of students.

Archives, I explained in the first lecture, must have what the archival theorist Theodore Schellenberg describes as an "organic" relationship with a records creator. In the case of the National Archives this relationship is with the federal government. The National Archives can only *receive* records from federal agencies and courts. NARA then *arranges* and *describes* (organizes and catalogs, in library terms) these records in the context of their relationship to their creator, not by the subject(s) of the records. The key to locating records in the archives is to determine which federal court or agency's activities intersected with the person, subject, or event one is researching. There will be much more on this in the next section.

Libraries, on the other hand, *collect* what Schellenberg calls "discrete items"—books, journals, audiovisual materials, or manuscripts. The "significance [of the discrete item] is wholly independent of [its] relationship to other items," Schellenberg writes.[3] In other words, the books on the shelves can come from different authors, different publishers, or different countries. There is no "organic" relationship dictating from whom the library can collect items. Moreover, the "discrete items" assembled in libraries are unrelated except by subject (or author) and are thus cataloged individually under specific subject headings according to a logical scheme, such as the Dewey Decimal or Library of Congress classification systems.

Another important distinction between libraries and archives hangs on the uniqueness of the archives holdings. Unlike a library, which might have ten copies of the same ghostwritten political memoir that every other library in the country has, an archive's holdings exist in one version and in one place. For instance, if you want to see the papers filed in the *Brown v. Board of Education, Topeka* school desegregation case, you must come to the National Archives–Central Plains Region in Kansas City. We alone have the originals.

In the next lecture a staff member used the following example to show the teachers how the individual elements of a complete scholarly citation can be read as a map to the archives facility holding those unique records. For example, Complaint, Case File T-316; Civil Case Files, 1938–1977; U.S. District Court for the District of Kansas, First Division (Topeka); Records of District Courts of the United States, Record Group 21; National Archives and Records Administration-Central Plains Region (Kansas City).[4]

Read in reverse order, the citation takes the researcher to the city, the facility, the Record Group, the Subgroup, the Series, and the Item. A good citation, she told them, allows other scholars to retrace your steps, to discover the same research gold for their students. In this case, the treasure is the Complaint filed in the *Brown v. Board of Education, Topeka,* case. There will be more on Items, Series, Subgroups, and Record Groups in the second section.

Another staff member then discussed how archival records could be used to create visual displays that might capture the imagination of students unmoved by the experience of discussing the contents of historic documents. Linking the past to a topical event or to something in the popular culture is one way to do this. Specifically, this staff member's lesson showed how she put together an exhibit composed of NARA records relating to individuals featured in the popular HBO series *Deadwood,* a fictional portrayal of the settling of Dakota Territory. Despite *Deadwood*'s fictions, most of the show's major characters were based on real people. Our exhibit employed census, court, and other records to bring characters such as Calamity Jane and Wild Bill Hickok to life, showing where the facts of history corroborated the producer's version of events or contradicted its inventions. "The Real Deadwood" remains one of our most popular exhibits and is a prime example of how historical documents can be utilized to catch the interest of even the most reluctant history student. With these lessons in mind, the teachers entered the research room.

The lectures and worksheets had prepared the teachers to a point, but did not guarantee them a successful trip to the archives. The teachers' experience with archival research was mixed.[5] Some teachers found they were so interested in the records on their own merit that they had difficulty getting through them in the allotted time. But too many teachers went through the first few carts of records they requested without finding anything they thought suitable for their classroom needs. They expressed frustration at finding records related to the subjects they were interested in based on the archival finding aids they had used to request them.

The problem was clear: The TAH teachers were still thinking in library terms, about the *subjects* of their research instead of about *who* would have *created* the records relating to the subjects of their research. My lecture on the differences distinguishing archives from libraries had not been enough to overcome the habits of thought and practice inculcated upon them by years of library experience. The next section seeks to correct that shortcoming by making the idiosyncratic workings of archives and archivists even more familiar. The familiarization starts with a journey back to the deepest origins of written history.

Introducing Archives and Archivists to Teachers

Almost every contemporary First World human is a private repository of written and electronic records. Records are simply "all recorded information, regardless of media or characteristics, made or received or maintained by an organization or institution," including individuals or families.[6] Their briefcases, wallets, handbags, and "personal digital assistants" bulge with the detritus of economic transactions, the impedimenta of personal identity, the encumbrance of remembrance. These prosaic documentary relics are everywhere in modern life, as ubiquitous as air, and almost as important to human existence.

Humans began creating records not long after they established sedentary agricultural communities some 10,000 to 12,000 years ago. A new thing in the world—surplus food—provided the impetus to preserve information. Tracking who had bartered for this or deposited that in the village grain bin soon exceeded the capacity of individual brains to remember. Records evolved to augment memory.[7]

Objective long-term memory grew in importance as the local transactions of storage and barter expanded to include strangers. Records established the trust necessary for different groups to coordinate their exchange and production activities, to grow in scale and complexity, with hierarchies of rank and a division of labor. To make a millennia story short, records "civilized" us, write Sidipta Basu and Gregory B. Waymire in their study of the evolutionary impact of transactional records on human development.[8]

The first records created to document economic transactions were clay tokens, molded to represent different crops and quantities. The early "plain" tokens were shaped into cones, disks, spheres, and other simple dimensions to signify agricultural produce. Later, "complex" tokens of varying sizes and inscriptions evolved to represent more precise enumerations of agricultural products and finished goods. Where a single plain token might represent a basket of grain, a cluster of complex tokens could signify the trade of six ewes and thirty lots of textiles.[9]

Records of these transactions, for trust and depressingly soon, tax reasons, were preserved in archives. "Archives" may be defined in a general way as the "non-current records of an organization or institution preserved because of their continuing value."[10] Archives are also the place where valuable noncurrent records are stored. The archives of the Mesopotamian world of the fourth century BCE utilized clay envelopes to hold the multifarious tokens. To distinguish one envelope from another, early archivists, if you'll pardon the anachronism, scratched or impressed representations of the tokens on the outside of the container. In time, they quit making the clay tokens altogether and instead recorded the token shapes on clay tablets.[11] These abstract inscriptions may have been but a short scratch of the scribe's stylus, but they were the proverbial giant leap for humankind. For it was from these homely inscriptions that the first pictographic symbols took shape, which evolved into phonetic cuneiform script, which in turn matured into what we recognize as "writing," an invention that surely ranks in importance with the discovery of fire and the domestication of animals in the annals of human history.[12]

This then is the history of records and archives, as well as a preliminary lesson to be learned: records were essential to establish the trust necessary for simple small-scale human organizations to grow into complex large-scale ones, and archives stimulated the development of writing. When teachers and students use historical records in the classroom, they are doing more than just "studying history." They are engaging the products of a process that is literally as old as civilization itself, and as essential to its life as the air they breathe.

Records Creators as the Key to Understanding Archives

The inhabitants of Mesopotamia may not have realized it, but they also created the category that is at the center of the modern organization of archival holdings. Their great invention, although perhaps unrecognized by them as such, was the record *Series*. A Series is defined as "a body of file units or documents, arranged in a unified filing system or maintained by the records creator because of some relationship arising out of their creation, receipt, or use."[13] The Ancients created separate Series when they devised plain tokens for agricultural staples and complex tokens for finished products. Plain tokens were stored in the hollow clay envelopes described above; complex tokens were secured by string to a larger piece of clay bulla. Plain tokens are found largely in the archaeological remains of agricultural compounds; complex tokens are found in administrative settings. Different records creators with different purposes resulted in different Series, despite the superficial similarities of the records themselves.[14]

Later archivists followed suit and formulated a theory to back up the practice. Based on the observation that knowing who created a record (e.g., the village scribe or the temple scribe) is the most important thing about it, the theory is referred to as the *principle of provenance*. The principle states that the "records created or received by one record keeping unit should not be intermixed with those of any other."[15] Why is this important? Because if the principle of provenance is violated, the paper trail between the record and its creator, as well as the context in which it was created, is lost. In terms of a government record, if you lose the connection binding it to the creator and the context, you unleash elected and appointed officials from the bonds of accountability. (To paraphrase James Madison, if public officials were angels, no records or archives would be necessary.) Like the role of records and archives in advancing civilization, the importance of records and archives to good governance is another lesson archivists could share with teachers.

The creator-based organization of records dictated by the principle of provenance additionally governs the level of description. The National Archives organizes (or "arranges" in archives nomenclature) its records at the Record Group, Subgroup, and the aforementioned Series level. Record Groups, generally referred to in NARA shorthand as "RG," are the big divisions: agencies, bureaus, courts, commissions, departments, and the like. The Bureau of Indian Affairs is a Record Group (RG 75). The National Recovery Administration is a Record Group (RG 9). Record Group 237 comprises the records of the Federal Aviation Administration. RG 129 contains the records of the Federal Bureau of Prisons, to cite but a few examples. The Record Groups comprise Subgroups, which are the literal creators of record Series. (The Subgroups employ the officials and workers who make the actual inscriptions on paper or other formats.) For example, Haskell Indian Nations University is a Subgroup of the Bureau of Indian Affairs, RG 75. Among the Series created by Haskell is "Student Case Files, 1884–1980." The United States Penitentiary-Leavenworth is a Subgroup of the Federal Bureau of Prisons, RG 129. One of the most popular prison record Series is "Inmate Case Files, 1895–1952."

This is the point where it starts to frustrate researchers. The finding aids have pointed them in a general direction, but not to specific documents. Since federal agencies and courts stop the arrangement of their records at the Series level, we stop our description ("cataloging") of their records at the Series level. The Series are thus described in the aggregate, *not* at the individual case file or item level (and *not* by subject). In practical research terms this means that while we know we have 68,937 Leavenworth Inmate Case Files and 1,108 boxes of Haskell Student Case Files, we cannot tell you specifically what is in each file or box. If you were looking for political prisoners in the Leavenworth files or students who received "Honors" in American History at Haskell, you would have to survey the items in the files individually to find those data. Nor would we extract that specific information from all the records creators from across the spectrum of the federal government whose activities might have brushed those subjects and place it in a spurious "Special Collection." To do so would violate the principle of provenance.

"Archives," a resigned researcher concludes in the pages of *The New Yorker* magazine, "are like books without indexes: you know in a general way if you're interested in the [records]…but there is no shortcut to finding out if what you're really looking for is in there."[16] So how do you narrow the search? The Series description, an overview of the Series' contents, is the place to start. And at the heart of the archives Series description is the "Scope and Content Note." Basically, the Scope and Content Note defines what the records are, and what they are about. This element typically provides information on the types of documentary materials it contains, the geographic locations it concerns, the activities and subjects it touches, and the dates it spans. Here, for example, is the Scope and Content Note for the Haskell Student Case Files series: This series consists of individual student case files of Indians from throughout the country who attended Haskell, an off-reservation boarding school. The early files (1884–ca. 1910) typically consist of one page that lists the following information: student name, age, tribe, parent, post office box, date entered, and date dropped. While the content of later files varies from student to student, most files include the student's name, photograph, date of birth, tribal affiliation, degree of Indian blood, home address, and dates of attendance. They may also include applications for enrollment, transcripts of grades, attendance records, class schedules, reports of grades, deportment, and medical or disciplinary problems. Some files include correspondence between school officials with students, parents, and reservation officials.[17]

The Scope and Content Note element helped the teacher-researchers to both find records Series of interest to their research and to eliminate unpromising leads before they asked the archives staff to bring them records. For example, a teacher interested in a World War II ordnance plant in his community discovered that the most helpful records were contained not in the Records of the Office of the Chief of Ordnance (RG 156), but in the Records of the War Assets Administration (RG 270), the agency responsible for disposing of excess government property after the war.

An additional key element to understanding the Series description is the "Arrangement Statement." The Arrangement Statement tells you how the files are ordered. The most common arrangements are alphabetical, chronological, numerical, or some combination thereof. The Haskell Student Case Files are arranged chronologically by date span and there-under alphabetically by student name. The Leavenworth Inmate Case Files Series noted above is arranged numerically by inmate registration number. Most court records follow a numerical arrangement as well.

Technology can also help narrow the search. NARA's online "Archival Research Catalog" (ARC) makes it possible to link subjects across different Record Groups. ARC has subject search capabilities keyed to the "Index Terms" element of the Series description.[18] A keyword search for the terms *Education, Health, Indians of North America*, or *Boarding Schools* would result in the Series description for the Haskell Student Case Files, as well as the descriptions of several hundred other records Series created by a score of different federal agencies. Some description formats also have an element for "Related Records" that list which federal agencies might have overlapped in function and programs, suggesting additional Records Groups and Series for study. For philosophical reasons I favor this method over subject-based "Index Terms" as it keeps the importance of records creators and context in the foreground.

Learning the arrangement and description practices of the archives may bewilder new researchers, but it also teaches them a lesson: archives research takes time. There are, as the *New Yorker* writer above reminds us, no short cuts. One of the most interesting attempts to save research time in our facility occurred when a man looking for records relating to the father of a famous Native American warrior fashioned a dowsing rod from a piece of string and a key. He swung the device back and forth over a box of documents, encouraging his talisman to lead him to the right document. This innovative effort failed, but the researcher was almost on the right track. The archives textual research room, notwithstanding its similarity to a library reading room, works more like a scientific laboratory. (Rational) persistent experimentation marks the path to success. This may require several trips to the archives before the desired records are found. Research gold rarely unearths itself in the first folder of the first box.

In addition to finding aids, time, and experimentation, successful archives research requires a unique mental approach. The next section introduces a conceptual primer designed to help researchers identify potential records of interest by "thinking" archives.

The Iron Law of Successful Archives Research

> As every man goes through life he fills in a number of forms for the record, each containing a number of questions…. There are thus hundreds of little threads radiating from every man, million of threads in all. If those threads were suddenly to become visible, the whole sky would look like a spider's web, and if they materialized like rubber bands, buses and trams and even people would lose the ability to move and the wind would be unable to carry torn-up newspapers or autumn leaves along the streets. (Alexander Solzhenitzyn, The Cancer Ward)[19]

Ah, if only it were so. If only we could snare our research prey so completely and observe it so easily. But in the real archives, the threads—the connections binding records to research subjects—are still invisible. They must be imagined before they can be seen as vividly as Solzhenitzyn's catchy metaphor.

The process of imagination begins with a question so crucial to archives success that it merits legislation. I call it the *Iron Law of Successful Archives Research.* It commands that the researcher's first question must always be: *Where did my research subject intersect with the actions of the federal government?* Whether you are researching the life of a Civil War veteran, the techniques of professional bank robbery, or the treatment of indigenous peoples, you must first establish the connection to the records creator(s). As noted above, in the case of the National Archives the records creator is always the courts and agencies of the federal government. The *Iron Law,* moreover, applies to the records of other archival institutions, be they the records of local and state governments or private organizations. In any case, the answer to the *Iron Law's* question will tell you where to look for records.

The key to applying the *Iron Law* question is to think of the broad functions of the federal government and the agencies that executed its policies, to consider how and where the trajectory of the research subject's "career" arc might have intersected with the actions of the state. This exercise should result in the identification of numerous NARA Record Groups. One example from our experience with the TAH teachers comes to mind. The researcher was interested in farm and labor protest movements of the 1890s. She reasoned that some of their activities, including the disruption of interstate commerce, might have led to federal criminal action. This reasoning resulted in her finding relevant cases heard by federal courts in Kansas and Nebraska, as well as correspondence discussing other possible related court actions in the records of the United States Attorneys.

But the connections are not always so logical. "Status," such as indigenous, alien, resident, or property owner; or "Service," whether voluntary or involuntary, can all serve to entwine persons and communities with the state, especially a state as expansive as the United States in the late nineteenth and early- to mid-twentieth centuries. States "see" people in different lights at different times based on the contingencies of their political, administrative, and security needs—taxes must be collected, nomads must be tamed, enemies must be identified.[20] This is all to the researcher's good fortune, for these needs are usually met by records-generating government actions.

Disparate state visions and actions sometimes collide in striking fashion in the same place or person, resulting in the creation of records in seemingly contradictory records Series. Take the case of William Mars: nonnaturalized U.S. resident, Civil War soldier, veteran, and federal pensioner. These categorizing facts of Mars's life correspond to concomitant state actions. As a U.S. resident, Mars is found enumerated in the decennial federal census, Records of the Bureau of the Census, RG 29.[21] His service with Company G, 50th Missouri Infantry, during the Civil War is documented in the Records of the Adjutant General's Office, RG 94. As a veteran of the Union Army, Mars received a monthly $22.50 pension payment; that paper trail starts in the Records of the Veterans Administration, RG 15.

Union veterans also qualified for residence in one of the regional branches of the National Home for Disabled Volunteer Soldiers. The "Soldiers Homes," as they were popularly known, were meant to be living memorials to the men who had saved the Republic during its darkest hour. Mars's individual record from his time with the heroes at the Western Branch of the home in Leavenworth, Kansas, is also located in RG 15.[22]

It was while residing at the Western Branch in 1917 that Mars received word that as a nonnaturalized German he must swear an affidavit to the federal government explaining his personal past, as well as his present ties to Germany. Wondering perhaps how he had ever arrived at this strange intersection of history, a seventy-six-year-old Mars stares glumly from the page of his "Alien Enemy Registration Affidavit" mug shot (Records of the US Attorneys, RG 118).[23]

The lesson here is that William Mars had not changed, but his status in the eyes of the government had changed because of a perceived threat to its security needs. This had the ironic effect of making him a putative enemy of the state at the same time he was being honored with accommodation in the Soldiers Home. And with work and residential zones restricting the free movement of German Americans, Mars was virtually a prisoner in a gilded federal cage; a cage suspended for our viewing in Solzhenitzyn's web of records.

Imagining the threads connecting records creators to the recipients of their actions is an important step in the research discovery process. This is an important practice to reinforce with teachers. Another is to find a good archivist.

Archivists

The archivist is important to research room success for two main reasons: the ongoing acquisition ("accession" in archives nomenclature) of new holdings, and the time it takes to describe them. The National Archives accessions thousands of cubic feet of records every year. The records are known to the archivists, yet are awaiting description in NARA finding aids. A good archivist will be aware of the new material. A good archivist also has a long institutional memory for old material, and for research problems encountered by previous researchers. The archivist will remember how this problem was solved, and where they found the records that proved helpful to the earlier researcher.

Establishing and maintaining a long-term professional relationship with a good archivist will pay future dividends. Some scholars describe this process as building up "social capital" with the archivist.[24] Teachers can forge postresearch relationships with archivists simply by staying in touch. They should share the products of their archives experience—articles, exhibits, or classroom lessons—with the archivist. A good archivist will respond by keeping the teacher's research interests in mind as they inventory new records, or discover links to the teacher's research in older records they discover anew while engaged in preservation projects or in answering other research requests. The link between William Mars's Civil War records and his registration as an "Alien Enemy" is an example of this. It is the sort of serendipitous data link that defies standard finding aid description. There was no logical connection between the processes of administering veterans' benefits and registering aliens. An alert archivist made the connection and shared the results with his researcher colleagues.

The people who will assist you in the archives are not as well known as their vocational cousins, the librarians, although they tend to be confused in the popular culture with them and are usually ascribed the same stereotypes. A study in *The American Archivist* found the typical archivist of modern fiction to be a bespectacled middle-aged male introvert, a poor dresser, a bad mixer, a bit of a snob, yet devoted to his duty to protect the records.[25] A 2004 survey conducted by the Society for American Archivists found some of this image to be a social fact, but concluded that the field is dominated by women, who make up about 65 percent of the archives workforce. Her age is around fifty-four years, and she has a more than 80 percent chance of being White. She makes about $50,000 a year. She did not enter the archives field until she was, on average, forty-three years old.[26]

The survey numbers are reflective of our staff. The Central Plains Region comprised eight employees at the time we hosted our TAH teachers: Seventy-five percent (N = 6) of the staff was female. The average age was forty-six. Five of the eight staff members had bachelor's degrees in history. Their graduate degrees varied: one held a master's in history; two held a master's in library science; one in historical administration; one in mathematics; one in music; and one was working toward a master's in public administration. None held degrees in Archives Administration, Information Studies, or any of the newer programs that claim to produce "professional" or "certified" archivists.[27] Like most human activities, the basic archival tasks of arrangement, description, preservation, and reference can be learned by any person of reasonable intelligence. The fact that archives work is not particularly glorified in popular culture probably has something to do with it attracting a largely middle-aged cohort of workers who have learned through life experience to appreciate the rigors of a job demanding research and descriptive writing skills, and who also appreciate the importance of providing access to that essential element of our civilization—the archival record.

Conclusion

But for all their varied background, the Central Plains Region staff lacked recent experience in the secondary history or social studies classroom. This realization was probably the biggest lesson learned in retrospect by archives staff members.

It was followed by the later admission of just how few teachers we attract to our research room. In fact, in 2004 and 2005, at the height of our TAH involvement, teachers made up only 4 percent of our total research room visitors. Most years it is less than 1 percent.

How can we change this? Fortunately, several good steps have already been taken. The first is the interest in "civic literacy" fostered by Allen Weinstein, the Archivist of the United States. Civic literacy may be defined as an understanding and awareness of how the federal government works, and its place in society. A specific NARA strategy to increase civic literacy is "to support teachers and students…creating a cadre of educators and researchers who use primary sources as teaching tools."[28] One result of the emphasis on civic literacy is the assignment of full-time "educational specialists" to NARA's regional archives staffs. The educational specialists attend in-service training days, curriculum fairs and conferences, coordinate IDL sessions, visit classrooms with facsimiles of records, and host students and teachers who come to the National Archives. Additionally, the National Archives–Central Plains Region's new Union Station facility (note: scheduled to open in 2009) includes more space for large groups in both its textual research and multipurpose rooms. The expansion allows the Central Plains Region to host more students and teachers than at any time its history. Other NARA regional branches will move to new facilities in the coming years. Their capacities for hosting large groups will also increase.

Another positive step would be for archivists to make more of their products available to secondary teachers and students, particularly their exhibits. As noted above, exhibits are successful in capturing the attention of even the most reluctant history student. These exhibitions should be accompanied by classroom visits where the archivist could explain the records used in the display, and in doing so point out those troublesome differences separating archives from libraries.

Finally, the continuation of *Teaching American History* and other similar grants that fund teacher travel to research facilities during the summer months will assure that the lessons of the archives are reinforced and maintained, and that the introductions of teachers to archives and archivists (and vice versa) remain fresh.

Note

This chapter reflects the writer's personal opinion and does not represent the official policy of the National Archives and Records Administration.

Notes

1. "National Archives History." NARA—About the National Archives. http://www.archives. gov/about/history/index.html, National Archives and Records Administration (accessed January 10, 2008).
2. "Our Mission Statement." NARA—About the National Archives. http://www.archives.gov/ about/info/mission.html, National Archives and Records Administration (accessed January 10, 2008).

3. T. R. Schellenberg, *Modern Archives: Principles and Techniques* (Chicago: The Society of American Archivists, 1956; Chicago: The Society of American Archivists/Kansas State Historical Society, 1998), 20.

4. *General Information Leaflet 17: Citing Records in the National Archives of the United States* (Washington, DC: National Archives and Records Administration, 2007), 2–3.

5. This would be true of any group conducting research for perhaps the first time. Reaction to archives research is based in part on temperament. People in general do not take to it. And most teachers, had they been so inclined, probably would have chosen a research career over a teaching one if it had been of primary interest. So it does not surprise me that of all the teachers who encountered NARA records through TAH grants in the Central Plains Region, only one has returned to conduct research on his own; another has contacted us to request records long distance. None of this should be construed as criticism of the teachers or their vocational interests.

6. Maygene F. Daniels and Timothy Walch, eds., *A Modern Archives Reader: Basic Readings on Archival Theory and Practice* (Washington, DC: National Archives and Records Service, 1984), 342.

7. Sandpit Basu and Gregory B. Waymire, "Recordkeeping and Human Evolution," *Accounting Horizons* 20 (September 2006): 201–229.

8. Ibid., 206.

9. Denise Schmandt-Besserat, *How Writing Came About* (Austin: University of Texas Press, 1996), 83.

10. Daniels and Walch, 339.

11. Schmandt-Besseart, 7, 55.

12. Ibid., 84.

13. Daniels and Walch, 342.

14. Schmandt-Besserat, 37, 41,; 83.

15. Daniels and Walch, 342.

16. D.T. Max, "Final Destination," *The New Yorker* (June 11 and 18, 2007): 66.

17. "Student Case Files, 1884–1980." Online version through Archival Research Catalog (ARC Identifier 592971) at http://www.archives.gov (accessed January 11, 2008).

18. "Search the Archival Research Catalog." NARA-Archival Research Catalog (ARC). http://www.archives.gov/research/arc/index.html, National Archives and Records Administration (accessed January 11, 2008).

19. Alexander. I. Solzhenitsyn, *The Cancer Ward.* Quoted in Heather Macneil, *Without Consent: The Ethics of Disclosing Personal Information in Public Archives* (Lanham, MD and London: The Society of American Archivists and The Scarecrow Press, 1992), 35.

20. James C. Scott, *Seeing Like a State: How Certain Schemes to Improve the Human Condition Have Failed,* Yale Agrarian Studies Series (New Haven, CT: Yale University Press, 1998), 1–2.

21. William Mars, 1910 census, Delaware, Leavenworth County, Kansas, T624, roll 444, page 14B, ED 85, image 642, http://www.Ancestry.com (accessed December 28, 2007).

22. William Mars, File no. 15376; Sample Case Files of Members, 1885–1933; Records of the National Home for Disabled Volunteer Soldiers, Western Branch, 1885–1934, Record Group 15; National Archives and Records Administration–Central Plains Region (Kansas City).

23. William Mars, Registration Affidavit of Alien Enemy; Enemy Alien Registration Affidavits, 1917–21; Records of U.S. Attorneys, 1821–1989, Record Group 118; National Archives and Records Administration–Central Plains Region (Kansas City).

24. Catherine A. Johnson and Wendy M. Duff, "Chatting up the Archivist: Social Capital and the Archival Researcher," *The American Archivist* 68 (Spring/Summer 2005): 54–71.

25. Arlene Schmuland, "The Archival Image in Fiction: An Analysis and Annotated Bibliography," *The American Archivist* 62 (Spring 1999): 34–42.

26. "Archival Census & Education Needs Survey in the United States," The Society of American Archivists. http://www.archivists.org/a-census/index.asp (accessed January 10, 2008).

27. This is for the better in my opinion. The last thing the archives or any other endeavor for that matter needs is more artificial barriers blocking entrance into the work field. The urge to "professionalize" the archives field (and limit the competition), to complicate its theories and practices feeds into a snobbery encountered by far too many researchers. The result is the dreaded "Gatekeeper," the archivist who won't condescend to assist you in your humble research endeavors until you've proven yourself worthy of his (or the more statistically likely, her) attention. This usually occurs because the Gatekeeper has mistaken seriousness of purpose with seriousness of person—her person—and you are the one who will suffer for it. This is not something I like to admit, but it is a hazard of doing archives research, and it is something the teachers may encounter as they venture out into archives research rooms. Do *not* let the Gatekeepers discourage you.

28. *Preserving the Past to Protect the Future: The Strategic Plan of the National Archives and Records Administration, 2006 to 2016* (Washington, DC: National Archives and Records Administration, 2006), Part III: 11.

APPENDIX A

Teacher's Name: John Doe

NARA Investigation

CHART WORKSHEET

Topic 1

Tinker v. Des Moines—As I'm not sure yet exactly what the terms of this research project will be, I don't have a specific goal or question, but I'd like to take a look at both the district court proceedings as well as the appellate materials and figure out a way to use the case to explain to students how the First Amendment is interpreted as well as to demonstrate the workings of the federal judiciary. I notice that the records for the Iowa District Courts go only to 1965 and for the Courts of Appeal to 1968. The Supreme Court issued its opinion in *Tinker* in 1969, and I don't know when the case was originally filed, but there might not be anything in the district court archives. As you suggested, the depositions would be especially interesting (as a way to get the students involved), but those might be with the district records.

Related Record Groups (include NUMBER and NAME)
Record Group 21 "Records of the District Courts of the United States" and Record Group 276 "Records of the U.S. Courts of Appeals"

Kelly's Feedback
This is perfect, John! You sometimes don't know until you read the materials what you will find that will be useful in your classroom—it just takes going through the documents.

Archivists' Feedback (NARA will indicate which archivist handled your inquiry)
We have the Tinker case. There's plenty to work with.
Tim

Topic 2

I'll stay with the same record group here because several of the cases mentioned in the Guide sound intriguing. In particular, I'd be interested in doing something with *Dred Scott v. Sanford, Standing Bear ex rel v. Crook* and/or the materials relating to the criminal prosecution of Katherine "Red Kate" O'Hare for sedition during WWI.

Related Record Groups (include NUMBER and Name)
Record Group 21 "Records of the District Courts of the United States"

Kelly's Feedback
Excellent again....

5Archivists' Feedback (NARA will indicate which archivist handled your inquiry)
The O'Hare case is the richest in material. The early two are quite skimpy, but you're welcome to look at them while you're here.
Tim

Topic 3

I've had several conversations this year, especially with my advanced class, about conscription, both historically and prospectively. I'd be interested in doing a project with the WWI draft board records. There are all kinds of good issues and questions here about the relations of citizens to their government, mobilizing for modern war, and matters of due process and equity. I suppose it would most relevant to focus on the Kansas records. There might be a way to connect this project with the "Red Kate" case records under topic 2 and really, to *Tinker* as well. All of these could also be tied in with *Schenck v. United States*, another landmark 1st Amendment case that arose over opposition to WWI conscription. (It, however, is a Third Circuit case.) I'm also intrigued by the inclusion in the records of lists of deserters.

Related Record Groups (include Number and Name)
Record Group 163 "Records of the Selective Service System (World War I)"

Kelly's Feedback
Excellent explanation of what you will find in the records at NARA-KC....

Archivists' Feedback (NARA will indicate which archivist handled your inquiry)
We do have the deserters' lists, and the names of men who failed to report, for whatever reason. You may also want to look at the U.S. Attorneys' correspondence from that period. It's thick with tales of war-resisting intrigue.
Tim

Chapter 7

Teachers' Voices in *Teaching American History* Projects

David Gerwin
Queens College/CUNY

> How do we tell stories? It is about storytelling which is something we also don't talk about. We use sources not because we love sources—though some of us I guess do love sources—but most of us use sources in a more utilitarian fashion. We use sources to tell stories. And all history writing is about storytelling. Even in a textbook. It is about making up a story out of various materials. And so then we have to analyze things not just by sources but also by plausibility and by narrative power. (Scene from a TAH summer institute, Tuesday, July 10, 2007)

This was David Jaffee speaking. He is a historian at the CUNY Graduate Center and City College. He was sitting at the head of a conference table with about 30 other people in a room in the Julia Richmond Educational Complex. It was a Tuesday afternoon in July, a day and a half into our week-long "Inventing the People" summer institute.

He was speaking at the conclusion of an hour-long seminar discussion about an article in the March 2007 *Journal of American History*. Wendy Warren wrote this award winning essay in a distinctive voice that provoked heated discussion. The first paragraphs of her piece explain why David Jaffee was wrapping up this conversation by focusing on stories and sources. Here is how she began her article: "This is a story of a rape of a woman."

> Indefinite articles deliberately saturate that sentence. They mean to say: this is not *the* story, not the *only* story—not the only story of rape, not the only story of this woman. This is a story of a person whose sole appearance in historical documentation occurs in one paragraph of a 17th-century colonial travelogue. Given such paltry evidence, perhaps only indefinite articles capture the indefinite nature of this narrative.
>
> The facts are few. The approximate date and location of the assault seem fairly certain: early fall 1638, not far from Boston, in the Massachusetts Bay Colony. The central characters are equally clear: the slave owner, Samuel Maverick, an English merchant; John Josselyn, an English traveler; two enslaved African women; and an enslaved African man. About the first two, at least, some evidence exists. Their sex, race, class, and literacy combined to ensure that some record of their lives survived their times. As for the other three, no written document other than the paragraph above mentions their existence. We know only what John Josselyn related: when he

was a guest in Samuel Maverick's house, he encountered a slave woman anguished because another slave had raped her upon their owner's orders. (p. 1031)

In an incredibly speculative, yet documented article, Warren tried to reimagine the occurrence by consulting whatever evidence remained 400 years later, generalizing from what is known about life in the 17th century and other specific people, and guessing about the rest. Using lists of the property on the island where Maverick lived, she wonders where the rape took place. Drawing upon letters about the household that do not refer to this incident, Warren wonders if Amias Maverick knew about her husband Samuel Maverick's decision to "breed" his slave, or if she had perhaps ordered the rape. Was the unnamed male slave assigned to this task reluctant, or was this an opportunity to assert his masculinity? The author also includes graphic descriptions of well-documented slaver's practices, and wonders how this woman reacted to such treatment—even though there is no evidence that the slavers who transported her, specifically, used them. The lack of evidence for what the woman might have been thinking but the author's insistence on speculating nonetheless, and the graphic descriptions of slave treatment that truly happened to many slaves but may or may not have occurred to this woman, make this article unlike almost any other academic work they had read. Some loved it, while it provoked other teachers to wonder about how this article could count as history.

David Jaffee closed this section of the afternoon discussion by putting his finger on the very thing that the teachers were most concerned about in the conversation, the bold and graphic speculation, beyond the evidence, on the details of the rape of a woman in the Massachusetts Bay Colony.

> It is very interesting that there are now increasingly genres of writing that are much more speculative and that are much more messy. And this is not messy in a bad way. Something can be messy where it just reeks of a lack of sources or poor use of materials or so on. This is not messy in a bad way. This is deliberately, elegantly messy. She knows what she is doing and she does it deliberately.

Our conversation revolved around several different purposes, and Jaffee reframed the discussion about the limited evidence for each particular speculation into a broader focus about how sources are used to tell a story, and how we have to analyze historians' stories not solely by the number of sources they supply for each claim, but also by the plausibility of the source and by the narrative power of the story they allow the historical community to tell. This provided a wonderful conclusion to the discussion. As a historian and a history teacher educator I thought that emphasizing the narrative power of different stories captured a broad undercurrent in the conversation and allowed us to reflect on the very stuff of histories. My role as a history teacher educator, sitting across the table from a historian, was to ensure that while the conversation spoke to teachers as a community discussing their historical knowledge, it also involved considerations relevant to their roles in constructing historical knowledge for the secondary students in their classrooms.

Overview of the Institute

David Jaffee and I were not alone at the head of the table. We were sitting with our TAH grant directors: Richard Miller, a full-time history teacher at the Beacon School and Avram Barlowe, a full-time history teacher at Urban Academy. "Inventing the People" was a collaboration between the Secondary Education Department at Queens College/CUNY, and the Empowerment Zone of the New York City Department of Education. This Zone is a very recent creation—at the time we submitted our proposal in February 2006, it was still named the Autonomy Zone. Its premise was that principals and teachers will accept targets for specific improvements in results for their schools—in measures of student outcome achievements, educational equity, fiscal equity—that exceed New York City public school averages. These targets are termed "accountabilities." In return for these accountabilities, principals and teachers gain greater control over their curriculum, instructional methods, scheduling, professional development, educational budget, and interim assessments, termed "autonomies." The Zone was not geographic, but open to any public school in the city. While the Zone had a CEO and some central staff, Zone schools did not get professional development from a district office, and there were no curriculum specialists or supervisors in the central office. Schools worked together in partnerships to secure professional development or other assistance, so no one was displaced or threatened by having two full-time teachers serve as grant directors.

Their position as TAH grant directors afforded Miller and Barlowe, and through them other teachers in our project, a much stronger and decisive voice in the design and operation of the grant. They constructed an unusual summer institute by working with their colleagues to recruit a group of 20 high school students mostly from Urban, Beacon, and Fannie Lou Hamer high schools who earned $100 each for participating in a week-long, morning "summer school." Each of our five days began with a one-hour discussion-oriented class cotaught by Miller and Barlowe in a "fishbowl" fashion at the center of a large room, while all around, on the "outside" sat the 30 teachers and institute faculty. We were also filming these sessions, so there was a camera and a boom mike, and we were thus enabled to review quotations from the discussions. The student work centered on materials associated with the "Origins Debate" (Fields, 1990; Vaughn, 1995) in American history, the question of how slavery evolved in the early Chesapeake, and the relationship between slavery and racism. On Monday we had students write a bit about what they imagined life in the early Chesapeake was like, and then they looked through a packet of primary sources from the 1600s that included indenture contracts, laws, court cases, inventories, and other fragments of evidence that historians had assembled in order to cast light on the nature of work, life, class, and what we now call race in the early Chesapeake (Berlin, 1996; Gerwin & Zevin, forthcoming; Morgan, 1972). On Tuesday morning students discussed an excerpted version we constructed, with vocabulary, reading questions, and other comprehension aids, of Edmund Morgan's OAH presidential address "American Freedom/American Slavery." Students had been wondering about interracial relationships of all sorts (fraternization), average wages in Europe, what it cost to come to America, why it was preferable to go all the way to Africa for labor instead of capturing other Europeans, and what kinds of jobs people did in the Americas to make a living, where they lived and bought their food, and if a society of landless laborers had to be unstable.

After about an hour of class and a short break, the students worked one-on-one with the teachers in the institute, reading documents or adapted secondary sources, and doing the "homework" for the next class session. Sometime around 11 a.m. the students went home, and we moved downstairs to a conference room to evaluate what happened in "class" that day for another hour. In those conversations we explored what historical understanding students had reached; whether Miller and Barlowe imposed their concerns on the class or if student-led inquiry occurred; how Miller and Barlowe intervened in the conversations; what the questions and ideas were that remained unclear to the students; and how small groups or a writing exercise might have made a difference. Teachers compared their one-on-one sessions with the students to the ways that the same students participated or remained silent in class.

After lunch we moved into a more traditional seminar style discussion of readings that so far had focused on Jamestown, social and labor relations there, and on African servitude, indentured servitude, and slavery in an Atlantic world. The Warren article (2007) on a slave in New England was a late addition to a reading list for the teachers that included articles by Edmund Morgan, Ira Berlin, and selections from books on Jamestown by James Horn (2005), a suspected slave revolt in New York by Jill Lepore (2005), and the archaeology of Manhattan. But even as these sessions explored the historical issues, and what we were doing when we did history as per David Jaffee's comments, we were also trying to figure out what to teach tomorrow—literally, upstairs, to those high school students who would show up again. So our conversations about the historical material furthered our own understanding, but also focused directly on teaching a common group of students, as well as how these materials might relate to individual classrooms in the fall.

Content/Pedagogy, Teacher Community, and Teachers' Voices

In the *Inventing the People* summer institute the teachers read professional journal articles, conducted research in archives, planned lessons, taught high school students, reflected on the teaching, and utilized questions raised by students in the classroom to direct their historical research. They conducted historical research with one eye on what kinds of questions could be answered by the existing sources and one eye on how certain sources could help students see existing questions that matter to the historical community. We tried to meet Tom Holt's challenge to find a way to make "historians'...*way of working* and not just the content of their work visible to students" while checking to see if students could indeed "grasp what is being made visible" (Holt, 1990, p. 10).

The institute achieved this blend because of the strong voice teachers-as-directors had in planning the summer. Neither David Jaffee nor I had conceived of running a summer school, and in my other work on TAH grants I had not heard this proposed by any regional supervisor or master teacher from outside of a region, though other regions may include some form of summer school in their grants. In the "Inventing the People" project this arrangement owed its existence to the central position Avram Barlowe and Richard Miller occupied in the grant, and it worked out in practice because of the strength of their voices in the daily workings of the students' class and afternoon seminars.

Tuesday, July 10, 2007, Continued

On this Tuesday afternoon, while discussing the Warren (2007) article, we were considering giving the high school students a six-paragraph version of it the next morning, which would mean moving away from the colonial Chesapeake to look at an African woman in New England and responding to student questions about the structures of daily life in the New World, but we were also thinking that we should stick with our original plan and move forward in a narrative arc following *American Slavery/American Freedom* by providing material on Bacon's Rebellion. Many teachers felt the subject of rape along with graphic language and a speculative tone made the article too rough to give to our students, and the group chose to stick with material on Bacon's Rebellion. This is the conversation that David Jaffee had been bringing to a conclusion: a consideration of race, slavery, and social/labor relations in the Chesapeake as illuminated by this article about the Massachusetts Bay Colony and this single incident in the life of a slave; the nature of history as represented by this narrative; and what we should teach the following day.

Avram Barlowe, the high school teacher who had also been leading the discussion, jumped in to elaborate on Jaffee's comment on judging narratives by plausibility and narrative power. He changed the conversation to one about teaching.

> It raises a question. If a student of ours wrote a paper in this style [laughter] what would we say? What would we say? We usually like them to have a point of view, defend it, respond to an opposing view, and critique it on the evidence....
>
> And I think that what some people were alluding to earlier was not that they were objecting...that the messiness has two sides. That it shows the complexity of history. On the other hand it is always a concern that I think we have with kids that when the conversation gets very complex and there are many multiple answers—which we want to encourage—there are always the kids who say "well then you cannot know anything, can you?" and throw their hands up in frustration, and I think that that is another aspect of this that we have to think about in the classroom.

This built quite directly from David Jaffee's conclusion, and took the focus straight back to the high school classroom. Barlowe considered Jaffee's point, and then wondered aloud about how he and his teacher colleagues—who work so hard to get their students to reach conclusions supported by evidence, and to consider other views as possibly valid—would respond to a student paper that spent so much time imagining beyond the evidence. The group laughter came at the absurdity of the thought that their students might attempt and pull off such sophisticated writing. But it was a warm laughter at the thought that they do stress a particular brand of history writing. And Barlowe also followed-up on real fears, that judging historical writing by criteria broader than the source-based evidence for each claim will confuse students. Taking into account the plausibility of sources and the narrative power of the story you can tell will prove such a complicated standard for judgments that it will cause middle and high school pupils to give up on history out of sheer frustration about understanding what it is possible to know about the past. On the other hand these considerations demonstrate a complexity of history that the teachers want their students to grasp.

Historians know that what they write is provisional, subject to rebuttal and revision. David Jaffee's comments addressed people who produce narratives and critique each other's narratives based on a variety of criteria including the degree to which sources provide the evidence to support an argument, but also whether or not the argument matters, whether the sources allow the historian to speak about something important. One frequent result, Peter Seixas warned, of the normative separation of teachers from historians is that scholarly materials that are live and contested within the community of historians become dead and inert "facts" when they are translated into "knowledge" in other communities less involved in the give and take of scholarly inquiry (1993, p. 314).

In the morning class our high school students struggled, with assistance from Barlowe and Miller to use evidence from documents they have reviewed to form ideas about the nature of life, labor, and race in early America. They disagreed with each other, citing one document against another, or trying to read it more closely. They also struggled to understand the arguments Edmund Morgan made in his article, and under the prodding of their teachers to identify the evidence Morgan provided for his arguments about Virginia, and to see if the sources they had read confirmed or rebutted those arguments. In this way we attempted to provide the teachers with a model of teaching that preserved the live nature of historical interpretation.

Live Historical Knowledge and Student Tension

Here, in one teacher's reflection on the summer institute, is her description of Barlowe and Miller's teaching style, emphasizing the way they kept knowledge provisional and open to continual interpretation. A first-year teacher, she found it revealing:

> Interestingly Avram [Barlowe] did not try to convince students of one particular point of view. He did not provide any factual evidence to promote his ideas but rather allowed students to discuss with each other their arguments based on a broad array of documents. Students were in a sense their own teachers; if their arguments could withstand each other's scrutiny then it could be seen as coherent. Even if some arguments were historically incorrect. I found it rather interesting he did not correct their thoughts. In retrospect he did not want to impede their thinking. All the ideologies led to many different roads all of which could have been developed further.

The teacher who wrote this reflection attended Queens College and received preservice coursework that emphasized inquiry teaching, but even after a semester of student teaching and a semester in a school, this was her first experience of seeing sustained inquiry around challenging primary and secondary sources.

What this teacher saw in our summer workshop classroom came very close to what we wanted from the ideal classroom we were trying to develop. Teachers presented our knowledge of the past as partial with room for student interpretation. Teachers would not claim the authoritative knowledge of the past, but they would act as historians do, as the epistemological authority who defines how their classroom community will use evidence, determine significance, and, as in the case of the Warren article, set the boundaries of acceptable interpretation (Seixas, 1993, pp. 316–317, 320).

An article such as the one Warren wrote might increase the "deep sense of tension" beyond what the students could handle. Warren is explicit about the paucity of evidence, her choice to expose the gaps in her argument and the limits of her knowledge, and admits the possibility that she has misread the situation or that the memoirist John Josselyn made the entire story up and no rape occurred, although she believes it did. She argues that it is important to attempt to tell this particular story because the lives of Africans in 17th century New England are almost never told, "the last book to focus exclusively on the subject of Africans in colonial New England was published in 1942 and is now out of print" (2007, p. 1032).

Yet Barlowe and Miller, as a historian and a teacher, reacted in slightly different ways. David Jaffee addressed concerns central to the organized professional community that reviews articles, shows up to hear papers at conference sessions, and when he talked about whether or not we love sources or use them to advance narratives we are promoting, in important ways he addressed these teachers as he might address a group of doctoral students who were considering how to read professional articles and write their dissertations. In the hypothetical situation that Barlowe presented, the people constructing narratives will be the students of the people sitting in the room, rather than the teachers themselves. Once again they will be judging the quality of the narrative, and Barlowe rightly wonders if in their own classrooms they would accept standards other than source-based evidence as a major or equal criterion for judging a high school student's essay. Their exchange highlights two distinctive concerns, those of the academic historian discussing the structure of narratives, and those of the classroom teacher discussing the criteria for grading student narratives.

The Parallel Roles of Teachers and Historians

Yet the exchange also highlights parallels in the ways that teachers and historians operate. When David Jaffee speaks about loving sources and using them to advance narratives, he is absolutely speaking about concerns that matter to teachers too. Teachers must use sources in the classroom (another community of inquiry) to advance a particular narrative with their students, and they may love sources more than their students, or be tempted by a particular document that is cool and fun, even if it might be confusing for their students. Teachers also build narratives out of sources, but not for publication in historical journals. Teachers generally borrow their sources from others, but then so do historians, who locate the majority of their sources through the work of other historians, not solely through their own archival research. Meanwhile, teachers too have opportunities to locate sources in virtual archives, as we will see in a moment. When Barlowe discussed what teachers would accept in student essays he referred to a teacher role that was actually quite similar to that of historians who review and comment on manuscripts. In their own classrooms teachers review and comment on narrative constructions offered by students, define how their classroom community will use evidence, determine significance, and set the boundaries of acceptable interpretation.

Seixas explored these parallels in his work, and argued that the crucial distinction between the two communities is that historians assemble sources, construct and review narratives for their peers, and this constantly reinforces the provisional nature of the history they know. Teachers, compiling sources, constructing and reviewing narratives primarily for and from their students, stand outside the community of historian knowers. The lack of a peer community of teachers with the competence to challenge and affirm their uses of historical sources and evidence may explain why teachers construct classrooms where historical knowledge is composed primarily of received facts or at best two or three competing explanations that students may choose between, but not discard completely in favor of an alternative answer or a reframing of the question. Seixas suggests the need for an ongoing "teachers' community of historical inquiry" that includes appearances by professional historians (Seixas, 1993, pp. 314, 316–320).

Tuesday, July 10, 2007 a Third Time

Following Barlowe's comment on whether or not teachers would accept a speculative piece that moved as far beyond the evidence as Warren had done in her article, we shifted away from a discussion of secondary readings to an archival activity, further illustrating the parallel nature of the work that historians and teachers perform these days, although for different audiences. Rather than attempting to discuss the chapters about Pocahontas in the book on Jamestown written by James Horn (2005), we decided to turn the teachers loose on Virtual Jamestown to see what materials we could find for the students to use on Wednesday morning.

This turn to research in an archive on the Web is a staple of TAH grants and other professional development workshops. The distinctive element in this exchange is how the topics to investigate evolved. Normally they stemmed from interest expressed by the teachers in conversations about the seminar readings, or were planned in advance by the institute historians and history educators. In this moment they arise from questions that the high school students asked as they discussed the sources and readings in the morning session, and the debate the teachers had at 11:00 a.m. about what kind of materials we could provide in response.

In this conversation David Jaffee, historian, announced that we would not be pressing on to the reading he provided on Pocahontas, and then Richard Miller, teacher, listed the topics, pointing out which one was raised by teachers in the 11:00 conversation about the morning class, and which one became a major focus of student decision during the class he ran that morning with Barlowe.

Teachers' Community of Historical Inquiry

I propose that the more significant role of discussion between historians and teachers is as an illustration of one form of a "teachers' community of historical inquiry" with the participation of a historian. This collapses the usual distinctions between content and pedagogy. This group composed largely of teachers was discussing their own historical knowledge, what they particularly know about Jamestown, miscegenation, interracial fraternization, and the ability of Europeans to mobilize labor. They were reading more, and discussing with each other and David Jaffee the limitations of sources and knowledge in the historical community. Their conversation about the Warren article was an open consideration of how far they were willing to move away from specific evidence in order to speculate about issues of importance to us that were not addressed directly by the existing historical record. They were also asking questions about relative labor costs that are standard topics in the work of historians such as David Eltis (2000). They were inviting David Jaffe to provide them with directions to such material. And they were making choices about how the available sources affected the course they were teaching right now, as well as what they would have to use during their regular school-year courses. They were forming a community of inquiry as teachers, giving voice to their position at the intersection of historians and students and the ways that they function in the scholarly and pedagogic realm.

This occurred simultaneously as they discussed readings that at once informed their own understanding of the Atlantic world, exposed the limitations of current historical knowledge possessed by the professional community of research historians, and served as potential readings for their students, with footnotes to primary sources that, increasingly as archives put material online, they could expect to track down to give to their students, or require the students themselves to track down. In such a situation it is not useful to describe a separation between content and pedagogy but to recognize a moment when teachers are "doing the discipline" (Seixas, 1999, p. 329). Teachers searching an archive with a historian in the room are learning about the laws (or demographics or worker fraternization, etc.) of Jamestown, the nature of historical records, considering the suitability of what they find for a group of 20 students showing up the next day, and for possible use in their own classrooms. They will have an opportunity to compare notes with each other after this exercise, and to make recommendations to Miller and Barlowe about tomorrow's class.

Teacher Voice: Structure and Agency

For my analysis of teachers' voices the crucial moment was when a teacher turned a conversation led by a historian about how historians use sources into a reflection on how much high school students can be permitted to read into the evidence. Any teacher at the seminar who had read the Wendy Warren article could have posed the same hypothetical situation that Barlowe suggested when he speculated about what would happen if a student turned in a paper that was far removed from what the evidence directly supported. Any teacher could have interrupted David Jaffee, but no one else did. Avram Barlowe had a different voice because he was a TAH grant director and had been planning this conversation with David Jaffee and others for several months. Barlowe's position at the head of the table allowed him to interject when David Jaffee paused, and steer that point in a classroom direction. The comment helped develop a teacher community-of-peers because Barlowe was not a retired master teacher or teacher consultant coming from outside of the community, but rather a full-time classroom teacher in the same building as some of the teachers who were present, and he was famil-iar to others from many professional development moments.

How did Barlowe come to have the role of coleader of the historical conversa-tion and a codirector of the grant? How did Richard Miller have the same posi-tion at the head of the table, visible in his announcement canceling the discussion of a historical text and replacing it with an archival activity? Historical process has a possible answer for these questions.

My historical training leads me to think about voice in terms of structure and agency. Voice, the ability to speak, be heard, and even followed, is the product of the choices that an individual (or a group) makes, but is also enabled or hindered by the surrounding environment. The teachers' voices, in this grant, are particu-larly strong in part because, unusually according to my knowledge of the *Teach-ing American History* grant projects, two full-time teachers were the official grant directors. The interwoven voices of Barlowe, Miller, David Jaffee, and myself, and the history of the Empowerment Zone, are also the product of a few structures, and our personal choices.

One explanation for the nature of the team that put the "Inventing the People" grant together rests on the unique qualities of the different individuals leading the program. David Jaffee facilitated this process by virtue of his own comfort with discussing classroom teaching. He regularly presents at sessions of the American Historical Association and the Organization of American Historians on teaching, particularly with new media. He has published in the *Journal of American Historians* on how he has worked with undergraduates to help them learn to interrogate images with the same critical eye that the profession teaches them to bring to written sources (Coventry, Felten, Jaffee, & Weis, 2006). Avram Barlowe and Richard Miller have had an unusual amount of interaction with historians in the past decade. They were both lead teachers in an earlier TAH Grant ("Enlivening American History Through Primary Sources") partnering the Alternative Schools of the New York City Board of Education with Queens College and the New-York Historical Society. Over 3 years of this institute Avram

Barlowe, who already had a strong background in the period, read the equivalent of what one would read in a doctoral history course on the Revolution and published his own book on inquiry teaching and how he uses these materials in his high school course on the American Revolution (2004). I started out in a doctoral program in American history, dropped out and taught high school, and earned a master's in social studies while also completing my doctorate. I found a home in the Queens College Department of Secondary Education. I have spent my career working at the intersection of history and secondary teaching.

Since 2004 Avram Barlowe, Richard Miller, David Jaffee, and I have been working together with a diverse group of other historians to produce Web sites for the National Endowment for the Humanities EdSITEment project. This gives us a long relationship in working directly at the intersection of scholarship, sources, and the classroom. In order to produce any single lesson we all read historical scholarship, looked at primary sources, drafted lessons, commented on early drafts of the different lessons, and even tried some lessons out in the classroom.

While our personal interests in teaching led to our specific collaboration in the prior TAH grant and the NEH lesson plan project, there is also an institutional, structural history that brings us together. Avram Barlowe and Richard Miller both work in the Empowerment Zone of the New York City Public schools, earlier known as the Autonomy Zone, and before that their schools were part of the Alternative Superintendent for High Schools. Without getting into New York City public school organizational arcana, both Barlowe and Miller have spent their professional lives in structures that consciously attempt to foster change. When we spoke with the Superintendent of that Autonomy (now Empowerment) Zone about structuring the grant with two full-time teachers as the directors it made perfect sense to him and his office staff. The goal of the Empowerment Zone is to devolve as much authority as possible to the local schools in exchange for holding them directly accountable for their students' achievement. To some extent the New York City schools facilitated the leadership role of these two teachers.

Many of the schools in our TAH grant also belong to a state-wide consortium of 30 schools that have maintained a waiver from the New York State regents' exams in science and social studies. This leaves them free to offer innovative courses on the American Revolution, or slavery in the Atlantic world, or to choose depth over breadth in a more common American history survey since there is no "gotcha!" threat that a "fact" they do not cover will trip up their students on a standardized test of course content at the end of the year. Teachers at the consortium schools meet as a group on professional development days in New York City, so many teachers know each other, and they already have a common language about their portfolio evaluation process that they have articulated to each other and the New York State Legislature. Avram Barlowe has had a leadership role in this consortium, running professional development sessions for the consortium, and Richard Miller is well known and well regarded in the group. In this setting New York State and to some extent New York City, with their one-size fits all assessments, generally multiple-choice standardized examinations developed by large testing companies, are not supportive of the structures that empower these teachers, although the work of resisting the test has created the community that meets at our institute (Darling-Hammond, Ancess, & Ort, 2002).

These structures help explain how Miller and Barlowe came to direct the grant and filled a room with like-minded teachers, and how they were available when David Jaffee came looking for teachers to collaborate with him on the NEH project. Miller and Barlowe's roles as codirectors go beyond their roles in leading discussions. They conceived of an institute built around a summer school, and in their daily work lives they were quickly able to recruit the necessary students. Moreover, in planning meetings, David Jaffee and I never had to ask each other what the teachers would want to do—the teachers were at the meetings, or calling us to the meetings and asking us what the historians might want to do. For Miller and Barlowe, other teachers were not even a phone call away, but the people they saw in the hallway everyday. In order to allow them to attend our meetings we built a $40,000/year position of "mentee teacher" who either worked in their classroom or school, providing the classroom continuity or school capacity to release them for work on the TAH grant. This ensured that teachers always had a voice at the table, whether in budgeting, planning, or running the professional development. We worked on getting Miller and Barlowe into other teachers' classrooms to provide direct coaching follow-up to the institute we held in the summer of 2008.

Teachers' Voice in Contrasting TAH Grants

Teachers may not direct most other TAH grants, but many projects have roles that amplify teacher voices. At a national TAH gathering I learned about a grant incorporating Japanese Lesson Study. In that model a smaller group of teachers design lessons together, and then come during the school day to one school all together to observe implementation in one or more classrooms. Even if a grant leader who is not currently a teacher facilitates that process or a historian provides input on the lessons, teachers take a central role in the planning and discussion, forming another version of the community of history teachers. In a previous TAH grant project I was involved in, our structure included "lead teachers" who planned the institutes with the historians and history educators, even though they did not have an equal status in running the program. Teacher voice ranges across a spectrum in TAH grant programs.

Other TAH programs with which I've been involved stand at the far end of the spectrum from the "Inventing the People" program. The teachers have no role in planning or running the program. There are history content people, history education people (including me), and district office people who make all of the program decisions. Teachers have no formal or informal advisory role in the program. The program provides impressive historical content, interaction with historians, and innovative primary sources often ready for classroom use, and models a variety of new classroom strategies. Since teacher voices are absent from the planning, although certainly not silent during the meetings, this other TAH program affords a contrast that highlights the different places teachers' voices surface when they are not built into the administration of the program.

Grant Structure: Leadership Retreats, History Days, and Teaching Days

The structure of one particular grant includes an annual two-day leadership institute at the end of the summer. The team that put this grant together deliberately avoided the week-long summer seminars, spreading the sessions out during the school year in the hope of providing teachers with in-depth conversations with historians, innovative historical sources, and lesson planning time all at once, so that teachers could develop lessons that incorporate the cutting edge historical interpretations they have been discussing. In prior institutes that provided more summer planning time some teachers had struggled to recall what historians had said months earlier and were less able to incorporate new interpretations into lesson materials.

Teachers are released for eight full days during the school year, a significant commitment by their districts to this program. This project holds "history days" that open with an inquiry activity leading teachers to share their prior knowledge of a topic, frequently followed by a historian giving a talk illustrated with images and documents, and an afternoon modeling close readings of classroom-ready historical materials, led by historians with a lot of experience working with teachers. The Queens College team follows up with a "teaching the history" day. So we always have two days per topic; for example, a day specifically dedicated to the history of the Civil War and then a day about teaching the coming of the Civil War.

In nearly every way the program exemplifies the benchmarks for professional development in history. Teachers have a chance for extended questions and answers with the historians, they consider multiple interpretations, they "do history" with the historians by examining documents or other evidence, and they have opportunities to adapt these materials for their classrooms. But there is no formal structure that brings teachers into the planning process for the sessions.

Content/Pedagogy and Voice

This project does separate content from pedagogy by having the historian present on one morning and not attend the teaching day, but even here content is not entirely separated from pedagogy. The grant format places the historians at the front of the room alone, standing, while the teachers sit in rows facing them, although this doesn't stop teachers from interrupting a historian or a bunch of teachers from piling on about a point. Moreover, at least one featured historian spent the entire day with the teachers, sitting in on the afternoon discussions about specific primary sources and teaching. However, in two years no teacher has made the move Avram Barlowe made during the seminar on the Wendy Warren article, and interrupted a historian to initiate a group discussion about teaching. This part of the day is always structured as a conversation directed to the historian.

Teachers' Voice in Unofficial Channels: Affirmation

The lack of formal channels does not prevent the expression of teacher voice. During the "History Day" on the Civil War teachers strongly set the agenda for the day and the subsequent "teaching the Civil War" day during the conversation with the historian. The teachers pressed the argument that secession occurred over states rights and not solely over slavery. Investigating this question raised by the teachers' voices set the agenda for the "teaching day" as surely as if the teachers were included in our planning session. Whether given a formal role or not, teachers individually and collectively expressed their interests during sessions, and every professional development team responded to those teacher voices. Teacher evaluations were also used and were the only formal expressions of teacher input available.

Teachers' Voice in Unofficial Channels: Dissent

When we presented material on Jamestown we encountered a problem. Teachers liked the material, but said that they could not teach it. Middle school teachers announced that they could not discuss laws against interracial marriage or fraternization, or anything else that raised issues of sexuality, and they couldn't look at documents that talked about religion. The middle school parent body would not tolerate it. The teachers were not rude, they just informed us that they found this set of materials useless.

Another moment of teachers voicing dissent occurred during a 2-day leadership retreat. After 2 years of working with the theme of freedom we devoted some time to setting out a framework for unit development that incorporated aspects of the understanding by design model (Wiggins & McTighe, 2005) and Project Zero at Harvard University. In this conversation about units and assessment, teachers started talking about the administrative structures that inform instruction in their schools. One teacher spoke at some length about how she prepared an assessment that was not structured exactly like the eighth grade social studies end-of-year examination. Her assistant principal in charge of social studies opposed the examination that she was giving instead. Several other teachers spoke about a related grievance. Rather than discuss assessments they were talking about the pacing calendar, a list of what historical topics teachers should be covering each week in order to stay "on pace" to teach all of the content in the course by the end of the year. Teachers reported to us that the supervisors in their schools often adopted those pacing calendars in a dogmatic fashion, requiring teachers to cover either those precise events, or those precise periods more or less in weekly correspondence with the district calendar.

As project staff our only reaction was to suggest that a thematic approach can allow a unit to examine evidence over a broader period of years, even if you do not "cover" everything, to suggest alternating between some significant, deep units and some handouts that cover topics in a day instead of a week, and to acknowledge that the demands of coverage are real, and pressing, and in conflict with the approaches we suggest.

Contrasting Two Programs

Contrasting these two different programs suggests a complex and contradictory conclusion about teacher voices in the *Teaching American History* grant program and other professional development efforts. Strong teacher voices designed into the structure of the grant program offer powerful moments for combining content and pedagogy in ways that develop a strong teacher community. Yet while the partners who work with school districts, whether they are historians or history educators or groups that combine both types of expertise, may seek out a partnership with teachers, they are quite often powerless, or nearly powerless to implement one if such a role is not embedded in the organization of the local educational agency. In short, teacher voices are critical to the grants, but almost totally beyond the control of grant partners.

Barlowe's and Miller's strong teacher voices, built into the structure of "Inventing the People," and their places at the head of the seminar table during the grant activities, dramatically increased the moments when content and pedagogy combined, as teachers delved ever deeper into high quality historical content in the very act of producing high quality classroom instruction. The other grant program did not, by any means, lack moments that combined content and pedagogy, and teachers' voices can still drive the program. However, the lack of a teacher cochair in each discussion means that there are fewer moments when a reflection by a historian triggers a discussion on the pedagogy of historical interpretation by the teachers. A more integrated teacher leadership structure in the grant would not eliminate pacing calendars that made Jamestown impossible, while Barlowe and Miller teach in schools that won a vote of the New York State Legislature that allowed them some freedom from State testing in history.

The teachers in the "Inventing the People" grant could consider how they would receive a paper from one of their students that went as far beyond the evidence as Wendy Warren did in her essay on the rape of an African woman in 17th century New England, because it is up to them to set the rules for their assessments and classroom writing. They can consider assigning students a cutdown version of the Wendy Warren article because they have control over what materials they use in their classrooms. If they investigate Virtual Jamestown in a summer workshop for a few hours it is with the certain knowledge that they can take the time to have their students develop meaningful projects using the site in the fall. The work of planning and carrying out the grant that Barlowe and Miller did as the TAH project directors built upon and took advantage of the already strong culture of teacher voice in these schools.

Teachers speak from within the structures of their schools and their districts, the way that they are supervised, and what their lesson plans need to look like, and these bureaucratic structures can affect teaching as powerfully, or more powerfully, than any given state test (Gerwin, 2003; Grant, 2003; McNeil, 1988). The TAH grants operate within the structures of the districts they serve, and apply in partnership with those districts, within the boundaries of a memorandum of understanding that the leadership team in the LEA must approve and sign. At least in the experience of these two TAH grant programs, the striking contrast in teachers' voice, with its implications for minimizing a division between content and pedagogy and teacher community, directly reflects the reality of the schools and their administrative structure, not the choice of the partnering historical/ history education organizations.

Discussion: Teachers' Voices in Professional Development, TAH and Beyond

The relationship between historical content, doing history, history pedagogy, and teachers' voices that this chapter presents is central to the Benchmarks for Professional Development in Teaching of History as a Discipline (American Historical Association, 2002). Jointly developed by a small group drawn from the membership of the American Historical Association, the Organization of American Historians, and the National Council for the Social Studies (American Historical Association, 2002) in response to a request from the U.S. Department of Education, the document begins by emphasizing two fundamental assumptions: that content, pedagogy, and historical thinking must be interwoven, and that they must be related to classroom experience. Immediately below, the first collaboration benchmark declares that, "K-12 teachers should be involved at the beginning of planning," and the document then develops a variety of structures and roles for including teachers' voices. Two roles suggested in the Benchmarks document include advisory committees for professional development efforts while funding master teachers to give workshops in their own schools or recruiting teacher leaders who can serve as facilitators and leaders of the professional development efforts.

The *Teaching American History* grants avoid the pitfalls of much problematic professional development offered to social studies teachers. These are not brief workshops without outside speakers, generic in-service days that have no particular content, or conferences too far removed from a school's curriculum to influence daily teaching (Valli & Stout, 2004; VanHover, 2008). They share many characteristics found to be part of successful professional development in math and science, including multiple teachers from the same school, creating networks of teachers from the same discipline, and providing many contact hours over three sustained years (Garet, Porter, Desimone, Birman, & Yoon, 2001).

Historians, scholarly organizations, and history educators that partner with districts that provide teachers with less classroom authority and less autonomous decision making about curriculum and assessment, are likely to shape grant structures and activities in ways that minimize teacher voice. Teachers from such districts will, of necessity, check the historical content and the pedagogic strategies for promoting disciplinary goals such as having students gain experience with sourcing, interpretation, broader themes, or greater depth in some areas, for its compatibility with their district mandates. Local educational authorities are unlikely to seek federal funding in order to hire historians and history educators to organize their teachers against city hall. In New York City the Autonomy Zone includes schools that were explicitly organized against the structure of standard schools, designed to provide greater teacher voice and community, and the consortium schools and Zone have an institutionalized role of pushing against the New York City Department of Education procedures. Similar LEAs are likely to support the Benchmarks document call for structures and roles that promote teacher leadership within the grants.

The call from AHA, NCSS, and OAH for giving teachers a strong voice in professional development is not a hollow piety but a specific position in a debate about how to reform schools. Some efforts, of the more "teacher-proof" type mandate the teaching of core knowledge, efforts that script classroom time into workshop sessions, or that dictate the actual page number in a textbook that all teachers in a city should cover in a given day. These reform efforts move the focus of decision making outside of the classroom and place it elsewhere within the district. Invoking a support for teacher voice and the creation of articulate teacher communities implicitly critiques such efforts, and endorses the role of the teacher as the key instructional decision maker.

As the experiences I have presented in two TAH grant projects demonstrate, the history education community has good reasons for this advocacy. Teacher voice is critical in forming a community of practitioners who can discuss their own historical knowledge and the role they play in helping students see how historical knowledge is structured and created, and in erasing a divide between content and pedagogy. Historians, history department, museum and history educators are constrained by the norms in districts, but also have some room for advancing teacher voice as they design grant projects, craft memoranda of understanding, choose their district partners, and carry out their projects.

References

American Historical Association. (2002). *Benchmarks for professional development in teaching of history as a discipline.* Retrieved August 30, 2008, from http://www.historians.org/teaching/policy/Benchmarks.htm

Barlowe, A. (2004). *Teaching American history: An inquiry approach.* New York: Teachers College Press.

Berlin, I. (1996, April). From Creole to African: Atlantic Creoles and the origins of African-American Society in mainland North America. *The William and Mary Quarterly, 53,* 251–288.

Coventry, M., Felten, P., Jaffee, D., Weis, T., with McGowan, S. (2006). Ways of seeing: Evidence and learning in the history classroom. *Journal of American History, 92*(4), 1371–1402.

Darling-Hammond, L., Ancess, J., & Wichterle Ort, S. (2002). Reinventing high school: Outcomes of the coalition campus schools project. *American Educational Research Journal, 39*(3), 639–673.

Dew, C. (2001). *Apostles of disunion: Southern secession commissioners and the Causes of the Civil War.* Charlottesville: University Press of Virginia.

Eltis, D. (2000). *The rise of African slavery in the America.* New York: Cambridge University Press.

Fields, B. (1990, May/June). Slavery, race and ideology in the United States of America. *New Left Review, 181,* 95–117.

Gerwin, D. (2003). A relevant lesson: Hitler goes to the mall. *Theory and Research in Social Education, 31*(4), 435–465.

Gerwin, D., & Zevin, J. (forthcoming). *Teaching U.S. history as mystery* (2nd ed.). New York: Routledge.

Garet, M. S., Porter, A. C., Desimone, L. Birman, B. F., & Yoon, K. S. (2001). What makes professional development effective? Results from a national sample of teachers. *American Educational Research Journal, 38*(4), 915–945.

Grant, S. G. (2003). *History lessons: Teaching, learning, and testing in U.S. history classrooms.* Mahwah, NJ: Erlbaum.

Holt, T. (1990). *Thinking historically: Narrative, imagination and understanding.* New York: The College Board.

Horn, J. (2005). *A land as god made it: Jamestown and the birth of America.* New York: Basic Books.

Lepore, J. (2005). The tightening vise: Slavery and freedom in British New York. In I. Berlin & L. Harris (Eds.), *Slavery in New York* (pp. 59–89). New York: New Press,

McNeil, L. (1988). *Contradictions of control.* New York: Routledge.

Morgan, E.(1972, June). Slavery and freedom: The American paradox. *The Journal of American History, 59,* 5–29.

Project Zero. (n.d.). Retrieved January 9, 2009, from http://www.pz.harvard.edu/Research/HistUnd.htm

Seixas, P. (1993). The community of inquiry as a basis for knowledge and learning: The case of history. *American Educational Research Journal, 30*(2), 305–324.

Seixas, P. (1999). Beyond "content" and "pedagogy": In search of a way to talk about history education. *Journal of Curriculum Studies, 31*(3), 317–337.

Valli, L., & Stout, M. (2004). Continuing professional development for social science teachers. In S.Adler (Ed.), *Critical issues in social studies teacher education* (pp. 165–188). Greenwich, CT: Information Age.

VanHover, S. (2008). The professional development of social studies teachers. In L. Levstik & C. Tyson (Eds.), *Handbook of research in social studies education* (pp. 352–372). New York: Routledge

Vaughn, A. (1995). The origins debate. In *Roots of American racism* (pp. 136–174). New York: Oxford University Press.

Warren, W. (2007). The cause of her grief. *Journal of American History, 93*(4), 1031–1049.

Wiggins, G., & McTighe, J. (2005). *Understanding by design.* Alexandria, VA: ASCD.

Chapter 8

History in Every Classroom
Setting a K-5 Precedent

Elise Fillpot
University of Iowa

> Just a note to let you know BHH [Bringing History Home] is still going strong in Perry. 2nd graders just finished their awesome Ellis Island Day, 3rd graders are deep into segregation, and I heard a fifth grade teacher talking about the war (WWII). I am so pleased with the program, the workshops we received and the help from the Washington teachers, but mostly from the responses from the students and the connections they are making as we work through the unit. It was put together so well and can easily be modified for different groups different years. I love teaching it.[1]

Common sense and research suggest that as children learn, they gradually expand their abilities to understand and execute ever more complex concepts and processes. This understanding informs how children in the United States study math, science, and reading, in a year-by-year sequence that begins in kindergarten. Encountering ever-increasing complexity in these subjects, children meet these challenges because they have incrementally acquired the necessary skills and abilities. In contrast, history is not systematically taught through the elementary levels where the foundation is laid for all ensuing education. The research on teaching and learning history does not justify the delay in teaching this subject to children. Instead, it suggests elementary students are capable of learning historical patterns and sequences.[2]

In a recent review of the research on how students learn history, Keith Barton acknowledges that many educators assume elementary students cannot understand history, and he inventories various mistakes young students are inclined to make as they study history. Nevertheless, he concludes that research suggests instruction can allow students to overcome these challenges.[3] Similarly, when Bruce VanSledright taught a fifth grade class through a full spring term, he concluded his students were capable of constructing understandings of history from various and varied sources.[4]

Unfortunately, the research on how children learn history cannot also tell us how to prepare in-service teachers on a large scale to teach history in the youngest grades. The gap between research and classroom; the gap between what we know children can learn about history vs. the history they actually study—or do not study—in the elementary grades is something of an elephant in the living room of education. In order to face the elephant, I worked with K-12 teachers and postsecondary history and education faculty to design Bringing History

Home (BHH), an elementary history curriculum and professional development project (http://www.bringinghistoryhome.org/index.htm). To date, we have received three *Teaching American History* grants to implement the program, in 2001, 2003, and 2008. The project focuses on moving history from the margins of the traditional elementary curriculum into the mainstream of the school day by preparing *all* regular K-5 classroom teachers in participating school districts to teach sequential history units.

During the initial grant, the director and assistant director worked with teachers and faculty to develop a curriculum in which all K-5 regular classroom students study history every year using constructivist strategies. The curriculum consists of two instructional units per grade level, with lessons that center on trade books, historic images, documents and statistics, and activities to engage students in analyzing and synthesizing the information sources. Seven years after its inception, the BHH program is taught in six Iowa school districts, and elements of the curriculum are spreading to other schools in Iowa, Illinois, Michigan, Missouri, and North Dakota. With approximately one thousand student learning assessments collected from more than 120 K-3 elementary classrooms, the BHH project provides additional evidence for the growing body of research into how children learn history.[5] The story embedded in that evidence deserves focused and ongoing explication in the coming months and years. This chapter reveals the part of the story in which teachers in two TAH grants closed the gap between academic research and classroom practice in entire schools rather than in isolated classrooms or research venues. They did this by applying to their teaching what they learned from TAH professional development events and curricular resources. The question to be explored is how did history learning become a part of the K-5 classrooms that participated in the project?

The Project's Impact: Lessons Learned

A complete answer to that complex question would include explorations of the project's principles, the relationships between the district and grant administrators, the development of the project curriculum, the professional development model and its implementation, the teachers' attitudes and experiences, and the students' learning outcomes. Another recent literature review helps define our focus. In her examination of the research on history workshops and institutes, Stephanie van Hover asserts that

> Overall, the majority of research on professional development for history offers interesting insight into the different types of workshops/institutes available for teachers and provides anecdotal and self-report evidence that teachers enjoy and learn from these experiences. What is missing…is systematic evidence that demonstrates whether these workshops/institutes affect classroom instruction and student achievement/understanding of history.[6]

By exploring the intersection of our grant components with teacher attitudes and expertise, we may begin to take the measure of the project's impact on teacher classroom practices and begin to understand what inspired more than 170 elementary teachers to bring history into the mainstream of their classes. An inventory of that intersection includes the following lessons we either learned or had reinforced as we conducted TAH grants:

- The importance of district and school-wide teacher participation.
- The importance of teacher commitments to their own development and to curricular change.
- An effective professional development design is longitudinal and sequential.
- Teachers may learn the most about history in the process of adapting and teaching instructional units.
- It is essential to recognize and respect the reality of teachers' working conditions.
- When teachers encounter history as an interpretive, constructivist process, they become excited about teaching it.
- Student learning is turbo-charged when teachers are encouraged to adapt and enhance lessons for their own classrooms.
- Incorporating literacy and metacognitive strategies into history explorations can enhance student learning in history.
- When history timelines and maps are transformed from static resources into dynamic construction activities, they are powerful learning tools.
- Student learning enhances teachers' interest in history, and their ongoing explorations of history topics and classroom resources.
- When teacher leaders serve as mentors, they jump-start new teachers' interest in and preparation to teach history.

Pragmatic Considerations

Our TAH grant proposals centered on preparing all K-5 teachers in participating schools to teach history. In order to secure and inspire the universal participation of teachers, our project design team prioritized pragmatic considerations when designing curricular units, and when choosing workshop activities and resources for the teachers. Because we sought to involve all regular classroom teachers in all grades of the participating schools, we knew we had to keep expectations for teacher time commitments to a reasonable level. While we always secure teacher participation through recruitment rather than administrative edict, because of the overwhelming demands on teacher time and increasing expectations that teachers will need to focus on subjects other than history, we can't count on teacher self-selection arising from a love of history. We found that fairly significant monetary and book stipends seemed to be the most powerful sign-up motivations for the initial participants; but the participants in the second grant were swayed to join the project by the enthusiastic testimony of the initial group of teachers that had taught the BHH instructional unit sequence over the previous two years.

Regardless of the motives that led to their involvement, 100 percent of the regular classroom teachers in BHH schools participated in the program. This is an important element of the sequential model we use. The self-contained nature of most lower and middle elementary classes means that almost every regular classroom teacher conducts lessons in social studies. If only a few teachers in a school participated in the BHH workshops, only a fraction of students in a school would learn history each year. This would completely derail our curricular goal for students to develop increasingly more sophisticated skills and understanding in history from year to year throughout the elementary grades. Thus, I can't overstate our appreciation for universal, district-wide teacher participation in the BHH grants. While the project probably would not be successful if we didn't privilege pragmatic choices, our emphasis on the practical also stems from a desire to not take advantage of teachers' generosity of spirit and time. It is humbling to work with groups of people whose professional lives are already quite taxed, but who are willing to rise to the occasion of learning new skills and perspectives.

In our perception of important reasons for project success, teacher commitment looms large on the radar. Studies suggest that the only consistently significant change agent in teaching is teacher commitment or belief in the value of a topic or pedagogy.[7] As we continue to peruse the intersection between project components and teachers' experiences, I encourage you to keep this idea foremost in your mind.

Operating within a Broader Context

In seeking to eliminate the gap between research and practice, we immediately encounter a conundrum along the lines of the chicken and the egg. The universal absence of intensive K-5 history teaching in elementary schools is a perpetuating factor in the universal absence of intensive K-5 history teaching in elementary schools. Inertia, precedent, and policy all are pillars and posts in the fence keeping our metaphorical elephant in the living room. These forces don't just impact the administrative level, however; the absence of history in elementary grades is perpetuated at the teacher education level as well. In a fiercely effective circularity, K-5 history is largely absent from U.S. schools, and institutions of higher education marginalize history in elementary teacher preservice education programs.[8]

As a consequence of history's low priority in preservice teacher education, elementary teachers rarely have any significant amount of history coursework in their academic backgrounds, and the BHH participants were no exception to this rule. Aware of their lack of knowledge, most of the teachers originally viewed the prospect of teaching history with at least some trepidation. In addition to learning to teach a new discipline in which they had little background, the advent of the No Child Left Behind (NCLB) legislation in 2001 meant that teachers were simultaneously under high stakes pressure to improve their students' reading and math achievement, a pressure often accompanied by the adoption of new curricula in those areas.[9] And a third source of reluctance was teachers' skepticism about elementary children's abilities to effectively engage in the learning of history.

Bringing History Home Solutions

The first of these issues, the teachers' concern about their lack of formal history education prior to participating in the program, influenced how we focused the workshop history explorations. In one two-day workshop per summer over a two-summer sequence, grade-level teams studied just one unit topic per workshop. In the year following the first workshop, teachers implemented the first of two grade-level units. After the second workshop, teachers implemented both the first unit and the new unit they had prepared in the second workshop. Prior to the unit implementations, some grade-level teams received a half-day release from their school day to meet and prepare their lesson materials. To facilitate this process, the TAH grant covered the expense of substitute teachers for the planning sessions, and one of the project directors or teacher mentors met with the teams. The longitudinal, sequential nature of the two professional development years allowed teachers to engage in studying just one new history topic at a time. By limiting the amount of change occurring in a given year, we tried to respect the competing demands for teachers' time, and to limit the stress that can accompany both learning and learning to teach a new discipline.

While we were not universally successful, a substantial number of teacher comments collected in conversations and e-mail with the project director reveal how teachers' concern about their lack of knowledge abated over the course of the project and what led to that abatement. Interestingly, but not surprisingly, teachers learned the most about their history topics in the process of prepping and teaching their instructional units. In his evaluation of teacher learning outcomes in a 2002 to 2005 Montgomery County Public Schools TAH grant, Bruce VanSledright found this same phenomenon.[10] Our teachers not only expanded their understanding and skills but became more confident about their knowledge as they read for background understanding, formed questions for class discussions, and studied additional resources that could be part of their lesson planning process.

Third Grade Teacher Interview

TEACHER I think they (the students) were just amazed at some of the things that they learned.
EVALUATOR Right. Right. Were there benefits for you as a teacher in…?
TEACHER Same thing!
EVALUATOR Ok.
TEACHER I mean—I knew some of that but not to the depth that we got into it. You know?
TEACHER I didn't even know of much depth. So I'm like her. I learned a lot… along right with them. I thought also the kids had a lot of good questions. You know—as we were discussing or talking, they would bring up stuff. Sometimes I knew the answer and sometimes I didn't. You know? There's things that I didn't know and I was learning right along with them.[11]

Over the years of the project at every grade level in every BHH school, teachers shared new resources they discovered that either expanded their own understanding of the history they taught or that they could use to enhance their students' explorations. The anecdotal evidence provided informally by the teachers aligns with information formally gathered by the external evaluation team via surveys administered to all BHH teachers annually. The surveys served five main purposes:

> 1) to determine the teachers' self-described thoroughness of teaching different historical topics as part of the *BHH* curriculum, 2) to ascertain teachers' perceptions of their students' competence at performing skills or demonstrating content knowledge related to the *BHH* curriculum, 3) to gather teachers' opinions of the benefits and drawbacks of the curriculum for their students, 4) to determine teachers' perceptions of the utility of different pedagogical techniques and instructional practices for teaching history, and 5) to ask teachers' opinions on teaching history, interest in learning history, and self-efficacy concerning teaching history.[12]

In the earliest survey, teachers' confidence in their own knowledge is lower than in the final survey, when teachers had taught both units and had two years experience teaching history. The instances in which grade level teacher teams have designed additional BHH units offer vivid evidence of the growth in teacher confidence. Because the pilot district operates on a trimester system, in the year after they had taught both BHH units the second and third grade teachers in the district decided to create a third history unit. This allowed them to teach one history unit each trimester. As they planned their units, the teachers visited book warehouses, gathered materials from conference sessions related to the topics they chose to teach, consulted with the project's main historian and directors, and combed the Internet for relevant sources.

Gaining Historical Content Knowledge

While such teacher interest in expanding knowledge and their teaching repertoire was inspired and inspiring, perhaps predictably the process of learning by teaching did not always translate into teachers becoming personally enamored of history study. While extra commitment and enthusiasm characterized certain participants in the project, this degree of enthusiasm for independent discovery didn't always appear in the teacher focus groups conducted by the grant's external evaluator. Those conversations revealed that several teachers interviewed tended to be satisfied with knowing just enough to teach their units.

Second Grade Teacher Interview

TEACHER And I don't think at our grade level, we want somebody coming in that's—you know—going to give us so much information that it's so high above second grade level that we wouldn't teach it anyway, you know?

> I think the project staff gave us about as much as what we needed to have. Because otherwise, you just get too much and they're not going to get it. So, yeah. I don't know if we need some....

We may speculate about the limited scope of these teachers' curiosity at the conclusion of the two-year program. It may be a function of several factors; the chronic teacher time-shortage issue, the human inclination to take a break after a stint on a steep learning curve, the inability of the scope and sequence of the professional development activities to fully change the teachers' epistemology of history from that of a finite discipline to that of a discipline with infinite interpretive possibilities, and finally, the simple differences in individual interests in history. A common thread in the comments, though, is the teachers' reliance on the curriculum lessons not just to guide their teaching, but also to develop their own knowledge of history.

The teachers that made the comments included above seem to perceive that enhancing their own knowledge about history beyond what is useful in the classroom is not necessarily a useful endeavor. Speculation may suggest that the sheer challenge of teaching elementary students, with several disciplinary preps per day, leaves little time or energy for a teacher to invest in developing expertise in a particular area. Regardless of the source of teachers' inclination to study only that which has direct classroom application, respecting the reality of the inclination itself has influenced our BHH design choices. This doesn't mean, however, that we left unchallenged an all too common understanding of history as strings of facts or heritage myths.

Constructivist Pedagogy

The BHH paradigm of history instruction is constructivist, but the most common history paradigm teachers have encountered in their own education is mastery based and factoid centered. In order to immerse teachers in a constructivist paradigm, we began workshops with activities that make transparent the nature of history as evidence-based and interpretive. Some teachers embraced this activity, others, like the teacher interviewed below, did not see the value in activities that they didn't perceive to directly affect their teaching.

Fourth Grade Teacher Interview

TEACHER I don't know as if I'd need an extra half day if we could just take out some of—you know—some of the other stuff (out of the workshop). Like there was—I don't know—pretty much the morning of the first day...it was just all about "This is what history means. And this is why we're doing this. And this is...." And it was, like, ok, I knew I had this unit and I had to teach it. Let me get to the unit! (laughs) You know?

TEACHERS Uh-huh. Yeah.[13]

Given this often pervasive attitude, the program chose not to rely on workshop sessions alone to influence teachers' perceptions of history. We knew the teachers would be new to constructivist history processes and so we designed the lesson with this in mind. The BHH instructional units center on five processes inherent in doing history, which make transparent for teachers the interpretive nature of history as an exploration of diverse sources, should the workshop experience fail to do so. The five processes consist of reading for background knowledge, interpreting sources, mapping geographic historic information, constructing and interpreting timelines, and synthesizing learning to design a historical account. They are distilled from the list of Historical Thinking Skills and a similar list by the National Council for History Education titled History's Habits of the Mind initially developed by the Bradley Commission on the Schools.[14] By providing lessons in which varied processes for studying history align with specific history explorations, the curriculum has simultaneously introduced teachers to a constructivist history paradigm and provided concrete activities that immerse children in such a paradigm from the beginning.[15] The teacher cohorts in both TAH grants to date have all expressed appreciation for the preexisting curricular lessons and the creative possibilities for utilizing the five processes. In a third grade teacher's words,

> But you can expand on it easier than come up with it.... So, having it laid out like that is a godsend and having it...then, if you don't like the way it's taught, you can always adapt it or change it. But having that framework or the base to start with was very helpful.[16]

Curricular Adaptation: A Make-It-Your-Own Zeitgeist

The teachers' comfort levels with the lessons and the processes in the lessons were greatly enhanced by the project's make-it-your-own zeitgeist. Involving teachers in curricular adaptation was not simply a strategy to enhance teacher commitment; however; teachers contributed innovative, effective solutions to curricular problems. The project designers frequently foundered on the shoals of how to adapt a historical skill for the various elementary grades. To the relief and benefit of everyone involved, many participating teachers were adept at co-opting literacy and metacognitive strategies for history purposes. In this way, the KWL became the unit organizer and source analysis guide of choice for not just the middle and lower elementary but for the upper grades as well.[17] The KWL chart, a metacognition strategy, encourages students to activate prior knowledge, generate questions that shape and motivate study, and then connect new knowledge with prior knowledge. The acronym stands for:

K—students recall what they know about the subject.
W—students determine what they want to learn.
L—students identify what they learn as they read.

One teacher said that the highlight of the unit was watching the students construct an end-of-unit KWL chart, especially under the "learned" category as the students "just kept generating all these things that they had learned." The teacher continued:

> Things that before when we started and I looked through the books and thought, they are never going to understand this, they are never going to get this—and then that was kind of fun to see all the things that they had learned and to watch their eyes as the chart kept getting longer and longer.

In another metamorphosis, historic timelines began as discrete components of particular lessons, but became, in the teachers' hands, wondrous year-long works of art.[18] Many BHH rooms sport a messy, homemade, child-lettered and illustrated, primary source-laden strip of butcher paper that represents the class's learning for not just a unit but the entire school year. History discussions in these rooms are often punctuated by students jumping up to utilize the line as a reminder of particular events, of chronological relationships between events, and as a resource to enhance students' abilities to infer understanding from new sources.

Similarly, maps in BHH rooms began as simple laminated wall hangings. In short order, teachers steered their students to morph them into three-dimensional representations of natural resource extraction, social dislocation on the World War II home front, the dense distribution of Native American reservations, the trail to Bosque Redondo, and the migration routes of Dust Bowl refugees. Many elementary teachers seem inclined to engage their students in kinetic and constructivist activities, both of which may capture students' interest and imaginations. And almost all elementary teachers are now required to incorporate metacognitive literacy strategies in their teaching. When BHH teachers mined these areas of expertise for use with history lessons, the resulting student learning outcomes galvanized the teachers' belief in the value of teaching history. And in an empowering circularity, student learning seemed to enhance teachers' interest in further exploring the BHH history topics. For many teachers, expertise and experience seem to feed interest and commitment.

Mentoring and Collaboration: Positive Peer Influence

The belief in the value of teaching K-5 history emerged from the first TAH grant. It was jump-started in the second grant. In each grade level team of the initial project, at least one teacher took extra initiative to prepare and adapt the lessons for his or her fellow teachers. These natural leaders were invited to serve as mentors to teachers in the second TAH grant schools.[19] The resulting dynamic between mentors and new teachers in the second grant's workshops proved to be one of the most powerful components of the program. This open-ended question appeared on a 2004 BHH workshop survey: *In what ways (if any) did the workshop help prepare you to teach history successfully to your students?* Nearly all (93 percent) of the teachers responded to this question and about one third (34 percent) of those responding said the workshop helped them because it provided units and materials that were "ready to go." One teacher said the workshop was, "Well-organized and provided complete materials and lessons." These responses probably reflect teachers' ongoing battle with the clock, their hesitance to design lessons for a disciplinary area in which they have little prior expertise, and, related to the shortage of time for lesson planning, a trend in education to mandate change without providing teachers with the curricular materials and lessons to do so effectively and efficiently.

The second most common reason teachers gave for appreciating the BHH workshops was offered by about one fourth (27 percent) of the respondents, who said they found helpful the ability to work with the mentors from the pilot school district. One teacher said, "The examples from the other district were wonderful! You could see and hear what worked." Several teachers mentioned their mentors by name and said it was great to have them there and to see their examples of student work.[20] In the 2005 workshop survey, the opportunity to work with their mentor teachers was the workshop benefit most frequently listed by teachers (41 percent of respondents). In answer to the original question, one teacher wrote, "[The mentor] was excellent help and a great resource. Full of many useful ideas, knowledgeable, easy to talk to, and offered excellent feedback."[21]

When teachers first began implementing the BHH units, they approached the endeavor from a variety of attitudes. Some eagerly embraced the challenge of engaging their children in history explorations. At the other end of the spectrum, a few teachers in each school viewed the enterprise with a deep skepticism. The majority of teachers fell somewhere between the two extremes, which meant the success of the project, would be at least partially determined by whether enthusiasts or skeptics would exert the greatest influence over their peers. I say *partially* determined because another variable, student learning, most greatly impacted the attitudes of both wait-and-see and skeptical teachers. Student learning ultimately gave most of the BHH teachers confidence in and commitments to teaching history.

Collaboration among teachers has been part of BHH since its inception. The mentoring dimension of the project did not formally begin until the second grant disseminated the program into new schools. During the implementation of the BHH curricular units in the pilot district, however, at least one teacher in each grade emerged as a leader or set an example of exemplary engagement for the rest of their team. As these lead teachers shared their lesson adaptations and student learning outcomes with other teachers, excitement about the instructional units rapidly developed. True collaboration! During the second grant, we formalized the sharing process by hiring pilot lead teachers to mentor new teachers in the project workshops. Each grade level team in BHH-2 was assigned a mentor teacher that had taught students in the same grade in the pilot project. Through this direct contact and support, we sought to replicate the positive peer influence that was critical to the pilot success. Mentoring turned out to be an effective way to both prepare teachers to teach their individual grade units, and to excite new teachers about the learning their students, too, could experience in history.

Five Processes BHH Teachers Use to Teach History

Preparing new teachers to teach the BHH units is a balancing act between building their confidence to try practices that were created either by the curriculum designers or veteran BHH teachers, and encouraging them to devise their own adaptations of the lessons. By describing a few of the ways in which teachers have adapted the five processes at the heart of the curriculum, we begin to understand the effects of helping teachers move beyond adoption of curriculum to adaptation.

The original BHH units prescribe trade book read-alouds to build student background knowledge in a historic topic. Accustomed to the growing emphasis on metacognition in literacy education, many teachers reflexively incorporate such strategies in their history read-alouds. As they make their way from page to page, they ask students to predict, make inferences, draw conclusions, form judgments, make connections between the text and themselves, between the text and other texts, and to articulate how the story makes them feel and how they think people in the story feel.[22] These activities engage students in organizing knowledge, in critical reading, in emotional empathy, and in constructing knowledge via the intersection of various sources and prior knowledge. All of these skills serve history learners well, but none are specific to history alone.[23] As a consequence, teachers were more adept at engaging children in history books than they might otherwise have been.

Adapting Literacy Practices

This overlap between teachers' knowledge of effective literacy practices and various strategies for actively reading history enhanced the BHH lesson implementations, and enhanced teachers' commitments to those lessons. One district recently made the decision to adopt BHH in all its elementary schools, partly as a consequence of the program's impact on student literacy achievement in the district's pilot school. Several teachers in that building chose to teach a mandatory literacy strategies unit in conjunction with the BHH lessons. In those classes, student proficiency on a related literacy assessment disproportionately increased, prompting administrators to seek a TAH grant to incorporate history in the other three elementary buildings in the district.[24] It is important to note that the improved student achievements in literacy in this instance didn't come when time was taken from the part of the school day designated for social studies. The improvements came when history instruction extended into portions of the school day set aside for literacy learning. For history education advocates, this suggests that making transparent the similarities between literacy and history learning strategies is not just a way to help teachers become more comfortable teaching a new subject, but is also a means to expand the amount of time children study history in the school day. For literacy education advocates, this suggests that student literacy may be enhanced by history study.

Primary Source Analysis

Primary source analysis presented a more history-specific challenge to teachers' assumptions about children's capabilities in the various grade levels. Like the reading strategies, however, the solution to engaging middle elementary age students in source analysis emerged from a metacognitive strategy with which almost every elementary teacher is familiar; the KWL chart. In the upper elementary grades, teachers used question guides modeled after those provided online by the National Archives and Records Administration.[25] The activity format for analysis of sources varied from teacher to teacher, but tended to incorporate a whole-class demonstration followed by student work in pairs or small groups. The student work seemed to be most successful when the children examined visual rather than written sources. It is difficult to find primary sources written on a reading level that elementary students may successfully comprehend. In addition, written sources, perhaps also as a function of reading comprehension barriers, don't seem to engender as significant an empathic response as do visual pictures of injustice, oppression, or suffering. For these reasons, teachers gravitated toward visual sources and in the upper elementary grades expressed quite a bit of frustration with using the prescribed written primary sources. The reading comprehension problem may be surmounted with better document choices and through strategic abridgment of sources. For now, we have skirted the issue by substituting visual sources whenever possible.

Chronological Thinking: Timeline Variations

Basic comprehension is not, however, the only challenge for children's use of sources. Putting varied sources together to generate understanding of the past is part and parcel of history as a discipline, but for children that sort of synthesis may be described with Sam Wineburg's phrase "unnatural acts."[26] How do students make, much less keep track of the connections between the Thirteenth and Fifteenth Amendments, Jim Crow laws and customs, poll taxes and literacy tests, forms of civil rights protest, and the 1965 Voting Rights Act? The original curriculum design prescribed the use of mind maps to help students make connections.[27] Mind maps do not, however, include a representation of chronological relationships. To fill this vacuum, a couple of BHH pilot teachers devised a strategy of their own. They utilized timelines to frame and sustain students' ongoing synthesis of varied sources. After their students explored a new secondary or primary source, they placed a representation of the children's learning on a class timeline. The representations were actual visual sources, student art, or student writing. As a visual representation of learning, the timelines provided both a review tool and a tool for contextualizing new knowledge. They helped students make chronological sense of information from varied sources, and understand how various events and figures influence one another.

Students' spontaneous use of the timelines provides evidence of the extent to which students take ownership of the lines. When analyzing documents or images in groups, students frequently read the class timeline to inform their inferences about when a source was created. The idea to do so is usually accompanied with an air of excitement. During classroom observations, I have frequently seen minor variations on this turn of events: Students working together to analyze a source will think of an event related to their source, such as the Fifteenth Amendment when they are examining a literacy test. "When was the Fifteenth Amendment?" they briefly ponder. Quickly, one of the children exclaims, "Let's look on the timeline!" and is affirmed by a rush of other group members leaping to their feet to join the mission. Other times, students have referenced their class timeline without having a specific event in mind; in this case they use it as a reminder of events that will help them contextualize a source.

The pilot teachers' timeline innovations quickly became a staple element of the BHH curriculum, and adaptations still continue to evolve. BHH teachers typically now hang a blank timeline in their rooms at the beginning of the school year, and students immediately begin construction. The topics that make their way onto the line are by no means limited to history, although the bulk of the additions typically come from the history explorations. Because wall space is an issue in almost every classroom, teachers have been creative in their timeline designs. Some hang a clothesline in a low-traffic area and students clip their timeline elements onto it. Others hang butcher paper lines in the hallways outside their rooms. In a couple of instances, this has led to multiple rooms building timelines together, which has motivated students to investigate the differences between the different classes' postings on the line. Those differences are a representation of the interpretive, constructed nature of historic knowledge; no two people perceive the same history sources exactly alike, and often two different people don't even explore the same sources.

In younger elementary classrooms, second grade and below, teachers have chosen to make smaller timelines that illustrate change over time in just one area, such as the evolution of farm implements or household appliances. In kindergarten classes, pilot teachers decided to have one student each school day draw a timeline on the board to illustrate their life to date. Subsequently, the students began drawing timelines on the board during indoor recess, and using their history vocabulary—artifacts, long ago, museum—as they pretended to teach one another. When new BHH teachers have heard about these classroom experiences from their mentors, they have lost their skepticism about introducing history concepts to young children. Consequently, when they teach the BHH units, their own kindergarteners begin to draw timelines and to talk about artifacts and life long ago.

Second grade teachers devised vertical timeline charts. Each chart consists of two columns. In one, children place images of farming, mining, and logging long ago. In the other column, they place images of the same processes today. The tangible content of these charts—material things and endeavors and how they have changed—seems to help children grasp the meaning of change over time in a way that more complex narratives do not. Expanding this idea, some teachers have guided their classes to construct wall-sized cause-and-effect posters on environmental issues. On the poster, children glue images of the pollution aftermath of factories, forest clear-cuts, and mines. Clustered with the images, the children place images of people and legislation that grappled with the hazards pictured.

Smaller timelines on discrete topics caught on in older classes as well, with third grade students constructing posters to depict related events within a unit of study. During a third grade classroom visit in 2004, I saw a student reference one such timeline to dramatic and inspiring effect. The incident came near the conclusion of the class's six-week study of systematic discrimination against African

Americans. During part of the unit, the students had explored voting rights, and constructed a supplemental timeline, in addition to the large class line, that included the Fifteenth Amendment, poll taxes and literacy tests, and the 1965 Voting Rights Act. On the day I visited, the teacher wanted her students to think about discrimination close to home. With the children gathered in a semicircle, sitting cross-legged and facing her, she began, "I saw some students discriminating on the playground today." The students raised a chorus of "Oh, no! It wasn't our class!" When their teacher assured them it was their class, a couple of the girls cried out, "It was the boys! They wouldn't let us play basketball." Indignant, the boys bounced to their knees and protested, "We said they could play with us!" Interrupting the ensuing outcry, one girl leaped to her feet, pointed to the voting restrictions and rights timeline that hung on one of the classroom walls, and exclaimed, "It's just like the voting thing! They say we can play but they won't throw us the ball!" The instantaneous silence in the room suggested the other children understood the analogy, and understood its application to the situation at hand. The class discussion shifted gently into a consideration of how the playground injustice could be remedied.

It's important to recognize the role the timeline played in the anecdote I described. It did not help the young girl that gestured toward it draw a rather sophisticated analogy between racist voter discrimination and playground gender discrimination. It simply served as a reminder of what she had studied; it helped her concretely recognize how some elements of history—the Fifteenth Amendment, voting restrictions, and civil rights legislation—fit together into a story of White people telling Black people they could vote, but then not allowing that to happen. The knowledge itself, represented on the timeline, took several weeks to accrue. It emerged from reading trade books, studying written and visual documents, researching questions that spontaneously arose in class such as "If the Fifteenth Amendment gave African American men the right to vote, what about women?" and writing narrative accounts based on information gleaned from all of those sources.

Geographical Thinking: Getting Creative with Maps

As timelines help students understand and remember chronological relationships between events, maps help students understand geographical relationships between and among events and their places of occurrence. In our program, both components are used more often as visual representations or organizers than as initial sources of information. While maps created in various time periods may be used as primary sources, we did not incorporate historic maps in the lessons. Instead, we centered on mapping as a tool to help students understand relationships between place and event. As is the case with all the BHH processes, we hope that early mapping experiences will prepare students to eventually develop the maturity and skills to more fully examine maps as primary source documents.

From the beginning of their participation in the program, every BHH teacher receives an enormous laminated U.S map that includes state boundaries but no lettering. Given this resource, teachers have designed exponentially more creative, inspiring ways to incorporate maps than was prescribed in the curriculum. These teacher adaptations, like all the others, have been shared during subsequent workshops and almost universally adopted by other teachers. The second and third grade classes' year-long construction of a map is similar to the ongoing construction of timelines. In their environmental history unit, second grade students create three-dimensional relief maps that illustrate major biomes and topography around the United States, natural resources that occur in various regions, and finished products made from the resources. In a subsequent teacher-designed Native American unit, students locate tribes and add indigenous forms of housing to the map. As a piece de resistance, the children create keys explaining the symbols they have used for illustration. During their units, third grade classes map Louis and Clark's expedition route, the Union Pacific transcontinental railroad, the Chicago stockyards, steel mills and textile mills, and Confederate and Union states.

Assessing Student Learning: Historical Narratives and Source Analysis

As teachers dove into adapting and teaching the BHH units, they were rewarded by their students' engagement and by the substance and importance of the topics their students' understood. Many teachers' recognition of their students' learning was enhanced by the pre- and posttesting they adopted after exposure to an elementary social studies faculty leader in some of the workshops, and to the project's formal evaluation methods. In a number of classes, these assessments became at least part of the synthesis process that engaged students in putting together the various facets of a topic they had studied. The tests took two forms. One asked students to demonstrate their grasp of historic concepts and chronologies. These narrative tests consisted of terms and phrases related to particular BHH units. Students would use the terms and phrases to write a historic narrative. The other format required children to use prior knowledge, inference, and historical analysis skills to answer basic who, what, when, and where questions about photographs and documents. The "why" question in this process skill format asked students to consider why a particular source was produced or created.

The teachers' use of pre- and posttests evolved during the second grant. The difference in the pre- and posttest results provides strong positive reinforcement for teachers, concrete evidence of student growth from point A to point B. Because tests *are* so powerful, and have the potential to be either a positive or a negative influence on the instructional process for teachers, the forms they take must be carefully considered. The two assessments represent different elements of a chicken and egg issue that haunts history instruction; how do students construct an understanding of history they may use to construct and deconstruct subsequent understandings or narratives, without developing an assumption that the original narrative pieces they study are *the* history of a topic. The narrative terms assessment engages students in expressing their understanding of a particular topical narrative; it allows students on their own to put together and represent the pieces they have studied, and allows teachers to see if and how their students can do this. The drawback is that students may consider their narrative understanding of a topic *the* history of that topic.

The source analysis assessment allows students to use their knowledge to form inferences about a historic image or document. By its nature, such an activity conveys the interpretive nature of history, but without a narrative understanding of the sort that allows them to write a history using specified terms, students almost certainly can't accurately form inferences. It is interesting to consider that if a teacher carefully chose several image and documentary sources, she or he could probably determine a student's grasp of historic narrative components. On the other hand, a student's ability to write a narrative about related topical terms does not tell us whether that student could successfully make inferences from various types of sources. Nevertheless, a number of BHH teachers administer the narrative terms test only. This doesn't mean the teachers neglect to introduce their students to various sources, or to engage their students in constructing knowledge. It does, however, suggest that as teachers adopt an evidence-based, interpretive paradigm of history they do so on a continuum. And they do so in a job that is increasingly driven by mastery learning types of student assessment. In this context, an assessment that centers on transferable skills seems to be intrinsically less valued than one that centers on concrete accretion of detailed knowledge, which is more closely aligned with the narrative test format.

Bringing History to Scale: Evaluating Our Success

This conundrum brings us back to the elephant in the living room—to the reality of bridging the gap between research and practice by bringing constructivist history into elementary classrooms.

The Constructed Nature of History

By exposing teachers to the constructed nature of history and asking them to increase their knowledge of certain historic topics, by encouraging them to use their hard-won expertise teaching elementary grade children to adapt history activities for their students, and by creating workshop space for teachers to share their innovations and student outcomes, our program sought to bring history to scale in the earliest grades. In the process, we negotiated the sometimes painful compromise between quality and quantity that lurks perpetually in the wings of public education.

Teachers have intimate acquaintance with this compromise. Most suffer its effects every day, in the form of time constraints, curricular constraints, class size constraints, budget constraints, and constraints imposed by the limitations of their individual expertise and knowledge. In designing the BHH instructional units, workshops, and expectations for implementation, we were committed to meet teachers squarely in the real milieu in which they must teach. We were also committed to introducing history to children as a constructed understanding of the past, as an endeavor that consists of various and varied sources of information. In order to confirm what we were seeing internally the BHH external evaluation team gathered extensive information to determine whether those commitments were successfully met.

In focus groups and surveys, teachers were asked whether they were able to implement the BHH units to the extent they had hoped. While 46 percent of the respondents said yes, 54 percent said they had not implemented the curriculum to the extent they had hoped. Time constraints were the culprit for 44 percent of these negative respondents. External curricular constraints affected another 26 percent of the negative respondents in the form of requirements to spend more time on content areas other than history, NCLB, or assessments. Eleven percent of negative respondents cited not enough prep time or unfamiliarity with the lessons or topic to be taught, and another 10 percent cited unit-specific reasons such as the BHH lessons were too difficult for the children.

Time Constraints to Success

Because a majority of teachers in BHH schools indicated they were not able to implement the curriculum to the extent they had hoped, or,it is hard to argue that we were successful in meeting the teachers squarely in their real world milieu. In considering whether or how to adjust or adapt the program to address the problems that led to abridged implementations, the specificity of reasons for abridgment comes into play. To solve the time constraint issue from our side alone by foreshortening the instructional units would involve a compromise that would affect the project commitment to teaching history in adequate depth to help students develop real understanding and ownership of topics and processes. In the case of the third grade industrialization unit and the fourth grade progressivism unit, however, the units incorporated economic elements that a majority of teachers found too difficult and abstract for their students. This problem overlapped with the reported prohibitive difficulty a few units posed for students, and encompassed a natural solution. In the third and fourth grades, by changing the units to emphasize more social history and fewer economic concepts, we have been able to reduce the implementation time. In other instances, some teachers have tackled the time shortage independently, by incorporating history activities into their daily reading time.

Preserving History Instruction in the Face of Curriculum Pressures

Curricular constraints on subjects that are not tested for NCLB are perhaps the same thing as time constraints, just under a different guise; it is perhaps a simple matter of perspective whether a subject takes too much time for its allotted slot in the school day, or is not allowed an adequate slot in the first place. Our response to this issue in new adopting districts has been to conduct workshop sessions in which teachers align BHH activities with literacy strategies. Teachers subsequently have begun on their own to make school day connections between history and metacognitive literacy strategies. An e-mail message from a third grade teacher whose team was in its third year of teaching BHH describes the teachers' reactions to a new literacy curriculum in their school:

> In fact, we are now a Reading First School because of a grant, so we are having to implement new reading strategies. One of the strategies is using Read Alouds focusing on nonfiction, so we are in the process of developing several nonfiction read aloud lessons that tie into the Industrialization unit. Our consultant from the AEA, in fact, encourages us to use content to drive our reading instruction! YEAH! So our 2 BHH units fit that bill VERY NICELY!!!!!!

The members of the fourth grade BHH teacher team at the same school identified alignments between history and another subject when faced with the demise of their BHH units by a new geography curriculum. The teachers preserved a substantial number of their history lessons by identifying the regions in which the topics occurred and teaching them as part of those regional geography units. They were, nonetheless, frustrated with the abbreviations the new curriculum forced upon their history explorations, and with the rapid curricular changes they were asked to make from year to year. This frustration is well-founded, given the ongoing tendency of schools to add more and more mastery learning requirements that center on rote student memorization of decontextualized names, places, and dates. The teachers did, however, find a creative means to continue teaching elements of the Great Depression and the Progressive Era.

In a more dramatic example of teacher efforts to preserve history in the face of curricular pressures, kindergarten through third grade teachers in the BHH pilot district simply refused to stop teaching the BHH units when the new principal hired for their school requested that the history time be spent on reading. The principal adhered to a philosophy that reading mechanics cannot be learned or practiced in the context of studying a particular topic. In solidarity with the teachers, parents advocated for the history units, and a school board member whose children were in the lower elementary grades strongly suggested BHH remain part of the curriculum. The parents and teachers were successful and the children in the district continue to study history in K-5.

Constructing Stories of the Past

In BHH, students effectively develop their understanding of this and various other essential topics such as the interrelationship of technological change, the economy, and labor; environmental use, degradation and protection; and human migrations and encounters. They accrue knowledge by studying books and documents that depict social, political, and economic relationships; images and stories that elicit empathic emotional responses; and maps that illustrate relationships between events and places. This exploration of a range of sources engages students in economics, psychology, sociology, geography, and political science. In fact, the construction of stories of the past—all of which directly or indirectly shaped the present moment—incorporates all the various disciplines categorized as social studies. For this reason, history, when it is approached as an interpretive, multisource activity, is a natural organizing framework for exploring the human condition, for exploring how the world reached the ever-changing present moment in time.

While this chapter is not the appropriate venue in which to address the divide between proponents of elementary history education versus proponents of elementary social studies education, it is perhaps a good place to assert that history education advocates are not all cut from the same cloth. Unfortunately, history education is too often characterized as the purview of advocates for the uncritical memorization of dates and proper nouns. And 1980s curricula that incorporated myth and folklore are still being cited as history proponents' ploys to expand language arts instruction at the expense of the social studies curriculum.[28] The tablum of possibilities for history education is much richer than these generalizations imply. Perhaps this goes unrecognized because of the gap between isolated examples and a critical mass of classrooms in which students study history by interpreting various sources. In a growing number of schools, BHH offers justification for a more nuanced characterization of elementary history education advocates, and provides evidence of student learning that supports using history to integrate the social studies disciplines.

Conclusion

By any definition, this chapter is not a complete inventory of the ways BHH has impacted teachers and children, or the ways that teachers and children have impacted the program. I have not described how extensively the information gathered by the project's external evaluation team affected the project's development on an ongoing basis. Nor have I discussed the interactions between the project, families and communities, or the impact of the project on preservice teacher education. It occurs to me that more than one elephant metaphor could lurk in this chapter; if the reader senses the enormous extent of the BHH project and the impossibility of adequately describing it in a few pages, she or he may feel kin with the blind man encountering the elephant.

In the course of these pages we have, however, perused several elements of the project that contributed to whatever measure of success it has achieved: collaborative professional development that made realistic demands on teachers' time; the inclusion of all regular classroom teachers in all grade levels of participating elementary schools; curricular resources that embodied a paradigm of history as interpretive and multisourced; an emphasis on teacher adaptation of lessons; an identification of and reliance on teacher mentors to encourage and share effective classroom practices; a search for cross-curricular alignments, particularly between history and metacognitive literacy strategies; and an emphasis on student assessment that allows teachers to both enhance and celebrate their students' learning.

Have the Bringing History Home TAH grant projects successfully herded an elephant from the living room of history education? Have they bridged the gap between what research tells us children can learn vs. what is being taught in elementary schools? Evidence suggests that in the K-5 schools of six Iowa districts, the elephant has left the building. It remains to be seen whether the herd that fills thousands of other schools in the country will eventually also disperse.

Notes

1. Excerpt from a 2007 e-mail sent by Karen Menz, a teacher participant in the 2003 to 2006 Bringing History Home TAH grant, to Elise Fillpot, the project director.
2. A sample of relevant studies includes M. T. Downey & L. Levstik, "Teaching and Learning History," in *Handbook of Research on Social Studies Teaching and Learning: A Project of the National Council for the Social Studies*, ed. J. P. Shaver, 400–410 (New York: Macmillan, 1991); L. Shulman, "Those Who Understand: Knowledge Growth in Teaching," *Educational Researcher* 15 (1986): 4–14.; E. Yeager & O. Davis, "Understanding the 'Knowing How' of History: Elementary Student Teachers' Thinking About Historical Texts," *Journal of Social Studies Research* 18 (1994): 2–9; S. Greene, "The Problems of Learning to Think Like an Historian: Writing History in the Culture of the Classroom," *Educational Psychologist* 29 (1994): 89–96; B. VanSledright, "The Teaching-Learning Interaction in American History: A Study of Two Teachers and Their Fifth Graders," *Journal of Social Studies Research* 19 (1995): 3–23; *Doing History: Investigating with Children in Elementary and Middle Schools*, K. Barton & L. Levistik, xi–xii (Mahwah, NJ: Lawrence Erlbaum, 1997); K. Barton & L. Levistik, *Teaching History for the Common Good* (Mahwah, NJ: Lawrence Erlbaum, 2004).
3. K. Barton, "Research on Students' Ideas about History," in *Handbook of Research in Social Studies Education*, ed. L. Levstik and C. Tyson (New York: Routledge, 2008).
4. B. VanSledright. *In Search of America's Past: Learning to Read History in Elementary School* (New York: Teachers College Press, 2002).
5. The BHH external evaluation reports include extensive descriptions of teacher and student experiences and student learning outcomes in the BHH projects. J. Kearney and others, *Evaluation of the Teaching American History Project: Bringing History Home*, vol. 2 (Iowa City: The University of Iowa Center for Evaluation and Assessment, 2007). http://www.education.uiowa.edu/cea/tah/documents/FINAL.12-20-07.pdf
6. S. van Hover, "The Professional Development of Social Studies Teachers," in *Handbook of Research in Social Studies Education*, ed. L. Levstik & C. Tyson, 352–372 (New York: Routledge, 2008).
7. K. Barton & L. Levstik, "Why Don't More History Teachers Engage Students in Investigation?" *Social Education* 67 (2003): 358–361.
8. S. Brown and J. Patrick, *History Education in the United States: A Survey of Teacher Certification and State-Based Standards and Assessments for Teachers and Students* (Washington, DC: The American Historical Association and the Organization of American Historians, 2004). http://www.historians.org/pubs/50statesurvey/
9. There are many articles, papers, blogs, and policy statements related to the CLB legislation's impact on the teaching of social studies. The following articles offer recent overviews of the issue: L. Levstik, "What Happens in Social Studies Classrooms? Research on K-12 Social Studies Practice," in *Handbook of Research in Social Studies Education*, ed. L. Levstik & C. Tyson, 50–62 (New York: Routledge, 2008); K. Manzo, "Analysis Finds Time Stolen From Other Subjects for Math, Reading," *Education Week* 27, no. 25 (2008): 6; J. Pace, "Why We Need to Save (and Strengthen) Social Studies," *Education Week* 27, no. 16 (2008): 26–27; A. Klein, "Survey: Subjects Trimmed to Boost Math and Reading," *Education Week* 26, no. 44 (2007): 7.
10. B. VanSledright, "Evaluation 101 for History Educators" (Paper presented at the annual meeting of the Project Directors for the Teaching American History Program, U.S. Department of Education, Pittsburgh, PA, April 2005).
11. J. Kearney and others, *Evaluation of the Teaching American History Project: Bringing History Home, vol. 2* (Iowa City: The University of Iowa Center for Evaluation and Assessment, 2007). http://www.education.uiowa.edu/cea/tah/documents/FINAL.12-20-07.pdf

12. Ibid.

13. Ibid.

14. *Building a History Curriculum: Guidelines for Teaching History in Schools.* Bradley Commission on History in Schools (Westlake, OH: National Council for History Education, 1995).

15. E. Fillpot, "Bringing History Home: A K-5 Curriculum Design." Paper accepted for publication in *The History Teacher* (2008).

16. J. Kearney and others, *Evaluation of the Teaching American History Project: Bringing History Home*, vol. 2 (Iowa City: The University of Iowa Center for Evaluation and Assessment, 2007). http://www.education.uiowa.edu/cea/tah/documents/FINAL.12-20-07.pdf

17. There are many uses of KWL. The acronym description included in this article is found on ESOL online: http://www.tki.org.nz/r/esol/esolonline/classroom/teach_strats/kwl_e.php

18. J. Alleman and J. Brophy, "History Is Alive: Teaching Young Children about Changes over Time," *Social Studies* 94, no. 3 (2003):107–10.

19. K. Steeves, "Building Successful Collaborations to Enhance History Teaching in Secondary Schools," American Historical Association (2006), http://www.historians.org/pubs/Free/steeves/preface.htm; T. Guskey, "The Characteristics of Effective Professional Development: A Synthesis of Lists" (Paper presented at the annual meeting of the American Educational Research Association, Chicago, 2003); A. McCall, "Supporting Exemplary Social Studies Teaching in Elementary Schools," *The Social Studies* 97, no. 4 (2006); S. Paavola et al., "Models of Innovative Knowledge Communities and Three Metaphors of Learning," *Review of Educational Research* 74, no. 4 (2004): 557–576.

20. J. Kearney and others, *Bringing History Home. vol. 2, Project: Year One Evaluation Report* (Iowa City: The University of Iowa Center for Evaluation and Assessment, 2004). http://www.education.uiowa.edu/cea/tah/documents/YearOneFinalReport-web.pdf

21. J. Kearney and others, *Bringing History Home, vol. 2, Project: Year Two Evaluation Report* (Iowa City: The University of Iowa Center for Evaluation and Assessment, 2005). http://www.education.uiowa.edu/cea/tah/documents/BringingHistoryHomeIIProject.reportFINAL.pdf

22. Two examples of literacy programs used in BHH districts are the Picture Word Induction Model (PWIM) and Creating Independence through Student-Owned Strategies (CRISS™). PWIM uses image analysis to engage children in vocabulary acquisition, inductive reasoning activities, and writing. While some researchers consider it a program best-suited to the needs of English Language Learners, BHH teachers in a PWIM school have aligned the model with history resources. Because BHH extensively utilizes analysis of historic images, this was a natural fit. For a description of the PWIM framework, see E. Calhoun, "Designing Multidimensional Reading and Writing Instruction," in *Teaching Reading and Writing With the Picture Word Inductive Model* (Alexandria, VA: The Association for Supervision and Curriculum Development, 1999). http://www.ascd.org/portal/site/ascd/template.chapter/menuitem.ccf6e1bf6046da7cdeb3ffdb62108a0c/?chapterMgmtId=6f95177a55f9ff00VgnVCM1000003d01a8c0RCRD. The CRISS project centers on metacognition strategies. Because it emphasizes the activation of prior knowledge, the program activities also naturally align with BHH. Project Criss Principles and Philosophy are described online at: http://www.projectcriss.org/prc/pages/general_info/principles.html

23. B. VanSledright. *In Search of America's Past: Learning to Read History in Elementary School* (New York: Teachers College Press, 2002).

24. The school district cited here requires every regular classroom student in grades K-5 to be assessed for literacy proficiency using a PWIM instrument. In the classrooms of teachers that chose to use for the assessment an image aligned with one of their grade level BHH topics, student proficiency levels were some of the highest ever recorded in the school. One teacher reported 100 percent of her students achieved proficiency in this way.

25. National Archives and Records Administration. *Teaching with Documents: Lesson Plans: Analysis Worksheets,* http://www.archives.gov/education/lessons/; *Bringing History Home. General resources: Analysis worksheets,* http://www.bringinghistoryhome.org/general_resources.htm

26. S. Wineburg, *Historical Thinking and Other Unnatural Acts: Charting the Future of Teaching the Past* (Philadelphia: Temple University Press, 2001).

27. J. D. Novak & D. B. Gowin, Learning How to Learn (New York: Cambridge University Press. 1996).

28. J. Brophy & A. Alleman, *Powerful Social Studies for Elementary Students*, 2nd ed. (Belmont, CA: Thomson & Wadsworth, 2007).

Emerging Practices for Professional Development

Introduction

Part III addresses emerging practices from the *Teaching American History* projects that may be of primary interest to teacher educators and others involved in professional development for teachers. Both those currently working in *Teaching American History* projects and those who work with preservice and in-service teachers of American history will benefit from the insights detailed here. Those involved with mentoring, preparing, and working in other professional development capacities with teachers will also find useful information in these chapters.

Overarching Themes

In examining the chapters included in this section, four overarching themes emerge from the work of these projects relevant to those involved with teacher professional development. These are: (1) the importance of collaborative partnerships; (2) the importance of prior planning and preparing before embarking on a professional development project; (3) the importance of integrating content and pedagogy to achieve the best result; and (4) the importance of having teachers engage in practical application of their knowledge to curriculum and instructional design in their classrooms.

Partnerships and collaboration are at the heart of the *Teaching American History* process, and many projects have stressed the importance of using both history and teacher education faculty together as neither on its own is as effective in making changes in teacher practice. Conditions for effective collaboration explored in many projects include key transformations in history professor beliefs, expanded professional networks with museums and other partners, and the importance of responding to teacher feedback and ongoing follow-up and communication among partners. Collaborative planning and teaching were also found to be effective tools for professional development including coteaching, teachers presenting to professors in a reversal of the usual role, and collaboration among teacher colleagues.

A second practice that emerged from many projects described in this section is the necessity of prior planning and preparedness. This included developing historians and museum staff as teachers of teachers through processes such as meta-teaching, using teachers' expertise on advisory boards, and preparing historians to mentor teachers. Another key element to preparedness is the identification of common project goals. This process can be made effective by starting with agreed upon guiding principles, setting up effective evaluation with logic models and embedded program theory, and determining appropriate ways to collect data.

Many TAH projects have stressed the effectiveness of providing professional development activities that include the intersection of content and pedagogy. These programs focus on both content-rich professional development and developing teachers' pedagogical content knowledge and familiarity with effective pedagogical principles. The mix of content and pedagogy, including using a museum as a setting to combine content and pedagogy, deepens engagement with history content.

Finally, it proved to be a strong practice for effective professional development to provide opportunities for teachers to engage in practical applications that included hands-on experience with history involving primary sources. Teachers found reading this material to be inspirational and made many connections to their classroom practices. In addition, classroom observation by project faculty to verify that ideas are put into practice in classrooms was a valuable addition to many programs.

Emerging Practices Chapter By Chapter

In chapter 9, Rachel Ragland, Assistant Professor of Education at Lake Forest College, examines five different TAH projects in Illinois to determine common elements of successful professional development. The overarching themes of all the chapters in this section emerged in this analysis and are described in the "4 Ps" framework: Partnerships, Planning and Preparedness, Pedagogical Content Knowledge, and Practical Applications. Comparisons examined among projects include: what project goals were met by each project; what professional development activities were most commonly used; what professional development activities did participants rate highest and lowest; what forms of collaboration were most and least commonly used; what barriers to collaboration were cited; and what successful classroom teaching practices emerged and were implemented.

As noted above, successful collaboration and partnerships were found to be key processes for successful TAH projects, and in chapter 10 Lake Forest College Professor of Education Dawn Abt-Perkins describes conditions for effective collaboration between professors of history and professors of education based on her involvement in the McRAH project. Recommended practices include careful choice of staff, advance preparation for history professors, sessions on learning about history and learning how to teach history, keeping a core of teachers and faculty over the life of the project, and using collaborative planning. The key practice for success was developing history professors as teachers of teachers through collaborative teaching, developing mentor/mentee relationships, and preparing history faculty to mentor, having historians visit secondary classrooms, "meta-teaching," doing history hands-on experiences together, and developing common pedagogical principles. All of these led to transformations in the beliefs of history professors. These included new realizations that teachers and history professors share some of the same instructional dilemmas; teachers need to teach students how to "think historically" and come to value this way of thinking as their goal for teaching history. History professors need to understand where teachers teach, whom they teach, and the materials they are using to teach so that they can make more grounded connections to their classrooms and their teaching contexts. Abt-Perkins's story also stresses the value of paying attention to unexpected outcomes.

Ann Marie Ryan, Assistant Professor of Education at Loyola University, Chicago, and Frank Valadez, Executive Director of the Chicago Metro History Education Center of the Chicago History Project share conclusions from their work in chapter 11. Emerging practices include recommendations on ways to collect data, the value of responding to teacher feedback and providing deep engagement with content which leads to increased content knowledge and different ways of thinking about history as a discipline. CHP participants incorporated the ideas they learned about having students analyze primary sources and made connections to their classroom practice. The "Historian's Chair" practice helped teachers take a scholarly approach to teaching as they presented to the group and received feedback from colleagues and faculty. This project also made good use of classroom observations to verify changes in practice and the importance of ongoing follow-up and support. Emphasis on collaboration between historians and teacher educators also proved successful as neither group on its own was as effective in making changes among teacher colleagues.

Museum education is the focus of the Chicago History Museum's Lynn McRainey and Heidi Moisan's discussion in chapter 12. The Chicago History Museum developed a model for building sustained relationships with partners, including teachers. The way the museum teaches history was changed by their participation in TAH projects, and they refined their approach to professional development by expanding their professional network, redesigning learning experiences, using the inspiration found in artifacts and the contextual environment of the museum, and listening to teachers as pedagogical experts on their Teacher Advisory Board. The museum setting itself proved key to developing successful practices for teachers that included behind the scenes tours, active involvement with teaching using materials in exhibit spaces, and developing activity stations to create a more experiential field trip experience for students.

Finally, in chapter 13 Julie Kearney, Emily Lai, and Don Yarbrough of the Center for Evaluation at the University of Iowa describe an important framework for investigating, documenting, and improving the quality of TAH projects through systematic high-quality evaluation based on their work with Iowa projects. Emerging practices discussed in this chapter concern the importance of good communication in planning and controlling and assuring the quality of programs. Considering the types of evaluation necessary and matching them to the project's goals is essential for successful assessment. These elements include formative and summative assessment, monitoring and tracking, instrumental or process improvement, accountability, investigating of merit or worth, knowledge generation, and impact measurement. Logic models, a graphic depiction of the inputs, activities, outputs, and outcomes are recommended and explained. In addition, program theory that describes in detail the concepts and mechanisms by which identified TAH needs are addressed by the project should be embedded in the logic model as a best practice.

Chapter 9

Teaching American History Projects in Illinois

A Comparative Analysis of Professional Development Models

Rachel G. Ragland

Lake Forest College

Introduction

I participate[d] to come into contact with resources and materials as well as like-minded teachers. Through networking, sharing ideas & resources, I get ideas to improve my teaching and renew my love for it.

I wanted to be more familiar with local historians and archival collections....

[I wanted to] build a deeper cooperative relationship with the teachers from my school.

My goal was to increase professional network[ing] on historical topics.

[I wanted to] interact with teachers across the state of Illinois.

My goal was to get my students more actively involved in my history class and have them excited about coming to class. I wanted to stir an interest in them as well as myself and put together an "arsenal" of resources and lesson plans to implement in the classroom.

[I have] learn[ed] ways to better impact my students and excite them in a study of history.

I made changes that allowed the students an opportunity to "do" history.

I feel so much more confident now, and my students enjoy social studies so much more.

Statements such as the above made by participants in the *Teaching American History* projects in Illinois from 2001 to 2005 are representative of participants' goals and experiences in projects across the country. Teachers have reported anecdotally that they enter these professional development experiences with goals to improve their teaching of American history and the learning and engagement of their students through collaboration with history education colleagues in both secondary and higher education settings. These goals are sometimes in line with the goals of the originating legislation, to improve teachers' content knowledge of traditional American history, while in some cases they go beyond this goal. Teachers report achievement of these goals to varying degrees of success. Rather than rely on purely anecdotal reports, the research described in this chapter was designed to document this anecdotal knowledge with an objective evidence-based analysis of participant experiences. By collecting data and comparing results from five different Teaching American History projects in Illinois, the research was designed to see if there are similarities in terms of what was successful in each project both in achieving the goals set by the project and in terms of the types of professional development activities and collaborations preferred by the participants to achieve these goals. The research was also designed to determine if a correlation exists in terms of achieved goals and the types of collaborative professional development activities used by the projects.

A comparative analysis of five different Teaching American History (TAH) professional development programs was conducted in order to discover similarities in various approaches to professional development for in-service teachers and what types of professional development activities were most successful in helping projects achieve their goals and implement best practices for history teaching. The projects were investigated with consideration for the impact of discipline-specific professional development on classroom practices with an emphasis on the collaborative relationships that characterize the design of all Teaching American History projects. By looking at a series of projects with both similarities and differences in specific goals and types of professional development activites, more valid generalizations can be made about what constitutes recommended professional development for history teachers.

The five projects compared are: (1) American History Teachers Collaborative (partners: Urbana School District No. 116, Urbana Free Library—home of the Champaign County Historical Archives—Champaign County Historical Museum, and Early American Museum); (2) Creating a Community of Scholars: Raising Student Achievement through Partnerships and Content-Rich Professional Development (partners: Evanston Township High School, Northwestern University, the Newberry Library, the Constitutional Rights Foundation Chicago, and the Minority Student Achievement Network); (3) Connecting with American History Project (partners: Chicago Public Schools District No. 299, Newberry Library, Chicago History Museum (former Chicago Historical Society), Chicago Metro History Education Center, Constitutional Rights Foundation Chicago, and DuSable Museum of African American History); (4) McRAH: Model Collaboration: Rethinking American History (partners: Waukegan School District No. 60, Lake Forest College, Chicago History Museum (formerly Chicago Historical Society); and (5) Professional Development School Network for Learning and Teaching American History (partners: Lincoln-Way High School District No. 210, Illinois State University, McLean County Museum of History). Each project was designed to meet the general requirements of the Teaching American History originating legislation of the first three rounds of the TAH grant program, yet each tailored its specific goals and activities to its specific participants and partners, as have most Teaching American History programs across the country—there is no one "best" national model that will address all projects' individual goals. By taking a look at the similarities and differences and what worked across these differences in project design, we can draw a broader and more complete picture of successful professional development for history teachers.

In this chapter, I draw on my experiences with a TAH project, along with the work of others, to propose a model of professional development for history teachers. Professional development for teachers is now recognized as a vital component of policies to enhance the quality of teaching and learning in our schools. Consequently, there is increased interest in research that identifies features of effective professional learning. Relatively little systematic research has been conducted on the effects of professional development on improvement in teaching or on student outcomes and more specifically on the effects of the TAH projects. As Bransford, Brown, and Cocking (1999) comment,

> Research studies are needed to determine the efficacy of various types of professional development activities including … in-service seminars, workshops, and summer institutes. Studies should include professional development activities that are extended over time and across broad teacher learning communities in order to identify the processes and mechanisms that contribute to the development of teachers' learning communities. (p. 240)

This research was designed to look at various features compared to the perceived success of projects as a whole in order to propose an evidence-based professional development model and add to the knowledge of the field of professional development in history education.

At the time this chapter was written, over $838 million had been allocated to the Teaching American History program and policymakers are increasingly asking for evidence about its effects on classroom practice. A wide variety of professional growth experiences can be effective if they are designed to incorporate research–based features and are aligned with the users' context and goals. In this type of investigation, it is important to note that there is a difference between research and evaluation. This study uses the results of evaluation to do research. I look at several levels of evaluation of professional development, as described by Guskey (2000). Evidence was gathered on level 1—participants' reactions; level 2—participants' learning; and level 4—participants' use of new knowledge and skills. This study also combines several phases of research, according to Borko, largely focusing on phase 3 in which very little research has been conducted. Phase 2 researchers study a single professional development program enacted by more than one facilitator at more than one site. The phase 3 research focus broadens to compare multiple professional development programs, each enacted at multiple sites. This research also studies the relationships among four elements of a professional development system: facilitator, professional development program, teachers as learners, and context (Borko, 2004, p. 4). Borko says the central goal of phase 3 research is to provide comparative information about the implementation, effects, and resource requirements of well-defined professional development programs (p. 11).

Background

In order to put the current research into context and help determine the appropriate questions to investigate, an examination of previous research in several areas is helpful. Areas to be considered begin with the research on best practices in professional development in general to provide a background on the types of professional development that projects have used to increase teacher content knowledge and teaching strategies. These would include discipline-specific professional development for history education, improvement of best practices in history teaching strategies and resources, and teacher pedagogical content knowledge. Professional collaboration will be examined, including the nature of collaboration between project faculty, historians, and participants and between participants and their teacher colleagues and a determination of what specific types of collaborative contacts are most successful. This brief review of the research in each of these areas will provide a context for the more detailed description of the measures used in and conclusions developed from the analysis of this study.

Impact of Professional Development

We have evidence that professional development can lead to improvements in instructional practices and student learning (Borko, 2004, p. 3). Guskey (2000) identifies four principles of effective professional development: a clear focus on learning and learners; an emphasis on individual and organizational change; small changes guided by a grand vision; ongoing professional development that is procedurally embedded, that is, woven into the fabric of every educator's professional life (pp. 336–338). These elements are present in *Teaching American History* projects to a greater or lesser extent.

Research rates professional development as "effective" when it leads to desirable changes in teaching practices. Core features of professional development activities that have significant positive effects on teachers' self-reported increases in knowledge and skills and changes in classroom practice are: a focus on improving and deepening teachers' content knowledge; opportunities for teachers to become actively engaged through "hands-on" work in a meaningful analysis of teaching and learning; and integration into the daily lives of the school and coherence with other learning activities, including follow-up with continued professional communication among participants. Opportunities for active learning can take a number of forms, including the opportunity to observe expert teachers and to be observed teaching, and to plan how new curriculum materials and new teaching methods will be used in the classroom (Garet, Porter, Desimone, Birman, & Yoon, 2001, p. 925).

Other studies indicate that to be effective, professional development must be: experiential, engaging teachers in concrete tasks of teaching; grounded in inquiry, reflection, and experimentation that are participant-driven; collaborative and interactional, involving a sharing of knowledge among educators; connected to and derived from teachers' work with their students; sustained, ongoing, and intensive, supported by modeling, coaching, and collective problem solving around specific problems of practice; and connected to other aspects of school change. Professional development activities should be designed to reduce teachers' isolation; encourage teachers to assume the role of learner; provide a rich, diverse menu of opportunities for teachers to learn; attach professional development opportunities to meaningful content and change efforts; establish an environment of professional safety and trust; provide problem solving opportunities for everyone involved to understand new visions of teaching and learning; enable restructuring of time, space, and scale within schools; and focus on learner-centered outcomes that place priority on learning how and why, rather than emphasizing memorization of facts and rote skills (Darling-Hammond & McLaughlin, 1996).

There are additional design principles of a successful model of professional development: that it is driven by an analysis of differences between goals and standards for student learning and student performance; involves teachers in the identification of their learning needs; is organized around collaborative problem solving; is continuous and ongoing, involving follow-up and support for further learning and includes support from sources external to the school; and provides opportunities to develop a theoretical understanding of the knowledge and skills to be learned. Earlier research had indicated that an effective strategy is to ask teachers to try out new practices and see the effects on their students, rather than trying to change attitudes first in the hope that this will lead to change in practice. Selecting or implementing a new set of curriculum materials can be a powerful form of professional development, partly because it has one of the key characteristics listed above; it is focused on the content that students need to know and teachers are given the time to research, practice, try out, and then reflect on the effectiveness of high-quality materials. Evidence suggests that helping teachers to prepare for their classroom practice yields results that are most directly translatable to practice (Garet et al., 2001; Guskey, 2000; Hawley & Valli, 1999; Steiner, 2002).

Penuel, Fishman, Yamaguchi, and Gallagher (2007) have found that the most common form of school-based teacher learning—the district in-service day—does not help the situation much. "The episodic and piecemeal nature of typical professional development dooms any attempt to sustain intellectual community. By their very structure, scattered in-service days are confined to technical and immediate issues" (p. 948). When traditional formats such as workshops and institutes are longer, they have better core features and are more effective. Longer activities, such as the three-year extent of the TAH projects, are more likely to provide an opportunity for in-depth discussion of content, student conceptions and misconceptions, and pedagogical strategies…activities that extend over time are more likely to allow teachers to try out new practices in the classroom and obtain feedback on their teaching (Garet et al., 2001, pp. 921–922).

In addition, there is broad consensus among teacher learning researchers that "reform oriented" professional development tends to be more effective than "traditional." "Reform" activities such as study groups, teacher networks, mentoring, coaching, and other collaborative endeavors are believed to have more success in changing teaching practice. Reform types of activities may be more responsive to how teachers learn and may be more responsive to teachers' needs and goals. There is a need for more in-depth engagement than is typically provided in the standard workshop given to teachers. Planning, enacting, and revising curricular units engages teachers more deeply with their teaching, so that they can come to understand more fully the principles of effective curriculum. Professional development that incorporates time for instructional planning, discussion, and consideration of underlying principles of curriculum may be more effective in supporting implementation of innovations. A professional development activity is also more likely to be effective in improving teachers' knowledge and skills if it forms a coherent part of a wider set of opportunities for teacher learning and development (Darling-Hammond & McLaughlin, 1996; Garet et al., 2001; Penuel et al., 2007).

Discipline-Specific Professional Development

A study by Medina, Pollard, Schneider, and Leonhardt (2000) reports that "subject matter professional development plays an important role in teacher preparation—one that isn't replicated anywhere else" (p. 18). Teachers in the University of California-Davis History and Cultures Project clearly transferred their experiences from the institutes into their history classrooms, where subsequently their students demonstrated improved use of primary sources and the ability to identify multiple perspectives in these sources (p. 19). The teachers' experience with professional development activities specific to history teaching proved to be an important element in improving their practice in the secondary history classroom. Bruce A. VanSledright (2004) indicates that "[k]nowing what expertise looks like gives history teachers some targets for what they might accomplish with their students (assuming they desire to move those students down the path towards greater expertise in historical thinking)" (p. 230). Garet et al. (2001) also noted that content-focused activities had a substantial positive effect on enhanced knowledge and skills, as reported by the teachers in their sample. Whitehurst (2002) found that participation in professional development that focused on academic content and curriculum was second only to a teachers' cognitive ability in leading to the success of a project.

To foster students' conceptual understanding, teachers must have rich and flexible knowledge of the subjects they teach. They must understand the central facts and concepts of the discipline, how these ideas are connected, and the processes used to establish new knowledge and determine the validity of claims (Borko, 2004). History engages students only when their teachers possess deep knowledge. Wineburg (2005) reinforces that history courses made up of all facts and no interpretation are guaranteed to put kids to sleep. "The notion of history as a constructed account of the past is central to examining the discipline because this construction is the process that historian, teacher, and student have in common" (Seixas, 1999, p. 330).

Conveying the fascinating nature of history to others requires considerable ability, knowledge, and effort. For history to be taught differently requires teachers and students to look at history in a new light. Preparation of history teachers to be able to understand and to perform this role, therefore, is critical (Bohan & Davis, 1998). There are two closely related aspects of "doing the discipline" of history. The first is the critical reading of texts, both primary sources and secondary accounts of the past. The second is the construction of historical accounts (Seixas, 1999):

Teachers … are probably not accustomed to the kind of debates that we [historians] get in the professional circles which is a complete breakdown of narrative, of any kind of construction of reality and truth … not only is there not a narrative of American history anymore, but even constructing a narrative is probably wrong. (p. 322)

Therefore, the primary goal of professional development needs to be the engagement of participants so that they will convey their excitement to their students. Participants should be given opportunities to learn how historians conduct research, and in particular, how they evaluate the reliability of sources.

Variables in Teacher Background/Preparation in History Content

Research by Wilson (2001) indicated that effective teachers thought of history as both fact and interpretation and strove to create educational opportunities that capture those aspects of historical knowledge. When teachers who possessed considerable subject matter knowledge taught, they represented the subject matter in ways to help students see the complexity of historical understanding. Nonhistory majors have been shown to have naive and narrow views of history. The research indicates that for nonhistory majors, history and its teaching was much more likely to be viewed as arcane, dusty, and dull. Teachers who saw history as "the facts" or who had little historical knowledge fell into age-old routines of uninspired history teaching. Wineburg (2005) indicates that among high school history teachers across the country, only 18% have majored (or even minored) in the subject they now teach (p. 1) and in some individual districts there may be an even lower percentage.

Best Practices in History Teaching/
Student Engagement in the History Classroom

Tied to the research on the importance of discipline-specific professional development in history and the importance of teachers having a strong background in historical content knowledge is the related importance of including best practices in history teaching as part of the design of professional development for history teachers. Best practices in history teaching engage students with both historical understandings and historical thinking skills in the history classroom. Knowledge is viewed as being actively constructed by the learner, which in turn calls for a shift away from a "transmission model of teaching toward one that is more complex and interactive" (Prawat & Floden, 1994, p. 37). In these model classes, students learn how historical accounts have multiple perspectives and their contributions are welcomed as part of a shared learning process. These tenets, nonetheless, do not suggest that history courses should minimize factual information and acknowledge only personal and relativistic interpretation. (Bohan & Davis, 1998).

Historical pedagogy means leading students through the processes of "doing history." As Seixas (1998, 1999) explains, without such activities there can be no critical historical knowledge at all. The teacher must arrange for students to work with historical sources and accounts while pursuing paths in constructing new knowledge. Thornton (2001) emphasizes the importance of choosing methods of instruction specific to the methods of history. Michael Simpson (2002) emphasizes that "[t]he use of primary sources is one of the best methods of interesting students in history because it places them directly in the role of historians" (p. 389). Constructing a lesson plan to help students understand the distinction between history (the constructed account of the past) and the past (everything that has happened) is key to best practice in history teaching.

In contrast, Bruce A. VanSledright (2004) states,

> In fact, studies suggest that these [typical history instruction] practices actually retard the development of historical thinking because they foster the naïve conception that the past and history are one and the same, fixed and stable forever, dropped out of the sky readymade, that the words in the textbooks and lectures map directly and without distortion onto the past.... [H]istorians know that there is a distinct difference between history (the product of their investigations) and the past (traces and artifacts that remain—historical data, if you will).... Historians ... occupy themselves with reading and digesting the residues of the past left behind by our ancestors. Much of this residue remains in the form of documents or sources. "Source work" then becomes a staple in the investigative lives of these experts. (p. 230)

Pedagogical Content Knowledge

Hertzberg (1988), Dewey (1916), and Shulman (1986, 1987) remind us that content separated from pedagogy is an incomplete metaphor for knowledge, and such a dichotomy can be particularly problematic. In a setting where historians and teachers come together for professional development, the discourse of content and pedagogy can construct a certain set of relations between historians and teachers, with historians as content specialists and teachers as specialists in pedagogy (Luke, 1995). The encounter can also act to reinforce a conception of history teaching as a technical problem, where historians supply the content and teachers work out the pedagogy. Hazel Hertzberg's (1988) historical explanation for the dualism is that "historians were cast in the role of content experts" (p. 36). The separation of "content" and "method" and the distance between historians and teachers were thus closely connected problems. Dewey explains that

> the subject matter, or content, thus becomes inert knowledge, while pedagogy becomes a matter of its "delivery". The idea that mind and the world of things and persons are two separate and independent realms ... carries with it the conclusion that method and subject matter of instruction are separate affairs. (1916, pp. 164–165)

Teachers' content knowledge has been found to be critical to their ability to convey historical knowledge and is, therefore, fundamental to student understanding. At the same time, substantial knowledge of historical events, persons, and places does not translate easily into wise pedagogical practice. The dichotomy of content and pedagogy was reinforced by the need to ascribe separate but equal fields of expertise to both historians and teachers. The search for a way to define teachers' expertise, balanced with the more recognized expertise of the historian, ended up in a separate realm of pedagogy (Seixas, 1999, p. 323). This is a part of reforming the understanding of teaching as an intellectual (rather than a technical) endeavor.

Lee Shulman (1987) has used the term *pedagogical content knowledge* to describe the intersection of content and pedagogy for the teaching practices in specific content areas. Participation in professional development that focuses on general pedagogy alone has not been shown to be related to student achievement. Similarly, activities that are content focused, but do not increase teachers' knowledge and skills, have a negative association with changes in teacher practice (Garet et al., 2001; Guskey, 2000). Professional development that focuses both on subject-matter content as well as on how students learn is an especially important element in changing teaching practice. For example, social studies teachers' ability to teach students the uses of primary sources should lie squarely in the center of their pedagogical content knowledge (Seixas, 1999, p. 311). These two aspects of teacher development—one that focuses teachers' attention on the improvement of student learning, the other focused on the teacher as a student of subject matter—do not always mix harmoniously. Two foci of teacher learning must be "brought into relation" in any successful attempt to create and sustain teacher intellectual community in the workplace. Teacher community must be equally concerned with student learning and with teacher learning. Tension often develops between professional development geared to learning new pedagogical practices and that devoted to deepening teachers' subject matter knowledge in the disciplines of instruction These two facets of professional development must both be respected in any successful attempt to create and sustain intellectual community in the workplace (Grossman, Wineburg, & Woolworth, 2001).

Wineburg and Wilson (2001) note that "an instructional representation emerges as the product of the teachers' comprehension of content and their understanding of the needs, motivations, and abilities of learners" (p. 170). The dimensions of pedagogical content knowledge include choices of topics of potential historical significance to students, knowledge of students' capacity for understanding difference, and selection of documents appropriate for students' levels of interest and understanding. Teachers' knowledge of their students (and historians' knowledge of the teachers in professional development institutes) are obviously crucial in dealing with these concerns (Seixas, 1999, p. 332).

Learning history through investigation is a most promising means of transcending the ubiquitous content/pedagogy dichotomy; it is in the doing of the discipline that content becomes pedagogy and vice versa. Teachers feel empowered when crafting historical interpretations and exercises grounded in historical sources that were appropriate for their students' lives. To teach history effectively requires good history content and historical research, knowing and using the best in learning research and pedagogical technique, and the practical application of both those bodies of knowledge in the classroom. Wineburg and Wilson (1991) found that historians and high school students considered text differently. The historians corroborated information, employed a sourcing heuristic, and contextualized documents more frequently than did the students. Additionally, the students accepted documents as literal bearers of factual information more commonly than did the historians.

Collaboration in Professional Development

Historians and Teachers

Donald Schwartz (2000) has observed that for teachers, collaboration with college or museum based historians served to rekindle the teachers' intellectual spark and academic fervor. Bruce A. VanSledright (2004) indicates that

> ... historians can serve as a benchmark in relationship to which we can understand what the less sophisticated historical thinkers do. However, we must not unfairly hold novices to the standards set by the experts. The academic developmental distance between novices and experts is a gap that history teachers—through history education—can strive to close. (p. 230)

The key to effective history teaching is an understanding of how historians think and evaluate evidence, and the best way to achieve this is to have teachers work directly in collaboration with historians.

Christenson, Johnston, and Norris (2001) point out:

> One positive aspect of collaboration ... is the value of learning from each other. Because teachers and professors do different things, they have different expertise. There is value in sharing what we know and in learning from our differences ... [it] opens doors to new ideas and teaching practices.... Teachers learn ways to be more articulate about their theories; professors learn more about the specific application of theories in particular contexts. Collaboration has the potential to create dynamic communities of practice as we share debate, collaborate and build better contexts for our students. (p. 7)

"Teachers' experiences in practicing historical inquiry were seen as contributing directly to their teaching practices, whose goals included students being able to engage in historical inquiry ... it provided a far more productive basis for historians' and teachers' collaboration than did a conception of expertise distributed along the lines of content and pedagogy" (Seixas, 1999, p. 319), "Doing the discipline" establishes a basis for teachers and professors to work together in a way which recognizes the expertise of historians, not as dispensers of fixed content, but as practitioners of a craft into which others are welcomed. The work of the visiting historians helped to contribute to an intellectual climate where historical research was valued, whether it was presented as a research paper or as materials for elementary or secondary school lessons (Seixas, 1999, p. 330). Successful professional development institutes paid attention to both content and strategy: "We have historians giving background, lectures, they [the teachers] take notes and then meet together, based on these strategies that I will present before the historians come in. We then fit those strategies in to the content, or the content into those strategies" (Seixas, 1999, p. 328).

By modeling the way teachers and historians should work as colleagues, a special chemistry can develop among the team and the teachers (Kiernan, 2002, p. 7). It was not found to be helpful when history lecturers failed to discuss their work in terms of how to impart that work to students. Promoting professionalism and collegiality is important to successful professional collaboration. Ribar (2002) describes a successful project in which "[w]e did not want to be 'outside experts' coming to tell the locals how everything should be done, so we were consciously there to 'talk together,' to share our ideas and listen to our participants" (p. 6). Zilversmit (1993) echoed that sentiment as a historian working with classroom teachers in a new way. "We need to talk *with* teachers: not to dictate to them" (p. 3).

Accordingly, the goals of the historian and the history teacher reasonably may differ in several important respects. Although an historian seeks new knowledge or new ways of understanding events, a history teacher seeks "to create new understanding in the minds of learners" (Wineburg & Wilson, 1991, p. 335). In fact, a historian examines documents to evaluate the type and credibility of evidence represented, but a history teacher reasonably must consider, as well, how useful, interesting, and readable such documents may be for students (Bohan & Davis, 1998). In addition, teachers face increasing pressure to meet a lengthy list of state standards that tend to emphasize breadth over depth often at the expense of historical thinking skills.

Another approach to increasing teachers' familiarity with historical thinking is the desirable coordination between the work of history professors and history teacher educators (Bohan & Davis, 1998). A tripartite team of three equals—a classroom teacher, a historian, and a learning specialist—who are all treated as history professionals can be a successful form of collaboration (Ribar, 2002, p. 7). Historians, teachers, and students are all involved in a roughly analogous process, and the expertise of the historian, properly understood, might help to develop that of the teacher, and in turn the student. This differs from the more traditional pattern in which "few professors in any of the arts or sciences ever seem to consider that they are teacher educators" (Griffin, cited in Thornton, 2005, p. 89). As Thornton (2005) points out, "this neglect of the needs of teachers can be compounded by lack of or ineffective communication between arts and sciences faculty and education school faculty" (p. 89). Not all historians can or care to articulate *how* they know, as opposed to *what* they know. Seixas (1999) found that historians needed (and generally received) preparation for their visits to the institutes, so that they would be ready to approach knowledge for teachers from this perspective (p. 333).

To make the assumption that teachers do not possess adequate content knowledge would offend many high school teachers (Grossman et al., 2001, p. 962). Ribar (2002) recommends: "tailor[ing] the agenda to meet what the participants themselves told us ahead of time were their needs and desires" (p.7). Too often teachers return to their schools refreshed after a summer seminar, only to have their enthusiasm blunted because they have no one with whom to share their new ideas. Many previous programs have faltered because they created only superficial relationships between school teachers and scholars, relationships that lasted only for the duration of the short seminar or summer program. During the follow-up year, the participants (working with these college or museum based historians) are developing teaching units based on their own original research. Teachers appreciate time in the agenda to work on things that matter to them (Ribar, 2002, p. 7).

Teachers and Teachers

Teachers involved in professional development activities are overwhelmingly consistent in affirming that they needed to work with other teachers to discuss common needs, strengths, and challenges (Kiernan, 2002; Seixas, 1999). Face-to-face interaction, dialogue, and trust are necessary ingredients to building cohesion: "a group of people who are socially interdependent, who participate together in discussion and decision making, and who share certain practices that both define the community and are nurtured by it" (Bellah, as cited in Grossman et al., 2001, p. 946). Teachers speak loudly about the benefits and usefulness of providing opportunities for teachers to collaborate on a regular basis over an extended period of time. For teachers, having the opportunity to collaborate with their peers on a regular basis and in a meaningful manner was one of the most useful aspects of study group participation. These teachers reiterated that working with their peers helped them to reflect on their own teaching and build new pedagogical knowledge (Arbaugh, 2003, pp. 158–159). As Seymour Sarason recognized years ago, we cannot expect teachers to create a vigorous community of learners among students if they have no parallel community in which to flourish themselves (cited in Grossman et al., 2001, p. 993). Peer cohorts are another component of quality teacher induction programs. The usefulness of peer coaching (Glickman, 2002) and other forms of interaction have been documented and were judged to be effective by teachers, in that they create a community of learners among teachers.

Mentoring and Observation Feedback

Another element that has been found to be effective in professional development is the establishment of mentoring relationships that include classroom observations with feedback from mentors. A mentor is a teacher, advisor, sponsor, guide, coach, and confidante. By promoting observation and conversation about teaching, mentoring is believed to help teachers develop tools for reflection on and continuous improvement of teaching practice (McGlamery, Edick, & Fluckiger, 2005, p. 5). Investigations into mentoring indicate numerous benefits for the new teacher, as well as for the veteran teacher (Cochran-Smith, 1991; Feiman-Nemser, Parker, & Zeicher, 1993). One study found that 71% cited their mentor as the most useful part of the experience, whether or not the relationship lasted beyond the yearlong induction program. In addition, 16% found the peer support to be the most useful piece of the process for them. Five important aspects of the mentoring process are mentor preparation, reflective seminars on teaching practice, one-on-one coaching, trust between mentor and teacher, and having the mentor be a local professional who is already acculturated in the same schools/system. Acculturated mentors, including those who know the school culture because they have already taught in that setting, are better equipped to successfully coach teachers (McGlamery et al., 2005).

Part of the mentoring process involves nonevaluative supervision that consists of helping teachers improve instruction through giving feedback from classroom observations. Teachers need time together to observe and discuss each other's instruction. Some mentoring also involves the use of online collaboration in addition to face-to-face interaction. Many educators have found that online communication promotes professional development by breaking down barriers of time and distance (Zimpher & Grossman, 1992, p. 141).

Description of Study

An examination of the data collected from teacher participants in the projects surveyed yielded information that helped to answer the key question: What types of professional development activities were most successful in helping to achieve project goals and implement best practices for history teaching? Additionally, several more specific questions were examined to provide evidence-based support to answer the key question. These questions included: (1) According to participants, how successful were the projects in achieving their goals? (2) What variables within the participants affected the success of the projects in achieving their goals? How did the amount of undergraduate study of American history and the number of years of teaching experience that participants brought to the projects affect their opinions of the success of the projects in achieving their goals? (3) What professional development activities were preferred by participants? (4) What variables within the participants affected the professional development activities they preferred? How did the participants' amount of undergraduate study of American history and years teaching affect their opinions of the professional development activities they preferred? (5) What relationship exists between the projects' achievement of their goals and the professional development activities used to achieve these goals? (6) According to participants, what forms of collaboration were most successful? (7) What best practices in history teaching resulted from the projects?

Data Collection

Teachers surveyed were participants in the five previously identified *Teaching American History* projects in Illinois funded in the first three rounds of the program. Participants completed surveys distributed cooperatively by this researcher and the Project Directors of their individual programs. Surveys were distributed and returned either via e-mail, in person at project activities, or through the mail. The total number of participant surveys returned was 102. The number of participants in each project included in the data analysis is indicated on the data tables in this chapter.

The first stage of data collection took place in spring 2004 when participants

(N = 22) from the McRAH project (this researcher's own project) were surveyed at the conclusion of their grant's activities. The second stage of data collection took place in spring and summer 2005 when participants in the other four Illinois projects were surveyed (N = 80). The survey consisted of demographic background information and questions on: achieving project goals; collaboration with peers/fellow teachers, with faculty/college professors, and with non-TAH colleagues; and professional development activities experienced. The surveys for each project followed the same general format with parallel questions but the specific survey for each project was customized by the Project Directors to reflect the specific goals of each project and the specific types of collaboration and professional development activities included in each project.

Data Analysis

Quantitative analysis of the survey responses consisted of tallying response frequencies by rating for each listed item and rank ordering the items based on the tallies, as well as calculating percentages for each data field. Qualitative analysis of participants' reflective responses to open-ended questions consisted of organizing responses into categories that matched the data collection areas. Relevant data are reported in the tables below.

Comparisons examined include: what project goals were met by each project; what professional development activities were most commonly used; what professional development activities did participants rate highest; what professional development activities did participants rate lowest; what forms of collaboration were most commonly used; what forms of collaboration were least used; what barriers to collaboration were cited; and what best practices emerged and were implemented. Correlations between goals achieved and professional development activities used were analyzed for each project and for the combined projects. Correlations were examined between participants' years of undergraduate history study and the project goals achieved and the professional development activities preferred by those participants.

Results

Each project defined its own customized goals within the parameters of the overall goals of the *Teaching American History* grant program which are to improve the teaching and learning of American history and to ultimately raise student achievement by improving teachers' knowledge and understanding of and appreciation for traditional U.S. history.

What Common Goals Were Established For the Projects?

While the goals of each of the five projects were specific to their participants and partners, some common features emerged from an examination of all projects. The features can be categorized into the following common project goals:

- Using more engaging teaching strategies, including primary documents;
- Collaborating to support instructional change (museums/higher education/ colleagues);
- Improving teacher content knowledge of American history;
- Rethinking traditional American history courses/making historical connec- tions/thinking like a historian/improved historical literacy;
- Improving student engagement and achievement.

All projects had two goals in common: enabling the participants to collabo- rate to support instructional change and enabling the participants to use more engaging teaching strategies. Four of the five projects had two additional goals in common: rethinking traditional American history courses and improving teacher content knowledge. Only three projects listed improving student engage- ment and achievement as a goal. Although the use of engaging teaching strategies might imply more engaged students, these projects did not necessarily focus on student achievement as measured by standardized testing measures. It should be noted that these grants were funded before the invitational priority for collecting pre- and post data on student achievement was a part of project design.

Teacher comments added to the survey answers reinforced the importance of these goals for the individual teachers involved in the projects. Teachers com- mented that their goals for collaboration in joining the projects included: collabo- ration with other teachers and exploration of new ideas for lessons and resources; networking, sharing ideas and resources; getting ideas to improve teaching and renew teachers' love for it; wanting to meet other teachers of history interested in scholarly pursuits; and increase professional networking on historical topics. Teachers commented that their goals for the use of more engaging teaching strat- egies included: the ability to feel more confident so that students enjoy social studies much more; learn ways to excite students in the study of history; increase instructional strategies that can assist in the involvement of students and their investment in American history; improve teachers' ability to make history rel- evant and engaging; learn to be facilitators of learning rather than "dispensers of wisdom"; and help students take responsibility for their own learning and help them to think critically and historically.

How Successful Were the Projects in Achieving Their Goals?

Participant responses to the surveys expressed a range of opinions in terms of how successful they felt their projects were in achieving the goals that had been set. Survey respondents selected responses from a Likert-type scale with choices of either clearly met, met, somewhat met, or not met for each project goal listed. Table 9.1 indicates the percentage of teachers from each project who felt each particular goal was clearly met. Approximately 84% of teachers felt both the goals to improve teacher content knowledge in American history (the focus of the originating legislation) and rethink the traditional American history course/ make historical connections/think like a historian/improve historical literacy

Table 9.1 Achieving project goals (percentage of teachers indicating goal was clearly met)

Project goal	AHTC	CCS	CHP	McRAH	PDSN	TOTAL (average of all projects)
Using more engaging teaching strategies, including primary documents	54%	53%	74/47%	100%	100%	71.3%
Collaborations to support instructional change (museums/ higher ed/ colleagues)	96%	47%	58/42%	43%	56%	57%
Rethinking traditional courses/ making historical connections/ thinking like a historian/ improve historical literacy	100%	47%	N/A	100%	88%	83.8%
Improve teacher content knowledge	100%	53%	89%	N/A	94%	84%
Improve student engagement and achievement	N/A	6%	69/47%	N/A	69%	47.8%
TOTAL (average of all goals)	87.5%	41.2%	60.9%	81%	81.4%	

were clearly met. Of the four projects listing improved content knowledge, three of the four were rated by over 89% of teachers as clearly meeting this goal. Only one of the projects was rated by a lower percentage of teachers in achieving this goal (53%). Of the four projects that listed rethinking traditional courses, making historical connections, thinking like a historian, or improving historical literacy as a goal, three of the four had over 88% of respondents rating the goal as clearly met. Only one project was rated less successful in achieving this goal (47%). The same project was rated lowest in these two ratings.

A very positive picture of the achievement for the projects, both individually and as a whole, is revealed when responses were included from participants who felt goals were both clearly met and met (see Table 9.2). When clearly met and met ratings were combined, all goals received over an 84% success rating, except for improving student engagement and achievement, which was rated by only 41% of the respondents as successfully achieved. Some aspects of two of the overall goals for one project were rated lower that the higher overall rating for the goal. The Connecting with American History Project's (CHP) goal of increasing effective teaching strategies and development of school-based curricula was rated less successful than the related goal of strengthening teachers' use of new materials in the classroom, and the goal of establishing connections between American history teachers in various neighboring schools was rated less successful than

Table 9.2 Achieving project goals (percentage of teachers indicating goal was clearly or met)

Project Goal	AHTC	CCS	CHP	McRAH	PDSN
Using more engaging teaching strategies, including primary documents	95%	88%	95/79%	100%	100%
Collaborations to support instructional change (museums/ higher ed/ colleagues)	100%	100%	84/68%	86%	87%
Rethinking traditional courses/ making connections/ thinking like a historian/ historical literacy	100%	100%	N/A	100%	100%
Improve content knowledge	100%	94%	100%	N/A	100%
Improve student engagement and achievement	N/A	41%	95/89%	N/A	100%

the related goal of strengthening teachers' use of community resources in the classroom.

In terms of overall success in achieving project goals, three projects were rated highly effective, one was rated moderate on effectiveness, and one was rated low on effectiveness with less than half of participants rating overall goals as clearly met. AHTC, PDSN, and McRAH were all rated as over 81% successful in achieving their goals in total. CHP was rated overall at 60.9%, and CCS was rated least successful overall at 41.2% of respondents rating the goals as clearly met (see Table 9.1).

What variables within the participants' preparation, including the amount of their undergraduate study of American history and their years teaching, affected the success of the projects in achieving their goals?

Teachers varied greatly both among and between projects in terms of their previous study of American history at the undergraduate level and their years teaching. Participants were examined for the variables of whether their undergraduate major was history and the number of semester hours in American history that teachers reported. The responses from teachers who were history majors as undergraduates, and therefore presumably had more prior content knowledge, and their perception of goals achieved are shown in Table 9.3. In general, those projects rated most successful in meeting their goals had a lower percentage of history majors. The project rated most successful (87.5% of respondents rated project goals as clearly met) had the lowest percentage of history majors (24%). The project with the most history majors (CHP) was rated the fourth in overall achievement of goals.

In general, those projects most successful in meeting their goals had participants with the least number of undergraduate semester hours in American history (see Tables 9.4 & 9.5). Those projects with teachers with the most hours

Table 9.3 Relationship between goals achieved and undergraduate history majors (overall percentage of project goals clearly met and undergrad history majors)

	AHTC (87.5%)	CCS (41.2%)	CHP (60.9%)	McRAH (81%)	PDSN (81.4%)
Percentage of undergraduate history majors	24%	37%	63%	30%	44%

in American history were rated less successful in clearly meeting goals overall. The lowest rated projects, CCS and CHP, had respondents with the highest average of semester hours, 14 each. In the higher rated projects, AHTC, PDSN, and McRAH, the respondents averaged 12, 13, and 10 semester hours of American history respectively, While this pattern emerged, the differences in semester hours were minimal (10 to 14 on average.)

In terms of years teaching, no direct correlation was found. No significant range of average years of teaching was found among the projects (7.6–10.1). The project with the least experienced teachers (CHP) was rated moderately successful in achieving project goals. (See Tables 9.6 & 9.7.)

What Professional Development Activities Helped Projects Achieve Their Goals?

The most often used professional development activities were summer institutes, workshops, curriculum projects, and online collaboration (see Table 9.8). All

Table 9.4 Relationship between goals achieved and undergraduate semester hours in American History (overall percentage of project goals clearly met and undergrad semester hours of American history)

	AHTC (87.5%)	CCS (41.2%)	CHP (60.9%)	McRAH (81%)	PDSN (81.4%)
0 hrs	3%	0%	0%	0%	0%
<5 hrs	13%	6%	11%	15%	0%
5–8 hrs	27%	0%	5%	20%	0%
9–16 hrs	13%	23%	26%	40%	25%
>16 hrs	43%	59%	58%	25%	75%

Table 9.5 Relationship between goals achieved and average undergraduate semester hours of American History (overall percentage of project goals clearly met and average undergrad semester hours of history)

	AHTC (87.5%)	CCS (41.2%)	CHP (60.9%)	McRAH (81%)	PDSN (81.4%)
Average undergraduate semester hours of American history	12	14	14	10	13

Table 9.6 Relationship between goals achieved and years teaching (overall percentage of project goals clearly met and years teaching)

	AHTC (87.5%)	CCS (41.2%)	CHP (60.9%)	McRAH (81%)	PDSN (81.4%)
1–5 yrs	35%	29%	58%	54%	31%
6–10 yrs	24%	29%	16%	12%	19%
11–19 yrs	17%	29%	10%	19%	25%
20+ yrs	21%	12%	16%	15%	25%

Table 9.7 Relationship between goals achieved and average years teaching (overall percentage of project goals clearly met and average year teaching)

	AHTC (87.5%)	CCS (41.2%)	CHP (60.9%)	McRAH (81%)	PDSN (81.4%)
Average Years Teaching	10	10.1	7.6	9.5	9.9

five projects used summer institutes and school year workshops of some type—either after school, weekdays, or on Saturdays. All projects had participants who used online collaboration, even if the project itself didn't list this as a formal professional development activity provided by the project. Four of the five projects used curriculum projects—done in teams or individually. The activities least commonly used were peer observation, faculty mentor feedback on teacher work, and summer fellowships—used by one project each. Two projects used action research, classroom observations by faculty, and book discussion groups.

What Professional Development Activities Were Preferred by Participants?

Participants were asked to rate the professional development activities offered by the projects on a Likert type scale of very useful, useful, not very useful, and

Table 9.8 Relationship between goals achieved and PD activities offered (overall percentage of project goals clearly met and PD activities offered)

	AHTC (87.5%)	CCS (41.2%)	CHP (60.9%)	McRAH (81%)	PDSN (81.4%)
Summer institutes	Yes	Yes	Yes	Yes	Yes
Workshops	Sat/weekday	After school/Sat	Weekday	After school/ Sat	Sat/weekday
Online collaboration	Yes	Unofficial	Unofficial	Yes	Unofficial
Curriculum projects	Team/indiv	N/A	Team/indiv	Team/indiv	Team/indiv

Table 9.9 Relationship between goals achieved and PD activities preferred (overall percentage of project goals clearly met and PD rated very useful)

	AHTC (87.5%)	CCS (41.2%)	CHP (60.9%)	McRAH (81%)	PDSN (81.4%)	TOTAL (average of all projects)
Summer institutes	100%	41%	89%	36%	81%	69.4%
Workshops	88/33%	18/29%	48%	57/86%	65/75%	55.4%
Online collaboration	57%	6%	32%	43%	31%	33.8%
Curriculum projects	83/89%	N/A	26/53%	41/71%	44/37%	55.5%

not at all useful. The activity rated most useful was a summer institute, which 69.4% of respondents rated as very useful (see Table 9.9). School year workshops were rated very useful by 55.4% of respondents, and curriculum projects were rated very useful overall by 55.5% of those whose projects offered this activity. However, some variation was seen in the rating of curriculum projects of various types ranging from 89% rated very useful by AHTC participants to 26% rated as very useful by CHP participants. When ratings of very useful and useful are combined, summer institutes received an overall positive rating from 92% of participants and workshops received a positive rating from 81.4% of participants. Of the most often used professional development activities, online collaboration was rated lowest, with only an overall average of 33.8% of participants rating it as very useful, with a range from 6 to 57% from each project.

What variables within the participants' preparation, including the amount of their undergraduate study of American history and years teaching, affected the professional development activities participants preferred?

Participants were examined for the variables of whether their undergraduate major was history and the number of semester hours in American history that teachers reported (see Tables 9.10 & 9.11). Projects with the lowest percentage of history majors (AHTC and McRAH) rated online collaboration highest of all the projects. Projects with the lowest percentage of history majors gave highest ratings to the workshops and curriculum projects, except for AHTC which gave

Table 9.10 Relationship between undergraduate history majors and PD activities preferred (percentage of undergraduate history majors and PD rated very useful)

	AHTC (24%)	CCS (37%)	CHP (63%)	McRAH (30%)	PDSN (44%)
Summer institutes	100%	41%	89%	36%	81%
Workshops	88/33%	18/29%	48%	57/86%	65/75%
Online collaboration	57%	6%	32%	43%	31%
Curriculum projects	83/89%	N/A	26/53%	41/71%	44/37%

Table 9.11 Relationship between undergraduate semester hours of American History and PD activities preferred (average of undergraduate semester hours of American history and PD rated very useful)

	AHTC (12)	CCS (14)	CHP (14)	McRAH (10)	PDSN (13)
Summer institutes	100%	41%	89%	36%	81%
Workshops	88/33%	18/29%	48%	57/86%	65/75%
Online collaboration	57%	6%	32%	43%	31%
Curriculum projects	83/89%	N/A	26/53%	41/71%	44/37%

higher ratings to the summer institute, while projects with the highest percentage of history majors (CHP and PDSN) rated their summer institutes as the most useful form of professional development. In terms of participants' reported undergraduate semester hours of American history, AHTC and McRAH rated online collaboration highest of all the projects. Projects with lowest average semester hours in American history gave highest rating to the workshops and curriculum projects, except AHTC which gave high ratings to the summer institute. Projects with the highest average semester hours in American history (CHP and PDSM) rated their summer institutes as the most useful form of professional development. In terms of years teaching, no direct relationship was found between activities preferred by new and more experienced teachers (see Table 9.12).

What Relationship Exists Between the Projects' Achievement of Their Goals and the Professional Development Activities Used to Achieve these Goals?

Projects with Saturday workshops were rated higher in meeting goals, with the exception of the CCS project (see Table 9.9). Projects with team or individual curriculum projects were rated higher in meeting goals. CCS was rated lowest overall in meeting goals, and it was the project that did not offer a curriculum project as part of the professional development activities used. Projects using online collaboration were generally rated higher in meeting goals, even though participants didn't rate online collaboration as very useful compared to other professional development activities.

Table 9.12 Relationship between years teaching and PD activities preferred (average years teaching and PD rated very useful)

	AHTC (10)	CCS (10.1)	CHP (7.6)	McRAH (9.5)	PDSN (9.9)
Summer institutes	100%	41%	89%	36%	81%
Workshops	88/33%	18/29%	48%	57/86%	65/75%
Online collaboration	57%	6%	32%	43%	31%
Curriculum projects	83/89%	N/A	26/53%	41/71%	44/37%

Table 9.13 Collaboration with peers/fellow teachers (percent of participants reporting use of the collaboration strategy)

Collaboration strategy	AHTC	CCS	CHP	McRAH	PDSN	TOTAL (average of all projects)
Email about strategies	31%	37%	47%	50%	87%	50.4%
Email about content	17%	37%	26%	27%	44%	30.2%
Email about resources	55%	44%	63%	45%	81%	47.6%
Exchange resources	65%	69%	84%	54%	75%	69.4%
Co-teaching	14%	25%	42%	18%	25%	24.8%
Observing a colleague	7%	25%	32%	32%	25%	24.2%

What Forms of Collaboration Were Most Successful?

Participants' responses concerning the various forms of collaboration which characterize the design of all *Teaching American History* projects were gathered regarding collaboration with peers, faculty, professors, and museum and archive staff, and with nonproject teacher colleagues. First, in terms of collaboration with peers involved in the TAH project, exchanging resources with fellow teachers was rated highest by participants in every project (see Table 9.13). Exchanging resources via e-mail was the second highest rated. E-mail was shown to be used most to talk about strategies and resources, not history content. Coteaching and observing colleagues were least used, although a participant commented that "I wish [we were able to observe each other teaching]."

Second, in terms of collaboration with faculty, professors, and museum or archive staff, the participants were asked to report on the amount of contact, how the contact occurred, the results of the contact, how likely the contact was to continue, and any barriers to contact (see Table 9.14). The majority of participants in the highest rated projects rated the amount of contact with faculty as sufficient (50–60%), except for the McRAH project, in which only 23% rated their contact with faculty as sufficient. Participants in the lowest rated project (CCS) rated the amount of contact with faculty the lowest; 65% said they had none, and only 12% said it was sufficient. Participants in the medium rated project (CHP) rated their amount of contact as the most sufficient (74%).

Contact with faculty occurred overall most often by e-mail and was used most often in three of the projects (38–58%) (see Table 9.14). Teachers visiting the professor or the museum was reported most often by two projects—both those rated most successful in achieving its goals (AHTC) and least successful (CCS), with an overall reporting by 24.4% of participants. Faculty visiting the teachers' classroom was reported least frequent, ranging from 0% to 30%, with an average of 8.6% reporting its use. Contact with faculty most often resulted in an exchange of ideas (all five projects) and resource support, which was either second or tied for first. Discussion of instructional strategies was not reported by over 24% of participants in any project.

Table 9.14 Collaboration with faculty/professors/museum or archive staff (highest frequency response in italics)

Collaboration strategy	AHTC	CCS	CHP	McRAH	PDSN
Amount of contact	none 12% little 28% *sufficient 60%*	*none 65%* little 23% sufficient 12%	none 5% little 21% *sufficient 74%*	none 32% *little 45%* sufficient 23%	none 19% little 31% *sufficient 50%*
Contact occurred via	my class 3% email 28% *visiting the professor/ museum 59%*	my class 0% email 12% *visiting the professor 23%*	my class 30% *email 43%* visiting the professor/ museum 12%	my class 15% *email 38%* visiting the professor 12%	my class 5% *email 58%* visiting the professor 16%
Contact results	*exchange of ideas 34%* strategy ideas 24% *resource support 34%*	*exchange of ideas 20%* strategy ideas 10% resource support 15%	*exchange of ideas 32%* strategy ideas 21% resource support 29%	*exchange of ideas 33%* strategy ideas 11% resource support 22%	*exchange of ideas 38%* strategy ideas 8% *resource support 38%*
Likely to continue contact?	*yes 84%* no 4%	yes 29% no 0% *N/A 71%*	*yes 68%* no 21%	*yes 46%* no 27%	*yes 81%* no 13%
Barriers	commun 0% *scheduling 64%* N/A 28%	commun 10% scheduling 37% *N/A 42%*	commun 10% *scheduling 45%*	*commun 31% scheduling 31%*	commun 12% *scheduling 35%* N/A 35%

Third, none of the forms of collaboration suggested with non-TAH teacher colleagues were used by a majority of TAH participants, although sharing materials was used most often with 49.6% of participants reporting its use, and sharing strategies was reported by 45.6% (see Table 9.15). In all but one project (CCS) sharing materials was the most common form of collaboration between participants and their non-TAH colleagues, slightly higher than sharing strategies. Co-teaching was the least use form of collaboration. Only a little over a third

Table 9.15 Collaboration with non-TAH teacher colleagues (percentage of participants reporting participation in each collaboration activity)

Collaboration strategy	AHTC	CCS	CHP	McRAH	PDSN	TOTAL (average of all projects)
Shared strategies	44%	36%	52%	50%	46%	45.6%
Shared materials	51%	56%	41%	50%	50%	49.6%
Co-taught	12%	29%	26%	9%	13%	17.8%
Presented professional development sessions	36%	29%	37%	27%	63%	38.4%

Table 9.16 Additional individual collaboration activities resulting from TAH participation (overall percentage of project goals clearly met and PD additional activities)

Additional Professional Development Activity	AHTC (87.5%)	CCS (41.2%)	CHP (60.9%)	McRAH 81%)	PDSN (81.4%)
Attended conference/ workshop	86%	44%	53%	55%	81%
Applied for/received a grant	17%	0%	21%	18%	12%

Conferences/workshops attended: NCSS/ICSS, Local university/museum history conferences, OAH, IL Humanities Council, NCHE, History Alive

Grants: Summer fellowships, IL Humanities Workshop, Metro History Fair, Newberry, Gilder–Lehrman, Technology equipment, NEH

(38.4%) reported presenting professional development sessions, as compared to more information sharing, which was the most common form of participant collaboration with teachers not participating in the project. Participants were also surveyed about the nature of any additional individual collaboration activities in which they participated that resulted from their TAH participation. Higher numbers of participants extended their professional development activities by attending conferences and applying for grants in the projects rated higher at achieving their overall goals (see Table 9.16).

Finally, participants were asked to identify any barriers they experienced to collaboration within the projects (see Table 9.17). Scheduling was rated highest, with an average of 55.6% of participants rating it the biggest barrier to collaboration. Other barriers listed most often, in order of frequency mentioned, were lack of time, logistics/proximity/distance/geography, and school administration not providing adequate release time and/or money for substitute teachers.

Teacher comments added to the surveys indicated that individual teachers identified some specific barriers that need to be considered, including: not having a partner history teacher within a small school; scheduling difficulties and difficulties with communication between teachers that prevented peer observations; lack of time in general—"which is why [the TAH project] was so valuable"; and "it just doesn't occur to me to go outside of my building for support." All of these issues can be addressed with proper project design and implementation, such as the use of the recommendations discussed later in the chapter.

Table 9.17 Common barriers to collaboration

Barriers:	AHTC	CCS	CHP	McRAH	PDSN
Communication	0%	0%	35%	22%	8%
Scheduling	56%	76%	58%	34%	54%
Other	22%	6%	17%	10%	33%

Other: (listed in order of frequency mentioned) Time (lack of), Logistics/proximity/distance/geography, School administration/lack of release time/lack of money for subs, Differing curricula/lack of other history teacher in school, Faculty mentor not helpful, Not sure of protocol for method of contact, "Burned out" on professional development

What Best Practices in History Teaching Resulted from the Projects?

Participants were surveyed on the types of history teaching strategies and resources that they were now using as a result of participating in a TAH project. By performing a content analysis on the list, the strategies could be grouped in the following larger categories of instructional design most often used in history teaching: use of primary source documents/analysis (including art, photos, artifacts, and DBQ's); cooperative, small-group strategies (including hands on or "doing history" activities); use of graphic organizers and other conceptual organization tools; discussion techniques; use of technology; and miscellaneous strategies such as historical fiction, museums field trips, and oral history (see Figure 9.1). The strategy most mentioned was use of primary source documents, one of

---

Primary source documents/analysis (including art/photos/artifacts/DBQ's)
- Use of primary source documents (19)
- artifact analysis
- DBQ
- Use of art and photography

Cooperative, small group strategies (including hands on/"doing history")
- "Doing" history/perspective taking
- Historical simulations
- Role play exercise
- Debates
- Hands-on activities
- Jigsaw
- Think, pair, share strategies
- The "each one/teach one" strategy
- Using non-text and non-lecture approaches

Graphic Organizers and other conceptual organization tools
- Graphic organizers
- Historical head
- Interactive notebooks

Discussion techniques
- Civil conversations
- Socratic dialogue
- Questioning strategies

Technology
- PowerPoint

Miscellaneous
- Historical fiction
- Museums, field trips
- Oral history

Figure 9.1 Common best practices history teaching strategies

Technology (including CDs/DVDs/videos/websites/PowerPoint)
- Websites
- CD with music
- DVD's/videos
- PowerPoints

Primary sources/artifacts
- Original documents (inc. local census materials, cartoons, images)
- Artifacts, e.g. samples of quilt patterns
- Photos of local artifacts
- Maps

Analysis forms
- NARA analysis forms
- DBQ's
- Analysis forms

Figure 9. 2 Common best practices history teaching resources

the most important strategies for historians. The use of cooperative, small-group strategies, an effective strategy for bringing engagement with the content to the history classroom, was listed next most often.

A variety of types of teaching resources were listed by participants (see Figure 9.2). Again using content analysis of the data, the resources could be grouped into several larger categories. Primary sources were listed commonly as resources, just as the use of primary sources was listed most often under best practice strategies by participants. The list of analysis forms as a resource is also related to using primary sources effectively in the classroom.

Conclusions

Goals of the Projects

All identified projects had two goals in common: enabling the participants to collaborate to support instructional change and enabling the participants to use more engaging teaching strategies. The goal to achieve collaboration among project participants and staff is directly in line with the required project design of all *Teaching American History* projects in that the designated grantee, the local education agency, is required to partner with at least one of the following entities: an institution of higher education; a museum; a library; or other educational institution. Therefore, this goal is not an unexpected finding. However, the fact that all projects also had the goal of enabling participants to use more engaging teaching strategies is one that might not be expected based solely on the description of project design provided by the U.S. Department of Education's requirements for the TAH projects in the first three rounds of the program. The fact that all projects included goals relating to history pedagogy, as well as history content knowledge, indicates that grant designers recognized the importance of developing teachers' pedagogical content knowledge, as supported by the work discussed in the background sections of this chapter on pedagogical content knowledge.

Four of the five projects also listed rethinking the traditional American history course, making historical connections, thinking like a historian, and improved historical literacy as a major goal of the project. These elements also relate to the importance of teachers connecting pedagogy with content knowledge of history and improving historical thinking skills as well as historical content knowledge. The U.S. Department of Education (2005) report prepared by SRI indicated a similar list of historical methods addressed by TAH projects (p. xiii) and teacher gains in knowledge of historical facts but more limited ability to analyze and interpret historical data (p. xv).

Four of the five projects also specifically listed improving teacher content knowledge as a goal, whereas one might expect all projects to focus on this, given the project description and the stated underlying goal of the TAH grant project to improve teachers' content knowledge of American history as the way to ultimately improve student achievement. It should be noted that the emphasis on assessment and evaluation, including direct assessment of student learning, found in the legislation in later rounds of the program was not required in the project designs reported here, and consequently none of the projects focused on directly measuring student achievement gains as a result of the program. Project designers in Illinois, like others across the nation, seem to have recognized the need to combine the focus on content knowledge with a focus on pedagogy and make pedagogical content knowledge a focus of project design.

Success of Projects in Achieving Goals

Overall, the majority of participants rated their projects as successful in achieving the goals set. This was a similar finding to the preliminary U.S. Department of Education (2005) report, prepared by SRI, in which project directors and participants reported positively on the effectiveness and quality of TAH projects (p. xiv). Interestingly, participants as a group rated the projects as more successful in achieving the goals related to improving historical content knowledge and historical thinking skills, with approximately 84% of the teachers feeling both these goals were clearly met by their projects. When the clearly met and met responses were combined, respondents felt the projects were 100% successful in improving their historical thinking skills, and 98.5 % successful in improving their historical content knowledge. The U.S. Department of Education (2005) report indicated the "project directors reported a great deal of improvement in teachers' interest in teaching American history, as well as a substantial improvement in teachers' content knowledge" (p. 41).

However, the projects were rated slightly less successful in achieving the pedagogical goal of enabling use of more engaging teaching strategies, rated as clearly met and met by 92.8% of teachers and clearly met by 71% of teachers. This may be due to the participants, who were trained as teachers and had higher expectations in the area of pedagogy than in the area of history content, and therefore had higher standards for the pedagogy goals being met than the history goals. In addition, the lack of preparation in history content and historical thinking skills on the part of many teachers may mean that they had more room for improvement in content knowledge, and therefore felt more successful in moving toward this goal with any content knowledge and historical thinking skills they gained.

Also significantly, the goal of collaboration was rated as clearly met by only a slight majority of participants, 57%, although by combining ratings of met and clearly met the number of teachers who felt this goal was met rises to 87.5%, still lower than their satisfaction with other goal achievement. Again, perhaps the expectations were higher in this area based on previous experiences with professional development or working in collaborative teams within the school setting. It could also be due to the plans for collaboration being overly ambitious in the project designs, thereby resulting in projects that were not able to achieve the full collaboration intended in all areas. This will discussed more fully in the section to follow which focuses specifically on the results on collaboration.

Participant Variables and Goals Achievement

The project with the most history majors (63%) was rated fourth in overall achievement of goals, although it was rated as moderately successful in clearly meeting goals (60.9%) so it was not unsuccessful. Perhaps those teachers that had less background in history were able to gain more from the projects because they started at a point farther away from the goals, thereby seeing them as more clearly met. These teachers may feel that they got more from participation in the project. Similarly, the projects rated most successful in meeting their goals had participants with the least number of undergraduate semester hours in American history, and those projects with teachers with the most semester hours in American history were rated less successful in clearly meeting goals. While this pattern emerged, the difference in average semester hours is minimal (10–14 hours). By looking more specifically at the goal of improving content knowledge, those projects with teachers coming to the project with more preparation in American history, CCS and CHP, were rated lowest in achieving this goal, whereas those projects with less prepared teachers, AHTC and PDSN, were rated as successful in meeting the content knowledge improvement goal. While this trend is observable, the lack of significant difference in prior content knowledge as indicated by undergraduate preparation makes this finding a weak one.

The findings for average years of teaching and successful achievement of project goals do not show any significant correlation. The two projects with the most experienced teachers were rated both the most successful in achieving goals (AHTC) and the least successful (CCS). In examining the breakdown of years teaching in more detail, those projects with the lowest percentage of very experienced teachers (>20 years) were rated the lowest in clearly meeting project goals. This finding may mean that those teachers who came to the projects with a lot of teaching experience did not find the projects as helpful as did new teachers. It might be assumed that those teachers who were history majors were not only better prepared in content, but in doing history and using historical thinking skills.

However, this is true only if they learned history with an emphasis on historical thinking skills rather than on history as a collection of facts.

Professional Development Activities Offered

Summer institutes, workshops, curriculum projects (done by both individuals and teams), and online collaboration were the professional development activities used most often by the Illinois projects. Summer institutes were also the activity offered most frequently by the 2005 U.S. Department of Education report (p. 9), and the background research cited earlier in this chapter. A range of other activities were found in various projects including action research, classroom observations with feedback by faculty mentors and peers, book discussion groups, and summer fellowships. These "reform-type" activities are those most often used for professional development with teachers to improve both content and pedagogical knowledge and skills. The 2005 U.S. Department of Education report also indicated that the project activities displayed some, but not all, of the research-based characteristics of effective professional development. Classroom visits by faculty, follow-up activities, and workshops were generally lacking (p. xiii).

Professional Development Activities Preferred by Participants

Summer institutes were rated as the most useful type of professional development activity by the participants as a whole. While the institutes varied in length and content, they were found to be useful overall. Workshops were rated the second most useful activity, and they also varied by length and time offered, with some being weekday offerings and some offered on Saturdays. For projects that offered both Saturday and weekday workshops, the Saturday workshops were rated more useful by participants in four out of five projects. This may be due to the fact that holding the workshop on Saturday enabled the workshop to be longer in duration and thereby enabled facilitators to deal with topics in more depth or allow more time for hands-on practice experience with techniques and resources than after-school or during-school workshops.

The preference for summer institutes may be due to the increased time that was able to be devoted to the process in the summer, compared to the often brief time available during the school year on Saturdays or after school. In addition, teachers may be less distracted during the summer by the pressing responsibilities they also face during the school year, and thereby they are able to devote more time and energy to summer projects. However, this might be counterbalanced by the inability to immediately apply the new curriculum developed to a class they are teaching the next day or week. Instead, the implementation has to wait for the following semester. These factors may account for the variable preferences of teachers for different types of institutes and workshops.

While curriculum projects were rated very useful by the majority of teachers, there was a wide range of opinion, with some projects (AHTC) receiving very useful ratings by over 83% of participants, while the other projects received very useful rating by less than half of the participants. In terms of the nature of the curriculum projects, those that were done individually were generally rated as more useful than those that were done as a team. This may reflect the fact that by doing a curriculum project, such as creating lessons and unit to be used in the teacher's own classroom, the participants felt they were able to personalize and customize the curriculum created to better match their own individual needs for their students. Teachers want something practical they can take back and implement in their individual classrooms. Time is limited, and the teachers want to see concrete results from the time they spend and a definite change in their teaching as a result of their participant in TAH.

It is also worth noting that some of these professional development activities may have been combined in actual implementation of the projects, thereby causing the rating to be interrelated. For example, curriculum projects or book discussion groups may have been offered as part of summer institutes or workshops, and online collaboration may have been an extension or follow-up to either. As discussed previously, online collaboration/e-mail was not shown to create a community of practice the way in-person mentorship and partners did.

Participant Variables and Professional Development Activities Preferred

Projects with teachers that had less prior knowledge of American history, as measured by lower numbers of history majors and reported undergraduate semester hours in American history, generally rated online collaboration higher than those with teachers that had more prior content knowledge. The less prepared teachers also gave high ratings to workshops and curriculum projects, although this was not an exact correlation. The one project with the lowest number of well-prepared teachers rated their summer institute as the most useful. In terms of years of teaching, no direct connection emerged with activities preferred. This may indicate that the purpose or goal of the activity, as discussed above, seemed to be more important to the teachers than the type of activity undertaken.

Goals Achieved and Professional Development Activities Preferred

Projects in which participants engaged in curriculum development were rated highest in achieving goals. The use of curriculum projects may allow teachers to apply their new knowledge and skills, combine history content, pedagogy lessons, and pedagogical content knowledge in a real world application, while allowing teachers to receive feedback from history faculty and colleagues, and use collaboration among participants and faculty to achieve the best results. Projects that used online collaboration were generally rated higher in meeting goals, even though participants didn't rate online collaboration itself as very useful compared to other professional development activities structured into project designs. Teachers may have used online collaboration on their own to supplement established project activities, thereby using it to their own best advantage to continue important mentoring relationships.

Higher numbers of participants extended their professional development activities by attending conferences and applying for grants in the projects rated higher at achieving goals overall. These projects seemed to instill a desire for further professional development in their participants. The success of the activities in which they participated encouraged them to continue to pursue further professional development. The 2005 U.S. Department of Education report cited a lack of research on effective professional development for American history teachers which made the project directors' decisions about what professional development activities to offer and how to implement them somewhat subjective (p. xvi). This is why the evidence-based conclusions of this study are so important.

Best Practices in History Teaching

The strategy most mentioned by teachers as coming out of their participation in TAH projects was the use and analysis of primary source documents. This is an important finding because this is one of the most important and authentic strategies for historians. The use of cooperative, small-group strategies is an effective strategy for secondary classrooms, bringing engagement with the content to the history classroom. These two best practices resulting from participation in TAH indicate the dual focus of the projects on both historical content and thinking skills and pedagogical content knowledge for history. The 2005 U.S. Department of Education report indicated that "TAH participants had opportunities to employ many of the historical methods historians use" (p. 33), and these effective strategies were included. This is true even though, as mentioned previously, there are appropriate differences in the ways historians and teachers approach the use of primary sources, given that teachers have to identify ways to apply those to their classrooms, requiring different types of expertise. In addition, it should be noted that not all projects focused on curriculum development. Many instead focused on use of primary sources that could be integrated to support students' work. In some cases these elements were combined in a project's approach toward creating curriculum around analysis of primary documents, so that a project's reference to curriculum, primary source documents, and effective teaching strategies could be referring to similar best practices in history teaching.

Collaboration

No correlation was found between goals achieved and types of contact with project faculty. This could be the result of different designs of the projects and what they intended in terms of contact between faculty and teachers. While the most common result of contact with faculty members was the exchange of ideas, listed by all projects by between 20 and 38% of respondents, the most common result of the contact in general dealt with resources, which was rated first or second in each case. Exchange of resources with colleagues was rated highest, and two projects' participants also listed resource support as the most common result of contact with faculty. The least common result of collaboration with faculty was giving ideas for instructional strategies. This could be because the faculty members were largely historians, museum, library, or archive staff who are not considered pedagogy experts by the teachers.

In addition, the project in which continued contact was rated as least likely was also the project rated lowest in achieving its goals. This was the only project in which the majority of those answering this question said they would not be likely to continue contact with faculty members. This was also the only project in which the majority of respondents said they had no contact with faculty during the project activities. This could be a part of the project design which led to a less than successful project. A case study reported by the 2005 U.S. Department of Education indicated that a more successful project ensured open communication among all partners which helped the project provide "a more coherent professional development experience for participants" (p. 11).

Teachers' comments reinforced the importance of contact with colleagues to obtain practical help for specific classroom strategies and projects. Teachers in many projects have continued to use this important resource, even beyond the conclusion of the project. One college historian was contacted by a former participant teacher four years after the project to ask for assistance in finding appropriate books for a summer reading assignment for an AP U.S. history course he is teaching. The e-mail from the teacher to the history professor started with "I hope that you remember me, [TAH project] is something that stands out to me, and I just assume to all of those involved." The history professor was pleased to provide the teacher with a long list of suggested books and a series of framing questions to structure an essay about the summer reading, and e-mailed back that "It was very good hear from you. I am so very pleased that [TAH project] continues to affect your teaching of American history at [your] high school."

Teachers also indicated that their love of learning history was rekindled by their collaboration with the historians. Working closely together on a project as colleagues reinforced the special relationship between teachers of history at the K-12 level and teachers of history at the college level. "Doing the discipline of history" together established a basis for the teachers and professors to work together, value the process of constructing and then teaching history, recognize each others' expertise, and create products that were richer than either had previously produced alone. This was particularly true in cases where teachers had continuous and sustained contact with the historians rather than a one time exposure to a content lecture delivered by a visiting history professor.

Coteaching and observing colleagues were least used, followed closely by e-mailing about content information. However, a participant commented that that "I wish [we were able to observe each other teaching]." The barriers to collaboration cited by participants, such as time, scheduling, and logistics could account for the lack of collaborations of these types between colleagues. Classroom visits by professors were also infrequent. This could be due to the design of the project or a lack of interest or availability on the part of the historians. This lack of comfort with visiting K-12 classrooms is something that could be remedied through inclusion of this as a required part of the project's design. Perhaps this would be another opportunity for collaboration between historians and education faculty who are comfortable in classroom settings and could facilitate these visits. Participants also indicated a strong desire to continue contact with project faculty, except for the project where the majority of participants indicated they didn't have contact with faculty during the project.

Overall, none of the forms of collaboration were used by the majority of participants with their non-TAH participant colleagues. This finding could be because most of the American history teachers in a school or district were already involved with the project, thereby providing a dearth of colleagues with whom to collaborate. This could also be because opportunities for collaboration are not built into teacher's work life or are not a common practice in their professional life. Of those that did collaborate with non-TAH colleagues, sharing materials and strategies was the most common form of collaboration. All but one project listed sharing materials as most common, with a slightly higher occurrence of sharing materials and resources than strategies. This could be because it is easier to just give materials to a colleague than to explain or demonstrate a strategy. Only a little over a third of participants presented professional development sessions, but this could be a reference to formal sessions for a selected audience. This may not have included more informal sharing with colleagues which was the most common form of collaboration with teachers not participating in the projects.

Barriers to Collaboration

Not surprisingly, scheduling was listed as the most common barrier to collaboration. Time was listed second, and this appears to be another way of referring to scheduling which reinforces the idea that this is the most common barrier to collaboration. This is why Teaching American History projects are so important. They allow teachers to build in collaboration time and make it a priority in their teaching life.

Implications and Recommendations

My goal here is to tie together the research base presented and the results and conclusions obtained in this study to suggest several ways for improving professional development for history teachers. Based on this information, I propose a model for professional development in history education that is structured around 4 "Ps":

- Partnerships
- Preparedness and Planning
- Pedagogical Content Knowledge
- Practical Applications

Partnerships

Collaboration among educators, college or museum based historians, and K-12 classroom practitioners in all combinations is a key to the success of many TAH projects and therefore key to professional development in history education. In maximizing the effectiveness of these partnerships, it is important to be realistic about the expertise that each party brings to the partnership and what can be done with the time and resources available. It is important to realize the limits of time and scheduling as barriers to collaboration, and put into place a structured plan for collaboration among partners that will meet the needs of all parties. One recommendation to consider is to recognize the limits of electronic communication among partners. A well-designed professional development project should not rely on e-mail without building in a particular structure and purpose for it. It is also important to incorporate a planned structure for continued follow-up contact between teachers and faculty members, with enough time and administrative support to allow for effective implementation of the partnerships. Without this, partners are unlikely to maintain contact on their own. This will enable the mentoring relationship to support continued growth and development. This may be particularly important in situations where partners are separated by geographic distance.

Preparedness and Planning

The most important element to incorporate in order to prepare for successful history education professional development is to conduct a structured needs assessment before designing the project in order to determine participant goals and needs. As the 2005 U.S. Department of Education report indicated, between 45 and 61% of projects did this in a limited manner (p. 7). The needs assessment should determine the prior knowledge and preparation of the teachers with history content and skills, teaching experience, and personal goals and needs for the experience. It is then important to plan the professional development activity formats to match the goals and needs uncovered by the needs assessment. The preparation of the design should include using a variety of professional development activities because different formats meet the needs of the different participants and faculty. The design should also include extension activities that enable participants to attend conferences and apply for grants to continue to build on the new knowledge and skills developed within the structure of the project.

A second key element to incorporate into preparing for the implementation of a successful history education project is to prepare all partners for the process. This is particularly important for the historians who will be working, perhaps for the first time, with classroom teachers. It is important to select those that have comfort level in working in school settings. If the historians or other content providers do not have this experience, it is important to prepare them in a structured way to work with school teachers. This can be done through a workshop that presents necessary details of the profile of the participants with whom the historians will be working. The profile should include their level of prior preparation with content knowledge and skills, their identified goals and needs, the context of the schools in which the work, and any other necessary parameters that will impact the application of the professional development, such as state standards, high stakes testing requirements, or the nature of the school district in which the teachers work. Preparing the historians in this way is key to establishing a truly collaborative and useful partnership among all participants, including a useful mentoring relationships and sustained contact.

Pedagogical Content Knowledge

In order to achieve the goals of a well-designed history education professional development program, it is important to include activities that address both history content knowledge and best practices in history pedagogy. By structuring activities to reflect the intersection of these two concepts as pedagogical content knowledge (how to use knowledge to teach history specifically), a project will be more successful in achieving its goals to develop both content knowledge and teaching strategies, both of which are essential to improve history education for students at all levels. The history content should include both historical understandings and historical thinking skills. Making the content of the project discipline specific to history is also key to successful achievement of goals, as the planned activities should focus on best practice strategies of history teaching as determined by research from many sources, including TAH projects.

Practical Applications

Building in opportunities that enable teachers to complete a hands-on, practice application of the content and strategies learned during from project activities is an important element for classroom practitioners. This takes the theoretical ideas presented by historians and other faculty members and enables teachers to put these ideas into practice in the unique context of their individual classrooms and with their individual students, thus making it real working knowledge. Projects should include a well-structured element that helps teachers to create curriculum, such as lesson or unit plans that can be used in their individual classrooms. This can be done as an individual project or a team/group project, but the process should be mentored and supported through a collaboration of all partners each of whom brings a specific expertise to enrich the curriculum product and provide feedback to participants in both the creation and implement phases of curriculum development. This mentorship could also include master teachers if they can be included in the design of the project.

Recommendations for *Teaching American History* Projects

Future *Teaching American History* projects should look to research findings when designing their project structure and activities. Applying the history education "4Ps" recommendations above is a good starting point for that structure. In terms of partnerships, build in appropriate and clearly defined roles for each partner in terms of collaboration. Include follow-up activities for the partners, such as classroom observations with mentor feedback from peers, faculty, or both. In terms of preparedness, include training for those not already comfortable with working in school settings or the specific context of the district with which the project is partnering. In terms of pedagogical content knowledge, projects should include activities that build both history content and teaching strategies. Within the area of history content, both historical understandings and historical thinking skills should be included. In terms of practical applications, it is important to build in opportunities for teachers to apply new knowledge and skills to curriculum projects to be used in their own classrooms.

More specifically, it is important to use educators (both college professors and K-12 teachers) and historians with a good collaborative relationship. Each partner should be valued for the unique knowledge and skills he or she brings to the partnership. If partners do not come to the project with a strong prior relationship, opportunity to build this relationship should be built into the design of the project. Part of preparing the partners to work productively together is to conduct a comprehensive needs assessment before planning the details of the project. This way teacher variables and expressed needs can be accommodated. It is important to be aware of teachers' starting points both in content and pedagogy and to match the project's goals and activities with these needs and starting points. Not only is it key to create specify goals tied to participant needs, but it is important to clearly express these goals to all partners so that everyone is on the same page at the beginning of the project in terms of the goals to be achieved and how the project's activities will lead to this success. In addition, providing support for participants to extend their professional development experience beyond the duration of the grant project through conference attendance, grant application aid, and other elements will help to sustain the gains made by teachers during the project. Overall, it is important to include all these elements and examine their interrelationships in order to be successful in creating effective history education professional development that addresses the big picture.

Knowledge of the Field and Future Research

Research on history teacher education is an integral part of research on teacher education in general. This study adds to the field of research on teacher education and professional development by supporting previous findings with evidence-based conclusions and recommendations. The study demonstrates the importance of discipline-specific professional development, such as these *Teaching American History* projects which focus specifically on teaching of American history. The research also extends our knowledge of the importance of setting up good collaborative relationships for projects of this type. Structuring projects to include specific responsibilities for all partners, setting specific and clearly defined goals and activities is also key, as is building in specific follow-up contact and extension activities into the project design. This research has provided evidence-based substantiation for preliminary and anecdotal findings reported for the TAH program over the years of its existence. Future research in this area should certainly continue to explore these research questions with a larger number of TAH projects across the county beyond the state of Illinois, although the variety of projects in Illinois involved in this investigation reflects the general types of projects across the country as a whole.

Another promising area of future research involves applying the findings that derive from this model of in-service professional development to preservice preparation of history teacher candidates at the undergraduate level. This was recommended also by the 2005 U.S. Department of Education report (p. xvi) in order to provide a more comprehensive approach to the improvement of American history teaching and learning. The lack of prior knowledge of history content and pedagogy that was documented among the teachers in these projects has been seen in other studies of TAH participants. By providing better preparation of history teachers at the preservice stage, future K-12 classroom teachers of history will be better prepared to implement the research-supported best practices in history teaching.

A recommendation that emerges from this research is that future history teachers should be well prepared in history content by completing a full undergraduate history major program in addition to receiving full teacher preparation in pedagogy. This research-based model of professional development can be applied to the preservice level of teacher education. I have already begun to do this with the history education candidates that I teach at the undergraduate level. I have applied the McRAH strategies developed in my own TAH project as a framework for organizing my secondary social studies teaching methods course for future history teachers. The results have been promising, as the candidates now have a more unified and "big picture" view of history teaching strategies and curriculum design and have increased the use of these strategies in their own curriculum development both in lesson and unit plans done in the college classroom and during student teaching in the high school classroom.

Limitations

While the conclusions and implication from this study are important and worthy of implementation, there are, of course, limitations to this research. The limited sample size of the participants certainly provides a limitation to the strength of the conclusions that can be drawn. The voluntary nature of the TAH projects and their activities means that there is already a match between the programs offered and those who volunteer—a fact that raises questions about teachers who chose not to participate. In many cases, the teachers most in need of such an intellectually broadening experience are the least likely to volunteer to participate.

Summary

In conclusion, summer institutes, workshops, and curriculum projects were rated as the most useful activities in the *Teaching American History* projects that were rated as most successful. Curriculum projects were not used in the least successful program. Overall, projects were rated as successful in achieving projects goals, especially improving content knowledge and historical thinking skills and strategies. Those teachers with less prior preparation in history content and pedagogy rated projects as most successful in achieving their goals, but this was a small effect. Summer institutes were the most preferred form of professional development activity. Finally, the best practices in history teaching that emerged from the projects were the use of primary documents and primary document analysis and the use of small-group collaborative strategies for student engagement. The "4 Ps" model of professional development that has emerged from the comparative analysis of *Teaching American History* professional development projects provides a strong foundation for successful professional development with future history teachers.

References

Adler, S. A. (1991). The education of social studies teachers. In J. P. Shaver (Ed.), *Handbook of research on social studies teaching and learning* (pp. 210–221). New York: Macmillan.

Arbaugh, F. (2003). Study groups as a form of professional development for secondary mathematics teachers. *Journal of Mathematics Teacher Education, 6*(2), 139–163.

Bohan, C. H., & Davis, O. L., Jr. (1998). Historical construction: How social studies student teachers' historical thinking is reflected in their writing of history. *Theory and Research in Social Education, 26*(2), 173–197.

Borko, H. (2004). Professional development and teacher learning: Mapping the terrain. *Educational Researcher, 33*(8), 3–15.

Bransford, J. D., Brown, A. L., & Cocking, R. R. (Eds.). (1999). *How people learn: Brain, mind, experience, and school.* Washington, DC: National Academy Press.

Christenson, M., Johnston, M., & Norris, J. (2001). Teaching together: School/university collaboration to improve social studies education. *NCSS Bulletin, 98.*

Cochran-Smith, M. (1991). Learning to teach against the grain. *Harvard Education Review, 6*(10), 279–310.

Darling-Hammond, L., & McLaughlin, M. W. (1996). Policies that support professional development in an era of reform. In M. W. McLaughlin, Milbrey, & I. Oberman (Eds.), *Teacher learning: New policies, new practices* (pp. 202–218). New York: Teachers College Press.

Dewey, J. (1916). *Democracy and education.* New York: Macmillan.

Feinman-Nemser, S., Parker, M. B., & Zeicher, K. (1993). Are mentor teachers teacher educators? In D. McIntyre, H. Hagger, & M. Wilson (Eds.), *Mentoring: Perspectives on school-based teacher education* (pp. 147–165). Philadelphia: Kogan Page.

Garet, M. S., Porter, A. C., Desimone, L, Birman, B. F., & Yoon, K. S. (2001). What makes professional development effective? Results from a national sample of teachers. *American Educational Research Journal, 38*(4), 915–945.

Glickman, C. (2002). *Leadership for learning: How to help teachers succeed.* Alexandria, VA: Association for Supervision and Curriculum Development.

Grossman, P., Wineburg, S., & Woolworth, S. (2001, December). Toward a theory of teacher community. *Teachers College Record, 103*(6), 942–1012.

Guskey, T. R. (2000). *Evaluating professional development.* Thousand Oaks, CA: Corwin Press.

Hawley, W. D., & Valli, L. (1999). The essentials of effective professional development: a new consensus. In L. Darling-Hammond& Gary Sykes (Eds.), *Teaching as the learning profession: Handbook of policy and practice* (pp. 127–150). San Francisco: Jossey-Bass.

Hertzberg, H. (1988). Are method and content enemies? In B. R. Gifford (Ed.), *History in the schools: What shall we teach?* (pp. 13–40). New York: Macmillan.

Kiernan, H. G. (2002, September). Teachers as scholars: Professional development in the teaching history. *History Matters! 15*(1).

Kohlmeier, J. (2005). The impact of having 9th graders "do history." *The History Teacher, 38*(4), 499–524.

Luke, A. (1995). Text and discourse in education: An introduction to critical discourse analysis. In M. W. Apple (Ed.), *Review of research in education* (Vol. 21, pp. 3–48). Washington, DC: American Educational Research Association.

McGlamery, S., Edick, N., & Fluckiger, J. (2005, February 19-23). *The CADRE project: The role of mentoring in the development of beginning teachers.* Paper presented at the annual American Association of Colleges for Teacher Education meeting, Washington, DC.

Medina, K., Pollard, J., Schneider, D., &Leonhardt, C. (2000). *How do students understand the discipline of history as an outcome of teachers' professional development? Results of a 3-year Study: "Every Teacher an Historian."* (A Professional Development Research and Documentation Program). Los Angeles: Regents of the University of California.

Penuel, W. R., Fishman, B. J., Yamaguchi, R, & Gallagher, L. P. (2007). What makes professional development effective? Strategies that foster curriculum implementation. *American Educational Research Journal, 44*(4), 921–958.

Prawat, R. C., & Floden, R. E. (1994). Philosophical perspectives on constructivist views of learning. *Educational Psychologist, 29*(1), 37–49.

Ribar, J. P. (2002, January). The history colloquium: Continuing education for history teachers. *History Matters! 14*(5), 1–3.

Schwartz, D. (2000). Using history departments to train secondary social studies teachers: A challenge for the profession in the 21st century. *The History Teacher, 34*(1), 35–40.

Seixas, P. (1998). Student teachers thinking historically. *Theory and Research in Social Education, 26*(3), 310–341.

Seixas, P. (1999). Beyond "content" and "pedagogy": In search of a way to talk about history education. *Journal of Curriculum Studies, 31*(3), 317–337.

Shulman, L. S. (1986). Those who understand: A conception of teacher knowledge. *American Educator, 10*(1), 9–15, 43–44.

Shulman, L. S. (1987). Knowledge and teaching: Foundations of the new reform. *Harvard Education Review, 57,* 1–22.

Simpson, M. (2002, December). Editor's notebook. *Social Education, 66*(7), 389.

Steiner, L. (2002). *Designing effective professional development experiences: What do we know?* Naperville, IL: John Edward Porter Professional Development Center. North Central Regional Educational Laboratory with Association for Supervision and Curriculum Development.

Thornton, S. J. (2001). Subject specific teaching methods: History. In J. Brophy (Ed.), *Subject-specific instructional methods and activities* (pp. 291–314). Oxford, UK: Elsevier.

Thornton, S. J. (2005). *Teaching social studies that matters: Curriculum for active learning.* New York: Teachers College Press.

U.S. Department of Education, Office of Planning, Evaluation and Policy Development, Policy and Program Studies Service. (2005). *Evaluation of the teaching American history program.* Washington, DC: Author.

VanSledright, B. A. (2004, April). What does it mean to think historically…and how do you teach it? *Social Education, 68*(3), 230–233.

Whitehurst, G. (2002). *Research on teacher preparation and professional development.* Paper presented at White House Conference on Preparing Tomorrow's Teachers, Washington, DC.

Wilson, S. M. (2001). Research on history teaching. In V. Richardson (Ed.), *Handbook of research on teaching* (pp. 527–544). Washington, DC: American Educational Research Association.

Wineburg, S. (2001). *Historical thinking and other unnatural acts: Charting the future of teaching the past.* Philadelphia: Temple University Press.

Wineburg, S. (2005, February 24). A history of flawed teaching. *Los Angeles Times,* News/Opinion/Commentary section.

Wineburg, S., & Wilson, S. (1991). Subject-matter knowledge in the teaching of history. In J. Brophy (Ed.), *Advances in Research on Teaching* (Vol 2, pp. 305–347). Westport, CT: JAI Press.

Wineburg, S., & Wilson, S. (2001). Models of wisdom in the teaching of history. In S. Wineburg (Ed.), *Historical thinking and other unnatural acts: Charting the future of teaching the past* (pp. 155–172). Philadelphia: Temple University Press.

Zilversmit, A. (1993, January). Academic historians need new ways to work with schoolteachers. *The Chronicle of Higher Education, 39*(27), B3.

Zimpher, N. L., & Grossman, J. E. (1992). Collegial support by teacher mentors and peer consultants. In C. D. Glickman (Ed.), *Supervision in transition* (pp. 141–154). Alexandra, VA: Association for Supervision and Curriculum Development.

Chapter 10

Finding Common Ground

Conditions for Effective Collaboration Between Education and History Faculty in Teacher Professional Development

Dawn Abt-Perkins

Lake Forest College

> Initially, I saw myself as a content specialist who might give a few interesting presentations and pass along a few insights concerning historical inquiry. Now, I see myself more as a History Project Advisor and Teaching Mentor. (Henry Binford, Professor of History, Northwestern University)

Embedded in the title of the *Teaching American History* grant project for which I served as internal evaluator and as a member of the administrative planning team from 2001 to 2004— Model Collaboration: Rethinking American History (McRAH)—is the core concept of collaboration and creating a model for collaboration among historians, college professors of history, education faculty, and middle and high school teachers—http://learn.lakeforest.edu/mcrah. In this chapter, I describe our administrative team's efforts during the project planning stage and the adjustments we made throughout the three years of the project to build a collaborative teaching community with history professors and school teachers working alongside one another. As internal evaluator, I describe our collaborative model's evolution in three phrases where the conditions, roles, and expectations for collaboration developed over time to support the deepening commitment of professors of history to teaching teachers. As a teacher educator and staff participant, I share my insights about the instructional principles the college professors of history taught me that helped shape substantial changes in the feedback and direction I gave to teacher participants and have shaped my instruction of history teachers ever since. Conversely, I share insights from the history professors about what they learned from their collaboration with the teacher educators. While the focus of the project was on teacher change (Ragland, 2007a), we found equally interesting results in changes in the thinking and teaching practices of teacher educators and history professors. This was a surprising finding and one that should influence the development of future professional development projects.

From the beginning, McRAH's administrative team knew that collaboration between history professors and middle and high school teachers would be a challenge to accomplish. We had studied the literature on professional development that indicates that professional historians view themselves as the "knowledge givers" and teachers as the "knowledge receivers" (Hertzberg, 1988; Zilversmit,

1993). We also knew from studying previous research on professional development models that this type of framework did not result in substantive changes in practices of teachers. The research describes this as a "translation" problem (Seixas, 1999), that teachers find it too difficult to modify or draw from what they learn in a college lecture model of instruction from history professors to their active classrooms filled with junior high and high school students. We wanted to provide direct teacher support in the form of a site-based coach, a middle or high school teacher who could perform the role of "translator" of the concepts and ideas presented by the history faculty, as have other projects before ours (Berenson, 1993; Darling-Hammond, 1999; Sirotnik & Goodlad, 1988). But we wanted to go a step further and have the college professors work side-by-side with the teachers to influence their beliefs about the teaching of American history as well as adopt new practices directly modeled by project faculty (Ragland, 2007b). In other words, we wanted the history professors to take up the challenge of teacher instructional change. We believed this could be possible if we provided the right conditions or framework for this to happen. We did recognize, however, that there were substantive differences in the ways in which history professors and teachers conceived of and communicated their knowledge of teaching history. We were also cognizant of the power relationships embedded in the role of professor/teacher and middle and high school teacher/student that would work against collegial exchange of knowledge.

We believed that the structure of professional development experiences used in the past could reinforce these perceptions about who has valuable knowledge and what knowledge is considered to be of value, simply in how they were structured, the roles they expected participants to play, and the expectations they had for the work of participants. Through the design of effective evaluation methods and responsive design, we were able to successfully modify as necessary the collaborative structures and conditions we created to support the development of a more egalitarian relationship for the sharing of knowledge about teaching among history professors, teacher educators, and teachers. In the following, I describe the project's collaborative principles in three phases that correspond to the three years of the project. Each year, after careful examination of evaluation material that included interview data, classroom observation data, teaching project analysis, and survey feedback from the teachers, we redesigned the collaborative conditions of our work. While our main outcome goal was to improve middle and high school teachers' practices (cf. Ragland, 2007a, 2007b), we understood that our main tool for meeting that goal was to bring history professors into as close a relationship as possible with the school teachers so as to see how they were all "teachers-in-training." One surprising and unintended outcome from this set of collaborative conditions was that history professors improved their own teaching practices to better address an audience of school teachers; they also grew in their confidence as "teachers of teachers." In what follows, I share the evolution of the conditions for collaboration so as to provide a rationale for the development of each. In other words, we didn't replace our initial conditions; we refined and added to them as we learned from evaluation data collected from the participants. Data from interviews and surveys of the history professors are embedded into this discussion to show how their roles, perspectives, and practices were affected by the collaborative conditions.

Year One: Initial Conditions for Effective Collaboration

Choice of Staff

The goal of collaboration guided the selection of staff. Professors of history were selected not only for their expertise as historians but for their accomplishments as teachers. All of the professors were recognized as exemplary teachers by their institutions and colleagues. The teacher educators involved had experience in developing teacher/professor collaborations using needs assessment to guide instruction (Hall, Wallace, & Dossett, 1973) and using workshop models for professional development instruction (Abt-Perkins & Gomez, 1993). One of the historians on the team had worked with teacher development projects in many different contexts, including a "Doing History" project, a workshop model where teacher and professors worked on curriculum together (Zilversmit & Reed, 1993). Therefore, our initial design was based on our previous experiences and the values about professional collaboration and responsive instructional design embedded within those experiences.

Preparation for History Professors

Before the professors started to plan for their presentations to the teachers during the first summer institute, we made sure that they met each other and that the professors had school district demographic information and information about each participant, including educational background, career histories, subjects taught, and general goals for the project. Teacher educators discussed how the history and demographics of the students, schools, and the community could shape the choices the faculty made in materials and themes for the professor's presentations. We also discussed the key difference between teaching teachers and teaching college students—teachers will be learning from *how* you teach not just *what* you teach.

Professors felt they were already comfortable in the role of modeling good practices. They saw themselves as effective teachers of college-level students of history and thought they could rely on that experience to teach teachers. Our message that teaching teachers would require them to develop new practices and a different presentation style had little effect on how the professors planned for their teaching sessions that first summer institute. The message that they would be modeling for teachers didn't substantively influence their planning or teaching. The following comment by one professor sums up the perspective of the history professors as they entered the first summer institute, "As far as the teachers are concerned, they want and need good teaching models." Embedded in this perspective was reinforcement of the history professor as "expert teacher" and the school teacher as "apprentice." When professors reflected on the situation at the end of the first summer they saw that they needed to change. "There was a tension between treating the teachers as students or as colleagues."

Sessions on Learning about History and Learning about How to Teach History

In developing the first summer institute schedule, we included separate sessions on "content" of American history and sessions on the "teaching of" American history. While we unintentionally supported the dangerous and artificial separation of content and pedagogical knowledge (Shulman, 1986, 1987), we did do one thing that led to better collaboration in the second year—professors of history observed and helped facilitate the teaching sessions led by teacher educators just as teacher educators observed content sessions led by the professors of history. Besides sending the symbolic message to the participants that we respected each other's knowledge base enough to participate in each other's sessions, we also began to collaborate on ways to integrate our two knowledge bases in the ways we participated in each other's sessions. Professors were challenged by and enjoyed extending their role and knowledge base. "In giving my presentations, I learned from the teacher educators who were in the audience about my own teaching: goals, methods, and evaluations." "I learned to be conscious of what I'm doing, to reflect on my own practice as a teacher."

Longitudinal Design

The project began with a collaborative framework in the administrative team. The project directors believed in the importance of collaborative and responsive planning. The model required that we work with the same core group of teachers, teacher educators, history professors, and museum historians over a three-year period of time. While we added teachers in the second and third years, we kept a core group of teachers from the first year. Because the professors worked with this same group over time, their sense of responsibility to their progress—both in their understanding of history and in their understanding of history teaching—was more substantial. "I think a good deal of genuine collegiality could develop over the next several years." "I am very anxious to see how their projects work out in the classroom. I hope I can be a resource base, a sounding board, and a cheerleader for them." "I really feel that these teachers deserve our continued involvement and support."

Collaborative Planning

The administrative team, consisting of a professor of history, teacher educators, professional development experts, and the internal evaluator collaboratively planned all aspects of the project. Data from the internal evaluator and the site coordinator were used to make adjustments in the expectations placed upon the professors for their work in the following summer institutes and during the academic year.

Evaluation surveys from the first summer showed that teachers felt over-whelmed with the reading and learning expectations placed upon them. While they found the material interesting, they resented what they perceived as the pro-fessors "lecturing down" to them. They also wanted more time to discuss the material with the professors, but found that the professors were not available to them outside of their assigned lecture sessions. Despite our intention of having professors work with teachers, professors saw their role as dispensers of informa-tion and as resource bases for teachers. Teachers did not feel comfortable sharing confusion or teaching concerns with the professors and professors didn't see it as their responsibility to address teaching concerns. Wasn't that what the teacher educators were for? Teachers claimed that the professors had no real understand-ing of their instructional contexts and therefore could not teach them anything they could take into their classrooms. They thought it was important that profes-sors understood better where they taught and whom they taught. Despite our efforts to educate the professors about this before the institute, their teaching did not sufficiently reflect this.

Our observations of the professors showed that they were lecturing much as they did to their college students and had not modified their presentational style for this audience of teachers. Teachers were asked to take notes not only on the material but also on the teaching techniques modeled by the professors. We found teacher notebooks were empty of ideas to take back to their own teaching. While the professors thought they were actively modeling good practice, the teachers were not noticing what these good practices were. Data from our first year of class-room observations and interviews showed that teachers' practices were not chang-ing in any substantive ways, and teachers were unsure of what they were supposed to take away from their work with the professors back into their classrooms.

Year Two: Developing History Teachers as Teachers of Teachers

Collaborative Teaching—History and Teacher Educators

Historians cotaught with teacher educators in the practice workshop sessions. Teacher educators would present an instructional technique (fishbowl discus-sions or Web quests) or instructional concept (such as collaborative learning) and historians would provide the materials—primary documents and concep-tual framing. The teachers saw the historian and teacher educators as part of an instructional team. Content knowledge and pedagogical knowledge were equally valued and simultaneously taught. Our goal of developing pedagogical content knowledge (Shulman, 1987) was now enacted in our pedagogical approach.

Establishing Mentor/Mentee Relationships

As part of the second year, project faculty were assigned project participants as mentees to establish closer working relationships on particular classroom proj-ects. Initially professors were only interested in doing presentations at the summer institute, but after working with the teachers, they began to volunteer for more commitment. "I would be happy to be a mentor for those who are implementing their projects over the next year." "I do intend to visit several classrooms next year to see how the projects are going, and I would like to be present when my mentees are reporting back on their work."

Visits to Middle School and High School Classrooms

History professors visited classrooms of project participants. History professors were surprised that they had any meaningful feedback to give to teachers based on these visits, but teachers found what they had to say helpful indeed. Professors provided alternative resources to the textbook materials teachers were using. According to the teachers, they also made useful suggestions about key questions and organization of ideas for class discussion. More importantly, there was symbolic capital in having professors "come down from the Ivory Tower" and sit in a high school or middle school classroom desk. The historians were nervous about having to do this. Many asked that teacher educators accompany them to the classrooms to help them negotiate the school and know how to observe and give feedback in appropriate and helpful ways. The classroom visits were a real eye-opener for the historians. They were shocked by how little actual instructional time teachers had in their 45-minute periods. They were struck by the textbook content and the "quick and dirty" presentation of facts, the diversity of skill levels of the students, the need for constant "activity" to keep students focused, accountable, and engaged, and the demands of a full teaching day (three preparations and six periods of instruction, in some cases) for the teacher participants. Nonetheless, they were able to think of relatively simple, straightforward ways to improve the practices of the teachers by using accessible primary documents, critical thinking and reading activities, and discussion questions that would result in more ownership and authentic engagement by the students.

Metateaching

In the second summer, historians' presentations changed. They worked with the teacher educators in the planning and preparation of their presentations to be sure they were being explicit enough about the instructional choices and decisions that they made as part of the presentation itself. Teacher educators worked with all professors to engage in a process that I labeled "metateaching," or the ability to describe and make explicit the instructional decisions and dilemmas faced in constructing a lecture or discussion. Professors needed to be prepared in how to both teach and metateach, or share their thinking about teaching simultaneously. This was what was necessary for them to be effective models of good practices and of the type of historical thinking teachers must do as they plan instruction.

This took practice. At first, the teacher educators helped the professors do this by leading post presentation discussions where they explicated the practices they saw and made apparent the underlying instructional thinking that supported the teachers' recent learning experience. The discourse of the teacher educators—the way that they thought as well as the language they used to describe practice—served as a model for the history professors. The teacher educators gained the respect of the historians with their metateaching skills. They were able to take the presentations by the historians and decode them in terms of their instructional design and skill for the teachers. As a result, the historians stopped seeing the teacher educators as mere "technicians" but as expert interpreters of practice. The teacher educators gained respect for the historians because of the care they took in their practice—their discussion skills, materials development, and lecture design skills.

The historians thought it would be enough to present the major themes in a survey course and to address the question of "what to cover." They thought this was their main job and role. As the project progressed, they reorganized their presentations to make explicit the specific critical thinking goals (e.g. "Here, I want them to think about or rethink the common misconception of....") and make apparent the hoped for consequences of any particular reading or learning experience (e.g., "The reason I want them to read this article before this one is that I want them to investigate this bias or perspective before this one.").

Professors commented in the following ways about the changes in their practices in the second summer: "I commented on why I made the choices I did. I was much more schematic, thematic, and directive in lecture." "I thought more explicitly about the underlying purpose of the discrete lecture. I also tried to highlight instructional problems that I would not broach in a regular lecture." "In short, working with the teacher educators really pushed me to think about how I teach and why I make the commitment and presentation choices that I do. I doubt that I could have done this on my own." "I am much more reflective about my own teaching—about the reading I assign, the music, video clips, slides, and Web sites I integrate into my presentations—and why I do these things. I feel much more comfortable now talking about Web-based teaching strategies and multimedia models than I would have previously."

Collaborative Teaching Product

In the first summer, teachers were expected to develop their own instructional design products (e.g., unit plans and lesson plans and instructional change plans). In the second summer, they worked in teams led by history faculty focused on a particular theme and time period in American history to create a unit plan for the upcoming academic year. Professors were expected to provide both conceptual direction and resources. Professors became more involved in understanding and guiding the thinking of the teachers and saw their role as building historical understanding (What is important about this time period? What is the connection in these events? What types of interpretations are possible? Which documents would fit this critical thinking outcome?) rather than guiding pedagogical design per se (e.g., Should I lecture or use collaborative groups? Should I create a test or an alternative assessment? How should I structure this activity so that I can manage it properly?). The teachers working with each other and with the teacher educators on the staff were able to answer these types of questions. It was important that the professors be part of the instructional design teams because the questions about pedagogical thinking outcomes and pedagogical design were intimately linked. While the professors did not feel trained to address instructional design issues, they did come to appreciate the intellectual value of those decisions. They saw that if history professors wanted teachers to engage students in certain types of historical thinking (the ultimate goal of the professors involved), they did need to contribute to a team that would address design issues. "I expected to be comfortable as a 'content specialist.' What surprised me was that by working with teacher educators, I could be comfortable as a teacher of pedagogy, too."

Doing History Together: Collaborative "Hands On" History Experience

We incorporated a one-day institute led by museum educators where both professors and teachers were the student-participants. In this context, professors and teachers worked literally side-by-side in collaborative learning teams to "do history" or create historical narratives and conclusions based on primary material. By having teachers and professors share the role of learner, their relationship became more collegial.

Preparing History Faculty to Mentor

Professors wanted to know more about the participants. The administrative team thought the professors of history needed to know about teacher beliefs about history instruction, and they needed to have a profile of teacher instructional practices. We needed a way to discuss progress in teachers' practices and our goals for teacher improvement. To do this, we needed to engage the history professors in conversations about what types of instructional change we really wanted to see. As a result, we created a list of McRAH instructional practices and subsequently observed all teachers in their classrooms in terms of that framework. We also developed an ethnographic interview instrument to mine the belief systems of teachers about history instruction.

To prepare for the second summer, professors were provided a full history instructional profile of each participant based on this data. Now professors understood the teachers' strengths and weaknesses and, thereby, could challenge the teachers more. The agenda for the preparation workshop for project faculty differed substantively in year two, focusing on more specific ways to improve history lectures/presentations and expectations of faculty as teacher mentors.

Development of McRAH Pedagogical Principles

In reflecting on the values and messages from the history professor's presentations, teacher educators were able to articulate and summarize a set of pedagogical principles for historical thinking that guided their work with the teacher participants. In addition to a list of practices, from closely observing and working with the history professors teacher educators learned a set of concepts to reinforce necessary changes in their perspectives. They were principles that comprised the "pedagogical content knowledge" or perspective on the discipline that was necessary to sustain productive changes in teachers' practices over time. In other words, while we could require teachers to experiment with new tricks, techniques, and materials, we found that the teachers who made the most significant changes in their practices and could sustain these best over time learned the following powerful ideas to guide their thinking about their instruction. They learned these from the historians and the teacher educators who were able to consistently articulate these in all project activities. Again, the project staff did not start with these principles. Instead, through reflection on data and conversations and collaboration, the historians and teacher educators were able to articulate these and consciously reinforce these throughout all project activities.

One such principle was to fight presentism or recognize the importance of context in interpretations of historical data. History teachers, in their desperation to find "relevance" and "connectedness" to students' lives and psyches, have wanted to illustrate how history "repeats itself" and is shaping events in the here and now of their students' lives. But, this emphasis on historical relevancy can be misplaced and could lead to fallacies of historical thinking. Teachers learned ways to "respect the pastness of the past." They learned that it is much better, much more exciting to students, to stretch their analytic powers and their imaginations by transporting them back to a certain time, place, and context for understanding historical actors' decisions and the consequences of historical events. To judge Lincoln's decisions and discourses on slavery in the here and now would lead to misjudgments of his character and of his political skill and his moral conscience. To judge him in the context of when he acted and the America in which he lived requires students to engage their imaginations and to search for detailed evidence that supports the type of disciplined thinking that only history instruction can teach. We can replace the current, "I can relate to that," with "I understand why that happened." In McRAH we emphasized how to teach historical understanding (e.g., For whom was this true? When? Where? Under what circumstances? For how long?).

Teachers learned to critique the "givens" of American history. McRAH gave teachers license to rethink the values, structures, and timelines of textbooks in determining what was important to teach—which actors, which events, which ideas, in what order. McRAH participants started to question and reorganize their course structures and classroom projects to include key turning points, thematic instruction, and juxtaposition of key historical time periods.

Working closely with professors, teachers took license to leave behind some of what the textbook writers considered important in order to go in-depth on certain subjects and topics, knowing that such work would set the framework for quicker and more substantive understanding of other historical events. McRAH brought to the forefront one of the main choices teachers have at their disposal and one of the most powerful ways they can initiate curricular reform—the power to choose materials. With McRAH, there were readily available options for replacing textbook chapters with pictures, music, maps, primary documents, letters, diaries, online museum exhibits, and artifacts.

The articulation of key practices and key instructional values by all members of the project staff and participants took two years to accomplish. The collaborative conditions we established brought these values, positions, and practices to the fore and allowed us all to claim them for our own work—as professors, school teachers, and teacher educators. By articulating these through careful examination and discussion of the evaluation instruments (surveys, interviews, observations), we could communicate these more clearly in the feedback and guidance we gave the teachers in years two and three of the project. When teachers were developing and presenting their work to each other and to us, they used these principles to guide their work and to assess whether or not they were meeting project goals in their practices. No longer were teacher educators necessary "translators" of professors' practices and ideas. No longer were teachers recipients of knowledge. We had created a knowledge base together and had established the basis for a true teaching partnership.

Year Three: A Teaching Partnership

Coteaching: History Professors and Teachers

Based on their work in their classrooms, our first cohort of teachers (fellows) taught sessions with professors in the second summer institute where they combined content and pedagogy. The teachers who had been with us the previous year cotaught sessions with history faculty and education faculty to a new group of participants. Sessions focused on topics such as how to teach with historical documents, how to structure a concept-based lecture, and how to use maps, photos, and artwork in history lessons.

Teachers Presenting to Professors

In the final project event (a one-day symposium in the third summer), the teachers presented on their work in their classrooms to history professors and other teachers. In this way, the project had come full circle. Now it was time for the professors to learn from the teachers.

Conclusions

We did not anticipate how important it would be for the history professors to take on the role of fully collaborating in teacher development. In my experience with McRAH, I found that a transformation needed to occur with the history professors in how they came to view their work in relationship to the teachers in order for the teachers to make meaningful use of the concepts, ideas, and materials provided by the history professors. In other words, the professors had to change and learn how to teach teachers as much as the teachers needed to learn new ways to teach history. Teacher educators had to learn new ways to view the teaching of history from the models provided by the history professors.

During the first year, professors expressed appreciation for all of the opportunities to know the teachers before teaching them in the summer institute. They commented on the usefulness of the demographic data about the diversity of the school district; they were impressed with the enthusiasm of the teachers at the opening event to learn new ideas; they appreciated knowing the personal and professional backgrounds of the teachers. But, in the first summer institute, they designed traditional college lectures centered on topics in the American history survey course. Teacher educators—working, for the most part, separately from the history professors—designed workshop sessions on instructional delivery. History professors taught separately from teacher educators. Despite our attempts at integrating knowledge for the teachers and what they needed and wanted from the institute in our planning, we ended up delivering a traditional professional development workshop. And despite our efforts to join teacher educators and history professors together in an instructional team, we continued to view our content, expertise, and professional development roles as separate from one another.

The result for the teachers was they were not communicating with the history professors as instructional partners and did not feel comfortable approaching them for help. The teachers became a community onto themselves, and the professors were disappointed at the lack of engagement and understanding of the teacher participants in their lectures. All in all, the project wasn't meeting anyone's goals.

The historians were expert teachers who lacked the language and frameworks for describing and reflecting on their practices in ways that teachers could understand and make meaningful in their practices. Professors had never been challenged in their own teaching lives to make their practices explicit or to reflect systematically on their instructional design choices. The teacher educators played the important role of helping the historians communicate as fellow teachers with the institute participants. They helped them find common language and common questions: Which primary documents should I use and why? Why use this map or diagram vs. this one? Why use art interpretation in a history presentation? Why begin a lecture with these types of questions? What is the best way to structure a lecture on this topic? How do you check on student understanding before moving on? What do you do if students haven't read the material or haven't read it carefully enough? How do you build the necessary background knowledge for this approach to this topic? The historians did not expect to have to engage in discussions of these types of questions when they put together their presentations for the first institute. The teacher educators opened this dialogue and debate and thereby contributed to the collaborative relationship building that occurred in the next phases of the project. Professors revealed their concerns and decisions about instructional design as they lectured. They shared dilemmas of practice with the school teachers and discussed ways they have resolved them in their pedagogical choices. They found a language for sharing pedagogical content knowledge.

Pedagogical structures and contexts also changed as the project evolved and better supported productive collaborations. Professors worked with teachers in both presentational and workshop formats. They lectured to large groups and worked with teachers in small groups and individually on teaching project design. They mentored projects as they developed in teachers' classrooms. Summer institute lecture sessions were followed by discussion of pedagogical choices as well as content. Both teachers and professors presented their work to one another and commented on each other's work. "I see this kind of collaboration, in the words of one teacher, a kind of collective brainstorming about content and method, with specificity being essential."

Professors came into the project with a set of dispositions that allowed them to learn from the processes of the project to be teachers of history teachers. They valued teaching and took pride in their accomplishments as teachers. They had extensive experience teaching undergraduates. They wanted to be part of a project that transformed middle and high school teachers. None of the collaborative conditions or pedagogical structures would have had any impact without this foundational openness to support teachers' practices.

Key Transformations of Beliefs for the History Professors

Transformation 1

From: The teachers know how to teach middle and high school kids; we teach college students. We can't presume to know how to help them teach.

To: We share some of the same instructional dilemmas. We are always fighting the clock and do not have enough time to teach everything we want to teach on any topic. We all are working with readers who need more training in reading historical documents. We all have students without enough background knowledge. We all struggle with motivation issues.

Transformation 2

From: The teachers need most to develop a deep understanding of the content, as they have not studied enough history.

To: Teachers need to understand how to plan their lectures and activities to teach students how to "think historically" and come to value this way of thinking as their goal for teaching history. My goal as a teacher of history teachers is to help them think this way themselves so that they can do the same with their students. I need to make the processes of teaching and studying history more explicit in my presentations.

Transformation 3

From: We need to do all of the teaching, and the teachers really need to be our students for this to be successful.

To: We need to understand where they teach, whom they teach, and the materials they are using to teach so that we can make more grounded connections to their classrooms and their teaching contexts.

In this first phase of the project and in our learning to collaborate, professors often became the "sage on the stage" with a hidden belief that teachers' minds needed to be filled with historical information and understandings and the belief that it was the teacher educators' responsibility to support instructional change. Instead, history professors had an important role to play in changing teachers' practices and it extended beyond simply deepening teacher content knowledge of history.

As we progressed in the project, evaluated our data on teacher change, and collected feedback from the professors, we changed the context of the professional development experience and the roles of the professors and the teachers to move us along a continuum of collaboration. One of the key features of our project is that we worked with the same history faculty (with a few exceptions) and the same group of teachers for 3 years. We added members as we progressed, but the first group of teachers eventually progressed to become "fellows" and stayed with the project over time. This allowed us to build a learning community and to learn and grow with one another. It also added a form of responsibility for teacher growth for the professors that might not have been present had we changed the group of teachers every year. We came to know one another and to challenge one another and to, eventually, shape each other's instructional practices.

When college history professors agreed to participate in the project, they did not know there would be a significant difference between teaching the adult learners they taught in their undergraduate and graduate courses and teaching history in such a way as to improve the teaching of others. They also did not know that in learning to do so, they would become better teachers of history themselves. In feedback to project evaluators, many spoke about how increased consciousness about their practices from the metateaching process made them more consistent in their practices, more explicit with their college students about their goals and intentions, and more versatile because they gained ideas from the other professors and teachers in the project. "I reflected on the nature of teaching American history." "Participation made me a better teacher, and I hope that it assisted the teachers. It gave me a richer sense of the importance of doing history in the development of the individual." By implementing these key conditions, other professional development projects may experience similar successful collaborations and transformations.

References

Abt-Perkins, D., & Gomez, M. L. (1993). A good place to begin: Examining our personal perspectives. *Language Arts, 70*(3), 193–204.

Berenson, E. (1993). The California history-social science project: Developing history education in the schools. *Perspectives, 31*(9), 21–24.

Darling-Hammond, L. (1999). *Professional development for teachers: Setting the stage for learning from teaching.* Santa Cruz, CA: The Center for the Future of Teaching and Learning.

Hall, G., Wallace, R., & Dossett, W. (1973). *A developmental conceptualization of the adoption process within educational institutions.* Austin: University of Texas Press.

Hertzberg, H. (1988). Are method and content enemies? In B. R. Gifford (Ed.), *History in the schools: What shall we teach?* (pp. 13–40). New York: Macmillan.

Ragland, R. G. (2007a). Changing secondary teachers' views of teaching American history. *The History Teacher, 40*(2), 219–246.

Ragland, R. G. (2007b). Adopting and sustaining use of new teaching strategies for American history in secondary classrooms. *The Journal of Social Studies Research, 31*(2), 43–50.

Seixas, P. (1999). Beyond "content" and "pedagogy": In search of a way to talk about history education. *Journal of Curriculum Studies, 31*(3), 317–337.

Shulman, L. S. (1986). Those who understand: Knowledge growth in teaching. *Educational Researcher, 15*(7), 4–14.

Shulman, L. S. (1987). Knowledge and teaching: Foundations of a new reform. *Harvard Educational Review, 57*(1), 1–22.

Sirotnik, K. A., & Goodlad, J. I. (1988). *School-university partnerships in action: Concepts, cases, and concerns.* New York: Teachers College Press.

Zilversmit, A. (1993, January). Academic historians need new ways to work with schoolteachers. *Chronicle of Higher Education, 27,* B3.

Zilversmit, A., & Reed, E.W. (1993, September). *Doing history: A model for helping teachers. A report on the History Academy for Ohio Teachers.* College Park, MD: National Council for History Education.

Designing and Implementing Content-Based Professional Development for Teachers of American History

Ann Marie Ryan
Loyola University, Chicago

Frank Valadez
Chicago Metro History Education Center

> I learned how to incorporate a "historical argument" into more of my teaching, and to get students to read with a "critical eye." The use of primary sources in lessons also will benefit my students—I have learned strategies on how to choose appropriate and effective sources/documents.
>
> [The] [r]eadings helped [my] knowledge, discussion helped [my] understanding and collaboration gave me numerous ideas for strategies and [the] whole experience increased [my] appreciation [of American history]. [The] [f]ocus on inclusion of secondary sources made me rethink my teaching and realize [the] importance of scholar[l]y arguments in [the] classroom.

These reflections by teachers involved in the Chicago History Project (CHP; http://www.chicagohistoryproject.org/) offer a sense of how this professional development program affected participants' knowledge and teaching of American history. The project gave teachers a chance to rethink the use of primary and secondary historical sources in their teaching and to consider including scholarly arguments and disciplined inquiry in precollegiate American history classrooms. This chapter focuses on the CHP, which was funded by the *Teaching of American History* (TAH) grant program of the U.S. Department of Education in 2002. CHP was the first TAH grant received by the Chicago Public Schools (CPS). The project also involved several organizational partners, which included the Newberry Library (NL), the Chicago History Museum (CHM),[1] the Constitutional Rights Foundation of Chicago (CRFC), the Chicago Metro History Education Center (CMHEC), and the University of Illinois at Chicago (UIC).[2]

CHP evolved over time and increasingly provided teachers with useful programs, partnerships, and resources that allowed them to significantly increase the depth of historical content in their American history courses, including the use of sophisticated historical thinking skills. As noted by the teachers above, CHP created opportunities for teachers to rethink their approach to teaching American history. In this chapter we examine the evaluation data gathered over the four years of the CHP to better understand the specific design elements and implementation practices of that project that contributed to the effectiveness of the content-specific professional development it provided for middle and high school teachers of American history.

CHP's partner organizations provided professional development to seventy-eight CPS middle and high school teachers in three cohorts from 2002 to 2006 (see Table 11.1).[3] The forty-eight schools of participating teachers had an average enrollment of nearly fifteen hundred students and an average low-income rate over 80 percent in a district with historically low standardized test scores. The participating teachers had an average of five years of experience teaching history and the social sciences with a range of one to twenty-nine years. Over 60 percent of the teachers in CHP had taught five years or fewer during those critical years when many teachers leave low-performing high-poverty school districts like Chicago.[4] All of the participants were certified teachers, but only 40 percent had a specific endorsement in U.S. history. This particular characteristic of the teachers significantly shaped the work of CHP and has been the focus of considerable research.[5]

In response to recent research on teachers' historical knowledge, Keith Barton and Linda Levstik argued that "[i]f teachers do not understand the nature of historical knowledge, then they cannot design meaningful learning experiences for students, because they will not know what it is that students need to learn (much less how to help them learn from it)."[6] This concern over the lack of historical knowledge on the part of teachers was a driving force behind the *Teaching American History* program. The grant program aimed at addressing what it considered several problems in history education, including the lack of emphasis on history in the curriculum (and overemphasis on social studies), the lack of teacher preparation in the discipline of history, and students' unsatisfactory performance on standardized tests in history.[7]

CHP aimed at increasing student achievement in history by improving teachers' knowledge, understanding, teaching strategies, and appreciation of American history as a separate subject within the curriculum.[8] The project also focused on fostering professional relationships among American history teachers by creating a program that linked history teachers, grades seven through twelve, with university history professors, history education specialists, museums, and libraries. Evidence from teacher surveys, facilitator surveys, and classroom observations demonstrated that both of these goals were largely met. In addition, CHP offered several lessons on designing and implementing content-based professional development for teachers of history. First, seeking and responding to the

Table 11.1 CHP participants, 2002 to 2006

	CHP Cohort 1	CHP Cohort 2	CHP Cohort 3
Middle School Teachers	13	13	12
High School Teachers	14	14	12
Total	27	27	24

feedback from teachers in Cohort 1 had a significant impact on the design of the professional development program in subsequent years and was critical in shaping the teaching of American history to middle and high school students. Second, changes in the design and implementation of the project included deeper engagements for teachers with authentic historical work, which offered an even greater exposure to the discipline of history and enhanced teachers' pedagogical content knowledge.[9] Third, the emphasis on collaboration, which took different forms over the course of the grant project, assisted in developing communities of inquiry that also strengthened teachers' pedagogical content knowledge.

Program Design and Evaluation

The initial plan in CHP was for Chicago Public School teachers to apply to CHP in teams of two from their respective schools to CHP. Participating teams were then matched up with another team to form a quartet consisting of two middle and two high school teachers. The intent of the design was to facilitate better articulation between the middle and high school American history curriculum. These quartets created curriculum development plans for their schools, including how they intended to draw on the expertise of partner organizations and network with American history teachers in other schools. Although a unique and potentially valuable feature, the logistics involved in sustaining these cross-grade cross-school partnerships proved considerably challenging. In some cases, tensions between the high school and middle school teachers prevented the development of effective partnerships. In most cases, however, time limitations and geographic distance prevented quartets from meeting and working together. In subsequent years, the grant continued to involve both middle and high school teachers, but disbanded the quartet design.

The original design of the grant project required teachers to participate in an introductory symposium, a three-week summer institute, four follow-up colloquia, and school-based professional development sessions. CHP focused each of these professional development experiences on content typically included in an American history survey course including topics such as federalism, the making of the Constitution, slavery, progressivism, Chicago history, the Great Depression and New Deal, and the Civil Rights Movement. The three-week summer institute served as the core experience for teachers and offered them the opportunity to participate in sessions facilitated by scholars of American history and history education specialists, primarily from the CHM, CRFC, and CMHEC. During the summer institute teachers read and discussed secondary and primary sources, conducted historical research for use in lessons plans and developed curriculum plans with their teams.

CHP also called for smaller groups of teachers, from the first two cohorts, to be identified and trained as master teachers to assist in facilitating the summer institutes for Cohorts 2 and 3 respectively. Finally, the project planned to select several teachers from each cohort to serve as research fellows with the task of identifying useful primary sources to share with CHP teachers from all cohorts. In the implementation of the project, the master teacher and research fellow roles were merged due to the fact that many teachers were unable to continue their participation as a result of other school-related obligations.

The program evaluation involved the collection of several sets of data to assess progress on the overall goals of the grant project and to assess the effectiveness of the program as it was implemented. The evaluation included several instruments designed to collect data on teachers before, during, and after the grant project. These instruments included:

- a needs assessment completed by teachers,
- a pre-institute profile of teachers,
- pre- and post-institute content inventories of teachers' perceptions of their familiarity with historical content and confidence in teaching that content,
- pre- and post-institute lesson plans developed by teachers,
- teacher interviews,
- one pre-institute and three post-institute classroom observations of teachers, and
- a final survey of teachers.

In addition to the data collected specifically on teachers, there were ongoing evaluations for all symposia, colloquia, and institutes completed by participants to assess the effectiveness of these professional development sessions. There was also an annual survey completed by principals of participating teachers' schools and an assessment of the summer institute by program staff members, consisting of representatives from the organizational partners. These partners assessed the significant strengths and weaknesses of the institutes and made recommendations for future institutes.

Continuity and Change over Time: Teachers as Participants and Partners

Responding to teacher feedback during the implementation of the project proved to be a valuable lesson from CHP. This feature of the project reflected the emphasis on teacher involvement in shaping professional development outlined in the Benchmarks for Professional Development in Teaching of History as a Discipline by the American Historical Association (AHA), which actually calls for involving teachers in the initial design of professional development projects.[10] CHP did not include classroom teachers in the initial project design, although district-level personnel responsible for the history and social science curriculum worked with representatives from the organizational partners to devise the professional development plan.[11] The commitment of district-level personnel to the project and their ability to establish institutional support by connecting with schools and principals was critical to the success of the project. Both teachers and principals were required to sign letters of commitment for teachers to participate. Thirty-three percent of all of the principals from all three cohorts (n = 48) responded to annual surveys and rated the quality of CHP as high to very high (this translated to an average of 4.2 (n = 16) on a Likert scale of 1 to 5 with 5 indicating the very highest quality of professional development). Principals reported that CHP resulted in teachers providing better instruction, increased resources for the school, and collaboration among teachers in the school.

Although CHP did not include teachers in the initial project design team, it did integrate ways to elicit participants' feedback on the design and implementation of the project over the course of the grant.[12] The evaluation instruments assessed whether or not grant-related activities helped participants meet the goals of the project. Representatives from CPS and those from the partner organizations who comprised CHP program staff regularly reviewed evaluation reports and used them to make decisions about subsequent grant activities. This responsiveness to feedback resulted in the ongoing and constructive improvement of the project, another design element endorsed by the AHA's Benchmarks for Professional Development.[13]

Survey data gathered over the course of the project documented that teachers valued the content-rich professional development provided by CHP partners. Teachers consistently noted the quality of the scholars participating in the professional development sessions, the resources provided by the NL and CHM, and the readings and other materials provided were especially valuable. Pre- and postclassroom observations demonstrated how these teachers incorporated those things they regarded as valuable. This included an increased use of primary sources, which rose from an average of 32 percent of classes observed across all three cohorts before the summer institute (n = 75) and 48 percent of classes observed using primary sources after the summer institute (n = 195). This increase in the use of primary sources and allowing students to engage in the analysis and interpretation of those sources confirmed teacher self-reports of these developments in surveys.

Over the four years of CHP, teachers consistently reported in summer institute surveys, content inventories, and final surveys that the program had deepened their knowledge of history. Additionally, principals reported in annual surveys that the strong content focus of CHP was potentially helpful for increasing student learning. Although teachers appreciated the content-rich focus of CHP, Cohort 1 teachers clearly articulated that more focused time and attention needed to be devoted to translating this rich content into meaningful curriculum. In their regular meetings and annual survey, facilitators concurred with this assessment. This feedback shaped the follow-up colloquia for Cohort 1, which incorporated at least one session per colloquium for teachers to discuss how they were using CHP-related materials and strategies. At each colloquium, teachers were asked to share in small groups or with the group as a whole the CHP-related resources they had integrated or planned to integrate into their teaching of American history. This activity addressed teachers' concerns and reinforced the goal that CHP was intended to affect the teaching of American history in middle and high school classrooms in addition to enriching teachers' understanding of content.

The most significant change made based on teacher input was the redesign of the summer institute. In the first year teachers worked in quartets to develop curriculum plans to better articulate middle and high school programs in American history. They also conducted individual research and used that research to revise a lesson from their own teaching of American history. Although teachers continued to apply as teams of two from a particular school, the linking of teams into quartets was discontinued. (This change is discussed in greater detail later in this chapter.) The dissolution of the quartets caused a rethinking of the products teachers developed during the institute. First year participants designed a curriculum development plan, revised a lesson plan, and wrote a historical essay supporting the modifications to the content and resources of that lesson. The program staff decided to focus Cohort 2 teachers' time on revising the lesson and developing a historical essay as well as a pedagogical essay grounding that modified lesson. (The change in the lesson assignment is discussed in more detail later in this chapter.)

Teachers' requests for more time to explore the connections between CHP and their classrooms also caused the program staff to rethink the summer institute's structure. The first cohort of teachers generally participated in whole group seminars with an array of guest historians focused on content knowledge delivery. Teachers also participated in sessions with program staff from the NL, CHM, CRFC, CMHEC, and UIC, which often emphasized content along with strategies for teaching that content. Some time was set aside for Cohort 1 teachers to meet and discuss the connections between CHP and their classrooms, but it was divided between grade-level groups (middle and high school teachers meeting separately), partner groups (quartets of middle and high school teachers), and lesson plan groups (teachers working on similar topics or themes). Participating in multiple groups on these various tasks made sustained and meaningful work a challenge. In the redesign of the summer institute, the program staff attempted to rectify this situation and bring more coherence to the program's attention to the teaching of American history.

By disbanding the quartets, CHP was able to sharpen the focus of the teacher activities and the summer institute's schedule. To assist in this effort, the institutes for the second and third years continued to serve middle and high school teachers together, but created two sections of teachers (each with a balance of middle and high school teachers). Each seminar group had a historian from the NL or UIC as the primary facilitator. Teachers met with their seminar groups daily and also participated in whole group sessions. Teachers continued to read secondary and primary sources in preparation for seminars, but now had a consistent facilitator who could help them make connections between seminars and assist in building from one conversation to the next. One participant noted that the facilitator "was a constant resource in discussion." Another mentioned that "access [to the facilitator] and colleagues with more extensive history backgrounds…was invaluable". The redesign of the summer institute allowed for small groups with more focused facilitation, but continued to encourage teacher collaboration.

The historian-facilitators for the seminar groups provided guidance in the seminars and also presented content sessions, which decreased the number of guest historians. Program staff from the CHM, CRFC, and CMHEC continued to offer sessions where they modeled teaching strategies while examining rigorous content with teachers. The summer institute also began each day with a discussion facilitated by various program staff on how teachers approached the historical topic at hand. The facilitators shared their own techniques for teaching the topic and solicited ideas from participants as well, which allowed for a better integration of and emphasis on historical content and the teaching of history. Finally, as in the first year, teachers were given time to conduct research at the NL and CHM to modify their lesson. During this time the historian-facilitators were available to offer guidance and answer questions. Teachers were expected to present their research during the summer institute to their seminar group.

On summary evaluations of the summer institutes, Cohorts 2 and 3 rated the time devoted to discussing the teaching of history and the modeling of actual strategies as valuable to very valuable. A teacher from Cohort 3 commented that the summer institute had a "very useful mix of content and pedagogy." Many noted the contributions of the CRFC and the CMHEC as particularly effective on these elements. Their modeling of specific strategies assisted teachers in seeing how they might teach particular content. In evaluations of school-year colloquia teachers reported on the strategies they were using that they had participated in at the summer institute. They highlighted primary source analysis (used by several facilitators, including the CRFC and CMHEC), civil conversations modeled by the CRFC and historical heads demonstrated by the CMHEC.[14] Important to note is that the increased satisfaction in the amount of time and quality of the sessions devoted to teaching strategies did not result in a decrease in the satisfaction with the emphasis on historical content.

In the final survey administered at the end of the grant year for each cohort teachers were asked in an open-ended question what they gained professionally from CHP. In Cohort 1, 36 percent of teachers (n = 25) identified improved historical knowledge as a professional gain from CHP and only 16 percent believed that it resulted in improved teaching. For Cohort 2, 38 percent (n = 21) and 42 percent of Cohort 3 (n = 19) identified improved historical knowledge as a professional gain, while 43 percent of Cohort 2 and 53 percent of Cohort 3 thought CHP had improved their teaching. These responses confirm the value of CHP's efforts to bring together partner organizations with different and distinct strengths in the areas of history and history education. It also offers evidence that the changes made from the first year to later years of the grant addressed teachers concerns, as well as the goal of the project to improve the teaching of history.

Assuming the Historian's Chair: Deepening Teacher's Pedagogical Content Knowledge

Lee Shulman advanced the term *pedagogical content knowledge* in 1986 in clarifying the difference between "knowing one's content or subject matter, like American history, and knowing how best to organize and represent that subject matter so that others could understand it."[15] He considered this type of knowledge as a subset of content knowledge, since it consisted of choosing the content that was "the most regularly taught topics in one's subject area, the most useful forms of representation of those ideas, the most powerful analogies, illustrations, examples, explanations, and demonstrations."[16] The revisions to CHP in its second year reflected a move not only in the direction of deepening teachers' content knowledge in the area of American history but also expanding their pedagogical content knowledge. This change in the program demonstrated an important lesson in engaging teachers in authentic historical work with opportunities to translate that disciplinary knowledge into plans for instruction. The modifications to the professional development plan intended to enhance teachers' ability to transfer the content and pedagogy explored at the summer institute into classroom practice (their pedagogical content knowledge). The revision of the essay and lesson plan assignment demonstrated this shift in the program. The original assignment required teachers to submit a lesson in American history and revise it during the institute. In the revision, teachers were expected to develop essays that contextualized the lesson and integrated new primary and secondary sources into the lesson. In the essay teachers posed a research question, a thesis, and a historical argument that they then used as the basis for their revised lesson (see appendix A). Some teachers in Cohort 1 struggled with understanding the relationship between the historical essay and the revision of their lesson plan. In one instance, a facilitator asked a teacher how the research he or she was conducting at the summer institute would change his or her lesson. The teacher responded that the new research would have little impact, but followed by saying that, "maybe I would bring in more of these primary sources." This comment illustrated the need to have a more explicit link between the lesson and the research conducted to formulate the historical essay.

The revised essay and lesson plan assignment for Cohort 2 asked teachers to submit a lesson plan prior to the summer institute on a specific topic that would be addressed during the institute (see appendix B for sample lesson assignment). This plan gave teachers more direction and strengthened the connections between CHP activities and teachers' work in classrooms. As in the first year, during the summer institute teachers researched and selected primary and secondary sources to support their revised lesson. The essay assignment continued to require an in-depth analysis of the historical context of the lesson, but this time it also asked for: (1) rich descriptions of the primary sources used; (2) a reflection on why the primary and secondary sources new to the lesson were chosen; (3) a description of how the experience in CHP affected the changes made to the lesson; and (4) an annotated bibliography of suggested secondary sources.

An analysis of the changes made to lessons indicated that over the three cohorts of teachers (n = 58) the number of teachers making significant changes and adding primary sources to their lessons increased (see appendix C for lesson analysis guide).[17] Almost half of the lessons were modified significantly between the original and revised versions. In the post-institute lessons, 62 percent of the teachers increased the historical focus and depth; 65 percent integrated more or different primary sources; and 31 percent integrated new scholarly secondary sources. Most significantly, the integration of new or additional primary sources jumped from 41 to 72 percent between the first and second cohorts and then increased to 75 percent in Cohort 3.

For the final cohort the reflective section of the essay was slightly modified to assess what teachers considered the durable knowledge of the lesson for their students and of the experience in CHP for them as teachers. This aimed at identifying the knowledge, attitudes, and skills that would continue to influence teachers' classroom instruction five years after their participation in CHP. As in the final surveys, teachers were not given a list of possible gains to choose from, but rather were asked to identify them on their own in an open-ended question. Fifty-three percent of Cohort 3 (n = 23) identified improved content knowledge, 32 percent reported new teaching methods as the lasting influences, and 37 percent of teachers indicated that they had developed a more scholarly approach to teaching from their participation in CHP. While the percentages for the latter categories do not represent a majority of teachers respectively, those who identified one did not necessarily identify the other (with only two participants doing so)—as a result 63 percent of Cohort 3 teachers believed CHP offered new methods or perspectives on the teaching of history.

Taking a scholarly approach to teaching was fostered in many ways in CHP, but was the primary focus of the "Historian's Chair" sessions introduced in the second and third institutes. In these sessions, teachers presented the research for their essay and lesson to their seminar group. In this forum, teachers received feedback from fellow participants and the facilitator on the selection of their documents and how well those documents supported the lesson. This aspect of the summer institute was modeled after the "Author's Chair" strategy used to assist in developing students' writing. The strategy required each participant to don the role of the historian and participate in "doing history." Peter Seixas argues that "'[d]oing the discipline' establishes a basis for teachers and professors to work together in a way which recognizes the expertise of historians, not as dispensers of fixed content, but as practitioners of a craft into which others are welcomed."[18] The Historian's Chair sessions took place in the seminar groups with the historian-facilitators, which allowed teachers to enter into a community of inquiry and in this case the scholarly community of historians. According to Seixas, being a part of such a community can enhance a teacher's understanding of historiography and the practice of history.[19] In these sessions, teachers learned from an experienced historian in the field as well as one another as they presented their historical arguments and received feedback from the historian-facilitator and their colleagues.[20] One teacher commented that these sessions "gave me insight on how to teach different eras/themes in history. The various readings refreshed my knowledge." The consistently high ratings for the Historian's Chair sessions indicated teachers' appreciation of the focus on historical knowledge and analysis integrated with the focus on teaching history. On average, participants at the second and third institutes (n = 45) rated the value of these sessions at 3.7 (on a scale of 1 to 4 with 4 being very valuable).

The addition of the Historian's Chair strategy affected teachers' thinking about the discipline of history, and final survey data also shows that an overwhelming majority of teachers (96 percent) across the three cohorts (n = 65) indicated that their involvement in CHP affected their thinking about the discipline of history, most commonly by raising the importance of primary source analysis (48 percent). Teachers from all three cohorts consistently identified the use of primary sources and the integration of those sources into the teaching of history as one of the major contributions to their enhanced understanding of American his-

tory, and some teachers elaborated further on the ways CHP affected their understanding of history. They noted that the summer institute experience changed
their way of thinking about historical interpretation and mentioned the need to
focus on historical methods, keep up with new historical scholarship, and evaluate authors' biases. Others noted the importance of critiquing historical interpretations, examining the evidence underlying interpretations, and the tentativeness
of historical interpretations. The Historians' Chair sessions emphasized developing scholarly arguments based on secondary and primary sources and then
applying it to a lesson for students. One teacher noted that CHP "changed my
views on using secondary sources in my class. I really believe that incorporating
scholarly arguments into lessons is important."

These self-reports by teachers support Barton and Levstik's assertion that in-
depth experiences and projects that offer teachers an opportunity to examine
the epistemology of historical knowledge may have a significant impact on their
pedagogical content knowledge.[21] Indeed the deep engagements with history
through the seminars as well as the essay and lesson plan assignment, especially
in the later cohorts, affected how CHP teachers understood history, historical
research, and the teaching of history. In responding to how CHP affected their
thinking about history, a Cohort 3 teacher stated, "[t]o not to be afraid to expect
students to do more rigorous tasks and think more critically. To get them to *be*
like historians, not just read a textbook [and] answer comprehension questions."
For this teacher, the in-depth historical work done by teachers in CHP translated into higher expectations and plans for deeper engagements with history for
students.

Assessing Teachers' Content Knowledge and Pedagogical Content Knowledge

The relationship between teachers' knowledge of American history and their
teaching of it was a central concern outlined in CHP's first goal. Hence the
program evaluation included several instruments designed to assess teachers'
perceptions of their gains in historical knowledge and how that affected their
teaching of the content. In pre- and postcontent inventories teachers gauged
their familiarity with the content and their confidence in teaching it on a scale
from 1 (not very familiar or confident) to 4 (very familiar or confident). Cohort
1 teachers (n = 26) indicated that they had gained some familiarity and confidence in almost all of the topics addressed at the summer institute (see Table
11.2). The most frequent reason given for a gain in familiarity or confidence was
the exposure to and use of primary sources in the institute. For each topic 15 to
33 percent of teachers named primary sources as the overriding reason for their
gain. One participating teacher confirmed these findings by saying, "The more I
know about my subject the better my students will do. My increased knowledge
will help me to categorize and pace the course. This increased organization will
help the students frame U.S. [h]istory." Indeed, teachers reported gains in their
level of confidence in teaching these topics from 0.2 to 0.9 with almost half of the
topics increasing by 0.5 or more (see Table 11.2). This offers evidence of CHP's

Table 11.2 Pre- and post-institute content inventory CHP Cohort 1

Topic	Pre-Institute Average Level of Familiarity	Post-Institute Average Level of Familiarity (gain/loss)	Pre-Institute Average Level of Confidence	Post-Institute Average Level of Confidence (gain/loss)
	n=27	n=26	n=27	n=26
American Revolution	3.3	3.3 (no change)	3.2	3.4 (+.2)
Making of the Constitution	3.2	3.3 (+.1)	3.2	3.5 (+.3)
The Early Republic	2.6	2.9 (+.3)	2.5	2.8 (+.3)
Slavery	3.1	3.5 (+.4)	3.0	3.5 (+.5)
Reconstruction	2.8	3.3 (+.5)	2.5	3.2 (+.7)
Gilded Age	2.3	2.7 (+.4)	2.1	2.6 (+.5)
Haymarket	2.3	2.8 (+.5)	2.0	2.7 (+.7)
Progressive Era	2.6	3.0 (+.4)	2.4	3 (+.6)
Chicago History	2.7	2.8 (+.1)	2.5	2.7 (+.2)
Immigration	3.1	3.2 (+.1)	3.0	3.0 (no change)
New Deal	2.9	3.0 (+.1)	2.7	3.0 (+.3)
Japanese Internment	2.6	3.2 (+.6)	2.4	3.3 (+.9)
Cold War Era	3	3.2 (+.2)	2.9	3.2 (+.3)
Civil Rights Movement	3.0	3.4 (+.4)	3.2	3.4 (+.2)

contribution to the pedagogical content knowledge of Cohort 1 teachers, despite the relatively limited time focused directly on the teaching of history at the first institute.

The final survey asked participating teachers to identify the areas of American history about which they felt they gained the most knowledge as a result of their involvement in CHP. This question was open-ended and relied on teachers to supply the topics, rather than select them from a predetermined list. Comparing the gains identified by teachers following the summer institute and on this item on the final survey at the end of the grant year offers additional insight to the perceived gains in historical knowledge. On the summer institute pre- and postcontent inventory, Cohort 1 teachers noted no change in their familiarity with the American Revolution and only a slight gain in their confidence in teaching it (3.2 to 3.4). However, this same topic emerged as an area of growth in the final survey with 28 percent of teachers (n = 25) noting it as such. This gain was likely due to the fact that the first and second colloquia of the school year focused on the American Revolution and the Early National Period. Slavery, a topic addressed almost exclusively at the summer institute, was identified as an area of growth by teachers both at the end of the summer institute moving from an average rating of 3.1 to 3.5. Some eight months later, in the final survey, 20 percent of teachers named slavery as one of the areas in which they gained the most knowledge. A number of participants continued to identify slavery as a significant area of growth, nearly a year after the institute, which demonstrates the efficacy of its treatment during the institute, since it was not the subject of any of the follow-up colloquia. The assessment by Cohort 1 participants of the areas where they made the most gains included topics addressed in both the summer institute and the colloquia, attesting to the value of both professional development experiences in advancing the historical knowledge of teachers.

Teachers in Cohort 2 (n = 26) indicated that they had gained familiarity and confidence in all of the topics addressed at the institute. Teachers identified a gain in familiarity of 0.2 or more in all topics and 0.6 or more in the areas of Chicago history (2.1 to 3.2), the Federalists and Anti-Federalists (2.4 to 3.0), and the National Standards in Historical Thinking (1.9 to 3.0) (see Table 11.3).[22] Teachers identified a gain in confidence in teaching of 0.4 to 1.2 in all topics, signifying that Cohort 2 teachers believed CHP enhanced their pedagogical content knowledge. In some areas teachers noted a gain of 0.7 or more, which included researching and writing history (2.4 to 3.1), the National Standards in Historical Thinking (1.8 to 3.0), the Federalists and Anti-Federalists (2.3 to 3.2), and Chicago history (2.1 to 2.9). The most frequent reasons given for a gain in familiarity or confidence in historical topics was the exposure to secondary readings, primary sources, and lectures and discussions in the institute. In terms of research and writing history, participants found the use of the Newberry Library and the critiques from instructors as enhancing their familiarity and confidence. In the case of the national standards, participants attended a session focused on becoming familiar with the standards and noted that applying those standards to specific content and understanding where they fit in relation to state standards were responsible for gains in these areas.

Although teachers' knowledge of the Progressive Era for Cohort 2 participants only rose by 0.4 (2.8 to 3.2) between the pre- and post-institute content inventories, teachers' knowledge of the same era emerged as a significant area of growth in their self-report on the final survey. In an open-ended question, participants were asked to identify in which areas of American history they believed they gained the most knowledge and understanding. More than 40 percent (n = 21) reported that their knowledge of the Progressive Era improved as a result of their participation in CHP. The increase on this topic was probably due to the fact that the first and third colloquia of the school year focused on the Haymarket uprising, Jane Addams's Hull House, and the history of political, cultural, and artistic

Table 11.3 Pre- and post-institute content inventory CHP Cohort 2

Topic	Pre-Institute Average Level of Familiarity	Post-Institute Average Level of Familiarity (gain/loss)	Pre-Institute Average Level of Confidence	Post-Institute Average Level of Confidence (gain/loss)
	n=27	n=26	n=27	n=26
Issues in Researching and Writing History	2.6	3.3 (+.7)	2.4	3.1 (+.7)
The National Standards in Historical Thinking	1.9	3.0 (+1.1)	1.8	3.0 (+1.2)
The Constitution	3.2	3.4 (+.2)	3.0	3.5 (+.5)
The Federalists & Anti-Federalists	2.4	3.0 (+.6)	2.3	3.2 (+.9)
Slavery	3.2	3.4 (+.2)	3.1	3.5 (+.4)
The Progressive Era	2.8	3.2 (+.4)	2.7	3.2 (+.5)
Chicago History	2.1	3.2 (+1.1)	2.1	2.9 (+.8)
The New Deal	2.9	3.2 (+.3)	2.6	3.0 (+.4)
The Civil Rights Movement	3.0	3.2 (+.2)	3.0	3.5 (+.5)
Contemporary U.S. History	3.0	3.2 (+.2)	2.8	3.2 (+.4)

dissent in Chicago. The topics of slavery (with 38 percent of teachers noting it as an area of growth) and the Civil Rights Movement (29 percent) were addressed extensively at the summer institute. The strong growth in knowledge in all of these topics further suggests the efficacy of both the summer institute and colloquia sessions.

After the three-week summer institute, teachers in Cohort 3 (n = 20) noted gains in familiarity in seven of the ten summer institute topics and gains in confidence in teaching the content in nine of the ten categories (see Table 11.4). Teachers generally noted greater gains in confidence (from no change to 0.9) in teaching these topics than in familiarity (from -0.1 to +0.6) with the content of the topics, which may indicate that teachers believed they were fairly familiar with the content, but that the summer institute offered them additional sources, perspectives, or strategies for teaching that content. This demonstrates the contribution that CHP made to the pedagogical content knowledge of teachers in Cohort 3 and supports the trend in the responses of teachers from Cohorts 1 and 2.

Teachers in Cohort 3 made the greatest gains with regard to Chicago history, showing a 0.6 gain in familiarity (2.4 to 3.0) and a 0.9 gain in confidence (2.1 to 3.0). Regarding familiarity, teachers showed gains of 0.3 in the topics of research

Table 11.4 Pre- and post-institute content inventory CHP Cohort 3

Topic	Pre-Institute Average Level of Familiarity	Post-Institute Average Level of Familiarity (gain/loss)	Pre-Institute Average Level of Confidence	Post-Institute Average Level of Confidence (gain/loss)
	n=24	n=20	n=24	n=20
Issues in Researching and Writing History	3.2	3.5 (+.3)	2.8	3.4 (+.6)
The Constitution	3.5	3.5 (no change)	3.0	3.4 (+.4)
The Federalists & Anti-Federalists	2.8	3.1 (+.3)	2.4	3.0 (+.6)
Slavery	3.5	3.5 (no change)	3.1	3.5 (+.4)
Industrialization and Labor	2.8	3.0 (+.2)	2.5	2.9 (+.4)
The Progressive Era	2.6	2.9 (+.3)	2.3	2.9 (+.6)
Chicago History	2.4	3.0 (+.6)	2.1	3.0 (+.9)
The New Deal	3.1	3.3 (+.2)	2.8	3.1 (+.3)
The Civil Rights Movement	3.3	3.4 (+.1)	3.0	3.3 (+.3)
Contemporary U.S. History	3.1	3.0 (-.1)	2.8	2.8 (no change)

and writing history (3.2 to 3.5), the Federalists and Anti-Federalists (2.8 to 3.1), and the Progressive Era (2.6 to 2.9). On confidence in teaching, teachers reported an average gain of 0.6 in researching and writing in history (2.8 to 3.4), the Federalists and Anti-Federalists (2.4 to 3.0), and the Progressive Era (2.3 to 2.9), gains of 0.4 in the Constitution (3.0 to 3.4), slavery (3.1 to 3.5), and industrialization and labor history (2.5 to 2.9), and gains of 0.3 in the New Deal (2.8 to 3.1) and the Civil Rights Movement (3.0 to 3.3).

In the final survey, Cohort 3 teachers (n = 19) felt they gained the most knowledge on the topic of slavery. Although many reported that they were familiar and confident with their knowledge of slavery in the pre- and postcontent inventories from the summer institute, 42 percent noted it as the topic in which they gained the most knowledge and understanding overall in the open-ended question posed on the final survey. After slavery, teachers identified imperialism (32 percent), the Vietnam War (32 percent), conservatism (26 percent), the Civil Rights Movement (16 percent) and labor history (16 percent) as areas where they gained considerable knowledge. The perceived gains in knowledge across summer institute and colloquia topics reflect the efficacy of the sessions in these different parts of the program.[23]

CHP in the Classroom

Self-reports of knowledge gains in American history indicated that teachers who participated in CHP may have engaged in more content-rich teaching. The changes made to lesson plans offered evidence that teachers had developed a more solid sense of history and understood the value of making their lessons content-rich. Evaluation staff conducted classroom observations to assess if these changes in content knowledge and curriculum planning resulted in changes in classroom practice. One pre-institute and three post-institute observations were conducted for each participating teacher over the course of that cohort's grant year.

In post-institute observations of Cohort 1 students wrestled with historical information both independently and with groups of students. There was an overall increase in the time devoted to primary source analysis, from 19 percent in the pre-institute observations (n = 26) to 33 percent in the post-institute observations (n = 79). The use of lectures remained relatively low at 23 percent in the pre- and 22 percent in the post-institute observations. Cohort 2 had a slight increase in the use of primary source analysis, which was 44 percent in the pre-institute observations (n = 27) and in 48 percent post-institute observations (n = 65). Similarly, the use of secondary source analysis rose from 15 percent to 23 percent. Meanwhile the use of lectures declined from 30 percent to 23 percent. Although the classroom observations did not reveal a significant change in the use of primary sources, they confirmed teachers' self-reports of increased use of primary and secondary sources. In the final cohort, the use of primary source analysis increased from 18 percent (n = 22) to 35 percent (n = 51), as did the use of secondary source analysis, which rose from 14 to 25 percent, while the use of lectures declined from 32 to 10 percent. Classroom observations revealed some change in the use of primary and secondary sources, supporting teachers' reports of using these types of sources.

How successful was CHP given that no more than half of its participants observed changed their practice? In absolute numbers the data suggest that important changes were made by some teachers, but not all. This could have resulted from a sampling issue, but could also be due to the fact that less than half of participating teachers (40 percent) were endorsed to teach U.S. history. Despite their increased familiarity with the content and confidence in teaching it reported on the content inventories administered at the summer institutes, some may have had difficulty in applying this new knowledge within the grant year. This raises an important question in the design of follow-up and support during the first year of implementation. CHP did not offer instructional coaching, but that kind of support may have resulted in more consistent implementation. Further research to assess the long-term impact of content-focused professional development projects, such as CHP, is necessary to determine the success of such programs.

Classroom observations also gauged the percentage of students actively participating in the class and the level of interest and engagement they demonstrated. The overall trend in the methods used in the post-institute observations indicated increased student involvement and deeper engagement in the subject matter. These observations provided evidence of changes in teachers' approaches to teaching history with an increased use of primary and scholarly secondary sources with their students. The pre-institute teacher profile, given to all teachers before participating in CHP, and the annual final survey offer further indications of change in teachers' instructional practices when asked to assess which methods of teaching history they believed were most effective.

Over the course of their involvement with CHP, teachers encountered a variety of teaching strategies that emphasized primary source analysis. Only 7 percent of Cohort 1 teachers (n = 27) judged primary source analysis as an effective method of teaching American history before participating in CHP. At the close of the grant year, 60 percent of this group of CHP participants (n = 25) identified primary source analysis as the most effective method, making it the most highly rated strategy. In the pre-institute teacher profile 41 percent of Cohort 1 teachers identified lecture as the most effective strategy and in the final survey 40 percent still found it effective, indicating that teachers did not abandon strategies, but instead complemented them with additional methods. Indeed, in an open-ended question on the final survey asking which methods of teaching were most effective for teaching American history, 36 percent of Cohort 1 reported that the most effective approach to teaching history was using a variety of strategies, rather than relying on a few. Participation in CHP enhanced teachers' use of strategies and made them more aware of the strategies they employed.

In Cohort 2, 38 percent of teachers (n = 26) identified primary source analysis as an effective teaching strategy on the pre-institute teacher profile, whereas 57 percent (n = 21) identified it as such in the final survey. As with Cohort 1, primary source analysis was the most highly rated strategy in the final survey. Several other strategies made significant gains as well: Research projects moved from 15 to 43 percent, lectures from 15 to 38 percent, student-led discussions from 12 to 29 percent, debates from 19 to 29 percent, and student presentations from 8 to 19 percent. This trend indicated that teachers chose to use a variety of strategies, and increased their use of pedagogies intended to actively engage students in the subject matter. In the final survey when asked which methods they considered most effective for teaching American history, 53 percent of Cohort 3 (n = 19) participants identified primary source analysis, making it the most highly rated strategy in the final survey—whereas 38 percent (n = 24) rated it as such on the pre-institute teacher profile. Cohort 3 teachers continued to find research projects effective, moving from 25 to 26 percent. Twenty-one percent listed lecture, student-led discussion, and simulations as effective, which had a minimal presence in the pre-institute teacher profile and reinforcing the finding that teachers employed a variety of strategies in their teaching of history.

The significant number of teachers in all three cohorts identifying primary source analysis as the most effective method of teaching history accurately reflects the emphasis devoted to this activity in CHP. The final survey also asked whether CHP affected the ways they taught history. Along with reporting that CHP enhanced their overall understanding of history, 94 percent of all CHP teachers across the three cohorts (n = 65) said CHP had affected their teaching of history. Nearly half identified the use of primary sources as the major influence of CHP on their teaching.

Table 11.5 Pre-institute classroom observations: materials and resources used by CHP teachers

Materials and resources used by teacher	Cohort 1 n = 26	Cohort 2 n = 27	Cohort 3 n = 22	Average n = 75
Primary Source	19%	63%	14%	32%
Secondary Source	4%	37%	27%	23%
Textbook	27%	33%	36%	32%

Table 11.6 Post-institute classroom observations: materials and resources used by CHP teachers

Materials and Resources Used by Teacher	Cohort 1 n = 79	Cohort 2 n = 65	Cohort 3 n = 51	Average n = 195
Primary Source	43%	57%	45%	48%
Secondary Source	21%	25%	37%	28%
Textbook	34%	34%	25%	31%

In addition to understanding what methods CHP teachers were using and found effective, CHP assessed the types of materials and resources used by CHP teachers during classroom observations. There was an increase in the use of primary sources between the pre-institute (n = 26) and post-institute observations (n = 27) of Cohort 1 (see Table 11.5 and Table 11.6). This particular group moved from 19 percent to 37 percent of classes using these sources between the pre-institute visit and the first visit after the institute. While teachers continued to use textbooks at a somewhat steady rate, they increased their supplements to these texts with primary sources, additional secondary sources, and summaries of the text.

Unlike the observations of Cohort 1, the observations of Cohort 2 did not reveal significant changes in the frequency of primary source use after the institute. However, this particular group had a higher rate of using primary sources prior to their participation in CHP. Observations of Cohort 3 revealed significant changes in the frequency of the use of primary sources after the institute. Teachers in Cohort 3 dramatically increased their use of primary sources (from 14 percent pre-institute (n = 22) to 45 percent (n = 51) of classes observed after the institute) and complemented that with the integration of secondary sources outside of the textbook. This indicated a change in the approach to teaching history by using methods and materials that required intellectual work for both teachers and students.

The Challenges and Rewards of Collaboration

CHP leadership initially set out to develop a professional development program that put history at the center with the belief that the translation of the content to the classroom would be done largely by the teachers. For the most part, the design of CHP in its first year saw historians as the experts in historical content and the teachers as experts in pedagogy with history education specialists (facilitators from the CHM, CRFC, and CMHEC) having a foot in each of these arenas. The tendency to place content and pedagogy in separate and distinct spheres in the field of history education has been challenged by the TAH grant program.[24] In programs such as CHP, which are funded by TAH, historians, teachers, and history education specialists have had to reconsider these once rigid roles so pervasive in the field. This emphasis on collaboration proved to be another valuable lesson from CHP. The deliberate integration of collaboration that was responsive to teachers' needs assisted in developing communities of inquiry that strengthened teachers' pedagogical content knowledge.

The TAH grant program requires collaboration from the different sectors of history and history education. This emphasis on collaboration is consistent with another of the AHA's Benchmarks, which encourages professional development plans that allow teachers to collaborate.[25] CHP made a commitment in its design to bring middle and high school teachers together in quartets to better articulate the American history curriculum. Prior to the CHP summer institute in 2003, there was concern over the logistical challenges posed by these cross-grade level school partnerships. These challenges, including making time to meet and coordinating schedules, proved to be formidable for most groups. These difficulties led CHP program staff to base Cohorts 2 and 3 on school teams from middle and high schools. The project maintained the middle and high school balance in terms of the number of participants, but rather than pairing schools it decided to focus on school-based teams. This change allowed more flexibility in cross-grade relationships and allowed teachers and schools with particular interests to work together and successfully addressed a pragmatic concern without sacrificing the emphasis on increasing teacher collaboration.

To better understand the effect of CHP's collaborative efforts after shifting to the school-based teams, the summer institute evaluations for Cohorts 2 and 3 asked teachers what they learned from their colleagues. Fifty-six percent of Cohort 2 teachers (n = 25) identified teaching strategies as the most important content they gained from their peers and 96 percent stated that they would use strategies or resources suggested by a fellow participant. Sixty percent of Cohort 3 (n = 20) teachers responded that they had learned different teaching methods and strategies and 25 percent said that they had learned how to use primary and secondary documents in different ways. Finally, when asked if they planned to use any strategies suggested by other teachers, 52 percent of Cohort 3 said that they would. Although Cohort 1 experienced frustration over the lack of time to meet with their quartet groups and the difficulties in coordinating schedules, on the final survey 44 percent of the teachers (n = 25) in this cohort found gaining new ideas and perspectives on teaching American history as the benefit of this collaboration.

During CHP institutes and colloquia, teachers had opportunities to make connections between historical content and pedagogical content knowledge. At one such session, one of the quartets from Cohort 1 discussed possible themes for a curriculum unit they were developing. They focused on immigration for the topic and raised a question about the use of metaphors to describe the notion of "becoming American." They pondered the dominant metaphor of the "melting pot" used to describe America and wondered when it had changed from that to the "tossed salad." They also posed questions about the historiography of that transformation and in turn integrated their newer understandings of historiography into their development of curriculum. Their collaborative act of developing curriculum was informed by their experiences in CHP and demonstrated their enhanced pedagogical content knowledge.

In final surveys, some teachers noted specific benefits of collaborating with colleagues from their school and other schools. One teacher described it as providing "a richer sense of professional collaboration among fellow CPS teachers," while another saw the school partnerships as a way to ensure that materials from CHP would be integrated into the curriculum. Another teacher appreciated "the opportunity to have conversations with teachers that [are] not 'business-based' but content-based." Sentiments such as these reinforce Peter Seixas's argument that engaging in historical inquiry with historians and with other teachers of history provides for teachers of history a basis for a community of inquiry that enriches their pedagogical content knowledge.[26] In open-ended responses to the final survey, 39 percent of all CHP teachers (n = 65) found the opportunities to collaborate with other teachers as one of the greatest benefits of CHP, which rivaled their rating of gaining historical knowledge (39 percent) and just surpassed their rating of improved teaching (37 percent) as significant outcomes of the project. Indeed the community of inquiry established through the summer institute and colloquia sessions offered teachers a place to work together toward enriching their understanding of their subject matter and how to teach it.

CHP also provided collaboration across organizations and between teachers and historians and history education specialists. The partner organizations found participation in the Chicago History Project to be beneficial in a variety of ways. They appreciated the opportunity to interact with a group of dedicated teachers over a sustained period of time. The partner organizations forged closer relationships with many participants and saw significant crossover of CHP teachers participating in other professional development programs. Partners also noted that the long-term nature of CHP provided them with time to refine and tailor their offerings and materials to best suit the needs of CHP participants.

Since CHP was awarded in 2002, the Chicago Public Schools have received three more *Teaching American History* grants. Each of these grants has built on the work of CHP and used that experience to continue to meet the needs of American history teachers in the Chicago Public Schools. The Newberry Library, Chicago History Museum, Constitutional Rights Foundation of Chicago, Chicago Metro History Education Center, and the University of Illinois at Chicago along with others have remained active in these grants following the Chicago History Project.

Conclusion

The Chicago History Project demonstrated how responding to teachers' feedback assisted in developing a stronger professional development program with more potential for affecting the teaching of American history at the middle and high school level. The redesign of the program also allowed the project to offer greater exposure to the discipline of history and connect that with the teaching of history. This feature enhanced teachers' pedagogical content knowledge. The emphasis on collaboration among teachers, history education specialists, and historians fostered communities of inquiry that also strengthened teachers' pedagogical content knowledge.

The Chicago History Project provided teachers with professional development experiences intended to deepen their historical background in American history in order to enhance their teaching of American history. In the process, CHP increased teachers' knowledge of American history, honed their pedagogical content knowledge, and enriched their pedagogical practices. The commitment to a rich and rigorous content-based program and the collaborative structure of the professional development project were instrumental in leveraging these changes. The response to teachers' ongoing feedback and the commitment to providing teachers' deep engagements with historical content made the project at once more responsive and challenging. Indeed, most teachers welcomed that challenge. In characterizing the summer institute experience a teacher described it as "inspiring, informative, and incredibl[y] intellectually challenging." The teacher concluded, "At present I have so many *more* questions than when I began. I am *much* more enthusiastic about teaching history now [than] when I began."

Notes

1. In 2002 the Chicago History Museum was known as the Chicago Historical Society. It was renamed the Chicago History Museum in 2006.
2. At the start of the grant project Ann Marie Ryan served as Clinical Assistant Professor in the Department of History at the University of Illinois at Chicago. She moved to the School of Education at Loyola University Chicago in 2004 and continued to serve as the lead evaluator on the grant. For the duration of the grant period, Frank Valadez served as the Director of Professional Development Programs for Teachers at the Newberry Library and the CHP Project Director.
3. The Chicago History Project was awarded a *Teaching American History* grant in 2002, but the first cohort of teachers did not begin until spring of 2003. That cohort ran from spring 2003 to spring 2004; Cohort 2, from spring 2004 to spring 2005; and Cohort 3, from spring 2005 to spring 2006.
4. For more details on teacher turnover in Chicago see Gary Barnes, Edward Crowe, and Benjamin Schaefer, "The Cost of Teacher Turnover in Five School Districts: A Pilot Study," 2007, *National Commission on Teaching and America's Future*, http://www.nctaf.org/resources/demonstration_projects/turnover/documents/CTTFullReportfinal.pdf.
5. For research on teachers' background knowledge in history see Sam Wineburg, *Historical Thinking and Other Unnatural Acts: Charting the Future of Teaching the Past* (Philadelphia: Temple University Press, 2001); Peter N. Stearns, Peter Seixas, and Sam Wineburg, ed. *Knowing, Teaching and Learning History: National and International Perspectives* (New York: New York University Press, 2000).
6. Keith Barton and Linda Levstik, *Teaching History for the Common Good* (Mahwah, NJ: Lawrence Erlbaum, 2004), 248.
7. Alex Stein, "The *Teaching American History* Program: An Introduction and Overview," *The History Teacher* 36, no. 3 (2003): 179.
8. The goal of the grant, consistent with the aims of the *Teaching of American History* program,

was to raise student achievement. There was discussion of using state-based achievement test scores as indicators of this outcome, but the state of Illinois removed the social sciences from its achievement tests in the 2003–2004 school year. The first cohort of teachers in CHP began in spring of 2003.

9. Pedagogical content knowledge refers to a teacher's ability to transform his or her subject matter knowledge into classroom instruction. For a discussion on the origins of this term see Zongyi Deng, "Transforming the Subject Matter: Examining the Intellectual Roots of Pedagogical Content Knowledge," *Curriculum Inquiry*, 37, no. 3 (2007): 280.

10. American Historical Association, "Benchmarks for Professional Development in Teaching of History as a Discipline," http://www.historians.org/teaching/policy/benchmarks.htm.

11. Timothy Hall and Renay Scott, "Closing the Gap between Professors and Teachers: 'Uncoverage' as a Model of Professional Development for History Teachers, *The History Teacher* 40, no. 2 (2007): 262.

12. This is similar to other grants awarded in the early years of the TAH grant program. See Karen Kortecamp and Kathleen Anderson Steeves, "Evaluating Professional Development of American History Teachers," *Theory and Research in Social Education* 34, no. 4 (2006): 504.

13. American Historical Association, "Benchmarks for Professional Development."

14. The historical head activity was developed by James Percoco; see James A. Percoco, *A Passion for the Past* (Portsmouth, NH: Heinemann, 1998), 32.

15. Lee S. Shulman, "Those Who Understand: Knowledge Growth in Teaching," *Educational Researcher* 15, no. 2 (1986): 9.

16. Ibid.

17. This represents the number of participants who submitted both pre- and post-institute lesson plans across the three cohorts.

18. Peter Seixas, "Beyond 'Content' and 'Pedagogy': In Search of a Way to Talk about History Education, *Curriculum Studies* 31, no. 3 (1999): 328.

19. Peter Seixas, "The Community of Inquiry as a Basis for Knowledge and Learning: The Case of History," *American Educational Research Journal* 30, no. 2 (1993): 321.

20. Stan Pesick and Shelley Weintraub found that teachers, as well as historians, had an impact on enhancing teachers' content knowledge. See Stan Pesick and Shelley Weintraub, "DeTocqueville's Ghost: Examining the Struggle for Democracy in America," *The History Teacher* 36, no. 2 (2003): paragraph 31. *The History Cooperative*, http://www.historycooperative.org/journals/ht/36.2/pesick.html.

21. Barton and Levstik, 248.

22. The National Standards in Historical Thinking focus on the skills required for historical thinking and are available from the National Center for History in the Schools, http://nchs.ucla.edu/standards/. For a print version see Kirk Ankeney, Richard Del Rio, Gary Nash, and David Vigilante, *Bring History Alive: A Sourcebook for Teaching United States History* (Los Angeles, CA: National Center for History in the Schools, 1996).

23. These perceived gains by teachers are derived from self-reports and therefore do not represent measurable gains.

24. For a discussion on the perceived divisions between historical content and the teaching of history see Seixas, "Beyond 'Content' and 'Pedagogy.'"

25. American Historical Association, "Benchmarks for Professional Development."

26. Seixas, "The Community of Inquiry," 320.

APPENDIX A

CHP Revised Lesson Plan

The goal of this project is to produce a document/artifact-based lesson plan that could be used by one of your peers in the Chicago History Project, your colleagues in the Chicago Public Schools, or the larger profession of teachers of American history.

Each participant has submitted a lesson plan on one of the topics to be covered in the summer institute. During the institute you will revise your lesson plan in workshops with peers and CHP faculty, and at the end of the institute you will submit a revised lesson plan in the six-part format described below.

Part I: **Cover Sheet**: *Author, Date, Title of Lesson Plan, Table of Contents*

Part II: **Lesson Plan Outline**

Part III: **Introduction to the Documents and Artifacts** *(~750 word essay)*

Please address the following points in this section:

- Explain the historical argument/issue you will address with your students.
- Explain how these particular documents and artifacts support this argument or address this issue.
- Discuss what historical questions are raised but not answered by the documents and artifacts included in your lesson plan.

Part IV. Three Document Descriptions and Reproductions of Each Document (up to 250 words for each of three documents)

In this part, you will identify one primary source: a "focus source" that serves as the centerpiece of the lesson, and several "supporting sources" that provide context, complicate the story, etc. Each description should include the following information:

- Identify the nature of each source (i.e., what each source is: a diary, a photo, etc.); If possible, identify *who* created it, *when* and *where* it was created, and *why* it was created.
- Explain the subject matter of each source. Identify the keywords, focal points, or key phrases of the document.
- Explain how each source relates to your central historical argument/issue. Assess the significance of each source. Explain how each source compares or contrasts with your other sources.

Part V: Reflective Piece (~250 word essay)

Please address the following in this section:

1. Secondary sources: List new secondary sources you read and describe the role these works played in revising your lesson plan.
2. Primary sources: List new primary sources and describe how they fit into your revised lesson plan.
3. Summer Institute: Discuss how the summer institute workshops helped you revise your lesson plan.

Part VI: Annotated Bibliography of Suggested Secondary Sources

In this part, you will identify a set of secondary sources (i.e., works of historical interpretation) that help clarify the goals of the lesson. Your bibliography should include the following:

- Identify at least three secondary sources, two of which need to be from 1995 to the present.
- For each secondary source describe its importance in revising your lesson plan.
- Identify and describe at least three student-appropriate readings to include in your lesson plan.

APPENDIX B

CHP Sample Lesson

Please submit a U.S. history lesson plan that addresses the following items. The topic of your lesson plan must fit into one of the six subjects that will be addressed during the summer institute.

- Subject—What is the course? (U.S. history, Urban Studies, etc.)
- Grade Level—What grade level are the students?
- Topic—What topic are you addressing?
- Goal—What do you want to accomplish? This is generally a broad statement of what you hope students will gain from this lesson.
- Objectives—What are the two or three primary objectives of this lesson? In other words, what do you want students to *do*?
- Materials—What do you use to teach this lesson? (texts, primary documents, films, equipment, etc.)
- Activities—What activities do you use to address the goal and objectives of this lesson? Please be specific and provide detailed descriptions of these activities.
- Evaluation—How do you know that students have accomplished the objectives of the lesson? Describe the assessment(s) you use to document student learning.

Describe the larger curricular unit of which this lesson is a part. Please address the following:

- What is the central topic or theme of the unit?
- What is the essential content or knowledge addressed in the unit?
- What are the essential skills developed by the unit?
- What curricular resources and materials are used?
- How does the unit address the Illinois State Standards in Social Science?

APPENDIX C

CHP Lesson Analysis

Original Lesson Topic
Revised Lesson Topic

Did the lesson change from the first draft submitted before the institute to the final draft? (yes or no)

If it changed, to what degree did it change? (minimal, moderate, significant)

Type of changes made:

    ____ Different lesson altogether
    ____ Refined focus—narrower, more in-depth
    ____ More instructional cohesiveness—better organized,
          clearer description
    ____ Integrated primary sources
    ____ Integrated more primary sources
    ____ Integrated different primary sources
    ____ Integrated new secondary sources
    ____ Integrated new activities demonstrated at the institute
    ____ Integrated new activities
    ____ Integrated field trips to CHP partner sites
    ____ Integrated field trips

Chapter 12

Artifacts as Inspiration

Building Connections Between Museum Educators and Classroom Teachers

D. Lynn McRainey and Heidi Moisan
Chicago History Museum

Introduction

Similar to how a birthday offers an opportunity to celebrate life and a commemorative day recognizes an important event, an anniversary provides another milestone in time for celebration and reflection. During the years leading up to the Chicago History Museum's (formerly the Chicago Historical Society) (http://www.chicagohistory.org) 150th anniversary, the education staff embraced this opportunity to reflect on its own practices, to celebrate the museum's accomplishments in interpreting history for diverse audiences, and to envision the possibilities for the future of museum education. The museum's missions to collect, preserve, and interpret both the city's and nation's past has taken form over the years in a range of educational programs for both school and public audiences.

The Chicago History Museum marked its milestone sesquicentennial in 2006 with a major building renovation of more than 70 percent of its public spaces. These physical changes of galleries and visitor amenities resulted in new exhibitions and experiences for exploring Chicago history and showcasing the Museum's collection. Coinciding with building plans, education staff initiated a parallel path in 2003 to reflect on and redefine our role and work within and outside the museum. This process drew on research into historiography, educational theory, and museum studies; conversations with scholars and educators; partnerships with schools, universities, and other cultural organizations; and experimentation with new approaches to teaching history. Our research for school audiences was guided by questions that grappled with the multifaceted nature of our work as both a history museum and educational institution in the twenty-first century: What is the role of a museum in history education and lifelong learning? How can programs portray the dialogue and debate that are inherent to historical inquiry? How do we teach history at the Chicago History Museum?

Through partnering on *Teaching American History* initiatives, education staff was able to practice three core elements of teaching history: interpreting collections, engaging in collaborations, and facilitating conversations. Teachers became valued partners as we each grappled with the teaching of history, whether in a museum gallery or classroom. Collections were positioned as valuable teaching tools for analyzing, interpreting, and promoting individual discoveries. And finally, conversations with one another as museum educators, classroom teachers, and historians allowed us all to expand our practice and skills as history teachers.

What Is the Role of a Museum in History Education and Lifelong Learning?

As an educational institution, both our practices and products have continued to be shaped by historical scholarship, our diverse audiences, and partnerships with schools and other organizations.

Defining Our Guiding Principles

To explore education's role both inside and outside the museum, education staff in consultation with MEM & Associates devised a Strategic Direction for Education.[1] Since education's work serves broad audience groups—teachers, students, families, teens, and adults—the plan was organized to provide a unified approach to program design across all audiences. Six guiding principles emerged for considering how we teach history at the Chicago History Museum: diverse stories, the city as artifact, personal connections, the interplay between the past, present, and future, audience accessibility, and civic engagement. These principles became tools for guiding the research and development of programs for school and public audiences at the Chicago History Museum, including the *Teaching American History* grants with which we have partnered.

Diverse Stories

History is about everyone and takes place everywhere. The richness of history is revealed through powerful stories that capture the diverse people, events, and movements that have shaped the city and the nation. Stories give voice to the past and reveal the multiple perspectives of individuals and communities—from the notorious and monumental to grassroots and ordinary. Kieran Egan of the Imaginative Education Research Group encourages educators to utilize stories for their potential to engage students (and learners of all ages) both cognitively and emotionally.[2] Both historians and educators turn to stories for the intellectual and affective opportunities they afford the practitioner and learner. Stories though are not limited to "once upon a time" but are timeless in their representation of the contributions of all people—past and present. Each person is an active agent and character in an unfolding story as Elaine Wrisley Reed and Fran Lehr explore in *Helping Your Child Learn History*: "Children are born into history. They have no memory of it, yet they find themselves in the middle of a story that began before they became one of its characters."[3] As chapters in an ongoing tale, history allows each individual to find her connection and place in time. Chris Husbands explores the challenges storytelling poses for history education in *What Is History Teaching?* but he also identifies its benefits: "they can entrance the imagination, conjure a picture of the past which is vivid and immediate, give 'life' to the characters they describe, create excitement and interest."[4]

City as Artifact

The Chicago History Museum is about the entire city of Chicago—and the city is our most prized artifact. While the Museum's collection exceeds 20 million objects, the city itself is a treasured artifact for analysis and interpretation. The built environment offers multiple points of entry for exploration and discoveries, as content is drawn from the historical and current life of the city. The theme of place and identity is found in evidence throughout the urban landscape and chronicles the growth of the "Metropolis of the Midwest." At the same time, the city is a lens for exploring regional, national, and global topics. As venues for staging programs, the places and spaces around the city are extended galleries and classrooms beyond the Museum's physical building. History where it happened is found in evidence around every corner. From the John Hancock and other buildings that define Chicago's distinctive skyline to the churches, schools, and bungalows that shape each ethnic neighborhood, the city expands the possibilities for where programs can occur and the discoveries that can be made.

Personal Connections

Finding a personal connection to the past leads an individual to value history and to seek it out throughout life. Historical investigation is an active process that requires the student, learner, and museum visitor to be engaged through their wonder and curiosity. Programs are designed to develop participants' skills in historical inquiry and foster opportunities for finding personal meaning based on solid historical evidence. This approach moves the museum from being the solitary voice and invites our audience to become our partner in the discovery process. In *What Is History Teaching?* Chris Husbands explains that "it is more imperative than ever to engage pupils in enquiries into, and dialogue about, the legacies of the past."[5]

Participants' own stories and experiences are valuable assets for connecting and meaning-making as they process new information and perspectives to understand the way things were in relationship to their own lives. Programs are not one-way presentations. Instead, they encourage questions, debates, and discussions among presenters (scholars, museum staff, and volunteers) and program participants (teachers, students, and the museum visitor). For *The Presence of the Past,* Roy Rosenzweig and David Thelen researched how adults perceive the past and its connection and significance in their daily lives and future endeavors. In his afterthoughts, Roy Rosenzweig reflects on the challenges the scholar, teacher, and even the museum faces in creating exchanges with the past that are meaningful for diverse audiences and learners:

> The most significant news of this study is that we have interested, active, and thoughtful audiences for what we want to talk about. The deeper challenge is finding out how we can talk to—and especially with—those audiences. History professionals need to work harder at listening to and respecting the many ways popular historymakers traverse the terrain of the past that is so present for all of us.[6]

Interplay between the Past, Present, and Future

The purpose of programs at the Chicago History Museum is to use history to understand the present and envision the future. When one begins a journey, a map becomes an invaluable tool for identifying your current location in relation to where you have been and the possibilities for where you may go. Like a map, history is a similar tool for charting paths and relationships between the past, the present, and the future. In terms of identifying where we have been, stories of the past capture the rich and diverse journeys of individuals and groups of people who have traveled before us. At the crossroads of history, the past intersects with the present through the interpretation and analysis of these stories. At this intersection, stories of the past collide with the present, resulting in diverse perspectives, dialogue, debate, and personal meaning. Through historical interpretation, the past, present, and future are no longer segregated to their own boundaries of time but, rather, are part of a continuous exchange for understanding the way things were, are, and might be. In considering the relevance of history in our contemporary lives, Kenneth T. Jackson and Barbara B. Jackson come to similar conclusions that Rosenzweig and Thelen's research revealed: "through the study of the past, individuals are empowered to develop a more informed way of seeing, knowing, and coping with the larger human society in which they live."[7]

Audience Accessibility

Assuring access means providing a rich array of exhibition features and programs as well as learning spaces, publications, and educational tools to meet the cognitive, social, emotional, and physical needs of a diverse set of audiences. Each museum visitor and program participant brings his or her own distinct needs, expectations, and desires to the learning experience. Drawing on educational theories from Howard Gardner to Jean Piaget, museum educators create developmental frameworks to better understand our audiences. Programs acknowledge diverse learning styles through the definition of content, identifying appropriate formats, and staging and delivery of a range of educational experiences. Audience studies such as focus groups and written surveys are additional tools for assessing the impact of our programs. The voice of our audience guides staff in research, decision making, planning, scheduling, and creating products and experiences that will serve them on multiple levels. For example, written gallery guides, audio tours, hands-on demonstrations, and behind-the-scenes tours are among the interpretive tools used to provide visitors access to our collection.

Civic Engagement

As a public institution, the Chicago History Museum shares responsibility with other civic leaders for the health and well-being of the city and its residents. To achieve this goal the programs are designed to provide historical context to contemporary issues and to enhance the quality of life especially for the city's youth. Through this guiding principle, history projects a contemporary voice. The museum becomes a town hall where young and old can raise, discuss, and debate current events and issues we all face as residents of neighborhoods, citizens of a nation, and members of an expanding global society. Newspaper headlines, community newsletters, picket signs, and the stories broadcast through radio, television, and the Internet are the sources for program focus and catalysts for discussions. The museum offers a neutral space for these conversations, while also providing historical context to understanding contemporary events. For example, in the fall of 2004, the Museum broadcasted the three Presidential debates to sold-out crowds of 400 participants per program. Prior to each debate, audience members enjoyed a brief commentary by local journalists and political analysts on the candidates and issues.

How Can Programs Portray the Dialog and Debate that are Inherent to History?

In Agatha Christie's mystery *The Murder of Roger Ackroyd*, Dr. Sheppard laments, as we all have at one time or another, "if those walls could speak." The wise Detective Hercule Poirot reminds him of the potential of inanimate things, "'but do not be too sure that these dead things'—he touched the top of the bookcases as he spoke—'are always dumb. To me they speak sometimes—chairs, tables—they have their messages'!"[8] The "messages" embodied in objects are not limited to works of fiction and are powerful sources for the historian and the museum visitor. To reveal these messages, history becomes an exchange or dialogue between the present and the past. Like any conversation, the act must be a two-way exchange between the sender and receiver, between the historian and the sources. Edward Hallett Carr reminds us that the "facts speak only when the historian calls on them,"[9] and Roy Rosenzweig further explains "as our interviewees would insist, that historical practice needs to link the past and the present in an active and continuing conversation."[10]

Conversations with the Past

How then can a museum encourage visitors to "be a historian" and initiate a dialog with the past? The process that Carl Becker describes in *Everyman His Own Historian: Essays on History and Politics* illustrates how every individual (though unknowingly at times) draws on the practices of the historian to solve the mysteries the day may bring. Though Mr. Everyman begins the day remembering some things and not others, Becker assures us that this is not a problem since Mr. Everyman initiates his own historical research. Wanting to pay his coal bill, Mr. Everyman turns to his sources—a calendar entry, conversation with Mr. Smith—to create a picture in his mind of past events. Carl Becker says that, "Mr. Everyman would be astonished to learn that he is an historian, yet it is obvious, isn't it, that he has performed all the essential operations involved in historical research."[11]

Just as Dr. Sheppard and Mr. Everyman soon discover, museum visitors have the same opportunities to connect with artifacts. In museums, we turn to the tools of the historian to engage our diverse audiences in the analysis and interpretation of history. In *The Historian as Detective: Essays on Evidence*, Robin W. Winks explores the possibilities and challenges evidence poses through a collection of essays by historians reflecting on their own practice. In examining the complexity of the historical process, Winks notes that like those methods employed by a detective, "the historian must collect, interpret, and then explain his evidence."[12] Chris Husbands illustrates how this process takes form for teaching children to make sense of the past: "understanding the past is inseparably also about finding out what evidence exists, how it might be interpreted, what limitations it has, and about how historical events might be described by different commentators."[13] Museums translate this process into object-based activities to encourage visitors to identify, analyze, use, and interpret artifacts. Questions become key initiators and mediators of the conversation between the past and the present. For school groups, directed-looking questions encourage children to visually dissect and describe an object; for adults, questions extend the conversation between a presenter and the participants. Through posing questions and the conversation that unfolds, we are giving the museum visitor a voice and inviting them to become our partners in exploring and understanding the past and the present. With our audience at the forefront of our planning, programs are designed to develop participants' skills in historical interpretation through posing questions and sharing perspectives.

Reading Artifacts

To begin to establish a relationship with "real stuff" we frequently facilitate an activity called "Reading Artifacts" with our *Teaching American History* participants. This experience connects teachers with one another as they collaborate in small groups, and works as an introduction to material culture. The exercise opens with a group discussion about artifacts. During this conversation participants engage in a kind of word association to create a list that captures the words and phrases that they feel define or describe what an artifact is. Often words such as *old, valuable, dusty,* and *story* appear on the list. At the conclusion of this initial discussion, a definition is written, drawn from the attributes on the group list and with input from the facilitator. In general, the definition usually reads along the lines of "objects made and used by humans in the past."

The discussion then moves toward identifying the kinds of artifacts that participants have seen or expect to see in any kind of museum. A second list is made which is divided into two broad categories: two-dimensional and three-dimensional objects. Words such as *tool, furniture, clothing, letters, paintings,* and *maps* frequently appear on these lists. This opening conversation is an effective method to build upon prior knowledge, to share ideas, to group brainstorm, and to clear up common misconceptions (i.e., the difference between a fossil and an artifact).

Next, working in small groups, teachers touch, examine, and discuss authentic artifacts (in this activity turn-of-the-century household implements, such as an apple peeler, a fluter, and a button hook) from the Museum's teaching collection

Figure 12.1 Turn of the century household objects inspire teacher investigation in the Reading Artifacts activity. © Chicago History Museum.

(Figure 12.1). Teachers get excited when the artifacts are brought out and are intrigued to discover more about the mystery object they have been given. As they engage with the object they record their observations on a simple graphic organizer (Figure 12.2) that takes them through distinct phases of analysis from concrete observations (describing the physical qualities of the object), to higher-order thinking (who might have used the object). It is not unusual to see intense conversations and actual experimentation taking place: trying the clamp on the apple peeler, putting a piece of paper between the two sides of the fluter to see what impression will be made. The artifacts and the structure of the activity encourage this kind of inquiry-based learning. At this point, groups report their initial findings. Groups are then given documents that relate to the artifact they have been working with. The documents are reproductions of pages from turn-of-the century Sears Roebuck and Montgomery Ward mail-order catalogs. Group members begin to connect their objects to a specific time period and function. They start to develop empathy as they imagine using these implements to run a household, and often conversations include remarks about how time consuming household work must have been, how physically difficult it must have been to use these kinds of heavy cast-iron tools, or how much dexterity was required to take shoes on and off using a button hook. Groups report a second time, sharing how the document either confirmed their thinking and added new information, or changed the direction of their analysis entirely. After presentations, group discussion focuses on the experience participants had in building historical understanding and making an interpretation through the use of a variety of sources, rather than relying on just a single piece of evidence.

Extensions of this activity include brainstorming exhibition topics and writing label copy. It is often eye opening to participants how the same set of artifacts and documents can be interpreted in a variety of ways to explore different aspects of history. In this case, gender roles (the fluter, flat iron, stove lid lifter,

Reading Artifacts

Interpreting symbols made by humans
using sight and touch.

Objects made and used by humans
in the past.

DESCRIPTION

What is the object made of? _____

What is its size, shape, and color?_____

_____

ANALYSIS

List three characteristics that are important about this object.

1. _____

2. _____

3. _____

INTERPRETATION

How do you think this object was used? _____

_____

_____

_____

When, or on what occasion might this object have been used? _____

_____

_____

_____

Who might have used this object? _____

_____

_____

_____

ChicagoHistoryMuseum   www.chicagohistory.org

Figure 12.2 Reading Artifacts Worksheet. During the Reading Artifacts activity, teachers
record their observations on a worksheet. © Chicago History Museum.

and cherry pitter as evidence of women's work), household technology (comparisons between then and now in cleaning and cooking), advertising (the language and imagery used in the catalogs), consumerism (these objects as the "must have" gadgets of their time), and the mail-order business (how it worked, why Chicago was the center of it, how it was the forerunner to modern mail-order catalogs and online shopping) have all been proposed as potential exhibition topics by participants. This introductory learning activity taps into the romantic emotion that Whitehead wrote "is essentially the excitement consequent on the transition from the bare facts to the first realizations of the import of their unexplored relationships."[14] Prior to a museum field trip experience, this kind of activity lays a foundation for more thorough looking and questioning in gallery spaces.

The activity concludes with a discussion of possible classroom applications, how to obtain grade-appropriate objects and documents, and how to best utilize them in instruction. In *Far Away and Long Ago,* authors Monica Edinger and Stephanie Fins recommend beginning this work with students by analyzing a single object. They further note that it is important that teachers themselves try an observational activity (such as the one above) to build comfort and experience in working with objects prior to trying these techniques with a class. They conclude that "Analysis of visual evidence can be a way of getting students to think about the kinds of questions historians ask of objects. It can lead them to think about the kinds of inferences that can be made from a single object as opposed to a group of objects and help develop their ability to generate and test hypotheses based on visual data."[15]

How Do We Teach History at the Chicago History Museum?

Over the course of participating in *Teaching American History* grants, we have continued to consider how we as museum educators teach history.

Refining Our Approach to Professional Development

The Chicago History Museum is a place of inspiration. Monica Edinger writes in the preface of her book *Seeking History: Teaching with Primary Sources in Grades 4–6,* "Primary sources are real stuff, and real stuff is powerful stuff."[16] As a museum full of the "real stuff" history is made of, the Chicago History Museum provides teachers with the opportunity to both emotionally and physically connect with the past. This "stage of romance," as Alfred North Whitehead theorized, is when the "subject matter has the vividness of novelty; it holds within itself unexplored connections with possibilities half-disclosed by glimpses and half-concealed by the wealth of material."[17] The starting point for our teaching and learning is the Museum itself, the primary source materials in our collection, and the exhibitions that create contextual environments for displaying and interpreting these objects.

Teaching American History grant projects have provided the opportunity to design learning experiences in which partners do what they do best. In the case of informal learning institutions, like the Chicago History Museum, we use active participation that includes facilitative, constructivist, and reflective practices. Teachers are engaged in cooperative learning, discussion, guided inquiry, reciprocal teaching, and simulation to emerge with deeper understandings of history that go beyond skill building or recall of facts. Engagement with primary sources provides learners with the opportunity to make observations, create interpretations, and draw conclusions from historical sources.

The Chicago History Museum has a long tradition of providing professional-development programs for teachers that engage them as lifelong learners. These programs range from informal open houses that introduce teachers to new museum resources and exhibitions, to workshops that assist teachers in preparing for a field trip to content-focused seminars that deeply explore specific history topics and classroom applications. Often programs are developed in response to a perceived need. For example, as the Internet grew and began to have a greater impact on school instruction, the Museum offered a program for teachers that examined some of the best history Web sites, how to determine the reliability of Web sites for research purposes, and how teachers could instruct their students in citing online sources. On the first anniversary of 9/11 we held a forum-style workshop to provide a place for teachers to share ideas and support one another as they decided how to address the anniversary in their classrooms. Over the years, a real sea change has taken place from Museum staff as the sole planners and providers of the professional-development experience toward a more collaborative planning process, an important feature of the *Teaching American History* grants we have participated in. Today we routinely hire teachers to present at our professional-development programs, we work closely with teachers as developers and testers of new classroom resources, and throughout the school year we turn to the advice and expertise of our Teacher Advisory Board. This shift toward more collaboration has resulted in closer relationships with teachers and a rich array of offerings that meet both the needs of the Museum and that of the school community.

In planning professional-development programs, we draw on our knowledge of adult learning and what attracts participants to our public programs. Teachers, like other adult learners are looking for an exclusive experience, one that not everybody has access to. During *Teaching American History* grant sessions our president has visited gallery spaces with teachers, engaging in conversations surrounding the exhibitions. Behind-the-scenes tours with the Museum's staff provide teachers with the opportunity to see how and where the costume collection or the decorative arts collection is stored and organized. They have visited our conservation labs to learn about the painstaking process of physically caring for the collection and they have met with Research Center staff to learn about the archival and photographic holdings of the Museum and how teachers can access these materials. These unique and memorable experiences provide a depth of knowledge that may not translate directly into the classroom but nevertheless can inform how teachers organize and approach projects, such as history-fair research and the creation of student exhibitions.

Collaboration with and among teachers is a hallmark of our contributions to the *Teaching American History* grants. Grant projects typically include university partners who contribute expert academic staff and bring the most recent historical scholarship and research to the teachers. The Chicago History Museum, and any other museums that participate in these grants, serve as a pedagogical bridge for participating teachers, helping to link graduate-level reading and work with concrete examples of instructional applications of that content. When

Figure 12.3 Civil War Prisoners of War packet. Reproductions of Civil War era documents and photographs serve as primary sources for analysis of the conditions of Northern and Southern prisoners of war camps. © Chicago History Museum.

teachers are covering the Civil War era, the Museum is able to provide learning activities that utilize primary source materials from the collection to enrich that topic. For example, teachers were given packets of high-quality reproductions of photographs and documents (Figure 12.3) relating to Northern and Southern prisoner-of-war camps. University professors and classroom teachers worked together in small groups to order and analyze sources, to reflect on reliability, purpose, and perspective, in an investigation of the conditions and quality of life in prisoner-of-war camps. In this case, the compelling human and political story of the camps was not told to participants in an explanatory fashion, instead the historical narrative was revealed through the learning experience itself. As Jay McTighe and Grant Wiggins remind us in *Understanding by Design*, "Important learning, whenever possible, should be allowed to unfold and reveal themselves through the work, as opposed to a teacher telling students what they should see as important. Imagine if storytellers stripped a story of its engaging elements and simply told its meaning or moral."[18]

The Museum Setting

The *Teaching American History* grant projects gave teachers the opportunity to experience exhibition spaces like never before: rather than walking behind a guide during a tour, teachers were active interpreters of the space-posing questions, analyzing artifacts and documents, and sharing ideas and discoveries.

Teachers in Exhibition Spaces

With a focus on experiential learning, the Chicago History Museum provides teachers with a physical, intellectual, and emotional connection to history. The

Museum is also an environment that stimulates teachers to rekindle their own love of history and to begin to imagine new ways to communicate that passion to their students. Teachers find that the museum setting and resources inspire creative thinking about history and history teaching. Simulating the field-trip experience, professional development programs invite teachers to "do" history as they analyze and discuss documents, handle and examine artifacts, reflect on findings, and share ideas. In this approach, teachers are making choices; investigating and exploring; analyzing and interpreting; and most important, sharing their discoveries with peers.

Museum exhibitions themselves are interpretations of history, as are the scholarly texts that teachers read during the grant projects. *Teaching American History* grants give teachers the chance to spend extended time in exhibition spaces without their students. Repeat visits to the same exhibition with a different focus or purpose provides the opportunity for teachers to build nuanced understandings of the space and topic, much like close reading, rereading, and discussion of a text. Often interpretive activities within the exhibition spaces are designed to be applied to a later field trip with students or adapted to the classroom. However, sometimes classroom activities serve as the inspiration for museum learning. For example, James A. Percoco, author of *A Passion for the Past*, designed a classroom assignment called "historical head" as a way for students to "get into the mind of historical figures,"[19] in other words, to develop some empathy for the people and events of the past. In this exercise his high school students fill in a drawing of an empty head with the "thoughts, ideas, visions, and motivations"[20] of a particular person, such as Frederick Douglass. We found that with some modification, this activity worked extremely well in the museum setting. During our first *Teaching American History* grant (in collaboration with Lake Forest College and Waukegan (IL) Community Unit District 60, teachers were studying the American Revolution. In designing the teacher activity for our exhibition *We the People*, museum educators adapted Percoco's historical head for exploring the compelling biographical stories in the exhibition. This classroom tool was restructured as an effective vehicle for digging into the exhibition, connecting teachers to specific artifacts, and to the people to whom they once belonged.

With a refocusing toward drawing information from the artifacts on display, rather than from a textbook (Figure 12.4), this activity proved to be a compelling way to engage with the exhibition. After completing the activity, teachers moved through the exhibition presenting their historical heads in front of the artifacts that inspired them. They collaboratively taught each other about the people of the Revolutionary War era, both famous and not so famous, and the unique artifacts that brought to life each person discussed. As Percoco notes, not only does this activity allow participants to put themselves into the shoes of another person, it shows in a "clear and concrete way what knowledge they have acquired,"[21] and it is important to note, participants enjoyed doing the activity. Other ways to interact and learn in exhibition spaces that museum staff and *Teaching American History* teachers experimented with include directed looking and discussion, paired research and report, creative drawing, and reflective response writing. These kinds of activities in museum professional development programs model for

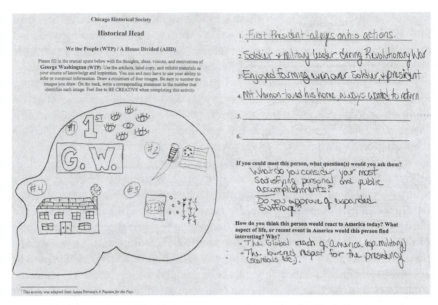

Figure 12.4 Historical Head: George Washington. The Historical Head classroom activity developed by high school teacher James Percoco was adpated for museum gallery exploration. Reprinted with permission from *A Passion for the Past: Creative Teachers of U.S. History* by James Percoco. Copyright © 1998 by James Percoco. Published by Heinemann, Portsmouth, NH. All rights reserved.

teachers how an exhibition can provide a space for students to create and share interpretations and ideas rather than the often held belief that true learning or understanding can only occur if an "expert" is leading a group on a guided tour.

When teachers explore an exhibition space multiple times, uncovering it bit by bit, like pulling apart the layers of an onion, it ultimately leads to a richer field trip for students. Teachers who participate in professional development like the *Teaching American History* grants become comfortable in the Museum and are prepared to create a focused field trip that is integrated with their instructional goals. This is a marked advantage over teachers less familiar with the Museum who may end up with a stand-alone experience disconnected from what is happening in the classroom and ultimately disorienting and uninteresting to students. The Museum supports teachers in developing memorable field trips by offering professional development programs for advance preparation, and through a new experience learning centered field trip program for students.

Students in Exhibition Spaces

As the Museum prepared for a major renovation, education staff began to question how the kind of visit we had developed for teachers participating in the *Teaching American History* grants, could be extended to students. How could the Museum provide an engaging and meaningful field trip? An interdepartmental team called the School Planning Group was convened and began to consider the field trip experience. A thorough research-and-development process led to the decision to move away from the formal guided tour, which was essentially passive, toward something more experiential. Eventually, activity stations emerged as the centerpiece of the new field trip.

Museums continue to broaden their understandings of learning theory and its application for working with diverse audiences. While once the primary staple for school audiences, the annual field trip visit with a guided tour has become just one of a range of experiences for students and teachers. Whether it is a hands-on analysis of artifacts, role playing and improvisational activities, small-group exploration at an activity station, or an audio tour written and recorded by teens, it is a variety of programs and experiences that leverages the Museum collection as a powerful instructional tool. At the Chicago History Museum, school group visits have evolved into facilitated experiences that engage children in the active side of history. We wanted children to become our partners in historical inquiry, similar to the collaborative and conversational approach used with teachers in *Teaching American History* programs.

To envision a new approach, Museum educators identified key characteristics that would allow students to become part of the historical process and engage in a conversation with the museum and with the past. Field trip experiences are designed to foster opportunities: (1) to examine and interpret primary sources— "the real stuff"; (2) to work both collaboratively in small groups for shared experiences and independently for personal connections; (3) to participate in diverse activities that challenge children cognitively, physically, and emotionally; (4) to converse with one another, student to volunteer, and even student to artifact; and finally (5) to express and share discoveries through creative writing, drawing, and role playing. In short, school group visits needed to empower children to be part of the historical process by sparking wonder, curiosity, and imagination.

The result was History à la Cart, seven mobile carts that each focus on one aspect of Chicago's history using primary source materials from the Museum's collection. Scattered throughout the museum galleries, the stations offer students twenty-minute activities facilitated by Museum staff and volunteers. Students act as historians as they pose questions, share discoveries, explore primary source materials, and work together to solve problems and meet challenges (Figure 12.5). The development of the stations allowed for the application of new learning techniques in the galleries including improvisation, game-style playing, tactile opportunities, and kinesthetic moments. At the Skyscraper station, students use their bodies to portray different elements of the John Hancock building during a charades-style game. At the Fire station, students sit around a giant map of the Great Chicago Fire to collaboratively tell the story of the fire as they fill the map with icon pieces that trace the path of the blaze. At the Bridge station, participants are challenged to design a bridge that spans the Chicago River. They test models of real bridges and discuss the drawbacks and benefits of each and compare the historic bridges to their own design solutions. At the Prairie station students imagine the vastness of the natural landscape by measuring and marking the height and depth of native plants and then comparing their own height.

Figure 12.5 At the Skyscraper station, students use improvisation techniques to act out different features of the John Hancock building, while at the Great Chicago Fire station, students collaboratively tell the story through charting the path of the fire. © Chicago History Museum.

Stations are now integrated into teacher professional development, too. During workshops teachers participate in the activities as if they were the student, which introduces teachers to the content of our new experiential field trip program better than any written description. They have a better ability to prepare their students for the field trip and also have a greater comfort level in the Museum than teachers who have not participated in a professional development program.

From the Museum Gallery to the School: Artifacts in the Classroom

Artifacts do not have to be the sole purview of museums; they can be effective and engaging in classroom instruction. In *Doing History* Linda Levstik and Keith Barton observed the important instructional benefits that emerged when teachers used artifacts in the classroom. Artifacts have the power to make memorable impressions, giving students "a more concrete understanding of life in the past"[22] and stimulating interest in a subject. Artifacts provide an element of authenticity to history instruction. They noted that when students engaged with artifacts over the course of the unit they became motivated to explore their own family artifacts, such as photographs and heirlooms. Barton and Levstik also observed that students who did not interact with artifacts had difficulty formulating meaningful questions because they did not fully grasp the use of questioning in conducting research. However, when children used artifacts, questions naturally arose as they engaged in the discovery process. Children were then able to write specific questions, to narrow their topic, and conduct focused research.

In *Teaching American History* grants, we have put interaction with artifacts at the center of our work. The museum itself is full of the "real thing" and is a welcoming place for teachers and, in turn, their students. We have also explored ways of integrating artifacts into classroom teaching. Expanding our reach beyond the Museum's walls becomes especially imperative given that *Teaching American History* grant programs are spread across the country. Some of the teachers who participate in these grants visit the Chicago History Museum from states such as Texas and California, and from across Illinois and the Midwest. They most likely will never have the opportunity to bring students to the Chicago History Museum. Making the collection accessible in the classroom via the Internet is one solution to the problem of geography and is a natural fit in the school environment. As noted in the book *Learning from Objects*, artifacts are "as much about classroom-based learning as…about visits to site, museums, and galleries, which is where people tend to think about studying objects."[23]

Museum Artifacts Online

One way to bring artifacts into the classroom is by posting high-quality digital reproductions on our Web site (http://www.chicagohistory.org). It is full of a variety of resources that teachers can download for free and use in their classrooms. These resources have all been developed in collaboration with local teachers. For example, the *History Lab* project spanned two summers and paid stipends to sixteen teachers who wrote and tested unit plans based on collection research. After testing with their students, teachers revised the units and they were posted on the Museum Web site. These units span a range of subject matter and grade levels. Many of the units relate specifically to *Teaching American History* institute topics and serve as a way to bring the Museum into the classroom. In addition, we asked teachers to present their units to the *Teaching American History* participants. Evidence shows that classroom instruction improves when teachers teach one another, in part because exemplary teachers can "inspire, as no outsider can, a vision of what's possible."[24]

The *Great Chicago Stories* project (Figure 12.6) provided us with another opportunity to deliver the Museum's collection to the classroom through the creation of a Website (http://www.greatchicagostories.org). *Great Chicago Stories*, developed in partnership with teachers (one of whom also participated in a *Teaching American History* grant project), brings Chicago history to life by integrating artifacts from the collection of the Chicago History Museum into powerful historical-fiction narratives for elementary and high school students. The narratives are points of entry for exploring key humanities themes and fundamental history concepts. These narratives allow students to explore critical American history content through the lens of Chicago. Stories about local history help students relate in more meaningful ways to the overarching American history themes covered in their textbooks and courses of study. At the elementary level students can explore transportation through the story *Joseph's Railroad*

Figure 12.6 The Great Chicago Stories website features a suite of historical fiction narratives based on the Chicago History Museum's collection and an accompanying interactive map that helps students make connections between history and geography (www.greatchicagostories.org).

Dreams, or they can delve into economics and culture when they read *Hot Dog!* High-school students can dig into labor issues and the complexity of the Haymarket Affair when they read *His Father's Namesake*, or they can consider issues of public housing and white flight by reading *Where the Neighborhood Ends*.

With the backdrop of broad American history themes, this resource has proven to be an effective teaching tool in our *Teaching American History* grant projects. For example, high-school teachers used *Great Chicago Stories* during a workshop about using narrative. Participants discovered how to use the story form to encourage students to critically engage with history, asking why things happened instead of memorizing rote facts, which leads to increased student interest and understanding. Teachers were oriented to the *Great Chicago Stories* site which provides the necessary resources for them to implement this instructional method in their classroom. The project uses artifacts as the primary tool for telling these stories and gives users access to them like never before. Students can locate story settings on an interactive history map, explore continuity and change through then-and-now photographs, and use zoom tools to see artifact details up close. Full audio recordings of all twelve narratives enrich the experience and meet multiple learning styles and needs. Classroom activities written by teachers involve students in developing their historical thinking skills as they examine and interpret primary sources.

Teacher-Made Classroom Artifact Kits

To continue building on the *Teaching American History* approach to collaborating with teachers, Museum educators explored ways to deepen our work in linking teachers and their classrooms with objects. During the *Teaching American History* grants we developed a range of learning activities that centered on objects which were used primarily in the Museum or that Museum staff took off-site to deliver to teachers in other settings. These activities had potential for use in the classroom, but only if a teacher developed his or her own collection of artifacts. During the *Teaching American History* workshops, we observed how artifacts could inspire teachers, leaving us pondering how could we help them build their own classroom teaching collection? Resources for further development such as funding to purchase objects, and guidance in locating and selecting artifacts was outside of the scope of the *Teaching American History* grants. Seeking to make this approach more realistic, the Museum secured a grant from the Polk Bros. Foundation to work with Chicago Public School third and fourth grade teachers over the course of a year and a half in a professional-development program called *History Connections & Artifact Collections* (Figure 12.7). In this initiative, teachers participate in a process that begins with the theory and practice of object-based learning and goes through the development and implementation of classroom artifact kits comprised of their own acquisitions. Author and fourth grade teacher Monica Edinger maintains that using primary sources enriches history instruction and allows students to "act as historians" and considers them "one of the most stimulating methods I use to make learning real and powerful for my young students."[25]

Figure 12.7 History Connections & Artifacts Collections teachers collaboratively investigate artifacts during a professional development workshop at the Chicago History Museum. In the outreach portion of the program, Museum educators visit classrooms to model object based learning techniques. © Chicago History Museum.

In this spirit, it is important to note that the Museum sought not to create a loan kit program administered through the institution, a more common practice, but rather to support teachers in developing a custom resource that will remain in their own classrooms. This approach encourages participants to form a true stake in the project through authentic activities and to create a flexible resource that they can add to and adapt over time. Project components include Saturday workshops with teachers, modeling by museum staff during classroom outreach workshops, field trip visits to the Museum, and joint planning and facilitation of two culminating Museum programs; a family day and a teacher symposium. Coplanning is essential to the success of the project, personalizing the process and involving participants in meaningful tasks that they can transfer to their classroom instruction. This approach is the key to effective professional development that promotes true learning, as outlined in the article in *Educational Leadership* by Grant Wiggins and Jay McTighe.[26] In the History Connections & Artifact Collections initiative, all the participants, teachers and museum staff alike, collaborate to set the objectives, formulate the program design, and develop the materials.

Lessons Learned and Benefits

Over the years of working on *Teaching American History* grants we have learned lessons big and small that have caused us to reevaluate our own practices. One key lesson that has emerged from the *Teaching American History* grants is a model for building sustained relationships between the Museum and teachers.

These kinds of working relationships which we have been able to apply to other initiatives outside of *Teaching American History* grants, allow us to practice the core elements of teaching history: interpreting the Museum collection, engaging in meaningful collaboration, and facilitating conversation. *Teaching American History* grants have also provided us the opportunities to expand our network of professional contacts, which has enriched our work with the school audience.

The Power of Long-Term Relationships

One strength common to all of the *Teaching American History* grant projects we have been involved in is that they offer the opportunity for long-term, close contact with groups of educators, often over multiple years. Early on we experienced first-hand the benefits of ongoing collaborative learning and the exchange of ideas. The opportunity to refine approaches over time produces an environment that not only allows for but encourages experimentation and chance taking. At the time of our first *Teaching American History* grant, the majority of our professional-development programs were either one-time workshops or five week seminars. A few programs took place for two weeks during the summer. However, *Teaching American History* grants provided us with a new model that linked summer and school year experiences.

Since that time we have implemented several grant-funded projects that involved more sustained contact between the Museum and teachers. For example, the formerly mentioned *Great Chicago Stories* project involved sixteen Chicago teachers who worked in collaboration with the Museum over a two-year period. Participating teachers chose the narrative topics, tested the stories in their classrooms, and wrote five lesson unit plans. Teachers helped to define and shape the multimedia feature on the site by drawing on their experience pilot testing the narratives and by critiquing a range of options. For the multimedia piece, teachers desired a tool that would expand their students' awareness of the geography of the city and where the historic events occurred; build on their curiosity of how those places looked at the time of the story compared to today; and provide a deeper interaction with the primary source materials. The project team (consisting of teachers, museum staff, and educational technology experts) eventually settled on developing an interactive map that met the expressed needs of the teachers. Teachers participated in the ongoing evaluation of the project that included testing the prototype versions of the interactive with their students, teacher logs, focus group discussions, classroom observation, analysis of student work, and peer review of unit plans. Similar to the *Teaching American History* grants, this collaboration enabled all the participants, Museum staff and classroom teachers, to form a learning community in which they could "look closely and analytically at teaching, and at how their teaching affects learning on an ongoing basis."[27]

Building on the notion of creating sustained relationships with teachers, we implemented a Teacher Advisory Board at the Museum. The charter document reads in part:

Bringing to the discussion their collective experience in teaching and learning Teacher Advisory Board members will review current offerings and will help
shape future initiatives that express the dynamic nature of history. The partnership
between Teacher Advisory Board members and Museum staff encourages educational excellence and produces programs and materials that are tailored to audience
needs and reflective of new approaches to teaching history.

This board of eighteen local educators includes pre-K to high school teachers
who work in a variety of school settings in both the city and suburbs. This group
has enabled the Museum to form our own learning community. For example,
when we began to consider the redesign of our field trip experience the School
Planning Group met with the board at key points in the process. At the beginning the board participated in a discussion about the qualities of exemplary field
trips, farther into the project the board critiqued activity station concepts, and
tested station prototypes. The board also consults on professional-development
programs, generating ideas for themes and topics and programmatic elements.
Other recent meetings have been devoted to developing curriculum resources.
For example, the board advised Museum staff on resources most useful to a
teacher visiting the temporary exhibition *Catholic Chicago*. With their advice,
gallery conversation cards and a user friendly map were produced. Select board
members who taught at the appropriate grade levels reviewed and critiqued the
draft text of the map and cards before production moved forward. The board is
also playing an instrumental role in analyzing the current educator section of
our Web site and offering ideas about better organization of information and
access to resources. Staff in such departments as Visitor Services, Collections,
and Research have benefited greatly from interacting with this group of educators to inform and further their work and to broaden their understanding of the
school perspective on various Museum initiatives.

Far Away and Long Ago: Young Historians in the Classroom is jointly authored
by a classroom teacher and a museum educator. This volume portrays two years
of cooperative history instruction in a fourth grade classroom. In one section of
the book the classroom teacher describes the impact of working with the museum
educator: "She became an extraordinary resource for me, seeking out new materials, doing special lessons in my classroom with artifacts and slides from the
museum and her own personal collection, and designing our field trips to the
museum to fit closely with our classroom work."[28] This description perfectly captures the quality of relationships and connections the Museum was inspired to
build as we took the lessons we learned from participating in *Teaching American
History* grants and applied them to other areas of museum education. In projects like *Great Chicago Stories, History Connections & Artifact Collections,* and
the formation of the Teacher Advisory Board, we have developed truly reciprocal relationships. The Museum has benefited by tapping into the professionalism
and expertise of classroom teachers to inform the development of resources and
programs. Teachers have benefited from experimenting with new instructional
strategies and from the knowledge and resources of Museum staff and collection
materials.

Expanding our Professional Network

Our participation in *Teaching American History* grants has yielded other, more subtle results. A major benefit is building professional relationships with partner institutions and networking with a wide range of teachers and colleagues from many different institutions. These relationships grow over time, widening to include more people and affect other projects. Our first *Teaching American History* grant with Lake Forest College began in 2001. Today, we continue to work with the college in a variety of ways, from meeting with professors and students to facilitating workshops for preservice teachers, and to working with College students through our internship program. We continue to turn to and draw on the expertise of colleagues from past grants. We called upon an education professor who had extensively worked on one of the *Teaching American History* grants to serve as both and advisor and instructor on *Great Chicago Stories*. She facilitated sessions that created a template for the unit plans the teachers authored. These sessions taught all of us—museum staff and classroom teachers alike—new skills in implementing the "backward design" approach developed by Jay McTighe and Grant Wiggins in their book *Understanding by Design*.

The teachers we have met through *Teaching American History* projects have spurred new relationships. Teachers broaden their understanding of the Museum and help spread the word to colleagues about our field trip and professional-development opportunities. Many of them attend programs at the Museum that are not part of the grant. Several teachers we met through *Teaching American History* grants have participated in other museum initiatives such as the *Great Chicago Stories* project, or have become members of the Teacher Advisory Board.

Conclusion

Teachers are key partners for the Chicago History Museum. The past two decades have brought changes to both history and museum education. The publication of *Building a History Curriculum: Guidelines for Teaching History in Schools* by the Bradley Commission in the late 1980s; the formation of the National Council for History Education and National History Standards; and most recently No Child Left Behind are all milestones in influencing how, why, and when history is taught in the classroom.[29] During this same period, the American Association of Museums was reflecting on its own practice with the publication of *Museums for a New Century* in 1984 followed by *Excellence and Equity: Education and the Public Dimension of Museums* and *Excellence in Practice: Museum Education Standards and Principles*. These reports defined the educational focus and public dimension of museums working with diverse audiences. As museum educators, our practice toggles between the worlds of classroom instruction and gallery interpretation. Program design for school audiences is influenced by such external factors of state standards, district priorities, and classroom course of study. In working with school audiences, museum educators must balance their own pedagogical approach and uniqueness of their own educational environment to that of the needs and priorities of the classroom.

It is, of course, impossible to know what the future holds for history instruction in the schools and for the relationship between formal and informal learning. In the wake of the Bradley Commission on History in the Schools, there was a renewed interest in history education in the United States. During the 1990s, our field trips and teacher programs were generally well attended and well funded. Since then, we, along with all museums, have had to learn to quickly adapt to changing education priorities and initiatives in order to stay connected with and relevant to our school audience. Since the advent of learning standards at the national and state levels, and as the worldwide standardized testing and accountability movements have taken hold, a challenging situation has developed for schools and subsequently for museums. Although writing about the United Kingdom, the points made by John Reeve in his essay *Prioritizing Audience Groups* also apply to current conditions in the United States.

> English children and their teachers are now the most assessed in the world, and as a direct result museums programs for schools have to meet precisely what teachers think is required or they are not adopted. Market forces now determine which exhibitions or galleries are "relevant" and such is the volume of demand and the financial clout of the customer that museums have no choice but to deliver. The curriculum is restrictive both in its view of the world and of learning. Many excellent museum exhibitions and galleries may not appear to "fit" it and are ignored as a result.[30]

Although this may sound bleak, it is actually a pragmatic view that serves as a warning, and if taken advantage of, provides opportunity.

In 2008, social science no longer appears on the Illinois Standards Achievement Test, which includes reading, mathematics, science, and writing.[31] Elementary teachers we work with report decreased classroom time devoted to history as the pressure to test well in other subjects, such as reading and math, increases. At the Chicago History Museum, we have tried to proactively address this situation by leveraging the interdisciplinary nature of history learning. As Sam Wineburg notes in his work *Historical Thinking and Other Unnatural Acts,* "There is a growing recognition by educators and policy makers that questions of historical reasoning carry implications that go well beyond the curricular borders of history."[32] For example, the *Great Chicago Stories* project aligns with the state language arts goals and the Chicago Public Schools reading and writing initiatives as well as meeting the state standards for history. Recently many organizations such as the National Council for History Education and National Council for the Social Studies have begun to mobilize members and organize lobbying efforts to strengthen the position of history in the schools. At the Museum, we continue to build lasting relationships with teachers, to grow our professional network, and to be responsive to the priorities of local districts to ensure that we are a viable resource and partner for our school audience.

As we wait to see what will happen next on the national scene, the *Teaching American History* grants take on new importance. In some cases they are the only school district sponsored history-focused professional-development opportunity available to teachers. They provide ongoing opportunities for school districts and cultural institutions to collaborate. Given the high-stakes environment that schools and museums are currently working in, it is vital that these grants continue to cultivate communities of learners and to develop new perspectives and practices on the teaching and learning of history. At the Chicago History Museum we look forward to our upcoming *Teaching American History* grants and the opportunities they provide to collaborate with teachers and other institutions and to continue grow in our own professional practice.

Notes

1. MEM and Associates in collaboration with the Chicago Historical Society. *Chicago Historical Society Strategic Direction for Education Programs, 2003–2007* (January 2004).
2. Kieran Egan, *Teaching as Story Telling: An Alternative Approach to Teaching and Curriculum in the Elementary School* (Chicago: University of Chicago Press, 1989), 29–30.
3. Elaine Wrisley Reed and Fran Lehr, "Helping Your Child Learn History," U.S. Department of Education, Office of Intergovernmental and Interagency Affairs, 1 (http://www.ed.gov/parents/academic/help/history/index.html).
4. Chris Husbands, *What Is History Teaching? Language, Ideas and Meaning in Learning about the Past* (Buckingham, UK: Open University Press, 1996), 49.
5. Ibid., 133.
6. Roy Rosenzweig and David Thelen, *The Presence of the Past: Popular Uses of History in American Life* (New York: Columbia University Press, 1998), 189.
7. Kenneth T. Jackson and Barbara B. Jackson, "Why the Time is Right To Reform the History Curriculum," in *Historical Literacy: The Case for History in American Education*, ed. Paul Gagnon and The Bradley Commission on History in Schools (Boston: Houghton Mifflin, 1989), 10.
8. Agatha Christie, *The Murder of Roger Ackroyd* (New York: Berkley Books, 1926), 114–115.
9. Edward Hallett Carr, *What is History?* (New York: Vintage Books, 1961), 9.
10. Rosenzweig, 188.
11. Carl Becker, "What is Evidence? The Realist View—Everyman His Own Historian," in *The Historian as Detective: Essays on Evidence*, ed. Robin W. Winks (New York: Harper & Row, 1969), 10.
12. Robin W. Winks, ed., *The Historian as Detective: Essays on Evidence* (New York: Harper & Row, 1969), xiii.
13. Husbands, 133.
14. Alfred North Whitehead, *The Aims of Education and Other Essays* (1929; repr. New York: Free Press, 1985), 18.
15. Monica Edinger and Stephanie Fins, *Far Away and Long Ago: Young Historians in the Classroom* (York, ME: Stenhouse, 1998), 19.
16. Monica Edinger, *Seeking History Teaching with Primary Sources in Grades 4–6* (Portsmouth, NH: Heinemann, 2000), viii.
17. Whitehead, *The Aims of Education*, 17.
18. Jay McTighe and Grant Wiggins, *Understanding by Design Handbook* (Alexandria, VA: Association for Supervision and Curriculum Development, 1999), 228.
19. James A. Percoco, *A Passion for the Past: Creative Teaching of U.S. History* (Portsmouth, NH: Heinemann, 1998), 32.
20. Ibid., 33.
21. Ibid., 32.
22. Linda S. Levstik and Keith C. Barton, *Doing History: Investigating with Children in Elementary and Middle School,* 3rd ed. (Mahwah, NJ: Lawrence Erlbaum, 2005), 89.
23. Gail Durbin, Susan Morris, and Sue Wilkinson, *Learning from Objects* (Swindon, UK: English Heritage, 1990), 3.

24. Mike Schmoker, *Results Now: How we can Achieve Unprecedented Improvements in Teaching and Learning* (Alexandria, VA: Association for Supervision and Curriculum Development, 2006), 118.

25. Edinger, *Seeking History*, viii.

26. Grant Wiggins and Jay McTighe, "Examining the Teaching Life," *Educational Leadership* 63, no. 6 (2006): 27.

27. Schmoker, *Results Now*, 108.

28. Edinger and Fins, *Far Away and Long Ago*, 4.

29. Jere Brophy and Bruce VanSledright, *Teaching and Learning History in Elementary Schools* (New York: Teacher College Press, Columbia University, 1997), 6–7.

30. John Reeve, "Prioritizing Audience Groups," in *The Responsive Museum: Working with Audiences in the Twenty-First Century*, ed. Caroline Lang, John Reeve, and Vicky Wollard (Farnham, Surrey, UK: Ashgate, 2006), 50.

31. Illinois State Board of Education, "Resources/ISAT: Student Assessment," http://www.isbe.state.il.us/assessment/isat.htm (accessed January 11, 2008).

32. Sam Wineburg, *Historical Thinking and Other Unnatural Acts* (Philadelphia: Temple University Press, 2001), 51.

Bibliography

American Association of Museums. *Excellence and Equity: Education and the Public Dimension of Museums, A Report from the American Association of Museums*. Washington, DC: American Association of Museums, 1992.

American Association of Museums standing Professional Committee on Education. *Excellence in Practice: Museum Education Standards and Principles*. Washington, DC: American Association of Museums, 2000.

Drake, Frederick and Lynn R. Nelson. *Engagement in Teaching History: Theory and Practices for Middle and Secondary Teachers*. Upper Saddle River, NJ: Pearson Merrill Prentice Hall, 2005.

Gerwin, David, and Jack Zevin. *Teaching U.S. History as Mystery*. Portsmouth, NH: Heinemann, 2003.

Krey, DeAn M. *Children's Literature in Social Studies: Teaching to the Standards*. NCSS Bulletin 95. Washington, DC: National Council for the Social Studies, 1998.

McTighe, Jay, and Carol Ann Tomlinson. *Integrating Differentiated Instruction and Understanding by Design*. Alexandria, VA: Association for Supervision and Curriculum Development, 2006.

McTighe, Jay, and Grant Wiggins. *Understanding by Design: Professional Development Workbook*. Alexandria, VA: Association for Supervision and Curriculum Development, 2004.

Munley, Marry Ellen and Randy Roberts. "Are Museum Educators Still Necessary? *Journal of Museum Education* 31, no. 1 (2006).

Weil, Stephen E. *Making Museums Matter*. Washington, D.C.: Smithsonian Institution Press, 2002.

Yell, Michael, M., Geoffrey Scheurman, and Keith Reynolds. *A Link to the Past: Engaging Students in the Study of History*. Bulletin 102. Silver Spring, MD: National Council for the Social Studies, 2004.

Chapter 13

How to Evaluate *Teaching American History* Projects

Emily Lai, Julie Kearney, and Donald Yarbrough
University of Iowa

> As a newbie TAH director in 2001, I didn't have any idea how to make full use of my project's external evaluation. Seven years later, I'm still learning. But I've come to use evaluation information constantly and reflexively in every stage of project design, much the way I'd use a compass to hike off-trail in the woods. The evaluation team shows me where my project is moving relative to my intended destination. Just about every project decision I make is somehow informed by assessment information and my evaluators' perspectives. (Elise Fillpot, TAH Project Director for Bringing History Home)

Many of the chapters in this book address the contexts, needs, and purposes for the *Teaching American History* (TAH) program or the best ways to design and implement TAH projects. The purpose of this chapter is to provide a framework for investigating, documenting, and improving the quality of TAH projects through systematic, high-quality evaluation. Because an exhaustive treatment of TAH project evaluation is not possible in one chapter, relevant references are included for additional guidance.

Types of Evaluation

There is never only one "correct" way to evaluate TAH projects. Evaluations can and should respond to the needs of sponsors and clients, project staff, and other stakeholders. In general, TAH evaluations often serve two broad classes of purposes: (1) formative purposes (i.e., to improve projects while they are being implemented), and (2) summative purposes (i.e., for decision making about the quality of completed projects; cf. Scriven, 1991). TAH evaluations can also serve a number of specific and somewhat overlapping purposes and uses (Alkin, 2004; Mark, Henry, & Julnes, 2000; Patton, 2008). For example, depending on situational needs, they can focus on *monitoring and tracking, instrumental or process improvement, accountability, investigation of merit or worth*, and *knowledge generation* for other conceptual, instrumental, and process uses (Alkin, 2004). In practice, many TAH evaluations serve multiple purposes that may change from year to year depending on the development cycle of the TAH project. In general, the value of an evaluation depends on its effectiveness and efficiency in meeting the needs of its users (Joint Committee on Standards for Educational Evaluation[JCSEE], 1994; Patton, 2008).

Most TAH projects are geared toward collecting at least some information to be used for *improving project performance* while implementation is still underway. Such formative evaluation investigates the question, "What can be done to improve project activities to better meet the identified needs?" For example, with TAH professional development projects, evaluators might survey participants about the most and least beneficial aspects of the project in order to inform staff where problems lie and how to deliver more effective programming. With timely feedback from evaluators, clients and staff may adapt the project to the needs of actual participants and their students.

Most TAH project evaluations also collect information regarding the *merit or worth* of the project after its conclusion. Such summative evaluation investigates project effectiveness: did the project produce desirable outcomes? (Rossi, Freeman, & Lipsey, 1998). For example, a summative evaluation of a TAH teacher professional development project might collect information concerning changes in teachers' historical content knowledge and skills or the growth in students' history achievement at the end of the project.

A somewhat different yet equally important evaluation purpose is to provide a complete and thorough description of the project as it was implemented and experienced by participants (monitoring and tracking; Mark et. al., 2000; Rossi et. al., 1998). TAH projects usually begin with a plan of the activities designed to occur during the grant period. In *monitoring and tracking* evaluations, the task is to answer the question, "What *actually* happened?" For this purpose, evaluators might observe teacher professional development workshops and meetings, interview the participants about what they experienced and learned, or collect other information documenting the project experience. In addition, evaluators might observe a sample of classrooms in which project participants are teaching in order to document student experiences and opportunities to learn. By combining multiple sources of information (Caracelli & Greene, 1997; Creswell, 2003; Mertens, 2005), the evaluator can craft a detailed description of the project that would enable project designers to assess fidelity of implementation—how closely the implemented project matched the planned and intended project outlined in the original grant proposal. The evaluation can document whether the intended resources were available and used, as well as whether and how proposed activities took place. Monitoring and tracking are especially important when conditions and resources change and project staff respond to unforeseen contingencies by modifying certain aspects of the project. Monitoring and tracking evaluations not only provide an accurate picture of what the TAH projects provided to participants, they also can support the *accountability* functions required by sponsors and other stakeholders. Especially when evaluations seek to document the outcomes or impact of a TAH project, it is crucial to know what participants actually experienced so that any outcomes that did or did not occur can be attributed to the TAH project as it was really implemented rather than as proposed. Monitoring and tracking also help with aligning outcomes assessment with the actual implemented project.

For example, perhaps the grant proposal initially included a unit on integrating primary sources into instruction but the workshop leader ran out of time. Knowing that teachers did not have the opportunity to learn this skill would assist evaluators and project staff in understanding why teachers subsequently did not appear to use many primary sources in their instruction. Likewise, if classroom observations revealed that some participating teachers were enriching the project-prescribed curriculum with additional activities and lessons, this finding could provide some insight into variations in the history accomplishments of students in different classrooms. Thus, developing a thorough TAH project description enables better interpretations to be made about the possible reasons for intended and unintended project outcomes.

Finally, in some cases, clients, sponsors, and other stakeholders are interested in determining outcomes and whether they can be attributed directly to the project. *Impact evaluations* investigate the question, "Would these outcomes have occurred in the absence of the project?" Impact evaluation requires an evaluation design that helps track outcomes over time and rules out alternative explanations for why they did or did not take place. Impact evaluations commonly rely on mixed methods or experimental or quasi-experimental designs with one or more control or comparison groups (Creswell, 2003; Mertens, 2005). For example, in order to investigate whether participation in a TAH project is responsible for increased student knowledge and skill in history, evaluators might compare the postproject student achievement with the achievement of similar students who did not participate. In the experimental design approach, students (or teachers, schools, etc., depending on the unit of analysis) are randomly assigned to alternative treatment or control conditions (Shadish, Cook, & Campbell, 2002). When randomization is not possible, quasi-experimental designs use a number of methods to approximate experimental designs (Shadish et al., 2002). For example, in some quasi-experimental designs, comparison schools are selected to be roughly equivalent in important ways that could affect outcomes, such as prior achievement levels, size and student composition, quality of instruction, socioeconomic status of the community, and other important factors. Well-implemented experimental and quasi-experimental designs with good monitoring and tracking help rule out alternative explanations to the conclusion that the TAH project did (or did not) produce identified outcomes.

Many evaluations are designed to fulfill both formative and summative purposes and may also suit descriptive or impact needs. For example, over the course of a project year, a TAH evaluation might create a thorough description of the project sufficient to guide replication of the project as actually implemented, collect information that can be used formatively to improve project performance, and collect evidence regarding teacher and student outcomes at the end of the project. Often, information addressing one purpose can at least partially address other purposes. For example, thorough monitoring of project implementation can provide alternative explanations for project outcomes that can then be tested in an impact assessment. To illustrate, suppose the evaluator noticed during school site visits and classroom observations that in addition to participating in a TAH project the school was also participating in other types of professional development programs aimed at improving instruction and boosting student achievement. Such alternative influences would need to be considered before project outcomes could be attributed directly to the TAH project.

Because effective TAH evaluations are responsive to specific clients' and stakeholders' information needs, the evidence provided by different evaluations may have unique features. For example, although most TAH projects with the goal of improving teachers' history content knowledge will entail an examination of teachers' knowledge prior to their participation and at various points during and at the end of the project, some clients may also want to know which context and project factors resulted in observed outcomes. Different projects may emphasize different knowledge bases and define what is meant by teachers' knowledge in unique ways. In effective TAH evaluations, the types of evidence collected (including the types of knowledge assessed as outcomes) will be aligned with the specific evaluation questions of interest and should reflect specific goals, for example, teacher knowledge, as conceptualized in the project.

In general, the types of information that may be useful to TAH stakeholders are quite varied, ranging from teacher and student needs at the outset of the project, to fidelity of implementation, to teacher and student outcomes, and even outcomes at the school or community level. Thus, although many people assume project evaluations are concerned only with outcomes that may be observed once the project is completed, in reality TAH evaluations may begin before the project has even started (in order to document participant needs), attend to every aspect of project participation and implementation, and continue to collect evidence long after the last professional development workshop is over.

Clarifying Evaluation, Assessment, and Measurement

Many people, including some educational researchers, are unsure of the true meanings of the terms *evaluation, assessment,* and *measurement,* and even consider them synonymous. However, these terms have different and useful technical meanings that help clarify what is required for quality TAH evaluations (JCSEE, 1994; Oosterhof, 1999). In brief, *evaluation* is the systematic investigation of the value of a TAH project, usually for decision making about improvement or final quality. For the purposes of this chapter, *assessment* refers to the investigation and documentation of characteristics or performances of persons, organizations, or other groups, especially with regard to important features of the project or its outcomes. For example, teacher and student knowledge, performances, skills, motivations, attitudes, and beliefs can all be assessed. So can the resources used to implement the project and the processes, facilities, and other characteristics of the project. Assessments sometimes rely on *measurement*—the systematic, technically precise attachment of numbers to describe levels of the characteristics being assessed. However, assessment may also be based on readings of project documents, formal observations, or interviews where no numbers are involved.

In summary, evaluation, assessment, and (frequently) measurement go hand in hand in TAH project evaluations. TAH evaluation requires systematic information, often from measurement or other assessment procedures, to produce judgments about the value of the project on specific dimensions of quality in a way that is useful to clients and other stakeholders. Evaluation, assessment, and measurement are all supported by extensive research and practice literature and require considerable expertise to accomplish with efficiency and effectiveness. It is essential that TAH evaluation teams possess that expertise (JCSEE, in press).

Logic Models

Regardless of the particular purpose of the evaluation, a logic model is often a useful evaluation tool (Frechtling, 2007; W. W. Kellogg Foundation, 2004). Formally, a logic model is a graphical depiction of the rationales and assumptions on which the project is based. More simply, the logic model depicts the story about how the project is expected to work by linking resources and project activities with the ultimate outcomes of the project through a chain of logic, or a series of rationales. Logic models can be straightforward and easy to understand. They often consist of only a few descriptions of elements linked together: (1) *inputs or resources;* (2) *activities;* (3) *outputs*; and (4) *outcomes*.[1] Figure 13.1 illustrates a logic model for teachers for a prototypical TAH project. Each element of the logic model is explained separately below. TAH project evaluations can investigate any element in the logic model, depending on the information needs of the evaluation users.

Project inputs or resources include human, infrastructure, financial, and other sources of support for the TAH project. For example, inputs may be individual persons, rooms, sources of funding, or complex bundles of resources, such as a community museum that will be available for workshops, training sessions, and field trips. Typical evaluation questions about project inputs direct investigation to whether the intended resources are actually available and used and which unintended or undocumented resources not in the original plan actually played a role in the implemented TAH project.

Project activities or processes include all services provided to TAH participants, such as professional development workshops, seminars and courses, curricular materials, technological support, mentoring, or work-release time. Activities constitute what is typically thought of as the intervention or treatment—the heart of the project. Typical evaluation questions investigate whether the intended TAH project was implemented with or without modifications, whether and how staff and other resources performed, how the participants experienced the TAH project (as compared with the description of the proposed project), and the actual detailed, day-to-day implemented project from various perspectives. Often, TAH projects have process goals (Stufflebeam, 2004) that specify activity schedules and milestones to be attained. Frequently, monitoring and tracking evaluations investigate process goal attainment for both formative and summative purposes.

Project outputs are the products directly resulting from project activities, such as the number of teachers receiving professional development, computers provided, lessons taught, students served, and so forth. How are outputs different from project activities? Outputs may include specifications of desired levels of

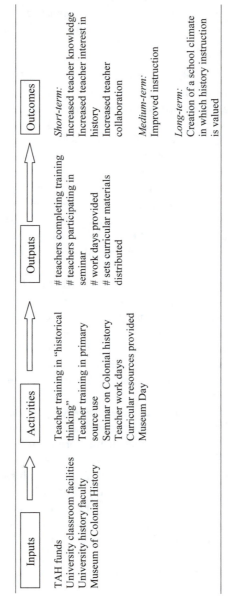

Inputs	$\Rightarrow$	Activities	$\Rightarrow$	Outputs	$\Rightarrow$	Outcomes
TAH funds		Teacher training in "historical thinking"		# teachers completing training		*Short-term:*
University classroom facilities		Teacher training in primary source use		# teachers participating in seminar		Increased teacher knowledge
University history faculty		Seminar on Colonial history		# work days provided		Increased teacher interest in history
Museum of Colonial History		Teacher work days		# sets curricular materials distributed		Increased teacher collaboration
		Curricular resources provided				
		Museum Day				*Medium-term:*
						Improved instruction
						Long-term:
						Creation of a school climate in which history instruction is valued

Figure 13.1 Simple logic model for (hypothetical) TAH project: Teacher model.

service. For example, if one project objective was to provide professional development to 150 teachers, documenting the output of the professional development activities allows evaluation users to determine whether activities met their mark or fell short with respect to this objective. Documenting outputs constitutes a simple accountability mechanism for determining whether certain aspects of project activities took place as intended. However, outputs should not be confused with project outcomes. Although all 150 teachers may have participated in the professional development, not all participants necessarily experienced an increase in content knowledge or pedagogical skill, or became committed to using their new knowledge and skills in teaching students.

Project outcomes depicted in the logic model typically focus on outcomes explicitly desired by the project planners. However, because the logic model depicts the project as it was intended rather than how it is ultimately implemented, it is also important for the evaluator to attend to unintended or unexpected consequences. For TAH professional development, typical outcomes to be investigated include teacher interest in or appreciation for American history, teacher knowledge of American history, and teachers' pedagogical knowledge and skill. Sometimes, outcomes are classified by the time frame associated with them. For example, a project may involve short-term, medium-term, and long-term outcomes. Short-term outcomes might include relatively immediate changes in teachers. For example, after a series of workshops that addressed Colonial America, project staff might expect teachers to be more interested in history and perhaps more knowledgeable about this specific time period. However, good teaching integrates multiple types of knowledge and skills. Most project staff would not expect teachers' instruction to improve after only a few workshops. Instead, improvements in instruction might be conceptualized as a desired medium-term outcome, occurring slowly and gradually as teachers are able to adapt and apply what they've learned in their own classrooms. Long-term outcomes might be investigated by examining whether teachers continue to read or study history after project participation. Finally, unintended or unexpected outcomes could include such positives as teachers encouraging students to sign up for and pass advanced placement exams in American history or such negatives as teachers spending too much time on specific aspects of American history that were emphasized in the TAH project while neglecting other teaching responsibilities. Good ways to explore these kinds of outcomes include asking teachers to complete surveys or take part in interviews near the end of the grant period.

The above example referred to teacher experiences and outcomes. However, many evaluations will also include an examination of student experiences and outcomes. The long-term goal or desired "downstream impact" (Davidson, 2005; Scriven, 1991) for many projects is increased student achievement. This brings to light an important point about any teacher professional development project— not just TAH: often, separate logic models should be constructed for teachers and students. Although teachers are the immediate targets of TAH projects, students are the ultimate beneficiaries of improved instruction. Moreover, teacher and student logic models should be nested, in the sense that outcomes at the curriculum and instruction level serve as inputs or resources at the student level. In the logic model for teacher professional development, increased knowledge is an *outcome* of the project, but in the logic model for students, increased teacher knowledge, skills, and practices serve as *inputs*. When the logic models are nested it provides an uninterrupted link in the chain between project inputs and resources and ultimate student outcomes. An example of a logic model for students that is explicitly linked to the teacher logic model is exhibited in Figure 13.2.

Logic models are useful for a variety of purposes. During the project design stage, a logic model can help clarify one's thinking about how best to achieve desired outcomes. The process of constructing a logic model can serve to facilitate communication among project staff about the project's goals and objectives. Creating the logic model can also help uncover important assumptions about the project that may need to be examined. Logic models can even be shared with project participants to help them develop an understanding of the long-term project aims and how the separate pieces of their professional development fit together. Having a logic model is also an aid to the evaluator, both in understanding the staff's vision for the project, as well as in designing the evaluation. The logic model can serve as a blueprint for the types of evaluation questions that might prove most useful to project staff.

Program and Project Theory

Program theory is closely related to the subject of logic models because program theories describe in more detail the concepts and mechanisms by which identified TAH needs are addressed by the project (cf. Chen, 1990, 2005; Rossi et al., 1998). At its simplest, program theory refers to the collection of theories, assumptions, and beliefs about what the problems or needs are, how and why the project will achieve its intended process, output and outcome goals, and how to define and assess the goals and outcomes (Chen, 1990, 2005; Donaldson, 2003; Rossi et al., 1998). These theories, assumptions, and beliefs may be based on scholarship, on practitioners' experiences, detailed knowledge of the setting, traditions, or on unfounded beliefs. For example, TAH program theories may be formal in nature and backed by extensive empirical research that demonstrates the effectiveness of certain instructional methods for improving certain types of student learning, such as Brown and Campione's classic study of cooperative learning methods (1994). Other TAH program theories may be less formal and may even consist of unexpressed, implicit assumptions on the part of project designers about the root causes of certain problems (cf. Gaynor, 1998).

TAH program theories are important because they constrain and define the needs the project serves and the questions the evaluation addresses. For example, a TAH project designed to improve student learning in American history by increasing teachers' historical content knowledge implicitly assumes that the root cause of students' low achievement in history is the inadequate preparation and knowledge of their teachers, rather than other plausible reasons such as poor instructional methods, low student interest in history, or subpar history curricula. A different project, focused on improving teachers' pedagogy, might have a

Inputs	Activities	Outputs	Outcomes

Inputs	Activities	Outputs	Outcomes
Teacher Inputs: Increased teacher knowledge Increased teacher interest in history Increased teacher collaboration Improved instruction *Project Inputs:* Curricular materials Local historical sites	Instruction on Colonial America Exposure to primary sources Exposure to curricular materials Field trip to local historical sites Field trip to Museum of Colonial History	# lessons delivered by teachers # students receiving instruction	*Short-term:* Increased student interest in history Increased student knowledge *Medium-term:* Increased student history achievement Increased # students participating in district's History Day *Long-term:* Increased # students enrolling in Advanced Placement History courses in high school

Figure 13.2 Simple logic model for (hypothetical) TAH project: Student model.

very different set of program theories, perhaps including the implicit assumption that teachers may know *what* to teach, but not *how* to teach it in the most effective way. Such a TAH program theory assumes that if the pedagogical need is addressed, students' achievement will increase.

Like logic models, the articulation of program theory is useful to the extent that it makes obvious what assumptions project designers and staff hold about the project (Donaldson, 2003). Exploring program theory also facilitates conversations concerning the theory of change for project participants—that is, the explanation of how participants are expected to change as a result of their interaction with the project (Chen, 2005). Program theories can form the basis of hypotheses to be tested in the evaluation of the project. For example, if a project were explicitly designed around the belief that turning students into historians is best accomplished by teaching them historical thinking skills rather than exclusive reliance on history content (as has been argued by Wineburg, 2001), the evaluation might compare students trained to "do history" with a comparable group of students receiving more conventional history instruction. If the group trained as historians outperformed the comparison group on tasks related to the work of "real" historians—independent of their level of content knowledge—this would provide some evidence to support the hypothesis that historical thinking skills, rather than knowledge of historical content alone, are necessary to turn novice historians into experts. To the extent that an important purpose of the TAH evaluation is additional knowledge about the factors affecting students' desired TAH project outcomes, articulated program theory (Chen, 2005) can be very important in guiding the evaluation.

Even when specific hypotheses are not being formally tested, examination of program theory can help focus the evaluation by drawing attention to questions of interest for project staff. The process of articulating program theory can consist simply of a series of interviews or informal conversations with project staff and other interested stakeholders about how they believe the project will achieve its intended goals (cf. Bickman, 2000). In addition, information about the theories undergirding the project is often also found in project documents, such as the original grant proposal.

Although the term *program theory* suggests a single, overarching theory that explains the entire project, in reality it may encompass multiple theories, each of which relates to a different aspect or phase of the project (Chen, 1990, 2005). For example, project staff may have theories about teacher needs (such as their need for supplemental training in historical content) that inform their selection of teacher professional development activities. There may also be theories derived from educational research about the best way to deliver effective professional development; for example, by focusing on specific instructional practices or providing opportunities for active learning (Desimone, Porter, Garet, Yoon, & Birman, 2002). Finally, theories regarding how students learn history best may guide the selection of instructional methods emphasized during professional development. These theories may all originate from different sources, resulting in a mixture of formal theories derived from academic literature and informal beliefs or assumptions held by project designers and project staff (Donaldson, 2007).

Combining logic models with program theory provides a rather complete picture of the project as intended (Donaldson, 2007; Davidson, 2005), which can greatly facilitate the generation of relevant evaluation questions. Embedding program theory into a logic model involves articulating, where possible, the assumptions, theories, and beliefs that support designated inputs, activities, and outcomes. Figure 13.3 illustrates an example of a logic model for teachers with embedded program theory for a prototypical TAH project discussed previously. In this example, college history faculty is listed as an input resource, with the explanation that history teachers often lack adequate college-level coursework in history, which causes them to approach their own history instruction as a forced march through the textbook rather than an academic discipline worthy of sustained inquiry. Likewise, teacher instruction in historical thinking corresponds to the argument that both teachers and students often lack historical knowledge because neither has been trained in historical ways of thinking.

With clear program theory providing a rationale for project inputs and activities, potential evaluation questions begin to suggest themselves. The evaluator could use the example outlined in Figure 13.3 to undertake a needs assessment for teachers prior to project implementation to determine whether participants actually lack historical thinking skills or suffer from deficient prior preparation. In this example, evaluation questions might include the following:

- What did participants have in terms of prior college-level knowledge and skills related to teaching history?
- To what extent are participants able to demonstrate historical thinking skills? To what extent do they lack these skills?
- What needs do participants report?
- What barriers to effective history instruction do participants identify?

Similarly, the evaluator might investigate whether variation in the extent to which teachers' knowledge and historical thinking skills improve is related to variation in the skill or thoroughness with which teachers implement prescribed instructional techniques and curricula. In other words, do higher levels of knowledge and skill predict better teaching? In this case, evaluation questions might include the following:

- What do teachers know at the conclusion of the project compared to their knowledge at the beginning?
- How skillfully and thoroughly do teachers implement new instructional techniques and curricula at the end of the project?
- What is the relationship (if any) between the historical knowledge and instructional skills of teachers as these concepts have been defined within the project?

There are a variety of different types of program theory that may be examined and many different ways in which program theory may be explored in an

Inputs →	Activities →	Outputs →	Outcomes
TAH funds University classroom facilities University history faculty Museum of Colonial History	Teacher training in "historical thinking" Teacher training in primary source use Seminar on Colonial history Teacher work days Curricular resources provided Museum Day	# teachers completing training # teachers participating in seminar # work days provided # sets curricular materials distributed	*Short-term:* Increased teacher knowledge Increased teacher interest in history Increased teacher collaboration *Medium-term:* Improved instruction
Program theory			
Teachers lack adequate college-level coursework in history, which leads to deficient instruction (Wilson & Wineburg, 1988). TAH projects that forge local partnerships with institutions of higher learning will foster vertical alignment of history content/skills emphasized throughout K-16 instruction. Partnerships with local museums optimize the use and value of existing resources and encourage interest in learning about history outside of the classroom.	Teachers lack historical knowledge because they are not trained in historical ways of thinking, including the use of primary source evidence (Wineburg, 2001). A prerequisite condition for the skilled teaching of history is for the teacher to "know" the subject. Teachers need time to collaborate with one another in order to facilitate growth in knowledge and instructional skills (DuFour et al., 2004). Teachers who are provided with curricular resources will be more likely to implement new instructional techniques than those who must create their own curricular units.		Training sessions and seminars will lead to improved teacher knowledge and skill and an increase in teachers' interest in teaching history. Providing work days and shared planning sessions will facilitate greater collaboration among history teachers. Improved knowledge, skill, and enthusiasm for history will eventually lead to improved instruction.

Figure 13.3 Logic model with embedded program theory for (hypothetical) TAH project: Teacher model

evaluation. These topics are developed more fully in the references cited above as well as in other scholarship (cf. Weiss, 1998, 2000).

Putting Logic Models and Program Theory into Action: Designing and Implementing the Evaluation

If one embeds articulated program theory into the logic model a wealth of possible evaluation questions and issues to address is presented. However, it is seldom feasible or desirable to address each and every one. In order to address TAH evaluation clients' and stakeholders' needs effectively evaluations usually focus on the most important evaluation questions that can result in useful knowledge. Knowing how to narrow the evaluation focus by tailoring evaluation questions to the information needs of project staff and other stakeholders can be a critical step in formulating a practical evaluation plan designed to provide maximally useful information.

Using Professional Standards and Guidelines

TAH evaluations (just like the TAH projects they evaluate) require design, planning, and implementation to succeed. A large body of evaluation practice literature can provide guidance to TAH evaluation teams. Many program and project evaluators rely on guidelines and standards to help them with their practice, for example, the *Guiding Principles for Evaluators* (AEA, 2004) and *The Program Evaluation Standards.* (JCSEE, 1994, in press). The *Guiding Principles for Evaluators* addresses the professional duties of practicing evaluators. The *Program Evaluation Standards* define and elaborate the four aspects of evaluation quality (utility, feasibility, propriety, and accuracy) with each aspect expressed through multiple supporting standards for evaluation quality. Although a complete discussion of these codes for quality is beyond the scope of this chapter, they are essential for high-quality TAH evaluations. For example, the utility standards focus on procedures for maximizing the likelihood that evaluation findings satisfy the information needs of sponsors, clients, and other stakeholders. These groups may use the information *directly* (e.g., to make project improvements or justify funding decisions) or *indirectly* (e.g., to further understanding about particular project elements that may be incorporated into existing conventional wisdom regarding "what works"; cf. Weiss, 1998). The feasibility standards provide guidance for keeping the evaluation scope bounded within reasonable limits, as defined by time, budgetary, human resources, and political constraints. Similarly, the accuracy standards convey how the data collection methodology and design can embody principles that result in less error, bias, and distortion. Propriety standards alert the TAH evaluator to legal, ethical, moral, and professional issues in evaluation. The *Guiding Principles* and the *Program Evaluation Standards* in their entirety are designed to facilitate good decisions about evaluation design, implementation, and selection of external evaluation teams. They are also useful for evaluating the quality of evaluation proposals, designs, and implemented evaluations (cf. Stufflebeam, 2001).

Maximizing Utility of Evaluation Findings

Ultimately, it is the quality and appropriate use of evaluation findings that justify the allocation of resources to TAH project evaluations (JCSEE, in press; Patton, 2008). There are a number of steps that can be taken to make evaluation findings more useful to project staff and other stakeholders. Many of these steps occur during evaluation design stages, when evaluation team members are gathering information about project and evaluation purposes, helping to articulate logic models, and identifying evaluation questions. For example, identifying and involving multiple client and stakeholder groups during these early stages can help to ensure that the diversity of information needs is adequately addressed. In TAH project evaluations, stakeholder groups may include sponsoring organizations and clients, project staff, consultants to the project, community leaders, teacher participants, school administrators, parents of participating students, history and other higher education professionals, and students themselves. Collaboration with stakeholder groups can help prioritize information needs, because the evaluation will almost certainly be incapable of addressing all of them. Identifying and prioritizing information needs will lead quite naturally to the development of relevant evaluation questions to guide evaluation design.

Similarly, time, budgetary, and resource limitations narrow the scope of the evaluation and focus attention on a subset of useful and feasible evaluation questions. Given the most important purposes that the evaluation serves, the available resources help determine evaluation planning and implementation. Considering evaluation feasibility during the planning stage allows project designers to ask themselves, "What are the most important things I want to learn about the effects of this project on students?" For example, a project planner may wonder whether students in a high school TAH project classroom improve their performance in school in general, but learning that would entail monitoring grades and gathering other data regarding academic performance, calling for additional time and resources. In order for the evaluation to be feasible, it may be necessary to narrow the scope in some way, perhaps by examining history performance only and not academic performance in other areas.

Once evaluation questions have been generated, reflected on, and selected in consultations among evaluators, clients, project staff, and other stakeholders, TAH evaluators must draft plans for collecting evidence to answer those questions. Methods for collecting evaluation evidence should correspond reasonably with the specific evaluation questions selected. For example, an evaluation question might be: "How skillfully and thoroughly did participating teachers implement prescribed instructional methods and curricula in their classrooms?" The ensuing evaluation, responding to that question, must investigate what occurs in the classroom. Methods could include classroom observations or self-reports (e.g., teacher interviews, surveys, checklists, rating scales, logs). Another common evaluation question is "Has students' history knowledge increased as a result of participating in the project?" Such an evaluation question requires appropriate methods for assessing students' historical content knowledge. The assessment must be aligned with the specific content and skill areas emphasized during instruction in order to document changes in student knowledge over time relative to some sort of comparison group. Because different evaluation questions will require different types of evidence, evaluators should be open to using methods that are best suited to answer a given question rather than limiting the evaluation questions to include only those that can be addressed with a prior, preferred method. Also to be avoided is the use of inappropriate evidence to support inferences and conclusions (for example, the use of student test score data to infer the quality of teachers' instructional practices without examining the practices directly; the use of unaligned data from existing assessment programs, etc.).

Sometimes, the evaluation methods may be adapted to make the desired evaluation more feasible. For example, if intended evaluation users need to investigate whether participation in the project resulted in greater use of primary source documents, evaluators might conduct a control group study investigating use of historical documents in actual classrooms. However, if the evaluation is to be completed in too short a time frame or the context does not support randomization or quasi-experimentation, this approach might not be feasible. To best meet users' needs, the evaluation might use a case study design (Stake, 1995, 2000; Yin, 2003), or focus on assessing participant outcomes and describing plausible factors that might also contribute to them.

Communication

A key feature of all high-quality TAH evaluations is good communications planning (Alkin, Christie, & Rose, 2006; JCSEE, in press). As is the case for other aspects of the evaluation plan, the purposes and uses that the evaluation serves should help guide communication strategies. Clear communication is important from start to finish. When planning the TAH evaluation, evaluators must clearly express the kinds of data to be collected, how and by whom it will be collected, the purposes the data will serve, and the nature of the conclusions that will be possible to extract from the data analysis. At the end of the grant period, when reporting student assessment results, the evaluator must provide findings to the stakeholders in a way that is appropriate and meaningful for each stakeholder group. For example, the way in which findings are reported to a research journal may be very different from how the same information is conveyed to a school board or parent group. Poor communication concerning the purposes and procedures for assessment or other information collection can undermine the quality and credibility of the entire evaluation. To avoid such problems, good communications planning is required from the start of the evaluation until the last report.

Most TAH evaluations require more frequent and distributed reporting than can be accomplished with annual reports only. For reporting to be most useful, it must be accurate, sufficient, and timely. Often, brief summaries and oral reports can communicate the most important findings for formative purposes almost as quickly as the findings can be accurately produced. Many TAH evaluations will require both formal and informal reporting, occurring regularly throughout the project as findings become available. Communication can also be enhanced through a series of short reports that are responsive to immediate findings. They can later be compiled in quarterly, annual ,or other reference reports. Reporting can also occur informally, through telephone conversations or e-mails. Just as project and evaluation staff consider utility (JCSEE, 1994, in press; Patton, 2008) during the planning phase, it should also be paramount in the reporting phase. For example, if audiences are more interested in hearing about conclusions reached than in particular methods used, attention to methods can be relegated to appendices or Web sites. Regardless of how it is packaged, sequenced, and presented, the information should be accurate, sufficient, clear, and understandable, and to the extent possible, encourage follow-through and use of evaluation results.

Controlling and Assuring the Quality of TAH Project Evaluations

From the perspective of the project management literature (Project Management Institute [PMI], 2000; Verzuh, 1999), TAH project evaluation has as its purpose the quality control and assurance of TAH projects. This last section addresses the issue of how to assure and control the quality of the TAH project evaluation itself. The process of evaluating the evaluation itself is called metaevaluation, and just like any other evaluation, it can serve both formative and summative purposes. Increasingly, program evaluators are calling for the systematic metaevaluation of all evaluation work (Stufflebeam, 2001; JCSEE, in press). To increase the quality of their TAH project evaluations, clients, sponsors and other stakeholders can take a number of important steps. First, they can be sure that those planning and implementing their TAH evaluations are familiar with the concepts from this chapter and from the standards and guidelines of the professional organizations (AEA, 2004; JCSEE, 1994, in press). Second, they can get involved in the evaluation planning and communication themselves to be sure that the evaluation is meeting the real needs of users. Third, they can review the planning and implementation of their evaluation and compare what is taking place to the principles outlined in this chapter and to the professional standards and guidelines.

Summary

Evaluations of TAH projects are important because they can document the quality of the projects and their outcomes, contribute to improvements during project implementation, lead to modifications that will increase future quality, document what has worked in one setting and might well work in others, lead to greater cost-effectiveness and efficiencies, and increase knowledge about how teachers and students gain knowledge and skill related to American history. However, high-quality evaluation work is different in important ways from most paradigm-driven educational research. Even though both research and evaluation rely on high-quality investigative methods and systematic information collection, analysis, and interpretation, the primary purpose of evaluation (in contrast to research) is to serve the needs of clients, sponsors, and other stakeholders and users.

In order to do their work competently, TAH project evaluation teams must possess or have access to the necessary expertise. This expertise includes experience with and knowledge of evaluation standards and guidelines, competence with multiple methods and designs from naturalistic and experimental, qualitative and quantitative perspectives, and experience with real-world evaluations in real-world settings.

Note

1. The Kellogg model also includes one final element—impacts. However, many evaluations will not include an examination of project impact.

References

Alkin, M. C. (2004). Context-adapted utilization: A personal journey. In M. C. Alkin (Ed.), *Evaluation roots* (pp. 293–303). Thousand Oaks, CA: Sage.

Alkin M. C., Christie, C. A., & Rose, M. (2006). Communicating evaluation. In I. F. Shaw, J. C. Greene, & M. M. Mark (Eds.), *The Sage handbook of evaluation* (pp. 384–403). Thousand Oaks, CA: Sage.

American Evaluation Association (AEA). (2004). *Guiding principles for evaluators.* Retrieved January 20, 2009, from http://www.eval.org/Publications/GuidingPrinciples.asp

Bickman, L. (2000). Summing up program theory. In P. J. Rogers, T. A. Hacsi, A. Petrosino, & T. A. Huebner (Eds.), Program theory in evaluation: Challenges and opportunities [Special issue]. *New Directions for Evaluation, 87*(3). San Francisco: Jossey-Bass.

Brown, A., & Campione, J. (1994). Guided discovery in a community of learners. In K. McGilly (Ed.), *Classroom lessons: Integrating cognitive theory and classroom practice* (pp. 229–272). Cambridge, MA: MIT Press.

Caracelli, V. J., & Greene, J. C. (1997). Crafting mixed-method evaluation designs. In J. C. Greene & V. J. Caracelli (Eds.), Advances in mixed-method evaluation: The challenges and benefits of integrating diverse paradigms [Special issue]. *New Directions for Evaluation, 74*(2).

Chen, H-T. (1990). *Theory-driven evaluation.* Newbury Park, CA: Sage.

Chen, H-T. (2005). *Practical program evaluation.* Thousand Oaks, CA: Sage.

Creswell, J. W. (2003). *Research design: Qualitative, quantitative, and mixed methods approaches* (2nd ed.). Thousand Oaks, CA: Sage.

Davidson, E. J. (2005). *Evaluation methodology basics: The nuts and bolts of sound evaluation.* Thousand Oaks, CA: Sage.

Desimone, L. M., Porter, A. C., Garet, M. S., Yoon, K. S., & Birman, B. F. (2002). Effects of professional development on teachers' instruction: Results from a three-year longitudinal study. *Educational Evaluation and Policy Analysis, 24*(2), 81–111.

Donaldson, S. I. (2003). Theory-driven program evaluation in the new millennium. In S. I. Donaldson & M. Scriven (Eds.), *Evaluating social programs and problems: Visions for the new millennium* (pp. 109–141). Thousand Oaks, CA: Sage.

Donaldson, S. I. (2007). *Program theory-driven evaluation science: Strategies and applications.* Mahwah, NJ: Erlbaum.

DuFour, R. (2004, March 1). The best staff development is in the workplace, not in the workshop. *Journal of Staff Development, 25*(2), 63–64.

Frechtling, J. A. (2007). *Logic modeling methods in program evaluation.* San Francisco, Jossey-Bass.

Fitzpatrick, J. L., Sanders, J. R., & Worthen, B. R. (Eds.). (2004). *Program evaluation* (3rd ed.). Boston: Pearson Education.

Gaynor, A. K. (1998). *Analyzing problems in schools and school systems: A theoretical approach.* Mahwah, NJ: Erlbaum.

Joint Committee on Standards for Educational Evaluation (JCSEE). (1994). *The program evaluation standards* (2nd ed.). Thousand Oaks, CA: Sage.

Joint Committee on Standards for Educational Evaluation (JCSEE). (in press). *The program evaluation standards* (3rd ed.). Thousand Oaks, CA: Sage.

W. W. Kellogg Foundation. (2004). *Logic model development guide*. Battle Creek, Michigan, W. W. Kellog Foundation. Retrieved January 20, 2009, from http://www.wkkf.org/Pubs/Tools/Evaluation/Pub3669.pdf

Mark, M. M., Henry, G. T., & Julnes, G. (2000). *Evaluation: An integrated framework for understanding, guiding, and improving policies and programs*. San Francisco: Jossey-Bass.

Mertens, D. M. (2005). *Research and evaluation in education and psychology: Integrating diversity with quantitative, qualitative, and mixed methods* (2nd ed.). Thousand Oaks, CA: Sage.

Oosterhof, A. (1999). *Developing and using classroom assessments*. Upper Saddle River, NJ: Merrill.

Patton, M. Q. (1997). *Utilization-focused evaluation* (4th ed.). Thousand Oaks, CA: Sage.

Project Management Institute. (2000). *A guide to the project management body of knowledge*. New York: Author.

Rossi, P. H., Freeman, H. E., & Lipsey, M. W. (1998). *Evaluation: A systematic approach*. Thousand Oaks, CA: Sage.

Scriven, M. (1991). *Evaluation thesaurus* (4th ed.). Newbury Park, CA: Sage.

Shadish, W. R., Cook, T. D., & Campbell, D. T. (2002). *Experimental and quasi-experimental design*. Boston: Houghton Mifflin.

Stake, R. E. (1995). *The art of case study research*. Thousand Oaks, CA: Sage.

Stake, R. E. (2000). Case studies. In N. K. Denzin & Y. S. Lincoln (Eds.), *Handbook of qualitative research* (2nd ed., pp. 435–454). Thousand Oaks, CA: Sage.

Stufflebeam, D.L. (2001). The metaevaluation imperative. *American Journal of Evaluation, 22*(2), 183–209.

Stufflebeam, D. L. (2004). The 21st-century CIPP model: Origins, development, and use. In M. C. Alkin (Ed.), *Evaluation roots* (pp. 245–266). Thousand Oaks, CA: Sage.

Verzuh, E. (1999). *The fast forward MBA in project management*. New York: Wiley.

Weiss, C. H. (1998). *Evaluation* (2nd ed.). Upper Saddle River, NJ: Prentice-Hall.

Weiss, C. H. (2000). Which links in which theories shall we evaluate? In P. J. Rogers, T. A. Hacsi, A. Petrosino, & T. A. Huebner (Eds.), Program theory in evaluation: Challenges and opportunities. *New Direction for Evaluation, 87*(3).

Wilson, S. M., & Wineburg, S. (1988). Peer at history from different lenses: The role of disciplinary perspectives in the Teaching of American History. *Teachers College Record, 89*, 525–539.

Wineburg, S. (2001). *Historical thinking and other unnatural acts: Charting the future of teaching the past*. Philadelphia: Temple University Press.

Yin, R. K. (2003). *Case study research* (3rd ed.). Thousand Oaks, CA: Sage.

Part IV

Emerging Practices in the Larger Perspective

Introduction

Part IV addresses emerging practices from *Teaching American History* grants that places them in the larger perspective of education and history education specifically and the realities of the contrasts between the outside pressures on the college and university classroom and the K-12 classroom along with providing a history of the intent and design of the federal government's grant program. Those interested in the history of the TAH program and those interested in learning more about making connections between colleges and universities and K-12 schools and classrooms will find something of interest in this final section of the book.

Overarching Themes

In examining the chapters in this section, an overarching theme emerges. We all need to learn more about what others in various capacities in our chosen professions of history and history education are doing. The *Teaching American History* grant program has an important place within the larger scope of federal grant programs but is unique in its impact and potential for bringing together practitioners of history at all levels, whether in the postsecondary setting or in the K-12 classroom. We can all benefit from working together to ensure that everyone's knowledge of history is expanded and that unreasonable demands from beyond our research and classroom walls don't make these important decisions for us. Instead, we can make these decisions for ourselves by effectively collaborating with our colleagues and go beyond teaching to continue to learn.

Emerging Practices Chapter By Chapter

In chapter 14, Towson University Professor and Chair of History Robert E. Rook examines the "clash of agendas" facing teachers each day as they struggle to not only improve student learning of American history but also to ensure that they are meeting the state standards with each lesson they teach, along with implementing appropriate assessments to prepare students for the state testing they will ultimately face. In contrast, many college and university history professors lack even a basic awareness of the daily struggles faced by teachers in the K-12 environment and do not understand the constraints under which they operate in order to teach American history. Rook further points out that college and university history professors have much to learn from their K-12 colleagues, especially in terms of the increasingly central role assessment is playing even in postsecondary education. As he points out, most graduate programs in history do not pay much if any attention to the scholarship surrounding effective teaching. Rook also discusses the challenges faced by college and university faculty who are still earning tenure or want to be successful in their next promotion bid.

In the final chapter in this collection, Cary Wintz of Texas Southern University, a historically Black college and university in Houston, traces the history of the *Teaching American History* program and places it within the larger context of similar federal efforts to support history and history education. As a frequent reviewer of TAH proposals and a guest historian for TAH institutes, he provides what he terms as an "outsider's assessment of the program" that begins by discussing the original intent of the *Teaching American History* program as envisioned by both Congress and the U.S. Department of Education. Wintz describes the evolution of the program along with its strengths and weaknesses and provides his assessment of how the TAH program has fulfilled and not fulfilled the original expectations placed upon it. He asserts that Senator Robert Byrd's vision remained constant but that it was left up to the U.S. Department of Education to translate this senator's vision into an actual program that would impact history teaching in classrooms throughout the country. Pointing out that the TAH program's location in this particular part of the federal government is fundamental to understanding the program itself. Additionally, he discusses the grant evaluation process and how it has evolved over time. This final topic is something of interest to almost anyone in any way connected to a *Teaching American History* grant.

Chapter 14

Mirrors, Mutuality of Interest, and Opportunities to Learn

The TAH Program, Assessment, and Faculty

Robert E. Rook
Towson University

In February 2008, in a rite of passage as regular as congressional recesses, another installment in the canon of concern about students' basic knowledge of history appeared in *The New York Times*. Reporting on the results of its recent telephone survey, Common Core, a nonpartisan research group dedicated to the teaching of liberal arts in American public schools, decried the state of history education in America's public education. One of Common Core's central arguments is that the "No Child Left Behind [NCLB]…has impoverished America's public school curriculum by holding schools accountable for students' cores on annual tests in reading and math" while requiring no similar tests for other disciplines, leaving the choice to assess student learning in those areas, history among them, to the states. While not directly indicting NCLB for the poor state of history knowledge among America teenagers, Common Core did argue that "the law has led schools to focus too narrowly on reading and math, thereby crowding time out of the school day for history, literature and other subjects." Indeed, this assessment echoed the results of the Center on Education Policy study, which indicated that "62 percent of school systems nationwide had added an average of three hours of math or reading instruction each week, at the expense of time spend on social studies, art and other subjects."[1] Such concerns mirrored those expressed elsewhere concerning the impact of NCLB with one report pronouncing one of the "worst-case scenarios" to be "a generation of youth who have good 'word attack' skills but who know little and care less about important facts, events, and concepts in history, science, and the arts."[2]

As if to anticipate the results reported by Common Core and addressing other related concerns, the Pennsylvania State Board of Education's unanimous approval of new requirements for high school graduation no doubt sent shudders down the spines of both high school faculty and building administrators. Under the new proposed requirements, students would be required "to pass a series of state exams before being allowed to graduate…." including an exam in American history. Contrary to Common Core's expressed concerns, history and other disciplines were back on the assessment agenda. If the Pennsylvania proposal becomes law then Pennsylvania will join more than twenty-five states that either have or will have (by 2012) content-specific exit exams for high school seniors.[3]

Pennsylvania's recent action is yet one more step down the road of assessment-based accountability, a reality driven as much by several decades of American educational history as by the more notable presumed culprit, the reauthorization of the Elementary and Secondary Education Act (ESEA) in 2001, more commonly known as No Child Left Behind (NCLB). In its original legislative form the ESEA (1965) not only constituted an element of President Lyndon B. Johnson's Great Society program but also represented a continuation of direct federal interventions in American public education that began in the early 1950s. Those early attempts reflected both domestic concerns over civil rights issues and Cold War fears that somehow American students, and the nation, were being left behind. Educational realities emerging from *Brown v. Topeka Board of Education* and Sputnik deserve as much, if not more, credit for the current shape of American educational policy and K-12 school curricula as any other individual or factor in the history of American public education. The ESEA's reauthorization at the dawn of the twenty-first century reflected similar concerns about equity issues in American public schools and nagging fears that somehow American schools, by not being measured carefully enough, were somehow not measuring up to the challenges of the new millennium. The nation at risk of educational mediocrity in 1983 seemingly remained at risk nearly twenty years later.[4]

NCLB and Teaching American History

The evolution of NCLB and its most recent reauthorization is of supreme relevance to the *Teaching American History* (TAH) program on many levels. Specifically, NCLB (2002) incorporated and institutionalized the TAH program within the framework of ESEA. Although the TAH program originated within a one year appropriations bill for the U.S. Department of Education, the program subsequently became a part of NCLB.[5] The irony of this fundamental reality is that on the one hand NCLB both fostered a culture of test-based assessment and strict accountability *and* charged school districts with placing well-qualified teachers in the classroom on the other hand. Seemingly these two goals are inherently compatible. The reality, however, is a bit more complicated. Deliverance from one dilemma created the context for subsequent dilemmas. Mastery of content is a necessary and great thing, for both teachers and students, but is only the first rung of the taxonomy of learning in general and historical understanding more specifically.

My experiences and the experiences of many other professional colleagues working with TAH grants has shown that many K-12 participants in TAH grant-funded programs are increasingly, and understandably, focused on the need for their students to do well "on the test." By test, I mean anything from a state-level assessment to a more local, district-wide assessment that certifies student proficiency in a specific subject area, in this case history. And, ironically, this performance need, for both students and K-12 faculty, creates an exceptionally challenging environment for many TAH grant-funded activities. The steady rise in the importance of assessment is evident within the TAH grant application and review processes with assessment constituting one of the required key areas for both applicant and grant reviewers. The panoply of activities, exercises, opportunities, and other truly wonderful possibilities that K-12 faculty have enjoyed, and continue to enjoy, courtesy of the TAH program is one of the great benefits that derive from the program. However, at the end of the day, teachers and, increasingly, university faculty and other local educational agencies (LEAs) find themselves thinking as much, if not more, about how the historical content will be assessed, and what that assessment will mean, than how to foster the kind of historical thinking and understanding that is at the core of good history education and the TAH program. The final irony within this circumstance is that despite the concerns over assessment and the stringency of some state history/social studies curricula, K-12 history teachers continue to desire high quality history content *and* welcome the opportunities funded by TAH grants to reconnect with history professionals and materials they last encountered in their undergraduate years.

TAH and Assessment: A Hall of Mirrors

Interestingly, TAH program language specifically highlights assessment by emphasizing measures of student achievement and other evaluations in requests for proposals over the past several years. Yet the specific relationships between TAH-funded programs and state assessments remain a largely underexplored topic. Moreover, placed with the additional contexts of assessment generally and related concerns in terms of faculty evaluation at the university level, TAH programming increasingly constitutes a "hall of mirrors" within which K-12 faculty, university faculty, states, and the general public see multiple reflections of issues that increasingly both define and confound educators at every level. And, each of these aforementioned constituencies has its own primary concern and agenda. Increasingly, for K-12 faculty student achievement and assessment emerge as primary concerns. For university faculty, particularly those early in their careers, it is tenure and their next promotion. Such an admission does not mean that university faculty members do not care about student achievement or refuse to consider assessment as essential to that process. However, it does indicate that there are different levels of priority, something that no department chairperson can afford to deny or ignore. And, in fairness, state legislatures and state boards of education, as democratically constituted arbiters and fiduciary agents, understandably focus upon quantitative data as a means of measuring relative success or failure both pedagogically and politically. The basic dynamics are not new. The immediacy and ubiquity of media and other forms of communication have increased the complexity and rapidity of those dynamics. Yesterday's report of assessments administered last spring becomes an immediate topic of conversation on the street and in the board room. Consequently, the interplay between curricular, assessment, instructional, and other critical aspects of the history education continuum at both the K-12 level and the postsecondary level suggests that the days of seemingly blissful, detached, and disconnected existences are long behind us.

The process by which history curricula are created, and subsequently assessed, in the United States is a constantly evolving, dynamic enterprise, one that is dramatically altering the American educational landscape. Yet this process generates as many anxieties as it does opportunities for the myriad constituencies involved. K-12 faculty participating in TAH grant-sponsored events and programs frequently find themselves caught between great opportunities to develop enhanced skill and content bases on the one hand and state-mandated assessment requirements on the other hand. Teachers at every level are asking the question that legions of students have asked and continue to ask, "Will that be on test?" The "test" in this case is a state assessment that can carry a range of consequences from delivery of a simple snapshot of student learning at a particular point in their educational program to denial of graduation, as the proposed Pennsylvania program suggests. For instructors, building-level administrators, and district officer personnel, assessment results can have equally significant professional consequences, ranging from reassignment to termination.

Given these realities, the question, "Will it be on the test?" is revealing on many levels in that it suggests something of the greatly changed circumstances that faculty face as they attempt to manage an increasingly complex set of tasks. Given the program focus for TAH, this question pertains primarily to K-12 faculty. However, circumstances at every stage of the American educational continuum are changing, and increasingly, postsecondary level faculty members, and particularly those at four-year institutions, are encountering realities that their graduate training did not cover. Moreover, in a further irony, many university level faculty and administrators are finding themselves facing some of the exact same challenges that their K-12 counterparts have been confronting over the previous decade. The working relationships and shared experiences fostered by TAH programs provide both constituencies with opportunities not only to learn more about one another but also to realize that in many ways they are all in the same boat. Hearing about common curricula and assessment realties in K-12 is often one of the first contacts that many new university-level faculty members have with these circumstances.

Assessment and Higher Education: Learning from K-12 Colleagues

Increasingly, assessment has insinuated itself onto university history department radar screens and into the professional lives of university faculty who never dreamed that they might be held directly and empirically responsible for student learning. Delivering daily classroom content, assigning grades, weathering student complaints, and providing guidance for the occasional advisee constituted the defining activities for postsecondary level student-faculty relationships. While these activities remain definitional, many factors long familiar to K-12 faculty are becoming increasingly common in the halls of higher education. From "helicopter parents" to "special needs students," the hallowed halls of ivy are being transformed by social, cultural, and political forces that are driving, among other things, assessment and curricular decisions in American educational society. As Peter Novick has argued, the last half of the twentieth century saw "the final collapse of the profession's original goal of having exclusive license to 'prescribe' history for schoolchildren and lay audiences."[6] While Novick's focus is primarily upon the historical profession and illuminates a portion of the great, and now shrinking, divide between K-12 history teaching and postsecondary history instruction, his explanation is only a part of the answer to a very complex question. Equally significant is the rise of a national culture of assessment, defined from both the top (ACT, SAT, Advanced Placement, etc.) and the bottom (Iowa Tests, state grade-level assessments) and other broad-based, widely implemented instruments that have acculturated generations of Americans into a bubble-sheet based definition educational success.[7]

In addition, more subtle but equally significant factors are likely at work. The proliferation of *Idiots Guides* and *History for Dummies* publications bespeak a culture that simultaneously acknowledges the vast complexity of topics but nonetheless expects that such topics be rendered facile and readily mastered. In the end the final product, in the case of history as a subject area, is usually a lengthy list of content that severely constrains any opportunity to develop true historical understanding.[8] Again, TAH sponsored programs present an opportunity both to ride against this tide and to provide frameworks by not only giving university faculty the chance to provide content expertise but for them to derive the benefit of knowledge and experiences that their K-12 counterparts have to offer, courtesy of their experiences with such phenomena as assessment and curricular issues, that have become both increasingly important and more open to scrutiny in higher education.

And, at the end of the day, gaining a greater appreciation and understanding of these realities is in the best interest of university faculty. As any faculty member who has encountered any aspect of either NCATE accreditation for colleges of education or regional accreditation processes for universities as a whole can attest, the culture of assessment is no longer revolutionary, it is the norm. And, university faculty members are well-advised to pay more attention to assessment lest they lose control of it. Better to address the issue internally at the course, departmental, and college level than to have it imposed from the university level or university system level. In this regard, TAH-sponsored activities provide a potentially fruitful two-way street along which both university level content experts *and* assessment experienced K-12 faculty travel and interact.

Impact on History Faculty of TAH Participation

Many university faculty members, particularly those early in their careers, are both likely participants in TAH grant activities *and* rightly concerned academic citizens in regard to how that participation will translate within their tenure-track evaluations. Similarly, assessment has become a major focus of regional accreditation organizations and processes, confronting universities and their faculties with assessment issues that K-12 faculty have faced for decades. As a department chairperson, I have been pleased by the willingness of university faculty to work in support of K-12 faculty, both within TAH activities and other similar programs designed to assist elementary and secondary level educators. Certainly, my experiences may be the product of a career in higher education thus far spent teaching at two state-comprehensive universities, both of which are former normal schools with well-established records as teacher-training institutions. Moreover, this experience does not suggest that history faculty at PhD-granting research universities are unwilling to work with the K-12 faculty. Indeed, they do work with K-12 faculty as any number of TAH grant-sponsored activities indicate. But, as any cursory glance, or rigorous statistical analysis, of job advertisements will reveal, the overwhelming majority of tenure-line jobs in academe are at institutions that are not Carnegie classification research universities. Rather, most entry-level jobs for recent PhDs in history are at comprehensive universities, many of them former normal schools, where one of the primary missions is to educate K-12 teachers and to support them via graduate programming.

According to psychologist Bruce Henderson, faculty at many state comprehensive institutions find themselves caught in a web of expectations, both real and perceived, that can limit their willingness to participate in TAH-sponsored activities, particularly when those activities occur during the summer and other academic breaks which are "prime-time" extended and protected moments for research, writing, and publication. Time spent in service to K-12 teachers is time not spent on dissertation revisions, article drafts, and book-length manuscripts, products much more likely to impress a tenure committee than service or curriculum contributions to secondary level social studies teachers. If institutions, and more importantly faculty-constituted promotion and tenure committees, recognize and credit the value of TAH opportunities or similar activities then, as Henderson suggests, faculty anxiety about and reluctance to participate in TAH may diminish.[9] Such an outcome holds forth great possibility not only for the immediate TAH grant period and funded activities but also for the long-term relationship of the academic institution and faculty members with K-12 constituencies, a result that offers enduring benefits for the entirety of the K-16 educational continuum.

Most faculty members want to know how they are doing and they want to know how their students are doing. What most faculty members fear is that somehow this information will be made specific to them and, subsequently, they will suffer significant consequences. These concerns are not limited to tenure-track faculty members who are the most vulnerable, or at least perceive themselves to be the most vulnerable. In reality, tenured faculty members also feel, and manifest, a certain sense of peril within the assessment process. While tenure-track faculty members fear a negative tenure decision, they also at least ponder the consequences of assessment outcomes on promotion, merit, and other award decisions. Moreover, many faculty members, regardless of tenure status are vulnerable to a loss of prestige or even self-worth in the face of negative evaluations.[10] With the increasing use of posttenure review, such results potentially could involve significantly more than the simple loss of prestige for more senior faculty.

In fact, university faculty members have much to learn through their participation in the process. Although it would be difficult to find university faculty who would argue, for the record, that student learning does not matter, American higher education has come late to the game of measuring what students actually know when they leave the university, something that both higher education administrators, private sector patrons, and public officials have increasingly begun to advertise. Regardless of the expressed or heartfelt beliefs, or political agenda, student learning, and the assessment of that learning, has become an increasingly important, visible, and, from the vantage of many university faculty, intrusive fact of life on-campus. Coupled with heightened awareness and concerns over other seemingly nonacademic measures, the traditional models for advancing and assessing student learning and other academic experiences while attending a university are quickly evolving on multiple axes in ways that, again, few faculty members expected, or were trained, to handle. From the National Survey of Student Engagement (NSSE) to service-learning to technologically driven changes in content delivery, the academy has become a much more dynamic environment than it was even ten years ago. As a chairperson, my list of agenda items has grown exponentially, along with those of my faculty.

Impact on K-12 Teachers of TAH Participation

Ironically, K-12 teachers often express similar reservations about including materials, pedagogy, and insights gained from TAH-sponsored activities. Just as students ask the predictable question "Will this be on the test?" K-12 teachers ask "Will the item or the concept be assessed?" Anyone who has served on a state standards or assessment committee is only too familiar with this reality in an era when quantifiable outcomes become the sine qua non of school districts' expressed, and perhaps equally importantly, perceived success. The taxonomy of teacher anxiety may become manifest in the classroom or the faculty lounge but the roots and variegated subtexts for that anxiety can be traced to powerful public sources. Governors, state legislators, state boards of education, local school boards, parents, editorial page editors, and authors of letters to the editor give voice to concerns about "the system," its successes and failures, and the myriad problems perceived by individuals whose last actual experiences with K-12 most likely ended decades before they voiced their concerns, when they received their high school diplomas. This statement is not an indictment. Taxpayers and the guardians of their tax dollars have a right to ask serious and often painful questions. However, there have been considerable changes in the rules and stakes of the game, particularly in terms of accountability and assessment, a clear and likely permanent legacy of the other epic event of 2001, No Child Left Behind (NCLB).[11] Although NCLB initially targeted basic competencies in reading and math the national and building level impacts of NCLB have altered both the culture and the behaviors in the K-12 world. Anecdotal evidence does indeed suggest that less time is being spent on other subject areas as a means of ensuring the greatest success rates in reading and math assessments. Indeed, the constituencies noted at the outset of this article have gone beyond the anecdotal and added a considerable body of empirical evidence. Consequently, one of the questions I have pondered, but which would likely require further assessment, is the degree to which students arrive at the sixth or even eighth grade levels with less actual historical knowledge than previous generations. Teachers in the classroom and professors in the lecture hall will be the first to attest to this probable result of teaching and scheduling to basic core competency testing.

A Personal Journey: Opportunities to Learn

Yet, as both an instructor and an administrator, I can still report that the multiple demands that I faced as a high school history and government teacher (and basketball coach) pushed and prepared me in ways that no graduate program could or did. In 1984 I left the United States and my job as a public high school social studies teacher in Schenectady, New York, seriously contemplating the possibility of spending the remainder of my professional career as an educator abroad. After two years in the classroom, I found myself increasingly bothered by the absence of opportunities to reconnect with the historical discipline at a level I enjoyed in my undergraduate and graduate experiences. I was under no illusions that teaching history at the high school level would be the same as what I experienced in the undergraduate history classroom or the graduate seminar. I truly loved, and still love, working with high school students. However, I confess to being ill-prepared and unable to weather the separation and distance I felt from the historian's tradecraft, a circumstance that thankfully TAH programs have addressed in any number of highly successful ways. Similarly, although the New York State Regents Exams constituted, and remain, a significant assessment tool, I was not convinced that I really knew what my students were learning on a given day, on any specific topic, particularly when it came to historical significance. In retrospect, I found myself challenging my own approach to teaching history, often asking, for example, to what degree a student's knowledge of New Deal programs actually revealed an understanding of the historical enterprise. Indeed, Sam Wineburg has raised similar concerns in the face of state assessments that require students to know a laundry list of historical personages and events.[12] Knowing the facts that constitute history and understanding the actual nuances of historical change and continuity can be two remarkably distinct, and often distant, realities. These professional factors, together with one major personal factor (a still unbridled wanderlust), facilitated my move abroad and a nearly decade-long career as a high school social studies teacher in American international schools in Israel and Egypt. Yet, even in these dynamic, stimulating environments I still found myself wanting more contact with the professional historical world, even as I was traveling all over the physical world. Subsequently, I returned to the United States in the early 1990s, completed a PhD in American history and, as a long-standing fugitive from the law of averages, landed a job immediately upon finishing my degree in 1996 and, to my great chagrin, found myself on the other side of the educational divide.

My K-12 days were done and my university career began, replete with all the privileges, hurdles, and pretenses I had never envisioned. And, as I made my way around the tenure track the same concerns I had as a K-12 instructor resurfaced as I taught my university history courses. How did I actually know what students were learning? The standard essay exams with the standard identification items, dutifully graded with all the requisite feedback ("significance?" "be more specific," "example?") simply did not assure me that I really knew what students were really learning. Moreover, I found myself missing the contact with K-12 teachers. My ability to teach was forged in the K-12 classroom and thankfully survived my doctoral program. University teaching was lecturing with learning presumed, illuminated as often by PowerPoint as by real teaching genius. I missed, and still miss, the opportunities to talk about teaching strategies with my social studies colleagues. Fortunately, I was smart enough to keep such concerns to myself until I was tenured. Most university departments beyond colleges of education quickly demarcate, and defend, the boundaries, both real and presumed, between primary research of discovery tied to an established academic discipline on the one hand *and* research associated with pedagogy and the teaching of a particular subject on the other hand. Yet, one of the questions that I and my faculty frequently encounter during TAH-sponsored activities is "How do you teach about this topic?" The presumption that good pedagogy and good content constitute the essential keys to successful instruction is both implicit and explicit.

Impact on History Faculty Revisited: A Two-Way Mirror

And herein lies yet one more supreme benefit of interaction between the constituencies frequently enlisted by TAH grants. While K-12 faculty have much to gain from postsecondary content experts, those same experts can gain much from their interactions with K-12 teachers, particularly master teachers whose classroom teaching experience and range of pedagogy may greatly exceed that of some of university faculty content experts. In short, university faculty members potentially have much to be gain from listening and asking the right questions of their K-12 counterparts. The basic concepts of lesson plan design and classroom management are topics rarely discussed in history graduate programs. Graduate students are much more likely to encounter the inner workings of the Freemasons than they are to hear about how to teach history to students who are not history majors.

Additionally, the interchanges between K-12 faculty and university faculty provide the latter with the chance to learn a bit about the dispositions and daily existences of the former. Teaching for five to six hours a day, five days a week, for nearly ten months is something that most university faculty do not understand and, in most cases, do not have the experience to appreciate. Understanding this simple yet critical difference can make for much more successful summer institutes and other professional development programs; that is, K-12 faculty simply do not have the time to prepare the detailed materials that many university faculty present in their lectures. Helping my own faculty to appreciate this reality led them to sharpen their presentations, align them with state curricula, and provide copies of their presentations to K-12 faculty attending the summer institute with the latter gesture being received by K-12 faculty as akin to a winning lottery ticket. Assessment is not just about the test. It is also about assessing where faculty members are in relation to one another within the K-16 continuum. And like any good assessment it has to be planned, implemented, and evaluated.

Recognition of Good Teaching

Professional organizations understand the efficacy and primacy of engaging K-12 constituencies or engage in rhetoric that at least expresses an interest in this enterprise. The creation of separate elements within both the Organization of American Historians (OAH) and the American Historical Association (AHA) dedicated to teaching is both an encouraging and troubling sign. On the one hand it attests to the significance of the classroom in promoting the professional historical enterprise. On the other hand such an approach has an unfortunate tendency to reinforce prevailing notions among many faculty members that research and publication are the most valued aspects of professional life. Regardless, the mere recognition of teaching as an endeavor worth recognizing, encouraging, and celebrating on the highest professional levels is both a symbolic and real indicator of interest in teaching, pedagogy, and activities directly related to the classroom. This interest changes over time, depending upon any number of variables, as David Noble has shown. However, the TAH program has generated fresh interest, affording both individual historians and departments of history with significant opportunities to reengage with the K-12 world in a manner that is more tangible and immediate than most historians have experienced. Teaching history courses, both for history majors preparing to teach and for education majors from a variety of disciplines, is the most common way in which most historians contribute to the K-12 community but it is far from the only way.

In 2006 the Carnegie Foundation funded a national conference which studied the preparation of history teachers at colleges and universities in the United States. As an outgrowth of the conference, The American Historical Association published *The Next Generation of History Teachers: A Challenge to History Departments and Colleges and University*. In detailing the background and prevailing circumstances surrounding the conference and the subsequent report, Edward Ayers and several other colleagues noted,

> Several assumptions underlie this message. We believe that the changes historians undertake should be departmentally focused, institutionally tailored, and community minded. We do not believe that historians need to revolutionize their teaching, their departments, or their institutions to accomplish these things, but that they do need to approach this part of their work in a more self-aware and coordinated way.
>
> One assumption underlies all the others: historians are uniquely qualified to assist prospective teachers in developing the habits of mind and instructional strategies necessary to teach effectively about the past. Long experience suggests that if historians do not assert responsibility for preparing future history teachers, others will.[13]

Although these assumptions speak admirably of the professional historical communities' willingness to engage, there remains much more that can be done, particularly when it is increasingly clear that *all* good history educators, regard-

less of degree, rank, or condition of employment share certain basic dispositions. One study suggests that, "the process of communicating knowledge about
the past is, above all, an epistemological and cultural act that conveys deep and
sometimes unintended messages about what it means to be historical in modern
society."[14] Such acts and their derived messages, unintended or not, constitute
the essence of what can, and frequently does, happen when the disparate worlds
of K-12 and postsecondary history instruction collide. TAH-sponsored activities bring together elementary and secondary history teachers, university historians, public history educators, and other actors who in their daily professional
lives channel the past in the service of the present and future. This confluence of
expertise provides benefits for all those involved, regardless of their place in the
great history education chain of being. Yet, to be truly successful in this enterprise requires a touch of subversion. Fortunately, history educators are usually up
to the task and the TAH program frequently provides the forum.

The Challenge of History Education Recognized

Robert Bain's tale of life as a high school history teacher by day and history graduate student by night provides a useful referential framework for two of the many
challenges that K-12 faculty face in their daily existence.[15] During the day, Bain,
like many other dual academic citizens, worked in a content-driven environment, teaching the facts as students, parents, and curricular coordinators defined
them. At night, Bain's life as a graduate student reminded him of the more real
and nuanced stuff of historical thinking and understanding, processes not easily
captured on a machine-scored state assessment. The Faustian bargain that most
K-12 history educators negotiate on a daily basis is transacted within this reality.
Too many state curricula advertise historical thinking but assess specific content
knowledge. The laundry list of facts serves as the substitute for a more tasteful,
and some would argue tasty, ensemble predicated upon a real understanding of
how things actually unfold in the historical enterprise. Sam Wineburg's long-
standing critique of such an approach is accurate and helpful in making an argument for doing things differently.[16] Alas, curricula and assessments continue to
stay the course as if governed by the television police detective whose weekly
proclamation, "just the facts, ma'am," reminded America that the real thinking
and analysis should be left to professionals elsewhere.

Fortunately, TAH-sponsored summer institutes and weekend workshops provide an opportunity for K-12 faculty and university historians to talk about the
use of historical content as elements within an expanded intellectual composition that is much larger, richer, and rewarding than any of the constituent parts.
The American Revolution and its curricular tyranny of the Sugar Act, the Stamp
Act, and the other intolerable acts became more vivid, and useful, when placed
within the framework of the Atlantic world, a milieu that was alive with far more
than rum, molasses, and slaves. The trans-Atlantic intellectual, commercial,
political, and cultural frameworks that generated both the American Revolution
and the international factors that ultimately joined several revolutions across an
ocean and over several decades, did not, and do not, surrender easily, if at all,

to easy item categorization. Good history educators at any level, whether in the employ of schools, colleges, or museums, intrinsically understand this reality. Both the substance but, equally important, the passion that underwrites good history instruction is reinforced when both stakeholders come together in grant-sponsored activities. This fortunate circumstance then provides both constituencies with additional ideas and language with which to convey ideas about history. Although the assessment and curricular mandates are omnipresent, it is essential to realize that true student understanding and historical thinking require both a firm grasp of the facts and a true leap of imagination. Work with documents, calibration of the right mix of technology and human touch, linking the media to the habits of mind, and developing a classroom that adheres to curriculum without becoming a lifeless enterprise, are hallmarks of TAH activities that I have seen. Many of the best activities combine the skills and experiences of K-12 instructors, master teachers, university faculty, museum educators, and other history professionals. If, as one history educator suggests, teaching history is "an epistemic activity challeng[ing] teachers to merge a substantive understanding of the discipline with an equally sophisticated understanding of learning," then TAH grant activities are one of the laboratories from which future epistemic successes can emerge.[17]

One of those future successes will I hope involve a reintegration of the American national narrative back into its original global framework. And, again, interchanges between various TAH grant constituencies have much to offer. Circumstances born of colonization but revivified by late twentieth century globalization and early twenty-first century consequences of that process further complicate the situation. Namely, as any U.S. history textbook will attest, the grand American experiment was the progeny of complex international, multiethnic, religious, political, and economic forces. Yet, as the conventional narrative unfolds both in the text and in real time throughout the school year, American history as a component a greater global historical narrative quickly succumbs to the national narrative. The occasional, mandated, and assessed forays abroad via imperialism, world wars, and the Cold War aside, American history is the tale of an isolated, independent hometown amid the global villages.

Fortunately, the previous decade has seen great strides in reattaching the American past with its global framework.[18] Ironically, based on both first-hand experience and anecdotal evidence furnished by colleagues reading TAH grant applications, the enabling legislation and subsequent requests for proposals (RFPs) at least suggested that "traditional American history" began and ended at the water's edge. That said, my own contributions in TAH grant-sponsored workshops as well as those of my colleagues and faculty over the years have made it clear that traditional American history has many global, international connections. Subsequent correspondence, conference conversations, and observation of classroom activities suggest the interchanges and opportunities provided by TAH grants have broadened the curricular and global horizons of the K-12 history classroom. Tempering this hopeful progress are continuing concerns that time spent discussing the international aspects of the Tennessee Valley Authority might be more productively spent covering some other assessed item in the state curriculum.

Looking Forward: Continued Collaboration

One absolutely key aspect of assessment within the partnerships underwritten by TAH activities is the assessment of relationships and frameworks vital for the continued development of history education in the future, post-TAH and post-NCLB. I am neither suggesting nor advocating that at some point one or both of these programs will disappear. Indeed, I anticipate their continued presence in some form for quite some time to come. However, consistent with TAH grant principles and subsequent guidelines, it is reasonable to expect and to suggest that partnerships and activities generated by TAH grants will, and should, endure beyond the funding timeline. Moreover, the mandated expectation of student and program assessment with TAH also suggests that there are many varieties and levels of assessment and it is in this regard that every TAH grant presents institutions of higher learning and other partners with the opportunity to assess where they are in the grand time–space continuum of K-16 education and beyond. As Robert Orrill and Linn Shapiro have noted, the overwhelming majority of doctoral level faculty and their doctoral students do not conceive of themselves within this continuum. Most of these faculty and students would be shocked to discover Frederick Jackson Turner's inclusive collective pronoun "we teachers" in his 1891 address to a group of K-12 teachers, two years prior to his epic address that began the transformation of America's conception of its frontier. The close relationship between K-12 educators and their university colleagues, once close, is now seemingly as distant and as remote as the American frontier.[19] Assessing the state of this relationship, or perhaps simply reestablishing it, seems to me to be one of the critical accomplishments of the TAH program. To date notable work has been done and significant evidence exists of a growing awareness and more importantly, sensitivity to the circumstances inherent to the K-16 environment. Although mere mention of this phrase alarms many post-secondary level professional historians, the circumstance is that K-12 realties increasingly are K-16 realities; the university has once again become part of a manifest universe with all of the destiny implied by this situation. Kathleen Anderson Steeves's overview of successful collaborations between university faculty and high school faculty is a testament to this possibility.[20] Equally significant, the AHA's recognition and endorsement of the challenges inherent in training "the next generation of history teachers" is a hugely positive development likely to carry even greater weight in departments of history, despite my near certainty that less than 5 percent of all university history departments devoted "at least one department meeting in the academic year 2006-2007 to a discussion of the preparation of teachers of history."[21]

Yet an additional and little appreciated factor lurks in the background and simultaneously envelopes everything in its midst while joining history educators and facilitating the assessment revolution. K-12 faculty and postsecondary faculty exist within the most technologically rich and demanding environment in the history of education. Student expectations of technological proficiency seemingly rival, and at times appear to eclipse, concerns over course content and grading, which has led one historian to predict that "not even the most unyielding among us will be exempt" from the consequences of the digital revolution.[22] On one level this reality confers many benefits, including greater access to information resources, significantly enhanced communications, and better coordination of curricula. Anyone who seeks data for an argument within a history framework need look no further than the Internet and the National Center for Education Statistics.[23] This fusion of technological means and assessment creates both a dynamic and a transparency that classroom instructors, regardless of level, did not previously face. While actual lesson plans remain, for the most part, very much under the control of classroom faculty, there has been an increasing trend for the results of classroom instruction to become immediately available to the public.

Additionally, the electronic revolution has transformed the myriad ways in which TAH grant are conceived, written, evaluated, announced, implemented, and assessed. However, these same benefits increase demands on faculty time, generate higher expectations of performance (for both faculty and students), and heighten awareness of assessment needs and outcomes. In the latter case, the awareness frequently foments anxieties both about what the assessment may reveal and what the actual assessment process may be. Knowledge of an expected outcome without the power to influence, much less control, and the process becomes one of the guarantors of faculty angst about assessment. Technology has multiplied both the possibilities and perils of assessment. In short, Intel, Microsoft, and the Internet have raised the bar and lowered the boom when it comes to assessment. Military historians studying technological change in warfare tell us that it is not so much "the revolutionary character of inventions and processes, but [the] creation of management and logistical system[s] that made the *application* of technological advantage possible."[24] In education, the management and logistical support for technology varies from district to district, from state to state, much in the same fashion that assessment processes vary across district and state boundaries. In each instance, whether it is technology or assessment, the variety and the apparent omnipresence of each within the professional lives of K-12 faculty create their own dilemmas while at the same time creating circumstances, yet again, where K-12 faculty and postsecondary level faculty have if not mutuality of interest at least common ground upon which to meet.

At the end of the day good history education is about facilitating historical thinking, despite the unfortunate reality that the possession, and subsequent recitation, of historical content will remain an all too facile means of measuring the effectiveness of history instructors. Regardless, as NCLB and the TAH move toward the second decade of the new millennium the realities inherent in both their design and their respective impacts will endure far beyond the limits of their legislative life. While the assessment of student learning and the enrichment of content and are likely to constitute their most likely respective programmatic legacies, the reconstruction of a genuine collegial community of K-16 educators is not only a necessity but also a real possibility given TAH sponsored activities.

Notes

1. Sam Dillon, "History Survey Stumps U.S. Teens," *The New York Times*, February 26, 2008, http://www.nytimes.com/2008/02/26 (accessed February 26, 2008).
2. Gordon Cawelti, "The Side Effects of NCLB," *Educational Leadership* (November 2006), 67.
3. Sean D. Miller, "Pennsylvania Acts to Bolster High School Requirements," *New York Times*, January 18, 2008, http://www.nytimes.com/2008/01/18/us/18graduation.html?_r=1&adxnnl=1&oref=slogin&adxnnlx=1200751694-abFXrlBTtxj0zekCWwaS3g (accessed February15, 2008).
4. The product of a blue ribbon panel experts, The National Commission on Excellence in Education, *A Nation at Risk: The Imperative for Educational Reform* (Washington, D.C.: U.S. Government Printing Office, 1983) warned Americans of a "rising tide of mediocrity" in their school systems.
5. Alex Stein, "The Teaching American History Program: An Introduction and Overview," *The History Teacher* (February, 2003), http://www.historycooperative.org/journals/ht/36.2/stein.html (accessed July 2, 2008). Also, Elementary and Secondary Education Act of 1965, as amended, Title II, Part C, Subpart 4 (2002).
6. Peter Novick, *That Noble Dream: The "Objectivity Question" and the American Historical Profession* (New York: Cambridge University Press, 1988), 368–370.
7. While the literature on this phenomenon is vast and disparate, Nicholas Lemann's *The Big Test: The Secret History of America's Meritocracy* (New York: Farrar, Straus and Giroux, 2000) is the best one volume treatment of the phenomenon.
8. See for example, Steve Wiegand, *U.S. History for Dummies* (New York: For Dummies, 2001) and Alan Axelrod, *Complete Idiot's Guide to American History* (New York: Alpha, 2006). An additional interesting feature of this phenomenon is the incorporation of these series within well-established, respected presses, John Wiley in the case of For Dummies and Penguin in the case of Alpha.
9. Bruce B. Henderson, *Teaching at the People's University: An Introduction to the State Comprehensive University* (Boston: Anker, 2007), 52–56.
10. These conclusions reflect anecdotal evidence gathered in a myriad of contexts beyond my own institutions, reflecting hundreds of conversations with university faculty members at annual professional conferences, Advanced Placement grading sessions, and other events where university faculty gather. Similarly, these conclusions reflect conversations with fellow chair colleagues at dozens of colleges and universities. This highly unscientific sample, however, does represent faculty from a variety of institutions (research, state comprehensive, community colleges, public, and private).
11. Although the actual act did not pass until January 8, 2002, NCLB has firmly embedded quantitative assessment in the K-12 educational landscape. Campaign promises during the 2000 electoral season and subsequent debates in Congress and state legislatures during 2001 provided the basic foundation for subsequent legislation in early 2002.
12. Sam Wineburg, "Crazy for History," *Journal of American History* 90 (January 1994).
13. Edward Ayers and others, *The Next Generation of History Teachers: A Challenge to History Departments and Colleges and University* (Washington, DC: American Historical Association, 2007), http://www.historians.org/pubs/Free/historyteaching/index.htm (accessed June 3, 2008).
14. Peter Stearns, Peter Seixas, and Sam Wineburg, eds., *Knowing, Teaching, and Learning History: National and International Perspectives* (New York: New York University Press, 2000), 3.
15. Robert E. Bain, "Into the Breach: Using Research and Theory to Shape History Instruction" in Stearns and others, 331.
16. Wineburg, "Crazy for History."
17. Bain, 335.
18. Some of the best, and most accessible, early work in this area was that of American historians focusing upon the African-American civil rights struggle, most notably Mary Dudziak, Thomas Borstelmann, and Penny Von Eschen. Daniel T. Rodgers's work on social reform

movements in the Atlantic community set an early and high standard, although it is less immediately applicable in the K-12 classroom. Thomas Bender's wide-ranging efforts to locate the entire breadth of American history within global history provide ample opportunities for one to think differently about the traditional American historical narrative. Finally, Peter Stearns and Noralee Frankel, eds., *Globalizing the Teaching of American History: The AHA Guide to Re-Imaging the U.S. Survey Course* (Washington D.C.: American Historical Association, 2008) constitutes an admirable start to a long overdue process.

19. Robert Orrill and Linn Shapiro, "From Bold Beginnings to an Uncertain Future: The Discipline of History and History Education," *American Historical Review* 110 (June, 2005): 750.

20. Kathleen Anderson Steeves, *Building Successful Collaborations to Enhance History Teaching in Secondary Schools*, http://www.historians.org/pubs/Free/steeves/preface.htm (accessed May 30, 2008).

21. Ayers and others, 7.

22. Barbara Weinstein, "Doing History in the Digital Age," *Perspectives: The Newsmagazine of the American Historical Association* 45 (May 2007): 5.

23. For further evidence of this reality, see http://nces.ed.gov/nationsreportcard/ushistory/ and http://nationsreportcard.gov/ushistory_2006/ (accessed July 28, 2008).

24. Allan R. Millett, "Patterns of Innovation in the Interwar Period," in *Military Innovation in the Interwar Period*, ed. Williamson Murray and Allan R. Millett (New York: Cambridge University Press, 1996), 348.

Chapter 15

Teaching American History

Observations from the Fringes

Cary D. Wintz
Texas Southern University

Introduction: A Disclaimer

This chapter is not about my experiences directing a model *Teaching American History* (TAH) project, or, for that matter about any single or group of the projects that this program has funded. Instead I intend to examine the *Teaching American History* project as a whole from the perspective of a historian. For this reason this chapter will be different from the other essays in this collection. This will be a historical piece that will reflect the thoughts and experiences of an individual who has danced around the fringes of the program, almost from its inception, and who has strong opinions about the program, both its strengths and weaknesses, and who has explored the history of the program. This chapter will provide an intimate but outsider's history of the program. beginning with a discussion of the original intent(s) from the perspective of both Congress and the U.S Department of Education, continuing with an examination of the evolution of the program and the degree to which the program fulfilled its original expectations or met other expectations, and concluding with a discussion of the program's strengths and weaknesses, successes and failures, again from the perspective of someone who has observed the program "up close."

I have not served as a director on a *Teaching American History* grant, and I have not written a proposal for a grant. However, I have served as a grant reviewer for the program, beginning with the first competition and continuing with four subsequent reviews between 2001 and 2006. During that period I read for every competition but one, which has given me a firsthand look at the program, the evolution of the program, as well as the evolution of the reviewing process. Twice I have committed time to serve as a "history faculty" or "content specialist" on TAH projects, and I been involved with numerous discussions of the program, both formal and informal. I have also consulted informally (i.e., gratis) with friends who were writing TAH proposals. I have attended or participated in three of the *Teaching American History* Symposia that have been held in conjunction with the Organization of American Historians annual meeting. So my knowledge of the *Teaching American History* program is fairly extensive, but it remains that of an interested and informed observer, a sometime participant, but not that of a project director. I also bring the perspective of a professor of history who has spent almost four decades teaching U.S. history, has worked extensively with

K-12 teachers in a variety of situations, and has contributed to the profession as a scholar, a researcher, and an author.

The Birth of the *Teaching American History* Grant Program: Byrd Legislation/Byrd Intention

Senator Robert C. Byrd of West Virginia introduced the *Teaching American History* program as an amendment to an educational appropriation bill in the early summer of 2000. Senator Byrd is something of a Senate phenomenon. On June 12, 2006 Senator Byrd became the longest serving Democratic Senator in the history of the Senate. He entered the Senate in 1959 and established a reputation as a defender of states' rights and segregation; over the years he moderated his earlier views, and became a master of the legislative process. By the late 1960s he had become part of the Democratic leadership in the Senate and for twelve years beginning in 1977 he served as Senate Majority Leader or Senate Minority Leader. Even today he remains a significant force in the Senate.

On June 30, 2000 Senator Byrd offered an amendment to Title X of the Department of Education funding bill to add $50 million to be used by the Secretary of Education to "award grants to develop, implement and strengthen programs to teach American history (not social studies) as a separate subject within the school curricula."[1] Senator Joseph Lieberman had already voiced concerns about the paucity of historical knowledge among American college students. In a speech to the Senate in support of the Byrd proposal, Senator Lieberman focused on the theme that the United States is at risk of losing its "civic memory" and that "historical illiteracy" was growing in the country.[2] He cited the report of the University of Connecticut's Roper Center which documented the lack of knowledge about American history among seniors at the top U.S. universities, and which reported that most major colleges do not require their students to take history courses. He also referenced "Losing America's Memory: Historical Illiteracy in the 21st Century," a report created by the American Council of Trustees and Alumni and based on the findings of the Roper survey, and he read into the Congressional record statements from prominent U.S. historians, including David McCullough, Oscar Handlin, and Gordon Wood, each of whom attested to the crisis in history education.

The initial legislation was an amendment to the appropriations bill. A year later, Byrd sponsored legislation to reauthorize and expand funding for the *Teaching American History* program, making it a component of the No Child Left Behind Act. This assured its continued funding; in doing this Byrd also doubled annual funding from $50 million to $100 million. In his speech supporting his proposal Byrd focused on what he termed "traditional" American history. Byrd's vision of traditional history contained two components. The first concerned how history was presented in the school curriculum. Byrd wanted history taught as a distinct and discrete discipline, and criticized the submerging of history into the broad category of social studies. "An unfortunate trend of blending history with a variety of other subjects to form a hybrid called 'social studies' has taken hold in our schools. I am not against social studies, but I want history. If we are going to have social studies, that is OK, but let's have history."³ Byrd also took issue with the content and direction of history. He wanted a history that celebrated the creation and development of the United States—one that would create the excitement and appreciation of American history that he had encountered as a youth in the classrooms of West Virginia. He complained that the current history textbooks used in the schools "gloss over the finer points of the American past" and promised that "my amendment provides incentives to help spur a return to the teaching of traditional history."⁴

What exactly was this traditional history? Byrd explained it clearly:

> American students, regardless of race, religion, or gender, must know the history of the land to which they pledge allegiance. They should be taught about the Founding Fathers of this Nation, the battles that they fought, the ideals that they championed, and the enduring effects of their accomplishments. Without this knowledge, they cannot appreciate the hard won freedoms that are our birthright.
>
> Our failure to insist that the words and actions of our forefathers be handed down from generation to generation will ultimately mean a failure to perpetuate this wonderful, glorious experiment in representative democracy. Without the lessons learned from the past, how can we insure that our Nation's core ideals—life, liberty, justice—will survive?⁵

Byrd cited broad support for his program among educational and historical professional organizations including the American Historical Association and the National Council for History Education.

Byrd further elaborated on his intentions in a series of press releases. Essentially he stuck to his original view of history as a subject area distinct from social studies, and as well as a vision of U.S. history that would strengthen American civic culture. On November 6, 2001, in conjunction with the Senate approval to expand the *Teaching American History* initiative, Byrd reiterated his purpose, to address a shortfall in the nation's educational system by placing emphasis back on traditional American history in the classroom, rather than lumping American history in with the other topics covered under social studies. He also introduced a new concept: that student achievement in American history would be enhanced by improving their teacher's "knowledge, understanding, and appreciation of the subject."⁶

Two years later Byrd added an addition $20 million to the appropriation bringing the total for fiscal year 2004 to $120 million. In his press release announcing this increased funding, he discussed two concerns. First he again argued that too many schools teach history as a part of a social studies curriculum rather than presenting them in stand-alone courses, a practice which Byrd argued failed to provide the "focused study that history deserves and requires" and consequently shortchanged students by failing to ground them in the "basic philosophies and values that served to form the constitutional foundation of America."⁷ Byrd linked this failure to the widespread illiteracy among college students in the basic content of U.S. history, a situation that he felt put at risk the Constitution and the institutions that protect the rights and freedoms of American citizens. In the fall

of 2007, a press release announcing the competition for the 2008 grants continued to voice these same themes.

Byrd's vision remained constant. The educational establishment had neglected
traditional American history, by subsuming it into a social studies curriculum that
failed to provide effective history education and assigning to these classes teachers
who had minimal academic preparation in American history. The resulting historical illiteracy among students threatened the civic health of the nation. His program
sought to address the problem by increasing the knowledge and understanding
of American history among the nation's teachers in the expectation they would
impart this knowledge to their students. Byrd also pursued a "traditional" vision
of the content of American history, meaning a return to a history that focused on
great Americans whose heroic and enlightened deeds created the nation and its
institutions. This vision was not exactly compatible with the direction most university-based historians took in their research, their writing, and their teaching.
Likewise, his insistence on divorcing history from social studies was not especially
welcomed by school administrators. Yet this vision and the political influence
behind the vision brought unprecedented federal funds to efforts to improve the
teaching of history.

The Legislation

The *Teaching American History* program was born with a five-line amendment
attached to the Education appropriation bill on June 30, 2000. The text of the
amendment was not very detailed:

> Providing further, That of the amount made available under the heading for activities
> carried out through the Fund of the Improvement of Education under part A of title
> X, $50,000,000 shall be made available to enable the Secretary of Education to award
> grants to develop, implement and strengthen programs to teach American history
> (not social studies) as a separate subject within school curricula.[8]

There are three significant points made in this short statement. First, $50 mil-
lion was going to be funneled into history or history education. From the perspective of historians this was an unprecedented level of funding for projects related to
history. For example, it represented almost 50 percent of the annual budget of the
National Endowment for the Humanities.[9] Second, the only indication of the organization or design of the project was the statement that history would be taught as
a separate subject and not part of social studies. Finally, and most important, the
project would be implemented through the U.S. Department of Education, and
the details of the program would be worked out by that Department.

So, it fell to the Department of Education to translate Byrd's vision into an
actual program for the enhancement of the teaching of American history. The
Department released plans for the new grants on May 23, 2001. For the most
part, the purpose and the major organization of the *Teaching American History*
projects have remained constant over the life of the program. The statement of
purpose asserted that the program will "raise student achievement by improving

teachers' knowledge, understanding, and appreciation of American History."[10] To accomplish this, projects would offer extensive professional development activities for teachers, which would be developed in partnership with "entities that have extensive content expertise."[11] The grant applicant would be a local education agency (LEA) which would be required to partner with one or more of the following: an institution of higher education, a nonprofit history or humanities organization, and a library or museum. Presumably these partners would provide the content expertise for the project. The statement of purpose and the partnership structure remained virtually unchanged in the notice for fiscal year 2008 applications.[12]

The initial announcement in the *Federal Register* of May 23, 2001 also included supplemental information about the *Teaching American History* projects. Under the category of "Program Description" the Department of Education repeated the concepts Senator Byrd emphasized in his discussion of the project, and added material related to pedagogy and teaching strategies. For example, the *Register* noted the link between knowledge of American history and the civic health of society and the civic responsibility of citizens; it also emphasized the importance of presenting history as a separate academic subject in the school curriculum. At the same time it linked student learning to the ability of teachers to make the subject "exciting, interesting, and engaging," and it indicated that in addition to elevating the content knowledge of teachers, the professional development activities should "reflect the best available research and practice in teaching, learning, and leadership" and that efforts to provide teachers with greater expertise in American history subject content should be accompanied by efforts to increase their expertise in "teaching strategies, use of technology, and other essential elements of teaching to higher standards."[13]

The Issue of Focus: Education and History

While on the surface there was nothing wrong with including enhanced teaching strategies along with efforts to upgrade the content knowledge of teachers, it opened up issues of whether the focus of the program centered on the content knowledge that professional historians could bring the teachers, or the teaching strategies that professional educators could bring to the program. This was further complicated by the designation of LEAs as the lead partner and applicant for the TAH grants, the designation of the Department of Education as the administrative agency for the program, and the interests of the school teachers who were the participants in the program, and ultimately the key to success or failure of the project. These issues, while not impossible to resolve, needed to be addressed by each project.

The location of the *Teaching American History* program in the Department of Education is fundamental to understanding the nature of the TAH program. First the Department of Education was a logical location for the program for two reasons, one practical and one related to the nature of the program. The most likely alternative location for TAH was in the National Endowment for the Humanities

(NEH). However, there were liabilities associated with the NEH and benefits connected with the Department Education that settled the issue. First, the size of the program would have strained the resources of the NEH. TAH also was significantly different from the NEH's other teacher education programs—the summer seminars for school teachers and the summer institutes for teachers. Each of these programs recruited groups of K-12 teachers for four- to eight-week seminars or institutes that were rich in specified humanities content. These programs, however, focused on individual teachers, recruited from across the country, and while some addressed topics in history they were not designed specifically to address shortcomings in K-12 history education. The TAH program, in contrast, addressed the needs of school districts, not individual teachers. While improving the content knowledge of individual teachers was important, the goal was to improve the knowledge of U.S. history among all the students in specified school districts. This task was more in line with the mission of the Department of Education that the National Endowment for the Humanities.

The requirement that the lead partner and grant applicant be a local education agency, usually a school district followed the same logic. Since the goal of the program was to improve the teaching and learning of history in K-12 schools, it seemed appropriate that school district play a leadership role in the projects.

Despite the logic of this structure, the leadership role of the Department of Education and LEAs would create some concern among university-based historians and others whose primary concern was history content knowledge. This situation contributed to a natural tension among the major players in the process: the advocates of history content information, those who focused on developing the instructional skills of teachers, and the interests of teachers themselves, many of whom entered TAH projects without a clear understanding of what the experience would be.

Implementation—Year I

During the implementation of the *Teaching American History* programs most of these concerns would be addressed, if not completely resolved. In the first year, however, things were a little ragged, in large part because the new program had to be rushed into place. After the legislation was approved by Congress in November, the Department of Education had to assign a staff, determine the details of the program, and publish the invitation for grant applications for the 2001 fiscal year. They issued their invitation for grant applications on May 23, 2001; proposals were due by July 23, and the review of applications would be completed by September 21, 2001. In their rush to meet deadlines, the description of the project and the selection criteria (issues which proposals must address and the standards by which proposals will be evaluated) in some places seem cobbled together combining components from other programs with issues specifically developed for the TAH program. In putting this material together, the Department of Education consulted with history groups. Of these the National Council for History Education (NCHE) was most involved in the process. Other groups, like the American Historical Association (AHA) played a smaller role.

The reaction of the history professional organizations is instructive. In the recent past the major academic bodies such as the AHA and the Organization of American Historians (OAH) had, by default, allowed issues related to K-12 history and history teacher education to pass to groups like NCHE and the National Council for the Social Studies (NCSS). The *Teaching American History* program would stimulate both the OAH and the AHA to reconsider this decision. In a June 2001 "Point of View" essay in *The Chronicle of Higher Education* Arnita Jones, executive director of the AHA, addressed the issue of the TAH program. She cited the unprecedented level of funding that Congress had made available to history. She also expressed concern that university-based history departments and other history institutions were ineligible to apply for these grants directly, and worried that this along with the language that seemed to emphasize "improving teaching, not improving the knowledge and expertise of teachers" might limit the program's focus to "teaching strategies or curriculum development."[14] Jones went on in her essay to suggest that it was a mistake for college and university historians to ignore what was happening in the public schools, and noted how math and science professors had established partnerships with the public schools, and participated in programs like the National Science Foundation's well-funded pre-collegiate education programs. She concluded by urging university historians to develop partnerships and submit TAH proposals.

The primary objective of Jones and other academic history organizations was to focus the program on history content knowledge and place responsibility for this with university history professors. In addition to the wording of the legislation, which Jones specifically referenced, the implementation efforts during the first year created some problems and established precedents that impacted the program.

Program Structure Requirements

As the details of implementation emerged so did the structure and organization of the program. First, as Jones noted, the Department of Education designated LEAs as only eligible applicants. History content would be derived from one of the partners the LEA was required to bring into their proposal. The structure of the partnership, linking the applying LEA to an institution of higher education, a nonprofit history or humanities organization, or a library or museum, was an "absolute priority" for funding. This collaboration had to be clearly defined and documented. The second feature of the program was the use of structured in-service or professional development activities to expand the historical knowledge of the participating teachers. While clearly content knowledge would be featured in the project, the initial language gave teaching strategies equal emphasis. Proposals "must" develop and implement "high-quality in-service and/or pre-service professional development that provides educators with content and teaching skills to prepare all students to achieve to higher standards in American history" and develop and implement strategies for sustained collaboration for a period of at least three years between teachers and outside experts to "improve instruction in American history."[15]

In addition to the structure of the partnership and the reliance on professional development activities, the initial invitation for applications included a number of other strategies that would be deemphasized or dropped from later applications. These included strategies to assist new history teachers in the classroom through mentoring and coaching and team teaching with experienced teachers, providing training on the use of technology to access primary documents, supporting school based collaborative efforts among teachers, creating networks and a forum among teachers for the exchange of information, and similar activities. In addition to the mandatory priority (the partnership between the LEA and a content-oriented institution), there was one invitational priority: application from high poverty rural and urban LEAs which contained chronically low performing schools.

The 2001 invitation for applications was distributed in late May, at a time when most schools and universities had ended or were ending their semesters. As a result LEAs interested in applying for grants had to scramble to structure partnerships at a time when many university faculty were unavailable for the summer. Consequently many applicants during the first funding cycle worked through their existing contacts, usually faculty from colleges of education, or those history or social studies faculty who had worked previously with education students in their districts. The results that first year included a number of proposals with poorly defined partnerships, imbalanced collaboration, and the utilization of content "experts" who lacked real documented expertise in the targeted areas of American history. The material distributed to grant applicants mentioned "traditional American history" but made no effort to include a clear definition of traditional American history; it mentioned history as a separate subject within the core curriculum, but did not specifically distinguish history from social studies. This resulted in proposals that did not effectively place history content, as distinguished from social studies content, at the center of their project, and which included as content specialists faculty with experience in political science, economics, sociology, anthropology, and other social science disciplines rather than history.[16]

Selection Criteria and Procedures

The selection criteria, which also were the basis of the rubric for evaluating proposals contained problems. For the first round proposals were evaluated on seven weighted criteria:

Need for Project	(10 points)
Significance	(20 points)
Quality of the Project Design	(25 points)
Quality of the Management Plan	(15 points)
Quality of Project Personnel	(5 points)
Quality of Project Evaluation	(15 points)
Adequacy of Resources	(10 points)

Most of the criticism of this evaluation design centered on two items: the failure to place sufficient emphasis on content, and the failure to assure the involvement of history content specialists with appropriate training and expertise.

While history content was mentioned in several of the evaluation criteria, there was no reference to traditional American history or to history as a discipline separate from social studies. In addition the distinction between history content and teaching strategies was blurred. For example, under the criteria for "Significance," statements relating to content included "the potential contribution of the proposed project to increase knowledge and understanding of effective strategies to improve instruction and student achievement in American history," and the degree to which the partnership with institutions with "expertise in the field" would contribute to the teachers' ability to "instruct students in American history in an engaging manner."[17] Under the criteria "Quality of the Project Design" the reference to content was equally vague: The extent to which professional development activities were sufficient to lead to "improved instruction in American history," and the extent to which the collaboration involved partners who had sufficient expertise in American history to "improve teachers' knowledge and instruction." The most direct discussion of history content (separate from teaching) was the statement under the criteria for Significance: the likelihood that the professional development activities would improve teachers' "knowledge, understanding and appreciation of American history." Finally, the criteria for "Quality of Project Personnel" included an evaluation of qualifications "including relevant training and experience in American history" of key project personnel—but this criterion was assigned only five points out of a total of one hundred points.[18]

The lack of specificity and clarity in these criteria impacted the initial proposal evaluation process. The evaluation process for the first round of proposals was on site in Washington, DC, August 12–17, 2001. Teams of three panelists read eight to ten proposals. Each team was expected to have at least one history scholar and one person with experience in K-12 schools or in teacher education. The fact that the program was new, the resulting inexperience of the panel monitors, the lack of clarity and consistency in the criteria and scoring rubric, the differing values and experiences of the panel members tended to lead to inconsistency in the evaluation process. While individual panels worked effectively toward consistency, differences among panels were significant—some panels rated similar proposals high, others low.

The National Endowment for the Humanities participated in the first proposal evaluation process. Program officers and other staff served as panel chairs (one of the three panel members who provided some guidance for the deliberations and made sure the scores were added accurately), or panel monitors; others worked with Department of Education staff proofreading panelists' comments and performing other tasks to facilitate the review process. The NEH also provided names of prospective readers to the Department of Education. NEH personnel were not involved in setting the standards or allocating points. They had concerns about the extent of content in the criteria, the weighting of content issues in the evaluation process, and the consistency of scoring. In spite of their concerns, the NEH did feel that the reading effectively ranked the proposals and that the proposals that were funded represented the best of the applications.

NEH participation declined significantly after the first year, and pretty much ended by the third or fourth year of the project. The reasons for the withdrawal of NEH from the process were varied and personal, not NEH policy. Essentially staff members stopped participating because of conflicts with their own work schedules, or with their summer vacation schedules (the first year review panels were held in August). The shift to remote conference-call review panels in 2004 also reduced the staffing needs. There were, of course, cultural differences between the way the NEH and the Department of Education conducted their grant reviews. For example, reviewers for NEH proposals read and prepared their comments at home, and then assembled in Washington usually in panels of five, and spent one day discussing proposals. There was no real effort to achieve consensus, written comments rarely exceeded one page in length, and there was no proofreading or editing process for the comments. During the initial cycles for the TAH proposals, reviewers spent a week in Washington reading and then writing extensive comments on the proposals. In panel discussions consensus (or near consensus) was sought. Readers' comments were carefully proofed for grammar and appropriateness. These differences in the review process also might have discouraged individuals from participating in cross-agency activities.

In spite of all the difficulties involved in implementing a new grant program, the short time frame for launching the program, the roughness of the written criteria and the grant review process, the first year of the *Teaching American History* program ended satisfactorily. The program funded sixty projects that first year, distributing $50 million to this first group of projects. The scoring rubric and panel process ended up working well to identify the best proposals.

Institutionalization and Issues

In the second and subsequent years, the *Teaching American History* program stabilized, and some of the rough spots evident in year one either disappeared or at least became less significant. In year two appropriations were doubled to $100 million and 114 projects received funding. The project was also attached fiscally to the No Child Left Behind Act, which made future funding more certain. As the program matured, the type of issues that affected TAH evolved. Also the criteria and other materials were better defined as the program responded to these issues.

Balancing Content and Pedagogy

One issue that persisted was the role of content and content providers in the projects. The appropriate balance between content and pedagogy continued to be an issue, as did the credentials and expertise of content providers. To some degree the manner in which this issue was resolved depended on the structure of the project partnership and the leadership of the project. Local education agencies (LEAs) are the applicant of record as defined by the *Teaching American History* program and beginning in fiscal year 2002, the authorizing legislation. In those projects where the LEA truly was the applicant and controlled the management of the project, there appeared to be a tendency to place more emphasis on the development of teaching strategies to deliver enhanced history content, and there seemed to be less concern about credentials and expertise of the content providers. Historians sometimes were recruited to provide content outside of their area of expertise—a small number of proposals designated historians of Europe, Asia, or the ancient world to direct or provide content for U.S. history.

On the other hand, some proposals were both written and managed by historians or history departments. In these instances the LEA partner signed off on the project but contracted with the history partner to manage the grant. The LEA recruited teachers for the project and perhaps provided a curriculum specialist and conducted sessions to develop teaching strategies and teaching materials, but this activity was secondary to the history content. The history partner wrote the grant, designed the project activities, and generally focused most resources on providing history content. Often these projects brought in top scholars to provide content in a carefully designed summer institute. However, sometimes content experts were merely colleagues with limited expertise.

In both the scenarios outlined above, the biases applicants brought to the project determined the way they addressed the balance between content and pedagogy and the attention placed on identifying and utilizing appropriate content providers. It is important to note than many good projects were developed using both partnership models, while the most egregious proposals of both models were unlikely to be funded.

The Nature of Content and Content Providers

As the TAH program developed, another issue related to content and content providers emerged. This involved contracting with outside agencies to provide content. Two types of content contracting appeared. The first involved utilizing historical organizations to provide nationally recognized scholars to TAH projects. The two organizations most frequently used for this purpose were the Organization of American Historians (OAH) and the Gilder-Lehrman Institute of American History. Both are highly respected organizations with an impressive record of accomplishments in American history. Both are able to provide access to first-rate scholars; both have a history of commitment to the teaching of American history. The Organization of American Historians provided content specialists through its Distinguished Lectureship Program, which allowed access to approximately 300 scholars in American history for a reasonable fee paid to the OAH and travel expenses for the speaker. The Gilder Lehrman Institute contracted with TAH projects to provide a set of historians appropriate to the content focus of the project. Their fees are substantial, as is the quality of historians they provide.

This approach to content has its strengths and its weaknesses. On the positive side, the OAH provides well-known scholars, many of whom authored the book or books that the teachers have studied. They brought prestige to the project and they provided teachers with access to leading scholars. Gilder-Lehrman also provides access to nationally recognized historians who have a record of combining scholarship with teaching expertise. There is no question that *Teaching American History* programs have benefited from having access to such historical talent. This is especially important for projects situated in small towns or rural areas and those partnered with small universities where the number of local historians is limited. However, these scholars come, stay a day or two, or perhaps a week, then leave. There is no opportunity for an ongoing relationship between historian and teacher that can occur when local historians serve as content specialists.

The second type of packaged content is more problematic. This involves packaged software-based or multimedia U.S. history curriculum materials, which provide specific lesson modules or complete history courses. These programs at their best provide rich and sophisticated history content geared to the grade level of the targeted classes. They can also include extensive supplemental materials— document sets, photographs, sound and film, access to Internet databases, and teacher lesson plans based on the content. While the quality of the content provided can be high, in other ways these packages run counter to the purpose of the TAH program—to increase teachers' knowledge and understanding of traditional American history so that they can impart this knowledge to their students. If this knowledge is digitized and presented directly to students, rather than imparted to the teachers, what role will teachers play in this process? Some supporters of this approach note the quality of the history content these packages provide and their ability to attract student attention; others argue that the teachers learn content from these programs enabling them to participate in their students' learning activities. Relatively few proposals using these software-based content packages have been funded and some review panels have viewed them negatively.

Formal Assessment of TAH

In 2005 the U.S. Department of Education released "Evaluation of the *Teaching American History* Program" prepared by a team of evaluators and SRI International, an independent, nonprofit research institute conducting client-sponsored research and development for government agencies and other organizations. The study was based on analysis of a sample of the first two cohorts of TAH Programs—those beginning in fiscal year 2001 and 2002. By 2005 these two cohorts had completed or were completing their three year projects, so they had amassed a full set of data. Data were collected from October 2002 to May 2005, and included surveys from project directors and participants, case studies of eight TAH projects, an exploratory analysis of teacher work projects, and the review of project documents.[19]

Among the key findings of the report were:

- The teachers who participated in the program were generally experienced teachers—those least in need of professional development. Thirty-eight percent reported having a major in history, 22 percent reported having more than ten college-level courses in history, and 23 percent reported having a minor in history.
- The participation of historians in the professional development activities seemed to be the key to successful projects.
- Professional development consisted primarily of summer institutes; the reliance of these development experiences on "traditional training formats" prevented them from attaining the characteristic of "research-based, high quality professional development."
- Internal evaluations of TAH projects lacked the rigor needed to provide an accurate measure of effectiveness.
- TAH teacher work products demonstrated factual knowledge of history, but limited ability to analyze and interpret historical data.[20]

The report made several suggestions to broaden the scope of the TAH program into areas that it concluded were essential to the improvement of teaching. These suggestions had significant policy implications. For example, the report's authors argued that focusing on the historical knowledge of teachers addressed only one element that led to ineffective American history education. It proposed that something needed to be done to address the poor quality of American history textbooks, and suggested that the wider distribution of the content rich lesson plans and other materials developed by the TAH projects might be a means of addressing this problem. The report also suggested that TAH should expand its scope to address the needs of teacher preparation programs. Specifically it suggested that historians should be involved in the preparation of new teachers.

The report's conclusions included several interesting statements. It suggested that TAH should play a larger role in the No Child Left Behind goal of placing a highly qualified teacher in each classroom, and suggested that the failure to attract less qualified teachers to its program may reflect the failure to structure TAH to provide training that is closely related to classroom needs. The report is interesting in what it proposes—more involvement of the history departments in teacher training, addressing the poor quality of history texts, and taking action to attract the most poorly prepared teachers—and what they do not propose, such as a requirement for history teachers to have a major in history. The report fails to recognize (or buy into) two fundamental principles that undergird the *Teaching American History* program: increasing the content knowledge of teachers in traditional American history, and teaching history as a separate discipline, distinct and separate from social studies.

Informal Assessment of TAH

In additional to the formal assessment conducted by SRI International, other far more informal discussions/assessments of the TAH program have taken place.

One setting where for the past several years project directors, consultants, evaluators, teacher participants, and others interested in the program have gathered is the annual *Teaching American History* symposium that has been held in conjunction with the annual meeting of the Organization of American Historians. At the Second Annual H-Net/OAH Teaching American History Symposium in Minneapolis in March 2007, I unsystematically and unscientifically gathered notes on the comments that were made in the meetings, both from panelists and from the audience. Many of these comments reflected concerns or issues that had not been resolved. Of course, this reflects more the nature of the discussion than any significant negative feeling or attitude about the projects. Indeed most of those present were enthusiastic about the *Teaching American History* program.

As I sorted through my notes from the meeting I noted that there were two separate but sometimes intertwined discussion threads, one from university history faculty and the other from K-12 or college of education faculty or administrators. Among academic historians most concerns centered on conflicts between historians and educators, problems understanding the needs of K-12 teachers, and issues related to assessment. For example, university history faculty were suspicious about prepackaged content and teaching materials, whether it involved outside agencies providing speakers, packaged content materials, or packaged lesson plans. They expressed concern with the quality and suitability of these materials, and raised questions about the best way to address the need of teachers for lesson plans. They also expressed concerns about effective assessment, especially how to get reliable quantitative and qualitative data. The most frequently expresses concerns centered on bridging the gap between academic historians and their colleagues in the teacher education world. These ranged from understanding exactly what teachers needed from them, establishing meaningful communication, especially with elementary teachers, and finding ways to more effectively recruit teachers into the program.

Teachers and university faculty concurred with their history colleagues that communication is one of the most important issues they face. They expressed this in several ways. First, they noted the disconnect between faculty in the departments of history and the college of education and the turf battles between the two groups of faculty that sometimes took place. K-12 teachers expressed concern about the apparent lack of respect that university historians have for their K-12 colleagues, especially those teaching history in elementary schools. They also questioned the role of historians in the project, especially the gap they perceived between the content knowledge that historians presented and what the teachers actually needed in the classroom. Others were concerned that the historians were not involved enough and sought ways to strengthen the connection between historians and classroom teachers, questioned how to embed historians in the schools so they would stay a while, and how to sustain these relationships after funding ended. One teacher raised the question about whether federal grants raised unrealizable expectations and fostered dependence, both on the federal funds, and on the partnerships that will likely fade following the end of the grant period. Educators also raised the issue of recruiting teachers to the program and the difficulty of convincing teachers to change their teaching strategies.

Adjustments to the *Teaching American History* Program

The *Teaching American History* program is an evolving process that has changed in several ways from the program that was inaugurated in May 2001. The changes have not been radical, but they have been significant. Most changes have been made to more closely align the program with the original intention behind the program or to address issues that have arisen on the review process or in the SRI International evaluation report. Many of these changes have been incorporated into the selection criteria. Rather that the seven criteria listed in May 2001, beginning in 2005 the list was reduced to four:

Project Quality	(45 points)
Significance	(20 points)
Quality of Project Evaluation	(20 points)
Quality of Management Plan	(20 points)

The first criterion, Project Quality, was expanded, given addition weight in the evaluation process, and recrafted to more clearly address issues related to content. For example the new wording included a definition of traditional American history that was conspicuously absent in the earlier version of the criteria. Referencing Senator Byrd's original vision, it defined tradition American history as addressing:

> the significant issues, episodes, and turning points in the history of the United States; how the words and deeds of individual Americans have determined the course of our Nation; and how the principles of freedom and democracy articulated in the founding documents of this Nation have shaped America's struggles and achievements and its social, political, and legal institutions and relations.[21]

The new selection criteria also detailed the qualifications expected of history content specialists: "their post-secondary teaching experience and scholarship in the subject areas relevant to the teaching of traditional American history."[22] The revised *Federal Register* posting also addressed the issue raised in the evaluation report regarding the need to attract less qualified teachers to the program. The Competitive Preference Priority encouraged proposals that address high needs districts and indicated that their needs assessment include the qualifications of individual teachers in the district.

There were two other changes in the program instituted in 2008. First, in the competition for that year, proposals were able to request five years of funding rather than the three years that had been allowed previously. Also the application material contained a statement indicating that quality proposals "should not be limited to the history of only one state or region, one ethnic group, or one time segment of American history."[23] The second of these changes addresses the issue of what is significant in history, and the needs of teachers who, at least in middle school and high school, are teaching courses that encompass the broad sweep of American history. This change is not at the level of a criterion—it is not mandatory—but it does address the expectation that these projects address American history, not just local history, the history of one racial or ethnic group, or only one small segment of time. However, it did not preclude projects that addressed such topics or utilized local resources, but it encouraged proposals to do this in a way that connected to broader themes of American history.

Impact

For all of its problems and imperfections the *Teaching American History* program has had a significant impact in several areas. First, the quantity of money and the number of grants awarded has had a significant impact on historians and history departments, especially those at second tier institutions. While some flagship research universities have participated in the program, most university and college participants have come from institutions where departments and faculty are more connected with teacher education, even if only because a significant percent of their students are pursuing teacher certification. As Table 15.1 indicates, at the time of the writing of this chapter the amount awarded to *Teaching American History* projects was over $838 million, and over 900 grants had been awarded. The size and scope of this program is unprecedented, and history departments are aware of the potential impact of these projects on their programs and budgets. For some departments applications for these projects have become a minor industry.

The impact on the schools and on actual teaching and learning in the nation's history classrooms is less clearly defined. According to the evaluation report, teachers who have participated in the program generally assess the program positively. The impact on their knowledge is less clear. The evaluation reports concluded that the work product of participating teachers indicated greater factual knowledge about history but did not indicate greater analytical skills. The impact on student learning is not clearly documented. Furthermore, the impact on student historical knowledge is limited by the relatively small number of school districts across the country that have been directly affected by these grants. Of the roughly 16,000 school districts in the United States only 650 have applied for and received TAH grants. Offsetting that number, approximately half of the 45 mil-

Table 15.1 TAH awards

Year	Total Award	No. of Projects
2001	50,000,000	60
2002	100,000,000	114
2003	99,350,000	114
2004	119,292,000	122
2005	119,040,000	129
2006	119,790,000	124
2007	116,000,000	122
2008	114,700,000	121
Total	$838,172,000	906

lion school children are in the districts that have been involved in the projects.[24] Only a very small percentage of the total school districts have participated in these projects.

The successes and the weaknesses of the program are fairly evident. Much like the National Defense Education Act of 1958, which, in response to the space race and the launching of Sputnik by the Soviet Union, pumped resources into science and math education, the *Teaching American History* grant program has provided significant funding for efforts to improve history education. While its overall effectiveness has not been clearly established, due primarily to the difficulty of proving improvement in teacher knowledge and student learning, the program has created partnerships between teachers of history and history scholars in those districts that have participated in projects. The major weakness is that the large majority of school districts have not participated, and likely will not do so in the future. Furthermore, because TAH is a grant program and there is intensive competition for awards, poorer school districts (and poorer colleges) which do not have access to professional grant writers are at a disadvantage when competing for grants. The disparity between large well-funded districts and poorer ones has been exacerbated by the shift to the "paperless" electronic submission system. This process has perplexed many potential applicants, even at the larger and wealthier districts. For the poorer districts (and the ones with the greatest need) this is another barrier they must overcome.

Future Prospects

What does the future hold for the *Teaching American History* program? In the short term the program will likely continue. Since *Teaching American History* is linked to No Child Left Behind, it will continue as long as NCLB does. If No Child is reauthorized with relatively minor changes, TAH will also likely be reauthorized for another five years or so. Until Congress takes action on No Child, both programs will continue under the current law. Obviously nothing is certain in politics. If interest grows to expand TAH to more school districts (or all districts) Congress could transform the program into a state grant. If that happens, each state will then distribute funds or resources to individual districts. At present there is no sign that this will happen to the *Teaching American History* program.

For the present, *Teaching American History* continues. Funding was awarded for the 2008 competition. Approximately $114 million was distributed among 121 successful applicants. The 2009 competition that will almost certainly follow should see the number of total awards since 2001 surpass a thousand and the total amount approach $1 billion.

Notes

1. Robert Byrd speaking for his amendment to Title X of the Department of Education Funding Bill (HR 4557), June 30, 2000, S.AMDT 3731, 106th Congress, 2nd Sess., *Congressional Record* 146, S6200.
2. Senator Joseph Lieberman speaking in support of Senator Byrd's amendment, June 30, 2000, *Congressional Record* 146, S6200.

3. Senator Robert Byrd speaking to his amendment to reauthorize and increase funding for his program "for the Teaching of Traditional American History as a Separate Subject," May 10, 2001, S.AMDT 402 to S.AMDT 358, 107th Congress,1st Sess., *Congressional Record* 147, S4810.

4. Ibid.

5. Ibid.

6. "Senate Passes Byrd's $100 Million for American History Initiative: Funds Expand Byrd's Teaching American History Grant Effort," press release from Senator Byrd's office, November 6, 2001. This and the other press releases cited in this study were provided by Senator Kay Bailey Hutchinson's office. Senator Byrd's office did not provide any information for this study.

7. Senator Byrd's office, "Byrd Focuses Funds on Teaching American History in Schools," press release, January 28, 2004.

8. *Congressional Record* 146, S6200.

9. In 2000 the NEH was funded at $115.3 million; in 2001 its budget increased to $120 million.

10. *Federal Register*, 66, no. 100 (May 23, 2001), 28429–28430.

11. Ibid.

12. *Federal Register*, 72, no. 195 (October 10, 2007), 57540.

13. *Federal Register* (May, 23, 2001), 28430.

14. Arnita Jones, "How Scholars Can Improve History Lessons," *The Chronicle of Higher Education* (June 8, 2001).

15. Ibid.

16. One proposal from this period asserted that it was taking an innovative approach to history by using only scholars from disciplines other than history as their history content specialists. It is also important to note that these cases represented a small number of extreme examples; most proposals involved historians as content specialists. A more pervasive problem was the limited role that many played in planning and implementing the proposed projects.

17. *Federal Register* (May, 23, 2001), 28431–28432.

18. Ibid., 28432.

19. Daniel C. Humphrey and others (SRI International), *Evaluation of the Teaching American History Program* (Jessup, MD: ED, 2005), 4.

20. Ibid., ix–xvi, 49–52.

21. *Federal Register* (October 10, 2007), 57543.

22. Ibid.

23. *Teaching American History: Application Information*, TAH Overview 2008, http://www.ed.gov/programs/teachinghistory/applicant.html

24. The number of districts involve is misleading because a number of grants have gone to LEAs that represent multiple school districts. LA County, for example, oversees about ninety school districts. Nevertheless, only a relatively small percentage of the nation's school districts have been touched by the program. On the other hand, since very large school districts are disproportionately represented in the program, about half of the nation's public school children are enrolled in districts that have been involved.

Contributors

Dawn Abt-Perkins, Professor of Education, Lake Forest College

Katherine Barbour, Program Coordinator, American History Teachers' Collaborative, Urbana, IL School District No. 116

Elise Fillpot, Director, Bringing History Home and The Grant Wood History Institute; Visiting Professor, University of Iowa Department of History; and Visiting Scholar, University of Iowa College of Education

David Gerwin, Associate Professor of Education, Department of Secondary Education, Queens College/City University of New York

Julie Kearney, Evaluation Project Leader, Center for Evaluation and Assessment, University of Iowa

Peter B. Knupfer, Associate Professor, History Department, Michigan State University

Emily Lai, Evaluation Project Leader, Center for Evaluation and Assessment, University of Iowa

D. Lynn McRainey, Elizabeth F. Cheney Director of Education, Chicago History Museum

Heidi Moisan, Schools Programs Manager, Chicago History Museum

Donald D. Owen, Project Director, American History Teachers' Collaborative; Director of Staff Development, Urbana, IL School District No. 116

Rachel G. Ragland, Assistant Professor of Education, Lake Forest College

Tim Rives, Supervisory Archivist, Eisenhower Presidential Library and Museum, Abilene, KS

Robert E. Rook, Professor of History and Chairperson, Department of History, Towson University

Ann Marie Ryan, Assistant Professor of Education, Loyola University, Chicago

G. L. Seligmann, Associate Professor of History, University of North Texas

Frank Valadez, Executive Director of the Chicago Metro History Education Center

Laura M. Westhoff, Associate Professor of History and Education, University of Missouri-St. Louis

Kelly A. Woestman, Professor of History and History Education Director, Pittsburg (KS) State University

Cary D. Wintz, Professor, Department of History, Texas Southern University

Donald Yarbrough, Director and Associate Professor, Center for Evaluation and Assessment, University of Iowa

Index

Page numbers in italic refer to Figures or Tables.